Jean G. Keetels, Hippolyte Dalmon

An Elementary French Grammar

For Colleges, High Schools and Academies

Jean G. Keetels, Hippolyte Dalmon

An Elementary French Grammar
For Colleges, High Schools and Academies

ISBN/EAN: 9783337159047

Printed in Europe, USA, Canada, Australia, Japan

Cover: Foto ©Paul-Georg Meister /pixelio.de

More available books at **www.hansebooks.com**

AN ELEMENTARY FRENCH GRAMMAR.

FOR

COLLEGES, HIGH SCHOOLS, AND ACADEMIES.

BY

PROF. JEAN GUSTAVE KEETELS,

AUTHOR OF "ANALYTICAL AND PRACTICAL FRENCH GRAMMAR," "A COLLEGIATE FRENCH COURSE," "AN ANALYTICAL FRENCH READER," "A CHILD'S FIRST BOOK IN FRENCH."

NEW EDITION,

EDITED BY

PROF. HIPPOLYTE DALMON,

UNITED STATES NAVAL ACADEMY, ANNAPOLIS, MD.

NEW YORK:
MAYNARD, MERRILL, & CO.,
29, 31, AND 33 EAST NINETEENTH STREET.
1898.

Prof. Keetels' French Series.

1. A Child's Illustrated First Book in French. 168 pages, 12mo, handsomely bound in cloth.

The aim of this book is to make the Study of the French language attractive and interesting to children, who have no knowledge of the English grammar. The object-lesson plan has been adopted. For this purpose the volume is handsomely illustrated by engravings especially prepared for the book.

2. An Elementary French Grammar. For High Schools and Academies. 340 pages, 12mo.

This work is designed for students of the academic and collegiate departments. Its purpose is to train them in the principles of French grammar, and to accustom them by oral instruction to the use of the French language.

3. An Analytical and Practical French Grammar. 524 pages, 12mo.

This book, containing the advantage of the oral and the analytical method of instruction, comprises all that is necessary to teach the French language successfully, both theoretically and practically. It is a complete grammar, in which the principles of the language are developed in a logical and efficient manner.

4. A Collegiate Course in the French Language, comprising a complete Grammar, with Rules on Gender; Reading-Lessons and Exercises for Translation; a Treatise on French Pronunciation; a Key to the Principal French Idioms; the Latin Elements, common to both the French and English; the whole being a compilation of the principles of the French Language, arranged and prepared for the study of French, in Colleges and Collegiate Institutions. 549 pages, 12mo. Cloth.

5. An Analytical French Reader: with English Exercises for Translation and Oral Exercises for Practice in Speaking; Questions on Grammar, with References to the Author's several Grammars. Notes and Vocabulary. In Two Parts. PART FIRST: Selections of Fables, Anecdotes, and Short Stories. PART SECOND: Selections from the best Modern Writers. 320 pages, 12mo.

A KEY TO THE ENGLISH EXERCISES IN THE ANALYTICAL AND PRACTICAL FRENCH GRAMMAR. (For teachers only.) 12mo. Cloth. 75 cents.

A KEY TO THE ENGLISH EXERCISES IN THE COLLEGIATE COURSE. (For teachers only.) Price, 75 cents.

Entered according to Act of Congress, in the year 1873, by MASON, BAKER & PRATT, in the Office of the Librarian of Congress, at Washington.

Entered according to Act of Congress, in the year 1873, by ALBERT MASON, in the Office of the Librarian of Congress, at Washington.

Copyright, 1881. 1884. CLARK & MAYNARD.

PREFACE.

THIS Elementary French Grammar is designed for students, who begin the study of French. Each part of speech is treated separately, and every subject is at once completed as far as the scope of the work permits. The rules and explanations are stated in simple language, which is believed to be within the comprehension of the youthful mind. The exercises are short, lively, and varied. To compose suitable sentences for practice, elements have been introduced which are outside of the order of development. These are given in the vocabularies, systematically arranged in order to engage the interest of the student, and with an occasional explanation when the subject absolutely requires it. The author has been careful, however, not to infringe the regular order of development, and to keep the subject-matter prominently before the mind, so as to leave an indelible impression.

Great attention has been bestowed on the treatment of the pronouns and verbs; the irregular verbs have been given in full, with copious exercises for practice.

The rules in Syntax are confined to elementary principles, in accordance with the plan of the work, which is intended as introductory to the author's Analytical and Practical French Grammar or Collegiate French Course. Students who have finished the present course, will be well prepared to take up either of the larger works, in which they will go over much of the same ground, but with the additional interest of the Oral Exercises. They will be enabled to advance rapidly, to understand more clearly the facts that come before them; and, in pursuing the course to its conclusion, will attain their aim: read, write, and speak the French language.

PUBLISHERS' NOTE.

The demand for this work has been so great that in the printing of many successive editions the plates had become badly worn.

New electrotype plates having become necessary, the publishers have deemed it proper to have the book carefully read, and such improvements made as suggested themselves to the editor.

The author of the work having died some years since, his friend Professor H. Dalmon of the United States Naval Academy undertook this work of revision, and has performed it with great care, so that it is believed that it is as nearly free from typographical errors as possible. No radical changes in the matter or form have been made, and the new edition can be used in the same classes with the old without the slightest difficulty.

The numerous teachers who have heretofore used the book with such satisfaction, will, we are confident, be glad to see it in this new and improved type.

CONTENTS.

	PAGE
PREFACE	3
INTRODUCTION.—CHAPTER FIRST	7
Alphabet and Orthographic Signs	7
Vowels. Nasal Vowels. Diphthongs	8–10
Consonants. Final Consonants	11–12
Division of Words into Syllables	12
Use of Capitals. Use of Accents	13
Exercises in Pronouncing	14

CHAPTER SECOND.

	PAGE
Parts of Speech, Definitions	15
Parts of Speech, Properties	17
Sentences	20
SUGGESTIONS	22

LESSON
		PAGE
I.	The *Noun*. The *Article*	23
II.	Plural Forms	24
II. (bis.)	Plural Forms, Continued	26
III.	Contraction of Article	28
IV.	Nouns. Partitive Sense	30
	Present Tense of Avoir	31
V.	*Qualifying Adjectives*	32
V. (bis.)	*Qualifying Adjectives*. Continued	35
VI.	Comparison of Adjectives	37
	Present Tense of Etre	38
VII.	*Limiting Adjectives*. Possessive	40
VIII.	Demonstrative	42
IX.	Numeral	45
IX. (bis.)	Numeral. Continued	49
	Days of the Week	51
	Months	51
X.	Limiting Adjectives. Indefinite	52
XI.	*Pronouns*. Personal	55
	Conjunctive	55
XII.	Conjunctive. Continued	58
XIII.	Collocation	62
XIV.	Disjunctive	64
XV.	Possessive	68
XVI.	Demonstrative	70
XVII.	Interrogative	74
XVIII.	Relative	77
XIX.	Indefinite	80
XX.	The *Verb*. Infinitive	84
XXI.	Participles	88
	Agreement of Past Participle	89
XXII.	Auxiliary Verb Avoir	91
XXIII.	Auxiliary Verb Etre	98

CONTENTS.

LESSON		PAGE
XXIV.	Regular Verbs. First Conjugation, Couper.	103
XXV.	First Conjugation. Orthographic Irregularities	108
XXVI.	Second Conjugation, Finir	111
XXVII.	Third Conjugation, Recevoir.	116
XXVIII.	Fourth Conjugation, Vendre.	121
XXIX.	Interrogative Conjugation	126
	Negative Conjugation	127
XXX.	The Passive Verb	129
XXXI.	The Neuter Verb	134
XXXII.	The Pronominal Verb	139
XXXIII.	The Impersonal Verb	145
XXXIV.	Irregular Verbs. First Conjugation	149
XXXV.	Irregular Verbs. Second Conjugation	154
XXXVI.	Irregular Verbs. Second Conjugation. Continued	159
XXXVII.	Irregular Verbs. Third Conjugation	165
XXXVIII.	Irregular Verbs. Third Conjugation. Continued	170
XXXIX.	Irregular Verbs. Fourth Conjugation	174
XL.	Irregular Verbs. Fourth Conjugation. Continued	180
XLI.	Irregular Verbs. Fourth Conjugation. Continued	184
XLII.	Irregular Verbs. Fourth Conjugation. Continued	189
XLIII.	Irregular Verbs. Fourth Conjugation. Continued	195
XLIV.	The *Adverb*	200
XLV.	The *Preposition*	207
XLVI.	The *Conjunction*	209
	The *Interjection*	210
XLVII.	SYNTAX. The *Noun*	212
	Idioms with Avoir	212
	Nouns as Adjectives	213
	Plural of Compound Nouns	213
XLVIII.	The *Article*	216
	Before Proper Nouns	218
XLIX.	The *Adjective*	221
	Adjectives as Nouns	222
	Place of Adjectives	222
	Government of Adjectives	223
	Numeral Adjectives	223
L.	The *Pronoun*	225
LI.	The *Verb*	228
	Agreement	228
	Use of the Tenses	229
	Use of the Conditional Mode	231
	Use of the Imperative Mode	231
	Use of the Subjunctive Mode	232
	Use of the Infinitive Mode	233
	Government of Verbs	233
XLII.	The *Participle*	236
	The *Adverb*	236
	The *Preposition*	237
	The *Conjunction*	238

APPENDIX.

Additional Vocabularies	241
Conversational Phrases	255
Vocabulary to the English Exercises for Translation	259
Conjugation of Verbs—Regular and Irregular	275
Idioms and Proverbs	315

INTRODUCTION.

CHAPTER FIRST.

1.—FRENCH ALPHABET.

LETTERS:	a	b	c	d	e	f	g	h	i
Old names:	ah	bay	say	day	ay	eff	jay	ash	ee
New names:*	ah	be	se	de	e	fe	gue	he	ee
LETTERS:	j	k	l	m	n	o	p	q	r
Old names:	jee	kah	el	emm	enn	o	pay	†	err
New names:*	je	ke	le	me	ne	o	pe	que	re
LETTERS:	s	t	u	v	x	y	z		
Old names:	ess	tay	†	vay	ix	egrek	zed		
New names:*	se	te		ve	kze	ce	ze		

The *w* is not a French letter. It is found in a few foreign words that have been introduced into the French language, and is pronounced the same as the *v*.

2.—ORTHOGRAPHIC SIGNS.

The written language has *accents, cedilla, diaresis, apostrophe, hyphen,* and the ordinary punctuation marks.

There are three accents, the *acute* (′), the *grave* (`), and the *circumflex* (ˆ).

The acute accent is used over the vowel *e* only. The acute *é* has the sound of *a* in *fate*.

The grave accent is used over *e, a, u*. The grave *è* has the sound

---

* The vowel *e*, joined to the consonants to give their new names, has nearly the sound of *u* in *burr*.

† The *q* and *u* have no corresponding sound in English.

of *ei* in *their*. The grave accent is used over *a* and *u* only as a mark of distinction (p. 13; 10, 2).

The circumflex accent is used over a long vowel, after which a letter has been suppressed (p. 13; 10, 3).

The cedilla (ˌ) is placed under the *c* (ç) before *a, o, u*, to indicate that it has the sound of *s*, as: ça, ço, çu.

The diæresis (¨) is placed over a vowel that begins a new syllable after another vowel; as, maïs (ma-is). It is also placed over final *e* that follows *u*, when the *u* is to be pronounced, as: aiguë; the *u* of the syllable gue is otherwise silent.

The apostrophe (') indicates the suppression of a vowel, as: l'ami, for le ami; l'homme, for le homme.

The hyphen (-) indicates the connection between two or more words, or parts of a word, as: ai-je; arc-en-ciel.

3.—VOWELS AND VOWEL-SOUNDS.

There are six vowels: *a, e, i, o, u, y*; but there are thirteen vowel-sounds; nine are pure, and four are nasal.

1.—Pure Vowel-Sounds.

The nine pure Vowel-Sounds are:

1	2	3	4	5	6	7	8	9
a	e	é	è ê	i y	o	u	eu	ou

These vowel-sounds have nearly all corresponding sounds in English.

a (*short*) has the sound of *a* in *hat*, as: sa, ma, malle, salle.
a (*long*) has the sound of *a* in *father*, as: âge, âme, mâle, sale.
e has the sound of *u* in *burr*, but faintly, as: de, le, me, se.
é has the sound of *a* in *fate*, as: dé, légal, métal, posé.
è has the sound of *ei* in *their*, as: dès, frère, mère, père.
ê has the sound of *ei* in *their* (broad), as: fête, frêle, même, tête.
i or y* has the sound of *e* in *me*, as: ami, mari, midi, si.

---

* The letter *y*, preceded by a vowel, has the value of double *i*, as: *pays* (pay-ee)

o (*short*) has the sound of *o* in *not*, as: **dot, mode, mol, notre.**
o (*long*) has the sound of *o* in *note*, as: **dos, mot, rôti, nôtre.**
u has no equivalent sound in English.
eu (*short*) has nearly the sound of *u* in *burr*, as: **fleur, sœur, beurre, heure.**
eu (*long*) has no equivalent in English, but has the sound of *ö* in German, as: **peu, feu, jeu, bleu.**
ou has the sound of *oo* in school, as: **mou, trou, sou, hibou.**
ou, before final *r*, has the sound of *oo* in *boor*, as: **jour, four, tour, amour.**

2.—Remarks on the Unaccented E.

The unaccented *e*, at the end of a word of two or more syllables, is silent, as: **abîme, trouve.** After two consonants, it is slightly pronounced—just enough to give utterance to the preceding consonant, as: **sable, sabre, cable.** This is also the case when it closes a syllable that is followed by a consonant: **demande** (d'mande), **samedi** (sam'di).

When *e* stands between two consonants that belong to the same syllable, it is sounded like *e* in *bed*, as: **bec, bel, mette, serre.**

Before a final *r* that is pronounced, *e* has the sound of *è* (grave), as: **mer, fer, hiver;** and before a final *r, z, d* or *f* that is silent, *e* has the sound of *é* (acute), as: **parler, parlez, bled, clef,** which are pronounced the same as if they were written **parlé, blé, clé.**

3.—Compound Vowels.

A compound vowel is a combination of two or more vowels, having the sound of a single vowel, as: **eu, ou.** The following compound vowels represent some of the pure vowel-sounds:

ai or eai has the sound sometimes of *é* and sometimes of *è*. ai has the sound of *é* when it closes a syllable, as: **j'ai, je mangeai;** and in **je sais, tu sais, il sait.** ai has the sound of *è* generally when it is not final, as: **plaie, j'avais, mais.**
ei has the sound of *è*, as: **peine.**
ea has the sound of *a*, as: **mangea.**
ée has the sound of *é*, as: **fée, épée.**
au, eau, have the sound of *ô*, as: **faux, beau.**
œu has the sound of *eu*, as: **bœuf.**

4.—NASAL VOWEL-SOUNDS

The four nasal vowel-sounds are:

an　in　on　un

m, preceded by a vowel, has the nasal sound of *n*.

e, before *m* or *n*, has the nasal sound of *an*; but *en*, preceded by *i*, (*ien*) has the nasal sound of *in*.

m and n are not nasal when they are double, or followed by a vowel.

The nasal sounds are represented by

$$\left.\begin{array}{l}\text{an}\\\text{am}\\\text{en}\\\text{em}\end{array}\right\} = \text{an} \quad \left.\begin{array}{l}\text{in}\\\text{im}\\\text{ain}\\\text{aim}\end{array}\right\} = \text{in} \quad \left.\begin{array}{l}\text{on}\\\text{om}\end{array}\right\} = \text{on} \quad \left.\begin{array}{l}\text{un}\\\text{um}\end{array}\right\} = \text{un}$$

The English language has no sounds exactly equivalent to the French nasal sounds. The nearest approach to them is heard in pronouncing, separately from the consonants that follow them, the nasal sounds *an, in, on, un*, contained in the following English words:

an is sounded as *an* in *want*, as: ruban, sang,* enfant.*
in is sounded as *an* in *angry*, as: fin, faim, pain.
on is sounded as *on* in *long*, as: bon, long,* façon.
un is sounded as *un* in *hunger*, as: brun, tribun, chacun.

4.—DIPHTHONGS.

A diphthong is a combination of two vowel-sounds, which are both heard in pronouncing.

Pure diphthongs: ia　ie　ieu　oi　oué　oui, etc.
Nasal diphthongs: ien　ion　oin　uin, etc.

5.—PRONUNCIATION OF THE DIPHTHONGS.

ia in fiacre, pronounced *fee-ah-kr*.
ie in lier, pronounced *lee-a*.
ieu in lieu, pronounced *lee-eu*. (See vowel-sounds for *eu*.)

---

* A final consonant after a nasal sound is silent.

oi in loi, pronounced *lou-ah*.
oue in ouest, pronounced *oo-ayst*.
ui in fruit, pronounced *fru-ee*. (See **vowel-sounds** for *u*.)
ien in bien, pronounced *bee-an* (*angry*).
ion in lion, pronounced *lee-on* (long).
oin in loin, pronounced *lou-an* (*angry*).
uin in juin, pronounced *ju-in* (*angry*). (See vowel-sounds for *u*.)

5.—CONSONANTS.

Consonants, when combined with vowels, have generally the same value in French as in English. The following are the principal exceptions:

c before *e, i, y* has the hissing sound of *s*, as: **ceci**. Befor *a, o, u*, and before a consonant, it has the sound of *k*, as: **cabas, colon, cure, crin**. But **ç** (cedilla) before *a, o, u*, retains the sound of *s*, as: **façade, façon, reçu**.

ch has generally the sound of *sh*, as: **charme**; but followed by a consonant, it has the sound of *k*, as: **Christ**. **ch** has the sound of *k* in words from the Greek and Hebrew, as: **écho, Cham**.

g before *e, i, y* has the sound of *s* in pleasure, as: **germe, gilet**; before *a, o, u* it has the sound of the English *g* in *grate*, as: **gant, gobelet**.

h is silent when a vowel may be elided before it, as: **l'homme** for le homme. It is called aspirate, when the vowel is not elided before it, although the *h* is not heard in pronouncing, as: le héros (le-ay-roh).

s has the hissing sound of *c* at the beginning of a word, as: **sa** (*ça*); between two vowels, it has the sound of *z*, as: **voisin** (vouah-zain).

ss between two vowels, has the hissing sound of *s*, as: **poisson** (pouah-çon).

sch is sounded like *sh*, as: **schisme**.

t is sounded like *c* in a few words ending in *tie*, as: **minutie**, and in those ending in *atie*, as: **diplomatie**; also before *ial, iel, ion*, as: **nation**; except when it is preceded by *s*, as: **question**.

th is sounded like *t*, as: **thé**.

x, initial, is sounded like *gz*, as: **Xavier**; also, **ex**, initial, when followed by a vowel, as: **examen**.

x is sounded like *ks* in **Alexandre, maxime,** etc.
x is sounded like *ss* in **soixante, six, dix,** etc.
x is sounded like *z* in **deuxième, sixième,** etc.

6.—LIQUIDS.

g, followed by *n,* and **l,** preceded by *i,* are generally pronounced so smoothly that their natural sounds are not heard; they are then called liquids.

The liquid sound of *gn* is heard in the word **mignonnette,** and that of *l* in the word **brilliant.**

7.—FINAL CONSONANTS.

A final consonant is generally silent; but a final consonant, followed by a word that begins with a vowel or silent *h,* is pronounced with the next syllable, when no pause takes place between the words, as: **mon ami, vous avez, un bel habit, il est** *(ee-lè),* **elle est** *(è-lè).*

Final **c**, before a vowel, is sounded like *k :* **du blanc au noir.**
Final **d**, before a vowel, is sounded like *t :* **quand il.**
Final **f**, before a vowel, is sounded like *v :* **neuf heures.**
Final **g**, before a vowel, is sounded like *k :* **rang élevé.**
Final **s** or **x**, before a vowel, is sounded like *z :* **ils ont deux enfants.**

8.—DIVISION OF WORDS INTO SYLLABLES.

In dividing words into syllables, a single consonant between two vowels belongs to the vowel that follows, as: **raser** (raser). If this vowel is an unaccented final *e,* the consonant is pronounced with the preceding vowel, as: **rase** (ra-se) pronounced *raz.*

The first part of a double consonant belongs to the vowel that precedes; the second, to the vowel that follows; the latter only is pronounced, as: **addition,** pronounced *a-di-cion.*

Two consonants in the middle of a word are separated, as: **parler** (par-ler), **rampant** (ram-pant); except the following combinations which are inseparable, and pronounced with the vowel that follows: *bl, br, ch, chl, chr, cl, cr, dl, dr, fl, fr, gl, gn, gr, gu, ph, phl, pl, pr, qu, rh, th, thl, thr, tr, vr.* Observe that they are principally *l* or *r* preceded by another consonant, but not by *m* or *n.*

9.—USE OF CAPITAL LETTERS.

The rules for the use of capital letters are the same in French as in English, with some exceptions.

Adjectives derived from proper names are not written with a capital initial.

The names of the months and of the days of the week are usually written with a small initial.

The personal pronoun of the first person singular, je, *I*, is written with a small letter, unless it begins a sentence.

10.—USE OF THE ACCENTS.

1. The acute accent (´) is used only over the *e*, in the following cases:

(1.) When it forms a syllable by itself, as: épi, écu, élu.

(2.) When it is followed by a vowel, as: réaction, réel, réélu, épée, fée, réunion.

(3.) When at the end of a syllable, or before final *s*, added by inflection, it has the sound of the English *a*, as: répété, vérité, vérités.

2. The grave accent (`) is used:

(1.) Over *e* preceding any consonant followed by unaccented *e*, as: lève, mène, chère; also before two consonants, when both belong to the unaccented syllable, as: règle.

(2.) Over the *e* of the termination *es*, when the *s* is an essential part of the word, as: après, excès, to distinguish it from the accidental termination *es*, as: les livres, tu chantes.

(3.) To distinguish

à, *to, at*, from a, *has;* où, *where*, from ou, *or;*
là, *there*, from la, *the, her;* dès, *from*, from des, *of the*.

(4.) Over çà, deçà, déjà, holà, voilà.

3. The circumflex accent (ˆ) is used over a long vowel, after which a letter has been suppressed, as: âge, épitre, tête, formerly written aage, épistre, teste.

REM.—No dot is placed over the *i* that has the circumflex accent, but the diæresis takes the place of the circumflex accent, in haïmes, haïtes.

11.—EXERCISES IN PRONOUNCING.

1.—VOWEL SOUNDS.

[Final consonants are silent, except those marked by an asterisk (*).]

a	=	la	ça	cabas	bal*	sac*
ă	=	lame	châle	base	âge	cage
e	=	le	ce	je	me	se
		table	cable	cadre	nacre	sacre
é	=	dé	j'ai	pied	parlé	parler
è	=	frère	mer*	fer*	air*	chaise
ê	=	fête	même	j'aime	chêne	chaîne
i (y)	=	qui	ri	crie	j'y	folie
o	=	dot*	mode	col*	sol*	choc
ŏ	=	dos	mot	gros	eau	chaud
u	=	du	lu	su	bu	connu
eu	=	beurre	heure	jeune	neuve	sœur
ĕŭ	=	bleu	deux	jeûne	jeu	peu
ou	=	cou	sou	chou	mou	hibou
		cour*	jour*	four*	tour*	amour*

2.—NASAL SOUNDS.

an	=	banc	enfant	empire	lentement
in	=	fin	faim	impie	rien
on	=	mon	garçon	rond	ponton
un	=	brun	parfum	chacun	humble

3.—DIPHTHONGS.

ia	=	fiacre	diacre	miasme
ie	=	ciel	fier	pied
ieu	=	Dieu	lieu	vieux
oi	=	loi	roi	croire
ouè	=	ouest*	fouet	louais
oui	=	fouine	oui	
ui	=	fruit	lui	bruit
ien	=	bien	lien	rien
ion	=	lion	nation	fluxion
oin	=	loin	foin	joint
uin	=	juin	suint	suinter

4.—LIQUIDS.

gn	=	Allemagne	champignon	poignard
ll	=	fille	brilliant	coquille
		œil	cueille	feuille
		soleil	sommeil	bouteille
		bétail	paille	Versailles
		bouille	fouille	mouille

CHAPTER SECOND.

1.—PARTS OF SPEECH.

There are ten parts of speech:

1. Noun
2. Article
3. Adjective
4. Pronoun
5. Verb
6. Participle
7. Adverb
8. Preposition
9. Conjunction
10. Interjection

DEFINITIONS AND SUBDIVISIONS OF THE PARTS OF SPEECH.

1. *a.* A noun is the name of a person, place, or thing, as: *Washington, Paris, city.*

b. Nouns are *proper* or *common;* a *proper* noun denotes a particular person or object, as: *Washington, Paris;* a *common* noun denotes one of a class, as: *city, tree.*

c. Common nouns include *collective* and *abstract* nouns; a *collective* noun is the name of several individuals together, as: *meeting, committee;* an *abstract* noun denotes some quality considered apart from its substance, as: *goodness, pride, frailty.*

2. The article is a word placed before a noun to limit its signification, as: *the tree.*

REM.—In French there is but one article, the equivalent of *the.*

3. *a.* An adjective is a word added to a noun, to describe or limit it, as: the *large* tree, *my* tree.

b. There are two kinds of adjectives, *qualifying* and *limiting.* The qualifying adjective adds a quality to the noun, as: the *large* tree; the limiting adjective limits its sense, as: *my* tree.

c. The limiting adjectives are either *possessive*, denoting possession, as: *my* tree; *demonstrative*, pointing out the object, as: *that* tree; *numeral*, indicating number or order, as: *one* tree, the *first* tree; or indefinite, as: *which* tree.

4. *a.* A pronoun is a word that is used in the place of a noun, as: *I* have your book, *you* have *mine.*

b. There are *personal, possessive, demonstrative, interrogative, relative,* and *indefinite* pronouns.

(1.) A *personal* pronoun represents a person in grammar, as: *I, you, he, it.*

(2.) A *possessive* pronoun denotes possession, as: *mine, yours,* etc.

(3.) A *demonstrative* pronoun points out an object, as: *this one, that one.*

(4.) An *interrogative* pronoun is used to ask a question, as: *who? what?*

(5.) A *relative* pronoun relates to a preceding noun, called the antecedent of the relative pronoun, as: the man *who* speaks; the tree *that* falls; the lady *whom* I admire.

(6.) An *indefinite* pronoun does not represent any particular person or thing, as: *every one, some one.*

5. *a.* A verb is a word that expresses action or being, as: *to write, to live.*

b. There are five kinds of verbs: *active, passive, neuter, pronominal, impersonal.*

(1.) The *active* verb expresses an action performed by the subject and is, or may be, accompanied by a direct object; that is, a person or thing that is directly affected by the action of the verb. An active verb is *transitive* when it is accompanied by a direct object, as: *he is writing a letter;* and *intransitive,* when it is not, as: *he is writing.*

(2.) The *passive* verb is the reverse of the active verb; the person or thing which is the object of the active verb, is the subject of the passive verb, as: *the letter is written by him.*

(3.) The *neuter* verb expresses a state or action performed by the subject, but cannot have a direct object, as: *I am, he works, he sleeps.*

REM.—We know that a verb is neuter when we cannot place *somebody* or *something* after it; thus, we cannot say *he sleeps somebody, he sleeps something.*

(4.) The *pronominal* verb is always accompanied by a pronoun of the same person and number as the subject, as: *I flatter myself,*

(5.) The *impersonal* verb is used only in the third person singular, as: *it rains.*

6. A participle is a part of the verb which partakes of the nature of the adjective, as: fields *covered* with snow, *glittering* in the sun.

7. An adverb is a word joined to a verb, a participle, an adjective, or to another adverb, and usually expresses *time, place, degree,* or *manner.*

8. A preposition is a word used to express some relation of different things or thoughts to each other, as: the book lies *before* me *on* the table.

9. A conjunction is a word used to connect words or sentences in construction, as: you *and* he are happy, *because* you are good.

10. An interjection is a word that denotes a sudden emotion of the mind, as: *Ah! alas!*

2.—PROPERTIES OF THE PARTS OF SPEECH.

1. A noun has *gender* to denote the sex, and *number* to indicate whether it means one, or more than one, person or thing.

2. The French language has only two genders: the *masculine* and the *feminine.*

3. The article and adjective agree in gender and number with the noun which they limit or describe; that is, their form is so varied as to indicate the gender and number of the noun.

4. The pronoun agrees in gender and number with the noun which it represents.

5. A noun or pronoun is of the *first* person, if it represents the speaker; of the *second,* if it represents the person spoken to; and of the *third,* if it represents the person or thing spoken of.

    1st person, I, me, we, us
    2d person, You
    3d person, He, him, she, her, it, they, them

6. A noun or pronoun is either the subject of a verb, or the object of a verb, or of a preposition.

7. The subject of the verb is the person or thing of which something is affirmed, as: *he writes;* *he* is the subject of the verb *writes.*

8. The object of the verb is the person or thing which is directly affected by the action of the verb, as: *he writes a letter; letter* is the object of the verb *writes.* The object which is thus directly governed by the verb is called the *direct object*, or *direct regimen.*

9. The object of a preposition is called an *indirect* object, or *indirect regimen*, as: *he writes to me*, or *he writes me a letter; me* is the indirect object of the verb governed by the preposition *to*, expressed or understood.

10. The prepostion and its object, dependent on a verb, noun, or adjective, are called the indirect object of the verb, noun, or adjective.

11. A verb agrees with its subject, in person and number; that is, the termination of the verb is so varied as to indicate whether its subject is of the first, second, or third person, and whether it is singular or plural.

12. A verb has *modes* and *tenses.*

13. *Mode* is the manner in which the action or being is represented by the verb.

14. By *tense* is meant the time to which the verb refers the action, whether *past, present*, or *future.*

15. Mode and Tense are indicated by modifications in the form of the verb.

MODES.

16. A French verb has *five* modes: the *infinitive*, the *indicative*, the *conditional*, the *imperative*, and the *subjunctive.*

17. The *infinitive* expresses the action without reference to person or number, as: *to write.*

18. The *indicative* expresses the action in an absolute manner, as: *I write, I have written, I shall write.*

19. The *conditional* expresses the action conditionally, as: *I would write, if I had time.*

20. The *imperative* expresses command or exhortation, as: *write.*

21. The *subjunctive* expresses the action in a subordinate and dependent manner, as: *I wish that you would write.*

TENSES.

22. Tenses are *simple* or *compound ; simple*, when they are expressed by the verb alone, as : *I write ; compound*, when they are formed with an auxiliary, as : *I have written.*

23. Each simple tense has its corresponding compound tense, which is formed of the simple tense of the auxiliary verb and the past participle of the principal verb ; thus, *I have*, is the simple tense, and *I have had*, the compound tense which corresponds with it.

24. Compound tenses always express completed action.

25. The *infinitive* mode has two tenses, a simple and a compound. It comprises also the *participles, present, past,* and *compound.*

26. The indicative mode has eight tenses.

27. The conditional mode has two tenses.

28. The imperative mode has one tense.

29. The subjunctive mode has four tenses.

INFINITIVE MODE.

SIMPLE.	COMPOUND.
Present.	Past.

PARTICIPLES.

Present.	Compound.
Past.	

INDICATIVE MODE.

Present.	Past Indefinite.
Imperfect.	Pluperfect.
Past Definite.	Past Anterior.
Future.	Future Anterior.

CONDITIONAL MODE.

Present.	Past.

IMPERATIVE MODE.

Present and Future.

SUBJUNCTIVE MODE.

Present.	Past.
Imperfect.	Pluperfect.

30. Adverbs, prepositions, conjunctions, and interjections are invariable words; that is, their forms are not varied to indicate gender, number, etc. They are sometimes called *particles*.

3.—SENTENCES.

1. A sentence is an assemblage of words making complete sense.
2. Every sentence consists of two parts: the subject and the predicate.
3. The subject is that concerning which something is said.
4. The predicate is that which is said concerning the subject.
5. A sentence is either (1) *affirmative*, (2) *negative*, (3) *interrogative*, or (4) *negative* and *interrogative*.

SUBJECT.	PREDICATE.	SUBJECT.	PREDICATE.
(1) Henry	is studious.	(3) Is Henry	studious?
(2) Henry	is not studious.	(4) Is not Henry	studious?

6. The rules which regulate the construction of sentences form that part of grammar which is called SYNTAX. They are comprised under the heads of *Government*, *Agreement*, and *Position*.
7. *Government* is the power which one word has over another, in requiring it to assume certain modifications, in order to express the relation in which the dependent word stands to the governing word.
8. *Agreement* is the correspondence of one word with another, in gender, number, and person.
9. *Position*, or *Collocation*, is the placing of the words in a sentence, in the order required by their mutual relations, or by usage.
10. In the sentence, *Henry is writing a letter to his father* (*Henry*, subject; *is writing a letter to his father*, predicate), the above three principles of syntax are illustrated in the following manner:

a. *Government.*—The subject *Henry* governs the verb *is writing* in the third person singular; the verb *is writing* governs the noun *letter*, directly, and the noun *father*, indirectly.

b. *Agreement.*—The verb *is writing* is in the third person singular, to agree with its subject, *Henry*.

c. *Position.*—In a declarative sentence, either affirmative or negative, the subject stands first, then the verb, next the noun which is the direct object, and then the noun which is the indirect object of the verb.

REM.—This is the natural or logical order in which the ideas present themselves to the mind: first, the thing about which we wish to say something; then the state or action which we wish to affirm of it; next the object; and lastly, the remote object of that action.

SUGGESTIONS.

The French Exercise may be recited in the following manner:— The teacher pronounces a sentence of the exercise to his class, and calls upon one of the students to repeat and translate it without looking in the book. When the student has done so, the teacher gives the English, and the student, or better the whole class, gives the French:

    Teacher. — **Le père et la mère de l'enfant.**
    Scholar. — **Le père et la mère de l'enfant.**
    The father and mother of the child.
    Teacher. — *The father and mother of the child.*
    Class. — **Le père et la mère de l'enfant.**

The students should be requested to prepare a written translation of the Theme, and to bring it to the class-room. The teacher should ask them to translate, each in turn, a sentence, and direct them to write their sentences on the blackboard, without looking at their written translations. If there are a sufficient number of blackboards in the class-room, several scholars may be writing their sentences at the same time, and the whole exercise may be corrected in a few minutes. When the teacher goes to the blackboard and corrects the sentences, in the order in which they are in the exercise, he should direct the pupils to correct, at the same time, their own exercises. The copy-books containing the corrected exercises should be examined from time to time, in order to ascertain whether they have been carefully and properly corrected.

FIRST LESSON.

The Noun.*—The Article.*

1. In French there are only two genders, the *masculine* and the *feminine*.

The article has two distinct forms; one for the masculine, and one for the feminine.

The definite article *the* is **le** for the masculine, and **la** for the feminine. Before a vowel and before a silent **h**,† it is **l'**.

Masculine.	Feminine.
Le père, the father.	**La mère**, the mother.
Le verre, the glass.	**La tasse**, the cup.
L'homme (*for* le homme), the man.‡	**L'eau** (*for* la eau), the water.

2. The indefinite article *a* or *an* is **un** for the masculine, and **une** for the feminine.‡

Un homme, a man.	**Une femme**, a woman; a wife.
Un verre, a glass.	**Une tasse**, a cup.

The article is repeated before each noun, as:

Le père et la mère.	The father and mother.
Un homme et une femme.	A man and woman.

Vocabulary 1.

Le père, the father.	**Un homme**, a man.
La mère, the mother.	**Une femme**, a woman; a wife.

---

* Introduction, p. 15. 17.

† There are some French words beginning with the letter *h*, before which the elision of the vowel does not take place; the *h* is then called *aspirate*, although it is not heard in the pronounciation. (See Introd., p. 11, 5.)

‡ Un, une, *a* or *an*, means also *one*, and is called, by most French grammarians, a numeral adjective. (See Less. 9.)

Un enfant,* a child.
Une maison, a house.
Une école, a school.
Un verre, a glass ; a tumbler.
Une tasse, a cup.
Le pain, the bread.
La viande, the meat.
Le lait, the milk.
L'eau (*fem.*), the water.
Et, and.

Est, is.
Où, where.
Ici, here.
Là, there.
A, to, at.
A la maison, at home ; home.
A l'école, at school.
De (d' before a vowel), of ; from.
Dans, in.
Pour, for.

Exercise 1.

1. Le père et la mère de l'enfant. 2. Le père est ici. 3. La mère est là, dans la maison. 4. Où est l'enfant ? 5. L'enfant est à l'école. 6. Le pain est pour la femme. 7. La viande est pour l'homme. 8. Un verre d'eau et une tasse de lait.

Theme 1.

1. The father of the child is here. 2. The mother is in the house. 3. The glass of milk is for the child. 4. The water is for the man. 5. Where is the woman ? 6. The woman is at home. 7. The bread and meat. 8. A glass and cup.

SECOND LESSON.

Noun and Article.—Plural Forms.

1. GENERAL RULE.—The plural of nouns is formed by adding **s** to the singular, as :

verre, glass ; *plural*, verres, glasses.

---

* Enfant, applied to a girl, is feminine ; une enfant, *a child (a little girl)*.

Exceptions.

Exc. 1. Nouns ending in **s, x,** or **z,** are the same in the plural as in the singular, as :

    fils, son ; *plural,* **fils,** sons.

Exc. 2. Nouns ending in **au** and **eu,** add **x** in the plural, as :

    gâteau, cake ;   *plural,* **gâteaux,** cakes.
    neveu, nephew ; *plural,* **neveux,** nephews.

Exc. 3. Nouns ending in **al,** generally change **al** into **aux,** as :

    cheval, horse ; *plural,* **chevaux,** horses.

REM. For other irregularities in the formation of the plural of nouns, see Second Lesson (*bis*), p. 26.

2.   PLURAL OF THE DEFINITE ARTICLE.

The plural of the definite article **le, la,** or **l',** is **les,** as :
Les hommes et les femmes.   The men and women.

Vocabulary 2.

Les parents, the parents.
Un fils, a son.
Une fille, a daughter ; a girl.
Un garçon, a boy.
Une église, a church ; **à l'église,** at church.
Une écurie, a stable.
Un cheval, a horse.
Un chien, a dog.
Un chat, a cat.
Un bateau, a boat.
Un gâteau, a cake.
Un livre, a book.
Une table, a table.
Un jardin, a garden.
Un arbre, a tree.
Charles, Charles.
Marie, Mary.
Sur, on, upon.
Sous, under
Sont, are.

Exercise 2.

1. Les verres et les tasses sont sur la table. 2. Les livres de Marie sont à la maison. 3. Les parents de Charles sont ici. 4. Le père et la mère sont à l'église. 5. Les filles sont dans la maison. 6. Les fils sont à l'école. 7. Le garçon est dans le jardin. 8. Le chat est sous l'arbre. 9. Où est le cheval? 10. Les chevaux sont dans l'écurie. 11. Le chien est dans le bateau. 12. Les gâteaux sont pour les enfants.

Theme 2.

1. The books of the child are on the table. 2. The parents are at church. 3. The sons are in the garden. 4. The daughters are in the house. 5. The boy is in the boat. 6. The dogs are in the water. 7. Where are the cats? 8. The cakes are for the girls. 9. The horse is in the stable. 10. The horses are under the trees. 11. Mary is at home, and Charles is at school.

SECOND LESSON (*bis*).

This second lesson (*bis*) is inserted, as all the lessons marked (*bis*) are, to complete a subject which is left incomplete in the preceding lesson. It is not intended that the students should study it in going through the course for the first time. They may do so afterwards, when they are reviewing.

PLURAL OF NOUNS.—EXCEPTIONS. (CONTINUED).

The exceptional rule 3, contained in the preceding lesson, does not comprise all the nouns that end in **al**. The following nouns in **al** follow the general rule.

Aval, surety for payment. **Cal**, callosity.
Bal, ball (*dancing party*). **Carnaval**, carnival.

Chacal, jackal.
Pal, pale (*in heraldry*).
Nopal, nopal.
Régal, entertainment.
Plural: **avals, bals,** etc.

Exc. 4. Seven nouns ending in **ou**, take **x** in the plural.

Bijou, jewel.
Caillou, flint.
Chou, cabbage.
Genou, knee.
Hibou,* owl.
Joujou, plaything.
Pou, louse.

Plural: **bijoux, cailloux,** etc.

REM. 1. Other nouns in ou follow the general rule.

Exc. 5. A few nouns ending in **ail**, change **ail** into **aux**.

Bail, lease.
Corail, coral.
Email, enamel.
Soupirail, air-hole.
Vantail, door-flap.
Ventail, ventail (*of helmets*).

Plural: **baux, coraux,** etc.

REM. 2. Other nouns ending in ail, follow the general rule, except ail, bétail (Exc. 6), and travail (Exc. 7).

Exc. 6. **Ail,** *clove of garlic,* has in the plural **ails** or **aulx**. **Bétail,** *cattle;* plural, **bestiaux**.

Exc. 7. The following four nouns have two plural forms, each with a different meaning:

Aïeul, ancestor, *plur.:* **aïeux;** aïeul, grandfather, *plur.:* **aïeuls**.
Ciel, heaven, *plur.:* **cieux;** ciel, tester; roof of a quarry; sky of a picture; climate; *plur.:* **ciels**.
Œil, eye, *plur.:* **yeux;** œil in œil de bœuf, ox-eye, *plur.:* **œils**.
Travail, labor, *plur.:* **travaux;** travail, minister's report; a brake for refractory horses, *plur.:* **travails**.

REM. 3. Nouns of more than one syllable ending in ant or ent, either change the final t into s, or follow the general rule: **l'enfant**, *plur.:* **les enfans**, or **enfants**, the children.

---

* The *h* of hibou is aspirated: le hibou, *the owl.*

THIRD LESSON.

CONTRACTION OF THE ARTICLE.—NE....PAS, NOT.

1. The definite article is subject to contraction.

De and **le** are contracted into **du**; **de** and **les**, into **des**.

A and **le** are contracted into **au**; **à** and **les**, into **aux**.

De and **la**, and **de** and **l'**; **à** and **la**, and **à** and **l'**, are not contracted.

2. **FORMS OF THE DEFINITE ARTICLE BEFORE NOUNS.**

(a.) BEFORE A MASCULINE NOUN.

SINGULAR.	PLURAL.
Le père, the father.	Les pères, the fathers.
Du père, of or from the father.	Des pères, of or from the fathers.
Au père, to the father.	Aux pères, to the fathers.

(b.) BEFORE A FEMININE NOUN.

La mère, the mother.	Les mères, the mothers.
De la mère, of or from the mother.	Des mères, of or from the mothers.
A la mère, to the mother.	Aux mères, to the mothers.

(c.) BEFORE A VOWEL.

L'enfant, the child.	Les enfants, the children.
De l'enfant, of or from the child.	Des enfants, of the children.
A l'enfant, to the child.	Aux enfants, to the children.

3. **Ne (n')....pas, NOT.**

Pas, *not*, or any other negative word accompanying a verb, requires **ne** (**n'**) before the verb. When the verb is not expressed, **ne** is not used.

Charles n'est pas à l'école.	Charles is not at school.
Les chevaux ne sont pas ici.	The horses are not here.

Vocabulary 3.

Un maître, a master; a teacher.
Un professeur, a professor.
Un général, a general.
Un soldat, a soldier.
Un mari, a husband.
Un chapeau, a hat ; a bonnet.
Une orange, an orange.
Un crayon, a pencil.
Une plume, a pen; a feather.
Paul, Paul.
Louise, Louisa.

Je (J'), I.
J'ai, I have
Ai-je ? have I ?
Je n'ai pas, I have not.
N'ai-je pas ? have I not?
Parlé, spoken.
Donné, given.
Prêté, lent.
Attaché, attached.
Eu, had.
Vu, seen.

Exercise 3.

1. Le fils du maître est dans l'école. 2. Les livres des enfants sont sur la table. 3. Le mari de la femme n'est pas à la maison. 4. Les mères des filles ne sont pas ici. 5. Le cheval du soldat est attaché à l'arbre. 6. Les chevaux des généraux sont dans l'écurie. 7. J'ai la plume du maître. 8. J'ai parlé au professeur. 9. J'ai donné les oranges aux enfants du professeur. 10. J'ai prêté le bateau aux fils du général. 11. Je n'ai pas eu le crayon de Paul. 12. Je n'ai pas vu le chapeau de Louise.

Theme 3.

1. The hat of the soldier is on the table. 2. The father of the girl is not at home. 3. The mother of the child is in the house. 4. The horses of the generals are under the trees. 5. The boat of the man is attached to a tree. 6. The husband and wife are not here. 7. I have the professor's book (the book of the professor). 8. I have not had the teacher's pen (the pen of the teacher). 9. I have spoken

to the general. 10. I have given the oranges to the girls. 11. I have lent the pencil to Louisa. 12. I have not seen Paul.

FOURTH LESSON.

Partitive Sense of the Noun.—Present Tense of Avoir, To Have.

1. A noun is used in a partitive sense when it is, or may be, preceded, in English, by *some* or *any*, as: *some* or *any bread*, or *bread*.

In French, a noun used in the partitive sense is preceded by **de** and the definite article; that is: **du, de la, de l'** or **des**, as:

Du pain,	Bread, some *or* any bread.
De la viande,	Meat, some *or* any meat.
De l'eau,	Water, some *or* any water.
Des gâteaux,	Cakes, some *or* any cakes.

2. **Omission of the Article before a Partitive Noun.**

The article is omitted, and **de** alone is used, before a partitive noun, in the following three cases:

(1.) After **pas**, or any other negative word, as:

Je n'ai pas de pain,   I have no bread (not any bread).

(2.) When the noun is preceded by an adjective, as:

J'ai de bon pain,   I have good bread.

(3.) When the noun limits another noun, or an adverb that denotes quantity:

Un verre d'eau,	A glass of water.
Un morceau de gâteau,	A piece of cake.
Une plume d'or,	A gold pen (a pen of gold).

PARTITIVE SENSE OF THE NOUN.

Un maître d'école, — A school-master.
Beaucoup de courage, mais peu de patience, — Much (of) courage, but little (of) patience.

3. Present Tense of Avoir, To Have.

J'ai,	I have.	Ai-je?	have I?
Tu as,	thou hast.	As-tu?	hast thou?
Il a,	he *or* it* has.	A-t-il?	has he *or* it?*
Elle a,	she *or* it* has.	A-t-elle?	has she *or* it?*
Nous avons,	we have.	Avons-nous?	have we?
Vous avez,	you have.	Avez-vous?	have you?
Ils ont,	they (*m.*) have.	Ont-ils?	have they (*m.*)?
Elles ont,	they (*f.*) have.	Ont-elles?	have they (*f.*)?

Rem. The letter t in *a-t-il? a-t-elle?* is inserted for euphony.

Vocabulary 4.

Du courage,† courage.
De la patience, patience.
De l'or (*m.*), gold.
De l'argent (*m.*), silver; money.
Du beurre, butter.
Du café, coffee.
Du thé, tea.
Du sucre, sugar.
Du sel, salt.
Du papier, paper.
De l'encre, (*f.*), ink.
Un morceau, a piece; a morsel.

Beaucoup (de), much; many.
Peu (de), little.
Un peu (de), a little.
Assez (de), enough.
Trop (de), too; too much.
Trop peu (de), too little.
Acheté, bought.
Apporté, brought.
Mangé, eaten.
Bu, drunk.
Mais, but.
Aussi, also; too,

Exercise 4.

1. Tu as du pain et de la viande. 2. As-tu de l'argent? 3. Je n'ai pas d'argent. 4. Charles a du papier et de

---

* As there is no neuter gender in the French language, *it* represents a noun which, in French, is either masculine or feminine. If the noun is masculine, *it* is *il*; if the noun is feminine, *it* is *elle*.

† Nouns which are preceded in the vocabularies by *du, de la, de l',* or *des,* in French, and by no determinative word in English, are taken in the partitive sense.

l'encre. 5. A-t-il des plumes ? 6. Il a acheté une plume d'or. 7. Marie a du beurre et du sucre. 8. A-t-elle aussi du café et du thé ? 9. Elle a assez de café et de thé, mais elle n'a pas de sel. 10. Nous avons mangé un morceau de pain et un peu de viande. 11. Les enfants ont bu trop d'eau. 12. Ils ont eu trop peu de lait. 13. Les filles ont apporté des oranges. 14. Ont-elles aussi apporté des gâteaux. 15. Elles n'ont pas apporté de gâteaux. 16. Vous avez beaucoup de courage, mais vous avez peu de patience.

Theme 4.

1. Thou hast courage and patience. 2. Charles has money, but he has no patience. 3. Has he brought paper and pens ? 4. He has brought paper and ink, but he has not brought pens. 5. Mary has bought much coffee and (of) tea. 6. Has she also bought sugar ? 7. She has not bought sugar. 8. We have sugar enough (enough of sugar). 9. Have you any salt ? 10. We have a great deal of (much) salt, but little butter. 11. You have too much courage, but too little patience. 12. They (*m.*) have eaten a piece of cake. 13. They (*f.*) have drunk water. 14. I have drunk a glass of milk.

FIFTH LESSON.

QUALIFYING ADJECTIVES.*—FEMININE AND PLURAL.

1. There are *qualifying* and *limiting* adjectives.

Qualifying adjectives add a quality to the noun, as: a *good* book, *bad* paper.

---

* Introduction, p. 14.

QUALIFYING ADJECTIVES.   33

Limiting adjectives limit the sense of the noun, as: *my* book, *this* paper.

All adjectives agree, in gender and number, with the noun which they qualify or limit.

2.   **FORMATION OF THE FEMININE OF ADJECTIVES.**

GENERAL RULE.— The feminine form of the adjective is obtained by adding **e** to the masculine form, as:

petit, *fem.* **petite,** small, little.

3.   Exceptions.

Exc. 1. Adjectives ending for the masculine in **e** mute, have but one form for both genders, as:

jeune, *masc.* and *fem.*, young.

Exc. 2. Many adjectives double the final consonant and add **e** for the feminine, as:

bon, *fem.* **bonne,** good; kind.

Exc. 3. Adjectives ending in **f**, change **f** into **ve**, as:

attentif, *fem.* **attentive,** attentive.

Exc. 4. Adjectives ending in **x**, change **x** into **se**, as:

studieux, *fem.* **studieuse,** studious.

For other irregularities in the formation of the feminine of adjectives, see Fifth Lesson (*bis*).

4.   **FORMATION OF THE PLURAL OF ADJECTIVES.**

The plural of adjectives is formed in the same manner as the plural of nouns (Lesson Second). The exceptional rules apply to the masculine forms of adjectives only; the feminine form always ends in **e**, and takes regularly **s** in the plural.

Les petits garçons,	The little boys.
Les petites filles,	The little girls.
Les mauvais crayons,	The bad pencils.
Les mauvaises plumes,	The bad pens.

See also Fifth Lesson (*bis*).

Vocabulary 5.

Un frère, a brother.	**Mauvais,** *f.* **mauvaise,** bad.
Une sœur, a sister.	**Bon,** *f.* **bonne,** good; kind.
Un oncle, an uncle.	**Gros,** *f.* **grosse,** big; large; stout; coarse.
Une tante, an aunt.	
Henri, Henry.	**Jeune,** *m.* and *f.*, young.
Henriette, Henrietta.	**Riche,** *m.* and *f.*, rich.
Jules, Julius.	**Pauvre,** *m.* and *f.*, poor.
Julie, Julia.	**Malade,** *m.* and *f.*, sick.
Alexis, Alexis.	**Attentif,** *f.* **attentive,** attentive.
Guillaume, William.	**Studieux,** *f.* **studieuse,** studious.
Petit, *f.* **petite,** small; little.	**Très,** very.
Grand, *f.* **grande,** large; tall.	**Qui,** who; which.

Exercise 5.

1. Le petit Jules* n'est pas ici. 2. Henri a une petite sœur, qui est malade. 3. Vous avez un grand jardin. 4. Nous avons aussi une grande maison. 5. J'ai acheté de bon papier et de bonne encre (Less. 4th—2). 6. Vous avez apporté des plumes, qui ne sont pas bonnes. 7. Les crayons ne sont pas mauvais. 8. Julie a un oncle, qui est très-riche. 9. Elle a aussi une tante, qui est très-bonne, mais qui n'est pas riche. 10. Le frère du soldat est pauvre. 11. Il n'a pas d'argent, et il est malade. 12. Le jeune

---

* In French, the article is used before a proper noun which is preceded by an adjective or title, as: *le petit Jules,* little Julius.

Alexis* n'est pas attentif. 13. Le gros Guillaume* n'est pas studieux. 14. La grosse Henriette* est une bonne fille. 15. Elle est attentive et studieuse. 16. Les enfants qui sont studieux, sont aussi attentifs.

Theme 5.

1. Little Henry* is a good boy. 2. He is studious and attentive. 3. Little Henrietta* is a good girl. 4. She is studious and attentive. 5. Good children† are studious and attentive. 6. Young Alexis* is not here. 7. He has a sister, who is sick. 8. The brother of Mary is sick too. 9. The father of Julius has bought a large boat. 10. It‡ is in the water, attached to a tall tree. 11. The uncle of (the) stout William has brought large (big) oranges, which are very good. 12. He is rich; he has a large stable and many (*beaucoup de*) horses. 13. Julia has an aunt, who is very kind, but she is poor. 14. You have brought bad paper and bad pens (Less. 4th—2). 15. He has brought pencils which are not bad.

FIFTH LESSON (*bis*).

FORMATION OF THE FEMININE OF ADJECTIVES.—EXCEPTIONS.
(CONTINUED.)

1. (Exc. 2, p. 33.) The adjectives which double the final consonant and add **e** for the feminine, are principally those that end in **el, eil, ien, on,** and **et,** as:

Tel, *f.* **telle,** such.	**Bon,** *f.* **bonne,** good; kind.
Pareil, *f.* **pareille,** similar.	**Sujet,** *f.* **sujette,** subject.
Ancien, *f.* **ancienne,** ancient.	

---

* See foot-note on opposite page.
† Good children, *les bons enfants.* The article is used in French before nouns that represent a class.   ‡ See foot-note *, p. 31.

And the following:

Bas,	f. basse, low.	Gros,	f. grosse, big; stout.
Gras,	f. grasse, fat.	Nul,	f. nulle, no.
Las,	f. lasse, tired.	Gentil,	f. gentille, pretty.
Épais,	f. épaisse, thick.	Sot,	f. sotte, silly.
Exprès,	f. expresse, positive.	Vieillot,	f. vieillotte, oldish.
Profès,	f. professe, professed.		

REM. A few adjectives in **et** do not double the **t**, viz.:

Complet,	f. complète, complete.	Secret,	f. secrète, secret.
Concret,	f. concrète, concrete.	Inquiet,	f. inquiète, uneasy.
Discret,	f. discrète, discreet.	Replet,	f. replète, corpulent.

EXC. 5. Five adjectives have three forms, two for the masculine, and one for the feminine:

Beau, bel, f. belle, beautiful; handsome; fine.
Nouveau, nouvel, f. nouvelle, new.
Vieux, vieil, f. vieille, old.
Fou, fol, f. folle, foolish.
Mou, mol, f. molle, soft.

Beau, nouveau, vieux, fou, and **mou,** are used before a consonant; **bel, nouvel, vieil,** (or **vieux**), **fol,** and **mol,** before a vowel and before a silent **h**.

EXC. 6. Four adjectives end in **che,** in the feminine:

Blanc,	f. blanche, white	Sec,	f. sèche, dry.
Franc,	f. franche, frank.	Frais,	f. fraîche, fresh.

EXC. 7. The following are peculiarly irregular:

Doux,	f. douce, sweet.	Tiers,	f. tierce, third (*part.*).
Faux,	f. fausse, false.	Long,	f. longue, long.
Jumeau,	f. jumelle, twin.	Oblong,	f. oblongue, oblong.
Préfix,	f. préfixe, prefixed.	Bénin,	f. bénigne, benign.
Roux,	f. rousse, reddish.	Malin,	f. maligne, malicious.

COMPARISON OF ADJECTIVES. 37

Caduc, *f.* caduque, decrepit.   Grec, *f.* grecque, Greek.
Public, *f.* publique, public.   Coi, *f.* coite, still; snug.
Turc, *f.* turque, Turkish.   Favori, *f.* favorite, favorite.
Traître, *f.* traîtresse, treacherous.

2. **Plural of Adjectives.—Exceptions. (Continued.)**

A few adjectives (Less. 5th—4) do not conform to the rules given for the formation of the plural of nouns in Lesson Second.

Bleu, *blue*, plural masculine: **bleus** (not *bleux*).

The following and some other adjectives in **al**, do not change **al** into **aux**, but follow the general rule and take **s**, as: **amical**, *amicable;* **fatal**, *fatal;* **final**, *final;* **initial**, *initial*, etc.; plural masculine: **amicals, fatals, finals**, etc.

The masculine forms (Less. 5th.—Exc. 5) **bel, nouvel, vieil, fol**, and **mol**, have in the plural, **beaux, nouveaux, vieux, fous, mous.**

SIXTH LESSON.

Comparison of Adjectives.

1. Adjectives are compared by means of the adverbs, **plus**, *more;* **moins**, *less;* **aussi**, *as;* **pas si** or **pas aussi**, *not so*.

The two terms of a comparison are connected by **que**, *than*, as:

Henri est plus grand que Charles.	Henry is taller than Charles.
Louise est moins avancée que Julie.	Louisa is not so far advanced as Julia.
Paul est aussi studieux que Marie.	Paul is as studious as Mary.
Il n'est pas si attentif.	He is not so attentive.

2. The superlative degree is formed by **le plus, le moins.**

Le plus studieux.   The most studious.
Le moins avancé.   The least advanced.

When the adjective in the superlative degree is placed after the noun,* the article is used twice, once before the noun, and once before the comparative adverb.

La fille la plus studieuse.   The most studious girl.

The noun that limits an adjective in the superlative degree, is preceded by **de.**

L'élève le plus avancé de l'école.   The most advanced scholar in the school.

3. Some adjectives are irregularly compared, as:

bon, good;	meilleur, better;	le meilleur, the best.
petit, little;	moindre, less;	le moindre, the least.
mauvais, bad;	pire, worse;	le pire, the worst.

The regular forms of **petit**, *small;* and **mauvais**, *bad;* that is **plus petit, le plus petit,** and **plus mauvais, le plus mauvais,** are also used.

4.   **PRESENT TENSE OF ÊTRE, TO BE.**

Je suis,	I am.	**Suis-je?**	am I?
Tu es,	thou art.	**Es-tu?**	art thou?
Il est,	he *or* it is.	**Est-il?**	is he *or* it?
Elle est,	she *or* it is.	**Est-elle?**	is she *or* it?
Nous sommes,	we are.	**Sommes-nous?**	are we?
Vous êtes,	you are.	**Etes-vous?**	are you?
Ils sont,	they (*m.*) are.	**Sont-ils?**	are they (*m.*)
Elles sont,	they (*f.*) are.	**Sont-elles?**	are they (*f.*)

---

* In French, the adjective is generally placed after the noun.

Vocabulary 6.

La ville, the city; the town.
La classe, the class.
Un élève, a scholar; a pupil (m.).
Une élève, a scholar; a pupil (f.).
Âgé, old; aged.
Appliqué, attentive; sedulous.
Avancé, advanced.
Fatigué, fatigued; tired.
Content, contented; satisfied.
Premier; première, first.
Dernier; dernière, last.
Ce matin, this morning.
Aujourd'hui, to-day.
Souvent, often.
Toujours, always.
Encore,* still.
Plus (ne),* no longer; no more.
Oui, yes.
Non, no.
Que (qu'), than; as.
Jean, John.
Pierre, Peter.
Élise, Eliza.

REM. The feminine form of the adjective is given in the vocabularies only when it does not conform to any of the rules contained in Lesson Fifth.

Exercise 6.

1. Je suis plus grand que Charles. 2. Oui, Paul, mais tu es aussi plus âgé que Charles. 3. Guillaume est le plus grand des enfants du maître. 4. Il est le plus avancé de l'école. 5. Julie, vous êtes moins avancée qu'Élise. 6. Élise est la meilleure élève de la classe. 7. Les bons élèves sont toujours les premiers à l'école. 8. Nous ne sommes pas les premiers ce matin. 9. Non, vous êtes les derniers aujourd'hui. 10. Nous ne sommes pas souvent les derniers. 11. Pierre est aussi appliqué qu'Alexis. 12. Henriette, vous n'êtes pas si attentive que Marie. 13. Êtes-vous encore malade? 14. Non, je ne suis plus malade, mais je

---

* *Encore*, still, and *plus* (ne), no longer, are adverbs of time. *Plus* requires *ne* before the verb; it is the responsive negative to *encore*: *Est-il encore ici?* Is he still here? *Il n'est plus ici.* He is not (*or* he is no longer here).

suis fatiguée. 15. L'oncle d'Élise est l'homme le plus riche de la ville. 16. Nous ne sommes pas riches, mais nous sommes contents.

Theme 6.

1. I am younger than Paul. 2. Yes, Charles, but you are also *less far* (moins) advanced. 3. Paul is the best scholar in (the) school. 4. Louisa is as tall as Henrietta. 5. She is not so old as Henrietta. 6. Julia, you are not very attentive this morning. 7. You are no longer sick? 8. No, but I am still tired. 9. Eliza is a good scholar. 10. She is the most advanced scholar (the scholar the most advanced) of the class. 11. Peter is less studious and less attentive than William. 12. We are contented, but we are not so rich as the uncle of Julius. 13. Julia is the first of the class to-day. 14. She is always the first. 15. Yes, Mary, and you are often the last.

SEVENTH LESSON.

LIMITING ADJECTIVES.—POSSESSIVE.

1. Limiting adjectives are of four kinds: *possessive, demonstrative, numeral,* and *indefinite.*

The possessive adjectives are:

SINGULAR.		PLURAL	
MASCULINE.	FEMININE.	FOR BOTH GENDERS.	
Mon	ma	mes,	my.
Ton	ta	tes,	thy.
Son	sa	ses,	his, her, its.
Notre	notre	nos,	our.
Votre	votre	vos,	your.
Leur	leur	leurs,	their.

LIMITING ADJECTIVES.—POSSESSIVE.

These adjectives are repeated before each noun:

Mon père et **ma** mère.	My father and mother.
Son frère et **sa** sœur.	His (*or* her) brother and sister.

Mon, ton, son, are used instead of **ma, ta, sa,** before a feminine word that begins with a vowel or a silent **h**:

Mon orange, **son** orange.	My orange, his (*or* her) orange.

Vocabulary 7.

Un cousin, a cousin (*m.*).
Une cousine, a cousin (*f.*).
Un neveu, a nephew.
Une nièce, a niece.
Un ami, (*f.*) **une amie,** a friend.
Une chambre, a room.
Une grammaire, a grammar.
Un mouchoir, a handkerchief.
Un gant, a glove.
Une montre, a watch.
Un parapluie, an umbrella.
Une ombrelle, a parasol.
Cassé, broken.
Trouvé, found.
Perdu, lost.
Vendu, sold.
Vif (p. 33, Exc. 3), lively.
Heureux (p. 33, Exc. 4), happy.

Exercise 7.

Pierre, tu* es mon cousin. 2. Oui, Jean, et je suis aussi ton ami. 3. Nous sommes heureux et contents; nous avons de bons parents. 4. Julie, vous avez ma grammaire. 5. J'ai trouvé votre grammaire dans ma chambre. 6. Avez-vous vu mes cousins aujourd'hui? 7. J'ai vu votre oncle et vos cousins ce matin. 8. Charles est très-vif; il a cassé sa montre d'or. 9. Ma cousine Élise a perdu son mouchoir. 10. Elle a aussi perdu ses gants. 11. Nous n'avons pas de classe ce matin; notre maître de français† est malade. 12. Nous avons vendu nos chevaux. 13. Nos amis ont

---

* The French use frequently *thee* and *thou* in conversation with children.
† *Un maître de français*, a French teacher.

vendu leur maison. 14. Mes neveux ont perdu leurs parapluies. 15. Notre tante n'est pas heureuse; elle est toujours malade. 16. Vos nièces sont les meilleures élèves de la classe de français.*

Theme 7.

1. Your cousin is my friend. 2. My cousin Mary is the friend of your sister. 3. Our uncle has lost his watch. 4. Our aunt has lost her handkerchief and (her) gloves. 5. Charles, I have found thy† umbrella in my room. 6. Louisa, I have broken thy parasol. 7. Thou art too (*trop*) lively, John. 8. Your nephews are my pupils. 9. Your nieces are the friends of my sisters. 10. Henry has found your grammar in his room. 11. Paul and Mary have lost their mother. 12. Our friends have sold their horses. 13. We have sold our boat to your cousins. 14. Your little niece is a lively child‡ (child lively); she is very happy.

EIGHTH LESSON.

LIMITING ADJECTIVES. (CONTINUED.) — THE DEMONSTRATIVE.

1. The demonstrative adjective is:

SINGULAR.		PLURAL
MASCULINE.	FEMININE.	FOR BOTH GENDERS.
Ce, cet,	cette, this, that.	Ces, these, those.

Ce is used before a consonant, **cet**, before a vowel:

Ce soldat.	This soldier; that soldier.
Cet arbre.	This tree; that tree.
Cet homme.	This man; that man.

---

* *La classe de français*, the French class.   † See p. 41, foot-note *.
‡ See p. 24, foot-note.

LIMITING ADJECTIVES.   43

The demonstrative adjective is repeated before each noun:

Cet homme et cette femme. That man and that woman.
Ces hommes et ces femmes. Those men and women.

To make the distinction which is made in English by *this* and *that*, the French use **ci** (from *ici*, here), and **là** (there). These words are joined with a hyphen to the noun:

Cet homme-ci.   *This* man.
Cet homme-là.   *That* man.
Ces enfants-ci.   *These* children.
Ces enfants-là.   *Those* children.

2.   Ce (C'), THAT; IT; *sometimes* HE; SHE; THEY.

Ce (C') must not be confounded with **ce, cet**: the latter is an adjective, and always precedes a noun; the former is a pronoun, and is much used before **est**, *is;* and **sont**, *are*.

C'est Monsieur et Madame D.   That is Mr. and Mrs. D.
Ce sont nos amis.   They are our friends.

3.   N'est ce pas? IS IT NOT SO?

N'est-ce pas? is added to a declarative sentence, to ask a question, when an affirmative answer is expected:

Nous sommes amis; n'est-ce pas?   We are friends; are we not?

Vocabulary 8.

Un monsieur, a gentleman.
Une dame, a lady.
Une demoiselle, a young lady.
Monsieur Delmar, Mr. Delmar.
Madame Delmar, Mrs. Delmar.
Mademoiselle D., Miss D.
Un capitaine, a captain.

Un médecin, a physician; a doctor.
Un voisin, a neighbor (*m.*).
Une voisine, a neighbor (*f.*).
Le facteur, the postman.
Un billet, a note.
Une lettre, a letter.
Du fruit, some fruit.

Une pomme, an apple. **Mûr,** ripe.
Une poire, a pear. **Vert,** green.
Un ananas, a pine-apple. **Ce (C'),** that; it (2).

Rem. **Monsieur,** abbreviated **M.**, is also used for Sir; **Madame,** abb. **Mme.,** for Madam; **Mademoiselle,** abb. **Mlle.,** for Miss. In the plural: **Messieurs,** abb. **MM.,** Gentlemen; **Mesdames,** abb. **Mmes.,** Ladies; **Mesdemoiselles,** abb. **Mlles.,** Young Ladies.

In addressing a person, it is customary to prefix the epithets **Monsieur, Madame, Mademoiselle,** to the names of his or her kindred: **Monsieur votre père,** your father; **Madame votre mère,** your mother; **Mademoiselle votre sœur,** your sister.

Exercise 8.

1. Ce monsieur est Monsieur Delmar, notre voisin. 2. Cette dame est Madame Delmar, notre voisine. 3. Cette demoiselle est Mademoiselle Delmar, leur fille. 4. Qui est cet homme-là? 5. C'est le facteur, qui a apporté des lettres de Paris. 6. Ce billet-ci est pour Mlle. votre sœur. 7. Cette lettre-là est pour Mme. votre mère. 8. Ces lettres-ci sont pour M. votre père. 9. Qui sont ces messieurs? 10. C'est le capitaine Duval et son frère, le médecin. 11. Ce sont nos amis. 12. Julie, vous êtes mon amie; n'est-ce pas? 13. Oui, je suis votre amie. 14. Charles, vous avez apporté du fruit, qui n'est pas mûr. 15. Mais ces gros ananas sont bons; n'est-ce pas? 16. Oui, mais les pommes et les poires sont trop vertes.

Theme 8.

1. Who is that gentleman? 2. That is Mr. Delmar. 3. That lady is Mrs. Delmar, his wife. 4. They are our neighbors. 5. That young lady is their daughter. 6. Miss Delmar is the friend of my sister. 7. The postman has

brought these letters. 8. *This* note is for your brother, the captain. 9. *That* letter is for the doctor. 10. *These* letters are for the professor. 11. I have bought some good fruit, apples, pears, and pine-apples. 12. These pears are good; are they not? 13. Yes, but your apples are too green. 14. These pine-apples are ripe. 15. They are not bad.

NINTH LESSON.

LIMITING ADJECTIVES. (CONTINUED.)—NUMERALS.

1. The numeral adjectives are of two kinds, *cardinal* and *ordinal*, they are:

CARDINAL.	ORDINAL.
1. **Un**, *fem.* **une.**	1st. **Premier**, *fem.* **première.**
2. **Deux.**	2d. **Deuxième**, *or* **Second-e.**
3. **Trois.**	3d. **Troisième.**
4. **Quatre.**	4th. **Quatrième.**
5. **Cinq.**	5th. **Cinquième.**
6. **Six.**	6th. **Sixième.**
7. **Sept.**	7th. **Septième.**
8. **Huit.**	8th. **Huitième.**
9. **Neuf.**	9th. **Neuvième.**
10. **Dix.**	10th. **Dixième.**
11. **Onze.**	11th. **Onzième.**
12. **Douze.**	12th. **Douzième.**
13. **Treize.**	13th. **Treizième.**
14. **Quatorze.**	14th. **Quatorzième.**
15. **Quinze.**	15th. **Quinzième.**
16. **Seize.**	16th. **Seizième.**
17. **Dix-sept.**	17th. **Dix-septième.**
18. **Dix-huit.**	18th. **Dix-huitième.**
19. **Dix-neuf.**	19th. **Dix-neuvième.**
20. **Vingt.**	20th. **Vingtième.**

21.	Vingt et un.	21st.	Vingt et unième.
22.	Vingt-deux.	22d.	Vingt-deuxième.
23.	Vingt-trois.	23d.	Vingt-troisième.
24.	Vingt-quatre.	24th.	Vingt-quatrième.
25.	Vingt-cinq.	25th.	Vingt-cinquième.
26.	Vingt-six.	26th.	Vingt-sixième.
27.	Vingt-sept.	27th.	Vingt-septième.
28.	Vingt-huit.	28th.	Vingt-huitième.
29.	Vingt-neuf.	29th.	Vingt-neuvième.
30.	Trente.	30th.	Trentième.
31.	Trente et un.	31st.	Trente et unième.
32.	Trente-deux.	32d.	Trente-deuxième.
33.	Trente-trois.	33d.	Trente-troisième.
40.	Quarante.	40th.	Quarantième.
41.	Quarante et un.	41st.	Quarante et unième.
42.	Quarante-deux.	42d.	Quarante-deuxième.
43.	Quarante-trois.	43d.	Quarante-troisième.
50.	Cinquante.	50th.	Cinquantième.
51.	Cinquante et un.	51st.	Cinquante et unième.
52.	Cinquante-deux.	52d.	Cinquante-deuxième.
53.	Cinquante-trois.	53d.	Cinquante-troisième.
60.	Soixante.	60th.	Soixantième.
61.	Soixante et un.	61st.	Soixante et unième.
62.	Soixante-deux.	62d.	Soixante-deuxième.
63.	Soixante-trois.	63d.	Soixante-troisième.
70.	Soixante-dix.	70th.	Soixante-dixième.
71.	Soixante et onze.	71st.	Soixante-onzième.
72.	Soixante-douze.	72d.	Soixante-douzième.
73.	Soixante-treize.	73d.	Soixante-treizième.
74.	Soixante-quatorze.	74th.	Soixante-quatorzième.
75.	Soixante-quinze.	75th.	Soixante-quinzième.
76.	Soixante-seize.	76th.	Soixante-seizième.
77.	Soixante-dix-sept.	77th.	Soixante-dix-septième.
78.	Soixante-dix-huit.	78th.	Soixante-dix-huitième.
79.	Soixante-dix-neuf.	79th.	Soixante-dix-neuvième.
80.	Quatre-vingts.	80th.	Quatre-vingtième.
81.	Quatre-vingt-un.	81st.	Quatre-vingt-unième.

LIMITING ADJECTIVES.—NUMERALS.

82.	Quatre-vingt-deux.	82d.	Quatre-vingt-deuxième.
83.	Quatre-vingt-trois.	83d.	Quatre-vingt-troisième.
84.	Quatre-vingt-quatre.	84th.	Quatre-vingt-quatrième.
85.	Quatre-vingt-cinq.	85th.	Quatre-vingt-cniquième.
86.	Quatre-vingt-six.	86th.	Quatre-vingt-sixième.
87.	Quatre-vingt-sept.	87th.	Quatre-vingt-septième.
88.	Quatre-vingt-huit.	88th.	Quatre-vingt-huitième.
89.	Quatre-vingt-neuf.	89th.	Quatre-vingt-neuvième.
90.	Quatre-vingt-dix.	90th.	Quatre-vingt-dixième.
91.	Quatre-vingt-onze.	91st.	Quatre-vingt-onzième.
92.	Quatre-vingt-douze.	92d.	Quatre-vingt-douzième.
93.	Quatre-vingt-treize.	93d.	Quatre-vingt-treizième.
94.	Quatre-vingt-quatorze.	94th.	Qnatre-vingt-quatorzième.
95.	Quatre-vingt-quinze.	95th.	Quatre-vingt-quinzième.
96.	Quatre-vingt-seize.	96th.	Quatre-vingt-seizième.
97.	Quatre-vingt-dix-sept.	97th.	Quatre-vingt-dix-septième.
98.	Quatre-vingt-dix-huit.	98th.	Quatre-vingt-dix-huitième.
99.	Quatre-vingt-dix-neuf.	99th.	Quatre-vingt-dix-neuvième.
100.	Cent.	100th.	Centième.
101.	Cent-un.	101st.	Cent-unième.
200.	Deux cents.	200th.	Deux centième.
210.	Deux cent-dix.	210th.	Deux cent-dixième.
1,000.	Mille.	1,000th.	Millième.
1,001.	Mille-un.	1,001th.	Mille-unième.
2,000.	Deux mille.	2,000th.	Deux millième.
2,500.	Deux mille-cinq cents.	2,500th.	Deux mille-cinq-centième.
3,000.	Trois mille.	3,000th.	Trois millième.
1,000,000.	Un million.	1,000,000th.	Millionième.

2.   **THE MULTIPLICATION TABLES.***

Combien font deux fois deux ?   How many are (in French, *make*) twice two?
Deux fois deux font quatre.   Twice two are (*make*) four.
Combien font deux fois trois ?   How many are twice three?
Deux fois trois font six. Etc.   Twice three are six. Etc.

Vocabulary 9.

Une année, a year.
Un mois, a month.
Une semaine, a week.
Un jour, a day.
Une heure, an hour.
Une minute, a minute.
Un dollar, } a dollar.
Une piastre, }
Un franc, a franc.
Un sou, a cent.
Un centime, a centime.
Une douzaine, a dozen.
Une fois, once; deux fois, twice.
Trois fois, three times.
La rue, the street.

La poste, the post-office.
La poche, the pocket.
Un mouchoir de poche, a pocket-handkerchief
La leçon, the lesson.
Combien (de), how much; how many.
Combien de fois, how many times.
Été, been.
J'ai été, I have been.
Jamais (ne), never.
Il y a, there is; there are.
Y a-t-il ? is there? are there?
Font (*ils font*), make (*they make*).
Ou, or.

Exercise 9.

1. J'ai cent-cinquante francs dans ma poche. 2. C'est trente piastres, ou dollars, de votre argent. 3. Le franc a vingt sous, ou cent centimes. 4. Il y a douze mois dans l'année. 5. Un mois a trente ou trente et un jours. 6. Vingt-quatre heures font un jour. 7. Soixante minutes font une heure. 8. Il y a une bonne école dans la onzième

---

* The pupils should learn the Multiplication Tables in French. The task is an easy one, when once the formula, and the numbers up to a hundred, are well known.

rue. 9. Combien d'élèves y a-t-il dans cette école? 10. Il y a treize élèves dans notre classe de français. 11. Jean a été le premier aujourd'hui ; Jules a été le deuxième ; et le gros Guillaume a été le dernier de la classe. 12. Nous avons eu la neuvième leçon. 13. J'ai été trois fois à la poste aujourd'hui. 14. Combien de fois avez-vous été à Paris? 15. Je n'ai jamais été à Paris. 16. Combien font sept fois sept? 17. Sept fois sept font quarante-neuf. 18. Julie a acheté une douzaine de mouchoirs de poche pour son frère.

Theme 9.

1. A year has twelve months. 2. A month has four weeks. 3. A week has seven days. 4. A day has twenty-four hours. 5. An hour has sixty minutes. 6. How many are (make) five times five? 7. Five times five are (make) twenty-five. 8. Five centimes make one cent. 9. Twenty cents make one franc. 10. Five francs make one dollar. 11. There is a large school in this street. 12. In that school there are eighty scholars. 13. The post-office is in (the) Eleventh* street. 14. How much money have you *with you* (sur vous)? 15. I have ten dollars, or fifty francs, in my pocket. 16. How many times have you been here? 17. *This is* (c'est) the first time *that* (que) I am here. 18. For *whom* (qui) have you bought that dozen of pocket-handkerchiefs?

NINTH LESSON (*bis*).

REMARKS ON THE NUMERAL ADJECTIVES.

1. The cardinal numeral adjectives are invariable, except **un**, **vingt**, and **cent**.

---

* No elision of the vowel takes place before *onze*, eleven and *onzième*, eleventh. See Less. 9 (*bis*)—4.

Un, fem. **une**, used in connection with **autre**, *other*, may take the plural ending (p. 81, 3).

Vingt and **cent**, when multiplied and not immediately followed by another number, take the plural ending.

Quatre-vingts piastres.	Eighty dollars.
Trois cents milles.*	Three hundred miles.

They are invariable when followed by another number.

Quatre-vingt-trois piastres.	Eighty-three dollars.
Trois cent-vingt milles.	Three hundred and twenty miles.

REM. **Vingt** and **cent** do not take the plural ending when they are used for **vingtième** and **centième**, as: **l'an huit cent**, in the year eight hundred.

2. **Mille**, *a thousand,* is written **mil**, in the ordinary computation of years, as:

Mil huit cent soixante-treize.	One thousand eight hundred and seventy-three.

3. **Second** and **deuxième**, *second*, are not to be used indiscriminately. **Second** indicates order; **deuxième** denotes one of a series, and is correctly used only when a third, a fourth, etc., are supposed to exist.

Au second étage.	In the second story (of a house).
La deuxième leçon.	The second lesson.

4. The elision of the vowel of the article and of other monosyllabic words, does not take place before **onze, onzième**, as:

De onze à vingt.	From eleven to twenty.
La onzième leçon.	The eleventh lesson.
Dans sa onzième année.	In his eleventh year.

---

* *Un mille*, a mile, is a noun; *mille*, a thousand, is a numeral adjective, and is invariable; *un milliard*, a thousand millions.

NUMERAL ADJECTIVES. 51

5.   THE NAMES OF THE DAYS OF THE WEEK.

Dimanche,	*or* **le dimanche.**	Sunday.
Lundi,	*or* **le lundi.**	Monday.
Mardi,	*or* **le mardi.**	Tuesday.
Mercredi,	*or* **le mercredi.**	Wednesday.
Jeudi,	*or* **le jeudi.**	Thursday.
Vendredi,	*or* **le vendredi.**	Friday.
Samedi,	*or* **le samedi.**	Saturday.

The article is used before the days of the week, to indicate the periodical return of something on a certain day of the week.

Nous avons le français deux fois par semaine, le lundi et le jeudi. We have French twice a week, Mondays and Thursdays.

No preposition is used before the days of the week.

Il était ici lundi. He was here *on* Monday.

6.   THE MONTHS.

Janvier, January.	**Juillet,** July.
Février, February.	**Août,** August.
Mars, March.	**Septembre,** September.
Avril, April.	**Octobre,** October.
Mai, May.	**Novembre,** November.
Juin, June.	**Décembre,** December.

The cardinal numbers are used for the days of the month, except for the first.

The preposition **de** before the names of the months is generally omitted, and no preposition is used before the date.

Le premier janvier. The first of January.
Le trois février. The third of February.
Le quatre mars. On the fourth of March.
C'est aujourd'hui le quinze mai. It is to-day the fifteenth of May.

TENTH LESSON.

Limiting Adjectives. (Continued.)—Indefinite.

1. The indefinite adjectives are:

Aucun, *f.* aucune, no.	Tout, toute, all; every; whole.
Pas un, *f.* pas une, not one.	Plusieurs, several.
Nul, *f.* nulle, no, not one.	Quel, *f.* quelle, which; what.
Autre, other.	Quelque, some.
Même, same.	Quelconque, whatever.
Chaque, each; every.	Tel, *f.* telle, such.

2.   Remarks and Examples.

(1.)   Aucun; Pas un; Nul (ne).

These are negative words; they require **ne** before the verb.

Aucun élève n'est absent.	No scholar is absent.
Nulle excuse n'est admissible.	No excuse is admissible.

(2.)   Autre, Other; Different.

J'ai d'autre papier.	I have other paper.
C'est une autre chose.	That is a different thing.

Rem. *Another*, meaning a *second one, one more*, is expressed by encore un.

Avez-vous encore un crayon?	Have you another pencil?
J'en ai encore un.	I have another one (one more).

(3.)   Chaque, Every; Each (*distributive*).

Chaque pièce est d'une qualité différente.*	Each piece is of a different quality.
Chaque chose est à sa place.	Everything is in its place.

---

* See foot-note, p. 38.

(4.) **Tout,** *pl.* **tous;** *f.* **toute,** *pl.* **toutes,** ALL; EVERY; WHOLE.

The article is placed between **tout** and the **noun**.

Tout le monde.	Everybody.
Tous les élèves.	All the scholars.
Toute une année.	A whole year.

(5.) **Plusieurs,** SEVERAL (*invariable*).

J'ai plusieurs grammaires.	I have several grammars.

(6.) **Quel,** *pl.* **quels;** *f.* **quelle,** *pl.* **quelles,** WHICH; WHAT.

Quel generally precedes a noun, either in an interrogative or an exclamatory sentence.

Quel jour du mois est-ce aujourd'hui ?	What day of the month is it to-day ?
Quelle leçon avons-nous ?	Which lesson have we ?
Quelle heure est-il ?	What hour (what time) is it ?

In an exclamatory sentence, **quel** is equivalent to *what a*.

Quel homme! Quelle femme!	What a man! What a woman!

The noun is sometimes understood after **quel**. It is then equivalent to **qui,** *who,* as:

Quel est ce monsieur ? *or* Qui est ce monsieur ?	Who is that gentlemen?

(7.) **Quelque,** SOME; *pl.* **quelques,** A FEW.

Quelque chose.	Some thing.
Quelques piastres.	A few dollars.

(8.) **Tel,** *f.* **telle,** Such.

The numeral adjective **un** precedes **tel**.

Un tel homme; une telle femme. Such a man; such a woman.

Vocabulary 10.

Une place, a place; a seat.
Une chose, a thing.
Une faute, a fault; a mistake.
Un thème, a theme; an exercise.
Un exercice, an exercise.
Une excuse, an excuse.
Une pièce, a piece.
De la mousseline, muslin.
La qualité, the quality.
Un mètre, a meter.
Une caisse, a case; a box.
Tout le monde, all the world; every body.
Absent, absent.
Présent, present.
Différent, different.

Exercise 10.

1. Aucun élève n'est absent de la classe. 2. Le professeur est dans l'autre chambre. 3. Nous avons tous la même leçon. 4. Il n'y a pas une faute dans ce thème. 5. Chaque chose est à sa place. 6. Jules a été absent lundi (on Monday). 7. Il n'a apporté aucune excuse. 8. C'est toujours la même chose. 9. Combien de pièces de mousseline y a-t-il dans cette caisse? 10. Chaque pièce est de trente mètres. 11. Toutes les pièces sont de la même qualité. 12. Il y a quelques pièces d'une qualité différente. 13. Tout le monde est dans la rue. 14. Tous les élèves sont présents. 15. Il y a plusieurs fautes dans votre thème. 16. Quel jour du mois est-ce aujourd'hui? 17. Quelle est cette dame? 18. Quel homme et quelle femme! 19. Je n'ai jamais vu un tel homme et une telle femme.

Theme 10.

1. Everybody is here. 2. Each student is in his seat. 3. No scholar has been absent to-day. 4. I have found a few mistakes in this exercise. 5. There are forty pieces of muslin in this case. 6. This piece is not of the same quality as the others. 7. Each piece is of a different* quality. 8. That is another thing. 9. Have you another pencil (2-2 Rem.)? 10. I have bought a whole piece of this muslin. 11. It is (of) thirty meters. 12. All my books are at home. 13. You have been absent several times. 14. It (Ce) is not my fault. 15. What an excuse! 16. What day of the week is it? 17. Which scholars are absent this morning? 18. Who is that gentleman? 19 I have never seen such a man.

ELEVENTH LESSON.

PRONOUNS.†—PERSONAL.

1. There are six kinds of pronouns: *personal, possessive, demonstrative, interrogative, relative,* and *indefinite.*

Pronouns agree, in gender and number, with the nouns which they represent.

2.   **PERSONAL PRONOUNS.— CONJUNCTIVE.**

Personal pronouns are of two kinds: *conjunctive* and *disjunctive.*

Conjunctive personal pronouns are used only in connection

---

* Place the adjective after the noun.   † Introduction, p. 16.

with verbs, as *subject, direct object,* or *indirect object,** or the verb. They are:

(1.) THE PRONOUNS USED AS SUBJECTS AND AS OBJECTS.

SINGULAR.

	AS SUBJECT.	AS DIRECT OBJECT.	AS INDIRECT OBJECT.
1st pers.	je (j'), I.	me (m'), me.	me (m'), to me.
2d pers.	tu, thou.	te (t'), thee.	te (t'), to thee.
3d pers. *masc.*	il, he; it	le (l'), him; it.	lui, to him.
fem.	elle, she; it.	la (l'), her; it.	lui, to her.

PLURAL.

	AS SUBJECT.	AS DIRECT OBJECT.	AS INDIRECT OBJECT.
1st pers.	nous, we.	nous, us.	nous, to us.
2d pers.	vous, you.	vous, you.	vous, to you.
3d pers. *masc.*	ils, they.	les, them.	leur, to them.
fem.	elles, they.	les, them.	leur, to them.

(2.)   **PRONOUNS USED AS OBJECTS ONLY.**

Se (s'), *himself, herself, itself, themselves, one's self* (direct or indirect object).

En, *some* or *any, of it, of them* (indirect object).

Y, *to it, to them* (indirect object).

Le (l'), *it, so* (invariable).

8.   **REMARKS AND EXAMPLES.**

The objective pronouns are placed before the verb, except when the verb is in the imperative mode.

Je connais.	I know *or* I do know.
Je vous connais.	I know you.
Je ne vous connais pas.	I do not know you.
Je parle.	I speak, I do speak.
Je lui parle.	I speak to him.
Je ne lui parle pas.	I do not speak to him.

---

* See Introduction. pp. 17, 18.

PRONOUNS.

When the verb is in the imperative mode, and used affirmatively, the objective pronouns stand after the verb.

Parlez-lui.   Speak to him.

But when the sentence is negative, the pronouns precede the verb.

Ne lui parlez pas.   Do not speak to him.

Vocabulary 11.

Je parle, I speak; I do speak; I am speaking.
Il parle, he speaks; he does speak; he is speaking.
Je donne, I give.
Il donne, he gives.
Je prête, I lend.
Il prête, he lends.
J'apporte, I bring
Il apporte, he brings.
J'appelle, I call.
Il appelle, he calls.

Je connais, I know; I do know.
Il connaît, he knows.
Je vois; il voit, I see; he sees.
Un camarade, a comrade; un camarade de classe, a class-mate
Un dictionnaire, a dictionary.
Une fleur, a flower.
Une pêche, a peach.
Les ciseaux, the scissors.
A présent, at present.
Tous les jours, every day.
Bien, well.

Exercise 11.

(In this Exercise, the pronouns representing the indirect objects are in *italic*.)

1. Je vous connais. 2. Je vous appelle. 3. Je *vous* donne ces fleurs. 4. Il me connaît. 5. Il *me* parle. 6. Je te vois. 7. Je t'appelle. 8. Je *te* prête ce livre. 9. Il nous voit. 10. Il nous appelle. 11. Il *nous* apporte des pêches. 12. Je vois votre camarade de classe. 13. Je le connais bien. 14. Je *lui* ai prêté un livre. 15. Je connais votre voisine. 16. Je la vois tous les jours. 17. Je *lui* ai parlé ce matin. 18. Je connais ces hommes. 19. Je les connais bien. 20. Je *leur* ai vendu un cheval. 21. Avez-vous mon

dictionnaire. 22. Je l'ai eu. 23. Je ne l'ai pas à présent. 24. Charles l'a. 25. Il ne l'a pas. 26. Nous l'avons. 27. Où sont mes ciseaux ; les avez-vous ? 28. Je ne les ai pas. 29. Vos camarades les ont. 30. Nous ne les avons pas. 31. Qui les a ?

Theme 11.

1. I know you. 2. I do not speak to you. 3. He sees me. 4. He has given me these peaches. 5. I see thee. 6. I give thee these flowers. 7. He calls us. 8. He speaks to us. 9. I know your class-mate. 10. I often* see him. 11. I have lent him my dictionary. 12. I know your cousin Mary. 13. I see her every day. 14. I often* lend her books. 15. I have had your pencil. 16. I have given it to your brother. 17. He has it. 18. He has it not now. 19. Julia has had your scissors. 20. I have them not now. 21. Louisa has them. 22. She has them not. 23. Have you them ? 24. We have them not. 25. The children have them.

TWELFTH LESSON.

Conjunctive Personal Pronouns. (Continued.)—Se; En; Y; Le.

1. **Se** is the reflective pronoun† of the third person, singular and plural, either as direct, or indirect, object of the verb: *himself, herself, itself, themselves, one's self,* or *to himself,* etc.

The reflective pronouns of the first and second persons

---

* Place the adverb after the verb.

† Reflective pronouns are so called because they receive the reflective action of the verb, as : I see *myself*. They are a subdivision of the personal pronouns.

CONJUNCTIVE PERSONAL PRONOUNS. 59

are, in form, the same as the objective pronouns given in the preceding lesson.

Me, myself, to myself.
Te, thyself, to thyself.

Nous, ourselves, to ourselves.
Vous, to yourself, to yourselves.

The reflective pronouns are used in the conjugation of pronominal verbs, as:

Se laver.	To wash one's self.
Je me lave.	I wash myself.
Il se lave.	He washes himself.
Vous lavez-vous?	Do you wash yourself?

2. EN, SOME *or* ANY; OF IT; OF THEM (*indirect object*).

The pronoun **en** expresses a part or quantity of the substance represented by the noun to which it refers: *some* or *any of it, of them; of it, of them.* It is used:

(1.) To represent a noun taken in the partitive or the indefinite sense, as:

J'ai du papier; en avez-vous?	I have paper; have you some?
J'en ai.	I have (some of it).
J'en ai encore.	I still have some.
Je n'en ai plus.	I have not any more.
J'ai des amis; vous en avez aussi.	I have friends; you have some too.
J'ai un livre; en avez-vous un?	I have a book; have you one?
Je n'en ai pas.	I have not.

(2.) To represent a noun taken in a definite sense, as:

Il parle de cette affaire; il en parle.	He speaks of that business; he speaks of it.

REM. In this latter sense, en is seldom used with reference to persons, **de lui, d'elle, d'eux, d'elles** being used instead.

3. Y, To it; To them (*indirect object*).

The pronoun **y** expresses the relation of the preposition **à** (*to*): *to it, to them*.

Pensez-vous à cette affaire ?	Do you think of (to) that business?
J'y pense.	I think of it (in French *to it*).

4. En and Y as Adverbs.

En and **y** are also used as adverbs, with reference to a place that has been previously mentioned: **en**, *from it, from there;* **y**, *there, to it, at it, in it*.

Avez-vous été à la poste ?	Have you been to the post-office ?
J'en viens.	I come from it.
J'y vais.	I am going to it.
Mon frère y est.	My brother is there.

5. The Invariable Pronoun Le.

The invariable pronoun **le**, equivalent to *it* or *so*, is used to represent an adjective or a sentence.

Etes-vous content ? Je le suis.	Are you satisfied ? I am (so).
Il est malade; vous le savez.	He is sick; you know it.

Vocabulary 12.

Je lave, I wash.
Vous lavez, you wash.
Je flatte, I flatter.
Vous flattez, you flatter.
Je blâme, I blame.
Vous blâmez, you blame.
Je trompe, I deceive.
Vous trompez, you deceive.
J'amuse, I amuse.
Vous amusez, you amuse.
Je pense, I think.
Vous pensez, you think.
Maman, mamma.
Je vais; il va, I go; he goes.
Je viens; il vient, I come; he comes.
Je sais; il sait, I know; he knows.
J'ai besoin de, I have need of.
Un couteau, a knife.
Une fourchette, a fork.

Un canif, a penknife.
Une affaire, an affair; a business.
La banque, the bank.

Pourquoi, why.
Parce que, because.
Quand, when.

Exercise 12.

1. Je me lave. 2. Je ne m'amuse pas. 3. Vous vous trompez. 4. Il se blâme. 5. Elle se flatte. 6. Il a de la patience ; j'en ai aussi. 7. Vous n'en avez pas. 8. Ils ont beaucoup d'argent. 9. Nous en avons peu. 10. Vous en avez assez. 11. J'ai un couteau ; en avez-vous un ? 12. Je n'en ai pas. 13. Charles en a deux. 14. N'avez-vous pas de fourchette ? 15. J'en ai une. 16. Marie n'en a pas. 17. Avez-vous besoin de ce canif ? 18. J'en ai besoin. 19. Où sont les ciseaux ; maman en a besoin. 20. Pourquoi parlez-vous de cette affaire ? 21. J'en parle, parce qu'il en parle. 22. Quand il y pense, il en parle. 23. Je n'y pense jamais. 24. Je vais à la banque. 25. J'en viens. 26. Henri y est. 27. Je le sais. 28. Vous êtes fatigué, et je le suis aussi.

Theme 12.

1. I blame myself. 2. You deceive yourself. 3. He amuses himself. 4. She flatters herself. 5. You have courage, and I have some too. 6. She has money, and you have none. 7. We have friends. 8. They have some too. 9. Have you a fork ? 10. I have one. 11. Louis has not. 12. I have no knife. 13. Mary has two. 14. I have your penknife; have you need of it ? 15. I have no need of it. 16. I think of (to) that affair. 17. When you think of it (to it), you speak of it. 18. Why do you speak of it? 19. Because I always think of it. 20. William is at the

bank. 21. I know it. 22. I come from there. 23. I go there. 24. He goes there too. 25. You are tired, and we are (so) too.

THIRTEENTH LESSON.

COLLOCATION OF OBJECTIVE PRONOUNS.

1. When two objective pronouns accompany a verb, the following order is to be observed.

The pronouns of the first and second persons precede the pronouns of the third person:

Me le, me la, me les.	It to me, them to me.
Te le, te la, te les.	It to thee, them to thee.
Nous le, nous la, nous les.	It to us, them to us.
Vous le, vous la, vous les.	It to you, them to you.

If both pronouns are of the third person, the direct object, **le, la** or **les**, precedes the indirect object, **lui** or **leur**; but the indirect object **se** precedes the direct object.

Le lui, la lui, les lui.	It to him *or* her, them to him.
Le leur, la leur, les leur.	It to them, them to them.
Se le, se la, se les.	It to himself, them to himself, etc.

POSITION OF EN AND Y.

En follows the other objective pronouns, and immediately precedes the verb:

M'en, nous en, vous en.	Some to me, to us, to you.
Lui en, leur en.	Some to him, to them.
L'en, les en.	It from there, them from there.

The adverb **y** follows the objective pronouns, except the pronoun **en.**

OBJECTIVE PRONOUNS.

M'y, nous y, vous y. — Me there, us there, you there.
L'y, les y. — Him, her *or* it there; them there.
Y en. — Some there.

REM. The negative particle ne immediately follows the subject; hence it precedes the objective pronouns.

Vocabulary 13.

Envoyé, (*past participle*), sent.
J'envoie, I send.
Il envoie, he sends.
Vous envoyez, you send.
Porté, *p. p.*, carried; taken.
Je porte, I take; I carry.
Il porte, he takes; he carries.
Mené, *p. p.*, taken; led.
Je mène, I take; I lead.
Il mène, he takes; he leads.
Raconté, *p. p.*, related.
Montré, *p. p.*, shown.

Un dessin, a drawing; a pattern.
Une gravure, an engraving.
Un bouquet, a bouquet.
Une bague, a ring (finger-ring).
Un violon, a violin.
Un concert, concert.
Une histoire, a history; a story.
Un oiseau, a bird.
Une cage, a cage.
Beau, bel, *f.* belle, beautiful,
(p. 36, Exc. 5) fine; handsome.
Joli, *f.* jolie, pretty.

Exercise 13.

1. C'est un beau dessin; me le donnez-vous? 2. Je vous le donne. 3. Qui vous a donné ce bel oiseau? 4. Ma tante me l'a apporté dans cette jolie cage. 5. Jules sait une belle histoire; il nous l'a racontée.* 6. Ce sont de beaux ananas; qui vous les a donnés?* 7. Mon cousin nous les a envoyés.* 8. Charles a un beau violon; son oncle le lui a envoyé de Paris. 9. Il nous l'a montré. 10. Julie a un beau bouquet; Henri le lui a donné. 11. Louise a une belle bague; son père la lui a achetée. 12. Vos neveux ont de belles gravures; leur oncle les leur a prêtées.* 13. Vous avez de belles fleurs; m'en donnez-vous? 14. Je

* The past participle agrees with the direct object of the verb. See LESS. 21, Sec. 4-3.

vous en donne. 15. Je lui en donne. 16. Je leur en donne. 17. J'ai été au concert; mon père m'y a mené. 18. Je vous y ai vu. 19. Jean est à la banque; je l'y ai envoyé. 20. Mes livres sont à l'école; je les y ai portés ce matin.

Theme 13.

1. You have a fine violin. 2. My uncle (has) sent it to me from Paris. 3. I have a beautiful pine-apple; I give it to you. 4. That is a fine ring. 5. My father (has) bought* it for me.† 6. *Those* (Ce) are fine drawings. 7. My aunt (has) lent* them to us. 8. Charles has fine engravings. 9. He has shown* them to us. 10. That is a beautiful story. 11. I have related* it to him. 12. This fine bouquet is for my cousin Henrietta; I send it to her. 13. Those pretty birds and that pretty cage are for Julius; his aunt sends them to him. 14. Your nephews have apples; I gave (have given) them to them. 15. Mary has bought oranges; she gave me one. 16. I have peaches; I give you some. 17. I give him some. 18. I give them some. 19. The money is *in* (à) the bank; I carried it there. 20. I go to the concert; my father takes me there.

FOURTEENTH LESSON.

Disjunctive Personal Pronouns.

1. The disjunctive personal pronouns are:

Singular.		Plural.	
Moi,	I *or* me.	**Nous,**	we *or* us.
Toi,	thou *or* thee.	**Vous,**	you.

---

* Make the past participle agree with the direct object of the verb, the same as if it were an adjective. See Less. 21, Sec. 4–3. † For me, *me* (indir. obj.).

Singular.		Plural.	
Lui,	he *or* him.	**Eux,**	they *or* them (*m.*).
Elle,	she *or* her.	**Elles,**	they *or* them (*f.*).

Soi, himself, herself, itself, themselves, one's self.

2. Remarks on the Disjunctive Personal Pronouns.

The disjunctive personal pronouns are used:

(1.) When the verb is not expressed, as:

Qui m'appelle? Moi.	Who calls me? I.
Qui appelle-t-il? Moi.	Whom does he call? Me.
Vous êtes plus grand que moi.	You are taller than I.

(2.) In apposition with other pronouns, for the sake of emphasis, and also to state separately the persons forming a compound subject or object.

Toi, tu es l'homme.	*Thou* art the man.
Lui et **moi** (nous) sommes amis.	He and I are friends.

(3.) After the verb **être,** when it is preceded by **ce.**

C'est moi. C'est lui.	It is I. It is he.

(4.) After prepositions.

Il parle de moi.	He speaks of me.

3. Chez, To, At *or* in the House of.

The preposition **chez** is used in the sense of *to* or *at the house of.*

Chez Monsieur Delmar.	To *or* at the house of Mr. Delmar.
Chez le médecin.	To *or* at the doctor's.

Chez is used with the disjunctive personal pronouns for *to* or *at my house, my home.*

Chez moi, to or at my house.
Chez toi, to or at thy house.
Chez lui, to or at his house.
Chez elle, to or at her house.

Chez nous, to or at our house.
Chez vous, to or at your house.
Chez eux, }
Chez elles, } to or at their house.

COMPOUND PERSONAL PRONOUNS.

The compound personal pronouns are formed of the disjunctive pronouns and the adjective **même**, *self*, connected by a hyphen.

Moi-même, myself.
Toi-même, thyself.
Vous-même, yourself.
Lui-même, himself.
Elle-même, herself.

Nous-mêmes, ourselves.
Vous-mêmes, yourselves.
Eux-mêmes, }
Elles-mêmes, } themselves
Soi-même, one's self.

These pronouns are used for the sake of emphasis.

Je l'ai vu moi-même.
Elle se blâme elle-même.

I have seen it myself.
She blames *herself*.

Vocabulary 14.

Un négociant, a merchant.
Un marchand, a storekeeper.
Un dentiste, a dentist.
Un artiste, an artist.
Un domestique, a man-servant.
Une domestique, }
Une servante, } a servant-girl.
Un magasin, a store; a warehouse.
Une boutique, a store; a shop
Un atelier, a workshop.
La rue du Temple, Temple street.

Un tableau, a painting; a picture.
Un miroir, a looking-glass.
Un journal, a newspaper.
Que? (Qu'), what?
Quelque chose,* something; anything.
Rien, (ne),* nothing; not anything.
Je demeure, I live; I am living.
Laissé, left.
Ce soir, this evening.
Avec, with.
Sans, without.

---

* *Quelque chose* is not used in a negative sense. *I have not anything*, is *Je n'ai rien*, not *Je n'ai pas quelque chose.*

Exercise 14.

1. Vous êtes plus âgé que lui. 2. Il est moins avancé que moi. 3. Vous et moi, nous sommes amis ; n'est-ce pas ? 4. Est-ce la servante qui est là ? 5. C'est elle. 6. Ma mère a besoin d'elle. 7. Je vais chez l'artiste ; j'ai quelque chose pour lui. 8. Qu'est-ce ? 9. C'est un tableau. 10. Qu'avez-vous pour moi ? 11. Je n'ai rien pour vous. 12. Moi, je vais chez les négociants ; ils sont à leur bureau. 13. J'ai de l'argent pour eux. 14. Ma sœur va chez le dentiste ; il demeure dans la rue du Temple. 15. J'y vais avec elle. 16. Elle n'y va pas sans moi. 17. Le dentiste n'est pas chez lui. 18. Maman a envoyé le domestique à la boutique. 19. Le marchand a laissé les journaux au magasin. 20. Henri vient chez moi ce soir. 21. Qui a cassé le miroir ? 22. C'est moi qui l'ai cassé. 23. Je me blâme moi-même. 24. C'est vous-même qui en avez parlé le premier.

Theme 14.

1. You are as old as I. 2. I am taller than you. 3. Is that the servant? 4. It is he. 5. My father has need of him. 6. He is in the office. 7. What is that? 8. It is a painting for the artist. 9. I am going to his workshop. 10. I am going there with you. 11. Have you anything for the merchant? 12. I have nothing for him. 13. The storekeeper (has) left his letters and newspapers at our house. 14. I am carrying them to his store. 15. Mamma has sent the servant-girl to the store (shop). 16. My cousin Lizzie is at the dentist's in Temple street. 17. I am coming without my sister. 18. She is going this evening to my aunt's. 19. I am now living at my aunt's. 20. My

cousins (*f.*) are not at home. 21. They are at my house. 22. Is it not you who broke (have broken) Mary's looking-glass? 23. It is not I; Mary broke (has broken) it herself

FIFTEENTH LESSON.

Possessive Pronouns.

1. The possessive pronouns are:

SINGULAR.		PLURAL.		
MASC.	FEM.	MASC.	FEM.	
Le mien,	la mienne,	les miens,	les miennes,	mine; my own.
Le tien,	la tienne,	les tiens,	les tiennes,	thine.
Le sien,	la sienne,	les siens,	les siennes,	his; hers.
Le nôtre,	la nôtre,	les nôtres,	les nôtres,	ours.
Le vôtre,	la vôtre,	les vôtres,	les vôtres,	yours.
Le leur,	la leur,	les leurs,	les leurs,	theirs.

Possessive pronouns agree, in gender and number, with the nouns which they represent.

Mon bien.	My property; my own.
Le mien, du mien, au mien.	Mine, of mine, to mine.
Ma fortune.	My fortune.
La mienne, de la mienne, à la mienne.	Mine, of mine, to mine.
Mes camarades.	My comrades.
Les miens, des miens, aux miens.	Mine, of mine, to mine.
Mes leçons.	My lessons.
Les miennes, des miennes, aux miennes.	Mine, of mine, to mine.

Vocabulary 15.

Un habit, a coat.
Un manteau, a cloak.
Un gilet, a waistcoat.
Une robe, a dress; a robe.
Une robe de chambre, a dressing gown.

POSSESSIVE PRONOUNS.

Une cravate, a cravat.
Neuf,* f. neuve, new.
Nouveau, nouvel, f. nouvelle,* new.
Vieux, vieil, f. vieille, old.
Facile, easy.
Difficile, difficult; hard.
J'aime, I love; I like.
Mieux, better.
J'aime mieux,† I like better.
Je préfère, I prefer.

Content (de), satisfied with; pleased with.
Je trouve, I find.
Je dis, I say; I tell.
Vous dites, you say.
Que (qu'), that.
Comme, like; as.
Comment, how.
Comment trouvez-vous? how do you like? (how do you find?)

Exercise 15.

1. Le manteau de Jules est neuf; le mien est vieux. 2. Le vôtre n'est pas moins beau que le sien. 3. La robe de Julie est neuve; la mienne est vieille. 4. La vôtre est aussi belle que la sienne. 5. J'aime mes parents; vous aimez les vôtres; chaque bon enfant aime les siens. 6. Nous avons un nouveau professeur de français, qui nous donne des leçons difficiles. 7. Les nôtres ne sont pas plus faciles que les vôtres. 8. Vous parlez des vôtres, et je parle des miennes. 9. Vous pensez aux vôtres; je pense aux miennes. 10. Ce nouvel élève pense aux siennes. 11. Comment trouvez-vous les dessins de nos nouveaux camarades? 12. Je les trouve beaux. 13. Que dites-vous des nôtres? 14. Je dis que j'aime mieux les leurs que les vôtres. 15. Ce nouvel habit est beau. 16. C'est un bel habit; je le préfère au mien. 17. Êtes-vous content de votre nouvelle cravate? 18. J'en suis content; elle est comme la vôtre.

---

* *Neuf, nouveau,* new. *Neuf,* new—what has not been used or worn; *Nouveau,* new to us—what we have not had, or seen, or heard of before.

† *J'aime mieux. Mieux* is not separated from *aime,* as *better* is from *like* in English. *J'aime mieux mon habit que le vôtre,* I like my coat better than yours.

Theme 15.

1. Your waistcoat is new; mine and his are old. 2. Your dress is new; mine and hers are old. 3. Your new clothes are handsome; mine and his are not so handsome as yours. 4. I like mine. 5. You are satisfied with yours. 6. He is satisfied with his. 7. Your lessons and mine are difficult. 8. His are easier than ours. 9. Every scholar thinks of his. 10. Your new coat is like mine. 11. I like the new drawings better than the old. 12. I prefer my engravings to yours. 13. I am satisfied with mine. 14. How do you like this new cravat? 15. It is very pretty; it is like mine. 16. What do you say of our new teacher? 17. I say that he gives us very hard lessons. 18. You are never satisfied. 19. Where is my cloak? 20. You (have) left it in my room.

SIXTEENTH LESSON.

Demonstrative Pronouns.

1. The demonstrative pronouns are:

Ce, *that; it;* **ceci,** *this;* **cela,** *that;* and the compounds of **ce,** formed by the addition of the disjunctive pronouns **lui, elle, eux, elles.**

Singular.			Plural.		
MASC.	FEM.		MASC.	FEM.	
Celui,	celle,	that, the one.	Ceux,	celles,	those.
Celui-ci,	celle-ci,	this (one).	Ceux-ci,	celles-ci,	these.
Celui-là,	celle-là,	that (one).	Ceux-là,	celles-là,	those.

DEMONSTRATIVE PRONOUNS.

2. **Ce**, THAT, IT; *sometimes* HE, SHE, THEY (p. 43-2).

Ce is used before **est**, *is*, and **sont**, *are*, to point out a person or thing.

C'est mon frère.	That is my brother.
Est-ce de l'or?	Is that gold?

Ce takes the place of a personal pronoun, *he, she,* or *they,* when **est** or **sont** is followed by a noun that denotes the same person or thing, to which **ce** refers.

Je connais ce monsieur; c'est mon voisin.	I know that gentleman; he is my neighbor.
Voici des livres; sont-ce les vôtres?	Here are books; are they yours?

Ce may represent a preceding sentence or a relative clause.

C'est vrai.	That is true.
Ce qui n'est pas clair, n'est pas français.	What (that which) is not clear, is not French.

3. **Ceci**, THIS (*this thing*); **cela**, THAT (*that thing*).

Ceci, *this,* is equivalent to *this thing;* **cela**, *that,* to *that thing*.

Ceci est pour vous.	This is for you.
Pour qui est cela?	For whom is that?
C'est (*for* cela est) pour lui.	That is for him.

REM. **Cela**, in conversational language, is often contracted into **ça**. **Ça ne va pas**, *that won't do;* **c'est ça**, *that's it*.

4. **Celui**, *f.* **celle**, THAT, THE ONE; **ceux**, *f.* **celles**, THOSE.

Celui, celle, *that, the one,* is followed by **de** and a noun, or by a relative clause.

Ce dessin et celui de Jules.	This drawing and that of Julius.
Cette gravure-ci et celle qui est sur la table.	This engraving and the one that lies on the table.
Les bas de laine et ceux de coton.	The woolen stockings and the cotton ones.
Les robes de satin et celles de velours.	The satin dresses and the velvet ones.

5. **Celui-ci**, etc., THIS; **celui-là**, etc., THAT.

Celui-ci, *this*, and **celui-là**, *that*, mark distinction and contrast.

Ce tableau-ci et celui-là.	This picture and that one.
Voici deux grammaires; celle-ci est pour vous, celle-là est pour moi.	Here are two grammars; this (one) is for you, that (one) is for me.

Vocabulary 16.

Un bas, a stocking.	Voulez-vous? Will you have? Do you wish for?
Un soulier, a shoe.	
Une botte, a boot.	Je veux, I will have; I wish for.
Du drap, some cloth (*broadcloth*).	Voici, here is; here are (*behold*).
Du coton, cotton.	Voilà, there is; there are.
Du satin, satin.	Cher, *f.* chère, dear.
Du velours, velvet.	Utile, useful.
De la soie, silk.	Agréable, agreeable.
De la laine, wool.	Vrai, true.

Ni....**ni** (ne), neither....nor.

Exercise 16.

1. Pour qui est cela? 2. C'est pour vous. 3. Comment trouvez-vous ceci? 4. C'est très-joli. 5. J'aime mieux ceci que cela. 6. Ce qui est utile, n'est pas toujours agréable. 7. C'est vrai. 8. Voici deux habits neufs, un pour

DEMONSTRATIVE PRONOUNS.

Charles et un pour moi. 9. J'aime mieux le vôtre que celui de Charles. 10. Quelle cravate voulez-vous, celle de soie ou celle de laine? 11. Je préfère celle qui est sur la table. 12. Voilà deux belles robes, une de velours et une de satin. 13. Celle de velours est la plus chère ; elle est pour ma cousine. 14. Celle de satin est pour ma tante. 15. Voulez-vous des bas de coton ou des bas de laine. 16. Ceux de laine sont plus chers que ceux de coton. 17. J'aime encore mieux ceux de coton. 18. Quel drap voulez-vous, celui-ci ou celui-là ? 19. Voici des bottes neuves ; celles-ci sont pour moi, celles-là sont pour vous. 20. Quels souliers voulez-vous, ceux-ci ou ceux-là ? 21. Je ne veux ni ceux-ci ni ceux-là.

Theme 16.

1. This is for you ; that is for me. 2. What do you say of that? 3. I do not like that. 4. What is agreeable, is not always useful. 5. Is that not true? 6. Here are two new cloaks ; the one of velvet is for my cousin, the one of cloth is for my aunt. 7. I like your cousin's (that of your cousin) better than your aunt's (that of your aunt). 8. These two dresses are beautiful ; the silk one (the one of silk) is for Mary, the satin one (the one of satin) is for Henrietta. 9. This one is dearer than that one 10. Which stockings do you wish, the cotton ones or the woolen ones? 11. I prefer the cotton ones. 12. There are new shoes ; these are for you and those are for me. 13. Which boots do you wish, these or. those ? 14. I will have neither these nor those. 15. These are too small, and those are too large. 16. Have you others? 17. Here are some.*

---
* En voici.

SEVENTEENTH LESSON.

INTERROGATIVE PRONOUNS.

1. The interrogative pronouns are:

Qui?	Who? whom? (*for persons, as subject or object.*)
Qu'est-ce qui?	What? (*for things, as subject.*)
Que?	What? (*for things, as direct object.*)
Quoi?	What? (*for things after prepositions.*)

And

Lequel, *f.* laquelle?	Which? which one?
Lesquels, *f.* lesquelles?	Which? which ones?

2.   EXAMPLES.

Qui m'appelle?	Who calls me?
Qui appelle-t-il?	Whom does he call?
Qu'est-ce qui vous amuse?	What amuses you?
Que voulez-vous?	What do you wish?
De quoi parlez-vous?	Of what do you speak?

The pronoun **lequel** is used with reference to persons and things, and agrees, in gender and number, with the noun which it represents.

Quel ruban?	Which ribbon?
Lequel? duquel? auquel?	Which one? of which? to which?
Quelle dentelle?	Which lace?
Laquelle? de laquelle? à laquelle?	Which one? of which? to which?
Quels dessins?	Which patterns?
Lesquels? desquels? auxquels?	Which ones? of which? to which?
Quelles étoffes?	Which goods?
Lesquelles? desquelles? auxquelles?	Which? of which? to which?

8. Que de....; Quoi de....

Que, quoi and the words **quelque chose** and **rien**, require **de** before the adjective to which they refer, as:

Qu'avez-vous de joli ?	What have you that is pretty?
Quoi de plus beau !	What is more beautiful!
Quelque chose de nouveau ?	Anything new?
Il n'y a rien de nouveau.	There is nothing new.

Vocabulary 17.

La porte, the door; the gate.
Le bruit, the noise.
Le goût, the taste.
La mode, the fashion ; à la mode, fashionable.
Le ruban, the ribbon.
La dentelle, the lace.
De l'étoffe, *f.*, cloth ; stuff.
Des étoffes, goods (*dress-goods*).
Un dessin, a pattern.
La préférence, the preference.
Durable, durable.
Dit, said ; told.
Fait, made ; done.
Il fait, he *or* it makes.
Il plaît, he *or* it pleases.
Il frappe, he strikes ; he knocks.
Il étonne, he astonishes.
Le plus, most.
Le mieux, best.
Rouge, red.
Bleu, blue.

Exercise 17.

1. Qui frappe à la porte ? 2. Qui a fait cela ? 3. Qui a dit cela ? 4. Qui blâmez-vous ? 5. De qui parlez-vous ? 6. A qui donnez-vous ces fleurs ? 7. Qu'est-ce qui vous étonne ? 8. Qu'est-ce qui fait ce bruit ? 9. De quoi parlez-vous ? 10. A quoi pensez-vous ? 11. Voici deux rubans ; lequel vous plaît le mieux, le rouge ou le bleu ? 12. Auquel donnez-vous la préférence, au rouge ou au bleu ? 13. Duquel parlez-vous, du rouge ou du bleu ? 14. Voici

de belles dentelles; laquelle est le plus* à votre goût, celle-ci ou celle-là ? 15. A laquelle donnez-vous la préférence ? 16. Quels dessins sont les plus jolis, les petits ou les grands ? 17. Lesquels sont le plus* à la mode ? 18. Desquels parlez-vous, de ceux-ci ou de ceux-là ? 19. Quelles étoffes sont les plus durables, celles de soie ou celles de laine ? 20. Auxquelles donnez-vous la préférence ? 21. Qu'y a-t-il de nouveau ? 22. N'avez-vous rien de nouveau ? 23. Votre tante a quelque chose de joli pour vous.

Theme 17.

1. Who lives in that house? 2. Who makes that noise? 3. Who strikes on the table? 4. Who has said that? 5. Whom do you call? 6. To whom do you speak? 7. What astonishes her? 8. What (has) made that noise? 9. Of (to) what do you think? 10. With what has he done that? 11. These ribbons are pretty; which one do you like best? 12. The blue one pleases me better than the red one. 13. Which one is most to your taste? 14. How do you like these patterns? 15. Which are the most fashionable? 16. Of which ones do you speak, of the small patterns or of the large? 17. Which goods are most fashionable? 18. Which are most durable? 19. To which do you give the preference? 20. What is more beautiful than this pattern? 21. What have you more beautiful than this?

---

* *Le* before *plus* is invariable when *plus* does not modify an adjective.

EIGHTEENTH LESSON.

Relative Pronouns.

1. The relative pronouns are:

Qui, who, which, that (*as subject for persons and things*).
Que, whom, which, that (*as direct object for persons and things*).
Qui, whom (*as indirect object, preceded by a preposition*).
Lequel, laquelle, *pl.* **lesquels, lesquelles,** who, whom, which.
Dont, of whom, of which, whose.
Quoi, what.
Où, in which; **d'où,** from which; **par où,** through which.

2.   **Qui,** Who, which, that (*subject*).

Le professeur qui parle.	The professor who speaks.
Les élèves qui écoutent.	The scholars who listen.
Les livres qui sont sur la table.	The books which lie on the table.

3.   **Que,** Whom, which, that (*direct object*).

L'artiste que je connais.	The artist whom I know.*
La leçon que je sais.	The lesson which I know.
Les livres que j'apporte.	The books which I bring.

4.   **Qui,** Whom (*indirect object for persons only*).

L'élève à qui je parle.	The scholar to whom I speak.
Les enfants avec qui il joue.	The children with whom he plays.

Lequel, Who, whom, which, that.

5. **Lequel,** preceded by a preposition, is used with reference to persons and things.

Les élèves auxquels (*or* **à qui**) **il donne une leçon.**	The scholars to whom he gives a lesson.

---

* *With whom I am acquainted.*

Les plumes avec lesquelles (*not* avec qui) j'écris. — The pens with which I write.

Rem. Instead of **de** and **lequel** (duquel, de laquelle, etc.), dont, is almost always preferable.

Dont, Of whom, of which, whose (*indirect object*).

Dont expresses the same relation as the preposition **de**. It is used with reference to either persons or things, for both genders and both numbers.

L'homme dont je parle.	The man of whom I speak.
La femme dont l'enfant est malade.	The woman whose child (of whom the child) is sick.
Les livres dont j'ai besoin.	The books of which I have need.
Le peintre dont je vous ai donné l'adresse.	The painter whose address I gave you (of whom I have, etc.)

Vocabulary 18.

Un peintre, a painter.
Une peinture, a painting; a picture.
Un auteur, an author.
Un ouvrage, a work.
Un outil, a tool.
Un voile, a vail.
Un nom, a name.
Une adresse, an address.
Une raison, a reason.
Une pension, a boarding house; a boarding-school.
Admiré, admired.
J'admire, I admire.
Travaillé, worked.
Je travaille, I work.
Joué, played.
Je joue, I play.
Quitté, left; quitted.
Je quitte, I leave.
Donné, given.
Lu, read.
Écrit, written.
Ce qui, what, that which (*subj.*).
Ce que, what, that which (*obj.*).
Si, so; si joli, so pretty.

Exercise 18.

1. Je vois le peintre qui vous a vendu cette peinture. 2. Je connais la dame qui a perdu ce voile. 3. Qui a apporté

les fleurs qui sont sur la table ? 4. Avez-vous lu le livre que je vous ai prêté ? 5. Est-ce moi que vous blâmez ? 6. Voilà les dessins que votre sœur trouve si jolis. 7. Sont-ce les étoffes que vous lui avez montrées? 8. Lui avez-vous dit le nom du négociant à qui vous avez écrit ? 9. Je ne connais pas le garçon avec qui il joue. 10. Je vais chez l'artiste pour qui j'ai une lettre. 11. J'ai vu le tableau auquel il travaille. 12. Il a vendu la maison dans laquelle il demeure. 13. Ce n'est pas la raison pour laquelle il a quitté sa pension. 14. Je ne connais pas l'homme dont vous parlez. 15. Avez-vous les outils dont vous avez besoin ? 16. C'est un ouvrage dont je suis très-content. 17. Voilà l'auteur dont vous admirez les ouvrages. 18. J'ai été chez le dentiste dont vous m'avez donné l'adresse. 19. Celui qui (he who) travaille est plus content que celui qui ne travaille pas. 20. Ce que je dis est vrai. 21. Ce qui est vrai, est beau.

Theme 18.

1. I know the painter who (has) made that painting. 2. I see the lady who was (has been) at our house this morning. 3. *This is* (Voici) the pattern which pleases (to) your sister. 4. There is the man whom I saw (have seen). 5. I have read the book which you (have) lent me. 6. The merchant (has) sent the vail which your sister (has) bought. 7. I have lost the address which he gave (has given) me. 8. I do not know the name of the physician to whom he has written. 9. I know the man *at whose house* (chez qui) he lives. 10. I have told you the reason for which I (have) left the boarding-school. 11. *These are* (Voici) the tools with which he works. 12. I see the lady of whom you speak. 13. I have the tools of which I have need. 14. There is the painter

whose pictures you admire (of whom you admire the pictures). 15. I know the author whose address he has given us (of whom he has given us the address). 16. I know what astonishes him. 17. I give you what I have.

NINETEENTH LESSON.

Indefinite Pronouns.

1. The indefinite pronouns are :

Autrui, others.
Chacun, every one ; each.
L'un l'autre, each other.
L'un et l'autre, both.
L'un ou l'autre, either.
Ni l'un ni l'autre (ne), neither.

On, one, some one, people, they.
Personne (ne), nobody.
Quelqu'un, somebody.
Quelques-uns, some; a few.
Quiconque, whoever.
Un de, one of.

The following indefinite adjectives are also used as pronouns:

Aucun (ne),
Nul (ne), } no one; none.
Pas un (ne),

Plusieurs, several ; many.
Tel, such a one.
Tout, all, everything.

2.   Remarks and Examples.

(1.) **Autrui,** Others (*used with reference to persons only*).

Autrui is always preceded by a preposition.

Les défauts d'autrui.   The faults of others.

(2.) **Chacun,** Every one ; Each (*distributive*).

Chacun pense à soi.   Every one thinks of himself.
Chacun de ces messieurs.   Each of these gentlemen.
Chacune de ces maisons.   Each of those houses.

INDEFINITE PRONOUNS.

(3.) **L'un l'autre,** Each other; *pl.* **les uns les autres,** One another.

Ils s'aiment l'un l'autre.	They love each other.
Ils se trompent les uns les autres.	They deceive one another.

(4.) **L'un et l'autre,** Both; **l'un ou l'autre,** Either; **ni l'un ni l'autre,** Neither.

J'achète l'un et l'autre.	I buy both.
J'achète l'un ou l'autre.	I buy either the one or the other.
Je ne veux ni l'un ni l'autre.	I will have neither.

(5.) **On,** One, some one, people, they.

On represents, indefinitely, some person or persons, as subject of the verb. It requires the verb in the third person singular.

On n'est pas toujours maître de soi.	One is not always master of himself.
On vous appelle.	Some one calls you.
Que dit-on de cela?	What do people say of that?
On n'en parle pas.	They do not speak of it.

After **et, si, ou, où,** and some other words, the letter l' is often used before **on** (**l'on**), for the sake of euphony.

On va et l'on vient.	They go and come.

(6.) **Personne,** Nobody (*requires* ne *before the verb*).

Je n'ai vu personne.	I have seen nobody.
Personne n'a parlé de cela.	No one has spoken of that.

(7.) **Quelqu'un,** Somebody, anybody.

Quelqu'un vous demande.	Somebody is inquiring for you.

Rem. **Quelqu'un** is not used in a negative sense. We should not say: je n'ai pas vu quelqu'un, but je n'ai vu personne, *I have not seen anybody.*

(8.) **Quelques-uns,** *f.* **quelques-unes,** SOME, A FEW.

Je connais quelques-uns de ces messieurs.	I know some of those gentlemen.
Je prends quelques-unes de ces gravures.	I take a few of these engravings.
J'en prends quelques-unes.	I take a few of them.

(9.) **Un de,** *f.* **une de,** ONE OF.

Un de nos élèves est absent.	One of our scholars is absent.
Une de ses sœurs est malade.	One of his sisters is sick.

(10.) **Aucun; pas un; nul (ne),** NONE, NO ONE.

Aucune de ces dames n'est ici.	Not one of those ladies is here.
Pas un de ces élèves ne sait la leçon.	Not one of those scholars knows the lesson.
Nul au monde ne le sait.	No one in the world knows it.

(11.) **Plusieurs,** SEVERAL, MANY.

J'ai vu plusieurs de vos amis.	I have seen several of your friends.
J'en ai vu plusieurs.	I have seen several of them.

(12.) **Tel,** *f.* **telle,** SUCH A ONE, MANY A ONE.

Tel rit aujourd'hui qui pleurera demain.	Many a one laughs to-day who will weep to-morrow.

REM. **Tel** is also used as a noun: **Monsieur un tel,** Mr. Such-a-one; **Madame une telle,** Mrs. So-and-so.

(13.) **Tout,** ALL, EVERYTHING.

Il a tout ce qu'il veut.	He has all (that which) he wishes.
Il m'a tout dit.	He has told me everything.

REM. **Tout** is also used as a noun. **Le tout produit un bel effet,** the whole produces a fine effect.

Vocabulary 19.

Le salon, the drawing-room; the parlor.
Un fauteuil, an arm-chair.
Une chaise, a chair.
Un éventail, a fan.
Un paquet, a packet; a bundle.
Un défaut, a defect; a fault.
Une composition, a composition.
Ensemble, together.
Seul, alone.

Frappé, knocked; struck.
Sonné, rung.
Il sonne, he rings.
On sonne, the bell rings.
Demandé, asked for.
Il demande, he asks for; he inquires for.
Il vaut, it is worth.
Parlez, speak.
Prenez, take.

Exercise 19.

1. A-t-on sonné? 2. On a frappé à la porte. 3. On vous demande. 4. On a apporté un paquet pour vous. 5. Ne parlez pas des défauts d'autrui. 6. Chacun a les siens. 7. Chacun est maître chez soi. 8. Chacune de ces maisons vaut dix mille piastres. 9. Ces deux élèves sont toujours ensemble. 10. On ne voit jamais l'un sans l'autre. 11. Ils sont l'un et l'autre très-studieux. 12. Voici deux éventails; prenez l'un ou l'autre. 13. Je ne veux ni l'un ni l'autre. 14. J'en ai déjà* plusieurs. 15. Plusieurs de nos élèves sont absents. 16. Y a-t-il quelqu'un avec M. votre père au salon? 17. Il n'y a personne avec lui; il y est seul. 18. On a apporté des fauteuils; en avez-vous acheté? 19. J'en ai acheté quelques-uns. 20. Quelques-unes de nos chaises sont cassées. 21. Pas une de ces compositions n'est sans fautes. 22. Nul ne sait cela mieux que lui. 23. Il m'a tout dit. 24. J'ai tout vu.

---

* *déjà,* already.

Theme 19.

1. The bell rings. 2. Some one calls me. 3. There is some one in the parlor who inquires for you. 4. They have brought the arm-chair. 5. Every one has his faults. 6. Every one works for himself (soi). 7. Each one of these paintings is worth five hundred dollars. 8. Those are two good friends; one always* sees them together. 9. The one is never without the other. 10. I am never alone at home; there is always somebody with me. 11. Take either of these two fans. 12. I don't like either (I like neither). 13. Have you seen anybody? 14. I have not seen anybody [see .(7.) Rem.]. 15. Nobody has been at the office. 16. Several of your friends have been here. 17. I have seen several of them. 18. Some of them have left the city. 19. I have bought a few of these chairs. 20. One of these compositions is without mistakes. 21. Not one of you has done better than Mr. Such-a-one. 22. He knows everything. 23. I have told him all.

TWENTIETH LESSON.

The Verb.†—Infinitive Mode.

1. There are four different classes or conjugations of verbs, distinguished by the endings of the infinitive mode.

The infinitive-endings are:

    In the 1st conjugation, **er**, as: **couper**, to cut.
    In the 2d conjugation, **ir**, as: **finir**, to finish.
    In the 3d conjugation, **oir**, as: **recevoir**, to receive.
    In the 4th conjugation, **re**, as: **vendre**, to sell.

---

* Put the adverb after the verb. † See Introduction, p. 18, 17.

THE VERB.—INFINITIVE MODE.

A verb consists of two parts, the root and the ending. The root is what remains after striking off the infinitive-ending, as: **couper**, root **coup**, ending **er**.

A verb is regular when it is inflected in all its modes and tenses, according to the model verb of the conjugation to which it belongs.

A verb is irregular when it deviates, in the formation of any of its modes or tenses, from the model verb of the conjugation to which it belongs.

The above four verbs: 1. **Couper**, 2. **Finir**, 3. **Recevoir**, 4. **Vendre**, are given as model verbs of the four conjugations respectively.

REM. Irregular verbs will be marked, in the vocabularies in this book by an asterisk, thus : *Aller, to go.

2. THE INFINITIVE MODE.

When two verbs are joined in construction, the one dependent on the other, the first verb governs the second in the infinitive.

(1.) Some verbs govern the infinitive directly, as:

Je veux couper l'arbre.	I will cut the tree.
Je vais le couper.	I am going to cut it.

(2.) Some verbs require the preposition **à** before the dependent infinitive.

J'ai beaucoup à faire.	I have a great deal to do.
J'aime à travailler.	I like to work.

(3.) Some verbs require the preposition **de** before the dependent infinitive.

Je cesse de travailler.	I cease working.
Je crains de vous offenser.	I fear to offend you.

REM. In English, prepositions, except *to*, are followed by the present participle; in French, prepositions govern the verb in the infinitive mode, except the preposition en, *in*.

3. THE INFINITIVE AFTER NOUNS.

A verb limiting the sense of a noun, is put in the infinitive, and is preceded by the preposition **de**.

Je n'ai pas le temps de sortir.	I have no time to go out.

4. POUR BEFORE THE INFINITIVE.

The preposition **pour**, *to, in order to*, is used before the infinitive to express a purpose.

Je viens ici pour vous dire.	I come here to tell you.
Il est trop malade pour sortir.	He is too sick to go out.
Je n'ai pas assez d'argent pour acheter votre bateau.	I have not money enough to buy your boat.

Vocabulary 20.

Trouver, to find.	Recevoir, to receive.
Copier, to copy.	*Voir, to see.
Étudier, to study.	Vendre, to sell.
Travailler, to work.	Attendre, to wait; to wait for.
Offenser, to offend.	*Dire (de),† to say; to tell.
Acheter, to buy.	*Lire, to read.
*Aller, to go.	*Écrire (de),† to write.
*Envoyer, to send.	*Faire, to do; to make.
Finir, to finish.	Je peux; il peut, I can; he can.
*Venir, to come.	Je cesse (de)†, I cease.
*Sortir, to go out; to come out.	Je prie (de),† I pray; I beg; I ask.
*Partir, to start; to leave.	Je crains (de),† I fear; I am afraid.

† These verbs require the preposition *de* before the dependent infinitive.

Le temps, the time ; the weather.   À midi, at noon.
L'intention, the intention.   Demain, to morrow.

Exercise 20.

1. Je veux couper l'arbre. 2. Je vais le couper. 3. Je vais finir mon ouvrage. 4. Je peux le finir ce matin. 5. Je ne peux pas recevoir ce monsieur. 6. Je n'ai pas le temps de le voir. 7. Avez-vous beaucoup à faire? 8. J'ai deux lettres à écrire, et trois à copier. 9. J'aime à lire, mais je n'aime pas à étudier. 10. Je cesse de travailler à midi. 11. Je vous prie de venir chez moi. 12. Je n'ai pas le temps d'aller chez vous. 13. Mon frère m'a écrit de lui envoyer les journaux. 14. J'ai l'intention de partir demain. 15. Il n'a pas la patience de nous attendre. 16. Vous n'avez pas le courage de lui dire cela. 17. Je crains de l'offenser. 18. Il est ici pour vendre son cheval. 19. Je n'ai pas assez d'argent pour l'acheter. 20. Je viens pour vous dire que le professeur est malade. 21. Il est trop malade pour sortir.

Theme 20.

1. He will cut the tree. 2. He is going to cut it this morning. 3. I wish to finish my work. 4. I can finish it at noon. 5. He will not receive us. 6. He says that he cannot see us. 7. He has too much to do. 8. I have several letters to copy. 9. I like to study, but I do not like to work. 10. I cease reading now. 11. I have no time to write this exercise. 12. He intends (He has the intention) to come here to-night. 13. I have no time to go to the post-office. 14. I am going to leave to-morrow. 15. I intend to send this letter to my uncle. 16. I beg you to do so. 17. *Tell him* (Dites-lui) to sell his boat. 18. I am

afraid to offend him. 19. Will you buy it? 20. I have not money enough to buy it. 21. I am too sick to go out to-day.

TWENTY-FIRST LESSON.

THE PARTICIPLE.*

1. A verb has two participles, the *present* and the *past*.

The present participle, which ends in English in *ing*, ends in French in **ant**.

The past participle of regular verbs ends, in the first conjugation in **é**, in the second in **i**, in the third and fourth, in **u**.

INFINITIVE.		PRESENT PARTICIPLE.		PAST PARTICIPLE.	
Couper,	to cut;	coupant,	cutting;	coupé,	cut.
Finir,	to finish;	finissant,	finishing;	fini,	finished.
Recevoir,	to receive;	recevant,	receiving;	reçu,	received.
Vendre,	to sell;	vendant,	selling;	vendu,	sold.

2. **THE PRESENT PARTICIPLE AND VERBAL ADJECTIVE.**

The present participle is not so much used in French as in English. It is principally used with the preposition **en**, *in*, which is the only preposition that may be followed by the present participle: **en allant,** *in going;* **en venant,** *in coming;* **en passant,** *in passing.*

J'ai vu votre frère en allant à la poste.	I saw your brother when I was going to the post-office.
J'y ai pensé en venant.	I thought of it while I was coming.
Il m'a dit le bonjour en passant.	He said good day when he was passing.

---
* Introduction, p. 17.

The present participle, qualifying a noun, is called a participial, or verbal, adjective.

Un enfant charmant. A charming child.
Une histoire intéressante. An interesting story.

   Rem. The verbal adjective is generally placed after the noun.

3. THE PAST PARTICIPLE.

The past participle is used in connection with an auxiliary verb, to form compound tenses (p. 92–2.).

J'ai cassé le plat. I have broken the dish.

The past participle of active verbs is an adjective when it is joined in construction with the verb **être**, and also when it is used without a verb. In the latter case, it is placed after the noun.

Le plat est cassé. The dish is broken.
Un plat cassé. A broken dish.

4. AGREEMENT OF THE PAST PARTICIPLE.

The past participle agrees with the noun to which it refers, in gender and number, the same as an adjective, in accordance with the following three rules:

(1.) The past participle, joined in construction to the tenses of the verb **être**, *to be*, agrees with the subject of the verb.

Le plat est cassé. The dish is broken.
Les plats sont cassés. The dishes are broken.

(2.) The past participle used without an auxiliary verb, agrees with the noun to which it refers.

Un plat cassé. A broken dish.
Une assiette cassée. A broken plate.
Des assiettes cassées. Broken plates.

(3.) The past participle of a transitive verb agrees with the direct object of the verb, when the direct object precedes the participle.

J'ai reçu *la lettre*.	I have received the letter.
Je *l'*ai reçue ce matin.	I received it this morning.
Voici la lettre *que* j'ai reçue.	Here is the letter which I received.

The direct object, in the above sentences, is in italic.

Vocabulary 21.

Abîmer, to spoil (a thing).
Gâter, to spoil.
Déchirer, to tear.
Mouiller, to wet.
Ôter, to take off; to take away.
Passer, to pass.
Rencontrer, to meet.
Saluer, to bow.
*Rire, riant, ri, to laugh, laughing, laughed.
Un horloger, a watchmaker.
Un bijoutier, a jeweler.
Une croix, a cross.
Une chaîne, a chain.
Bonjour, good morning; good day; dire le bonjour, to say good day.
Hier, yesterday.
Amusant, amusing.
Charmant, charming.
Intéressant, interesting.
Déjà, already.
Pas encore, not yet.

Exercise · 21.

1. J'ai rencontré votre frère en allant à la poste. 2. J'ai laissé votre croix chez le bijoutier en venant. 3. J'ai dit à Charles, en passant, de venir ici ce matin. 4. Le professeur nous a dit d'étudier la leçon en l'attendant. 5. Marie m'a salué en riant. 6. Je lui ai dit le bonjour en passant. 7. Nous avons lu une histoire intéressante. 8. C'est un livre amusant. 9. Votre petite nièce est charmante. 10. Elle a déchiré sa robe. 11. Elle va ôter sa robe déchirée. 12. J'ai ôté mon habit mouillé. 13. Mes gravures sont abîmées. 14. Jules les a mouillées. 15. Ce sont des enfants gâtés.

16. Ma chaine est cassée. 17. Je l'ai cassée hier. 18. Je vais porter cette chaine cassée chez l'horloger. 19. Voici la lettre que j'ai reçue. 20. Je ne l'ai pas encore lue. 21. Vous ne nous avez pas attendus. 22. A qui a-t-il vendu sa maison? 23. Il l'a vendue à M. Larue. 24. Vos sœurs sont ici; je les ai vues. 25. La pièce est déjà finie.

Theme 21.

1. I saw (have seen) Charles in coming. 2. He (has) bowed in passing, but he did not speak. 3. In going to the office, I (have) left your broken chain at the jeweler's. 4. Will you read the newspaper while waiting? 5. I met Julia this morning. 6. She said good-day laughing. 7. This is an interesting story. 8. I have read it twice. 9. That piece is charming. 10. Your drawings are spoiled. 11. That spoiled child tore (has torn) them. 12. That is very amusing. 13. My dress is wet. 14. I am going to take it off. 15. We have taken off our wet clothes. 16. My cross is broken. 17. Henry broke (has broken) it yesterday. 18. He is going to take it (carry it) to the watchmaker's. 19. I have received his letter, but I have not yet read it. 20. We have not yet sold our house, but we intend to sell it. 21. The lesson is already finished.

TWENTY-SECOND LESSON.

Auxiliary Verbs.— Conjugation of Avoir, To Have.

1. Verbs are subject to four different modifications, to indicate mode, tense, person and number.

These several modifications are, in some tenses, expressed

by the verb itself, in others, by the help of an auxiliary verb; the former are called *simple*, the latter *compound*, tenses.

2. AUXILIARY VERBS.

There are two auxiliary verbs: **avoir**, *to have*, and **être**, *to be*. They are auxiliary verbs, only, when they are used in the formation of compound tenses.

a. **Avoir** is used in the compound tenses of
(1.) All active verbs;
(2.) Most neuter verbs;
(3.) Those impersonal verbs which are not used as personal verbs, and which may be called *essential* impersonal verbs.

b. **Etre** is used
(1.) In the formation of the compound tenses of certain neuter verbs; those generally whose past tenses express a change in the condition or position of the subject;
(2.) In the formation of the compound tenses of all pronominal verbs;
(3.) In the formation of the passive verb.

3. CONJUGATION.

To conjugate a verb is to write or recite it, with all its modifications of mode, tense, person and number. This may be done in four different ways: 1. *affirmatively;* 2. *negatively;* 3. *interrogatively;* and 4. *interrogatively* and *negatively*.

In this lesson, we shall study the conjugation of the verb **avoir**, *to have*, and in the next, the conjugation of the verb **être**, *to be;* because these verbs are used as auxiliaries in the conjugation of other verbs.

4. Conjugation of AVOIR, To Have.

INFINITIVE MODE

Present.		Past.	
Avoir	to have	Avoir eu	to have had

PARTICIPLES.

Present.		Compound.	
Ayant	having	Ayant eu	having had

Past.
Eu, *m.*; eue, *f.*   had

INDICATIVE MODE.

Present.		Past Indefinite.	
J'ai	I have	J'ai eu	I have had
Tu as	thou hast	Tu as eu	thou hast had
Il a	he has	Il a eu	he has had
Nous avons	we have	Nous avons eu	we have had
Vous avez	you have	Vous avez eu	you have had
Ils ont	they have	Ils ont eu	they have had

Imperfect.		Pluperfect.	
J'avais	I had	J'avais eu	I had had
Tu avais	thou hadst	Tu avais eu	thou hadst had
Il avait	he had	Il avait eu	he had had
Nous avions	we had	Nous avions eu	we had had
Vous aviez	you had	Vous aviez eu	you had had
Ils avaient	they had	Ils avaient eu	they had had

Past Definite.		Past Anterior.	
J'eus	I had	J'eus eu	I had had
Tu eus	thou hadst	Tu eus eu	thou hadst had
Il eut	he had	Il eut eu	he had had
Nous eûmes	we had	Nous eûmes eu	we had had
Vous eûtes	you had	Vous eûtes eu	you had had
Ils eurent	they had	Ils eurent eu	they had had

FUTURE.

J'aurai	*I shall have*		
Tu auras	*thou wilt have*		
Il aura	*he will have*		
Nous aurons	*we shall have*		
Vous aurez	*you will have*		
Ils auront	*they will have*		

FUTURE ANTERIOR.

J'aurai eu	*I shall have had*
Tu auras eu	*thou wilt have had*
Il aura eu	*he will have had*
Nous aurons eu	*we shall have had*
Vous aurez eu	*you will have had*
Ils auront eu	*they will have had*

CONDITIONAL MODE.

PRESENT.

J'aurais	*I should have*
Tu aurais	*thou wouldst have*
Il aurait	*he would have*
Nous aurions	*we should have*
Vous auriez	*you would have*
Ils auraient	*they would have*

PAST.

J'aurais eu	*I should have had*
Tu aurais eu	*thou wouldst have had*
Il aurait eu	*he would have had*
Nous aurions eu	*we should have had*
Vous auriez eu	*you would have had*
Ils auraient eu	*they would have had*

IMPERATIVE MODE.

Aie	*have (thou)*
Ayons	*let us have*
Ayez	*have you*

SUBJUNCTIVE MODE.†

PRESENT.

Que j'aie	*that I may have*
Que tu aies	*that thou mayst have*
Qu'il ait	*that he may have*
Que nous ayons	*that we may have*
Que vous ayez	*that you may have*
Qu'ils aient	*that they may have*

PAST.

Que j'aie eu	*that I may* ⎫
Que tu aies eu	*that thou mayst* *have had*
Qu'il ait eu	*that he may*
Que nous ayons eu	*that we may*
Que vous ayez eu	*that you may*
Qu'ils aient eu	*that they may* ⎭

IMPERFECT.

Que j'eusse	*that I might have*
Que tu eusses	*that thou mightst have*
Qu'il eût	*that he might have*
Que nous cussions	*that we might have*
Que vous cussiez	*that you might have*
Qu'ils eussent	*that they might have*

PLUPERFECT.

Que j'eusse eu	*that I* ⎫
Que tu eusses eu	*that thou* *might have had*
Qu'il eût eu	*that he*
Que nous cussions eu	*that we*
Que vous eussiez eu	*that you*
Qu'ils eussent eu	*that they* ⎭

---

† The subjunctive mode in French is very different from the subjunctive mode in English. The English forms, *that I may have, that I might have*, do not give an adequate idea of the meaning of the subjunctive in French. The following sentence, taken from Exercise 22: *Je ne veux pas que tu aies mon dictionnaire*, if translated into English, according to the above form, would run thus, *I do not wish that*

REM. 1. The negative conjugation is formed with ne.... pas. Ne is placed before the verb, and pas after it (28-3). In compound tenses, ne stands before the auxiliary verb, and pas between the auxiliary and the past participle: **Je n'ai pas; Je n'ai pas eu.** See also Lesson Twenty-ninth.

REM. 2. A verb is conjugated interrogatively, by placing the pronoun subject, with a hyphen, after the verb. See, for full treatment Lesson Twenty-ninth.

Vocabulary 22.

Le bonheur, good luck; good fortune.
Le malheur, bad luck; misfortune.
Le plaisir, the pleasure.
La bonté, the kindness.
La prudence, the prudence.
Beau temps, fine weather.
La pluie, the rain.
De l'orage (*m.*), a storm.
Le prix, the price; the prize.
La promenade, the walk; walking; **aller à la promenade,** to go for a walk.
Congé, (*m.*), leave; permission; **avoir congé,** to have leave; to have a holiday.
Avoir besoin de, to have need of.
Avoir soin† de, to take care of.
Avoir envie de, to have a wish (for); a desire, a mind (to).
Fermer, to shut.
Perdre, to lose.
Dîner, to dine.
Dernier, dernière,‡ last.
Prudent, prudent.
Si (s' before il and ils), if; whether.
Je voudrais, I should like; I wish.

---

thou mayst have my dictionary, whereas the proper English is, *I do not wish thee to have my dictionary.* And again the following sentence taken from Theme 22: *He wishes that I should have pleasure,* might lead the learner to suppose that *should have* is to be translated by the conditional mode, whereas the present of the subjunctive is required. In translating from French into English, the student should, regardless of the French construction, give the correct English; and again, in translating from English into French, he should not adhere to the words in the English text, but rather be guided, for the present, by the heading of the section, and construe the French sentences accordingly.

† We say in French: *J'ai bien soin,* for, I take *good* care. using an adverb instead of an adjective, because the expression *avoir soin* is equivalent to a verb.

‡ *Dernier,* last, meaning the preceding, is placed after the noun; *lundi dernier,* last Monday.

Exercise 22.

IMPERFECT TENSE. 1. J'avais envie ce matin d'aller à la promenade. 2. Tu n'avais pas le temps de sortir. 3. Il avait à travailler pour son père. 4. Nous avions beaucoup à faire. 5. Vous n'aviez pas besoin d'acheter ce livre; nous l'avions déjà. 6. Ils n'avaient pas envie de venir avec nous.

PAST DEFINITE TENSE. 7. Hier, j'eus le plaisir de recevoir une lettre de mes parents. 8. Lundi dernier, nous eûmes le bonheur d'être tous ensemble. 9. La semaine dernière, ces enfants eurent le malheur de perdre leur père.

FUTURE TENSE. 10. Aurai-je besoin du parapluie? 11. Tu en auras besoin. 12. Aura-t-il soin de son petit frère? 13. Il aura bien soin de lui. 14. Aurons-nous beau temps? 15. Vous aurez de la pluie. 16. Ils auront de l'orage.

CONDITIONAL MODE. 17. J'aurais du plaisir, si j'avais congé. 18. Tu aurais un prix, si tu avais travaillé. 19. Il en aurait eu un, s'il avait été studieux. 20. Nous aurions eu nos thèmes, si nous n'avions pas été malades. 21. Vous auriez de l'argent, si vous aviez travaillé. 22. Ils n'auraient pas eu besoin de travailler, s'ils avaient été prudents.

IMPERATIVE MODE. 23. Aie la patience d'attendre. 24. Ayez la bonté de fermer la porte. 25. Ayons du courage et de la prudence.

SUBJUNCTIVE MODE, PRESENT TENSE.† 26. Il veut que j'aie soin de ces oiseaux. 27. Je ne veux pas que tu aies mon dictionnaire. 28. J'aime que vous ayez du plaisir. 29. Il ne pense pas que nous ayons du courage.

IMPERFECT TENSE.† 30. Je voudrais que vous eussiez un peu de patience, qu'il eût du courage, que nous eussions de

---

† See foot-note, p. 94.

l'argent, que vous eussiez de la prudence, et qu'ils eussent la bonté d'étudier leurs leçons.

Theme 22.

IMPERFECT TENSE. 1. I had to work. 2. Thou hadst a wish to go for a walk. 3. He had no time to go with thee. 4. We had letters to write. 5. You had not the patience to wait for us. 6. They had nothing to do.

PAST DEFINITE TENSE. 7. Last Monday, I had the good fortune to meet my friend Julius. 8. We had the pleasure of dining together. 9. He had the misfortune to lose his watch-chain. 10. Last week, my cousins had the kindness to send us some beautiful flowers.

FUTURE TENSE. 11. I shall have a holiday to-morrow. 12. Thou wilt have pleasure. 13. He will have need of an umbrella. 14. We shall not have any rain. 15. You will have a (de l') storm. 16. I think (that) they will have fine weather.

CONDITIONAL MODE. 17. I would have courage, if I had money. 18. Thou wouldst have money, if thou hadst worked. 19. He would have had a holiday, if he had had a prize. 20. We should have pleasure, if we had a holiday. 21. You would not take care of your money, if you had any. 22. They would have had a great deal of pleasure, if they had been with us.

IMPERATIVE MODE. 23. Have (*sing.*) the kindness to shut the door. 24. Have (*plur.*) the patience to wait for us. 25. Let us have prudence.

SUBJUNCTIVE MODE, PRESENT TENSE.† 26. He wishes that I should have pleasure, that thou shouldst have

---

† See foot-note, p. 94.

patience, that he should have courage, that we should have prudence.

SUBJUNCTIVE MODE, IMPERFECT TENSE.† 27. *I wish* (Je voudrais) that you had courage, that we had good luck, that he had patience, that they had all their books.

TWENTY-THIRD LESSON.

CONJUGATION OF ÊTRE, TO BE.

INFINITIVE MODE.

PRESENT.		PAST.	
Être	*to be*	Avoir été	*to have been*

PARTICIPLES.

PRESENT.		COMPOUND.	
Étant	*being*	Ayant été	*having been*

PAST.	
Été	*been*

INDICATIVE MODE.

PRESENT.		PAST INDEFINITE.	
Je suis	*I am*	J'ai été	*I have been*
Tu es	*thou art*	Tu as été	*thou hast been*
Il est	*he is*	Il a été	*he has been*
Nous sommes	*we are*	Nous avons été	*we have been*
Vous êtes	*you are*	Vous avez été	*you have been*
Ils sont	*they are*	Ils ont été	*they have been*

IMPERFECT.		PLUPERFECT.	
J'étais	*I was*	J'avais été	*I had been*
Tu étais	*thou wast*	Tu avais été	*thou hadst been*
Il était	*he was*	Il avait été	*he had been*
Nous étions	*we were*	Nous avions été	*we had been*
Vous étiez	*you were*	Vous aviez été	*you had been*
Ils étaient	*they were*	Ils avaient été	*they had been*

† See foot-note, p. 94.

CONJUGATION OF ÊTRE.

PAST DEFINITE.

Je fus	*I was*		
Tu fus	*thou wast*		
Il fut	*he was*		
Nous fûmes	*we were*		
Vous fûtes	*you were*		
Ils furent	*they were*		

PAST ANTERIOR.

J'eus été	*I had been*
Tu eus été	*thou hadst been*
Il eut été	*he had been*
Nous eûmes été	*we had been*
Vous eûtes été	*you had been*
Ils eurent été	*they had been*

FUTURE.

Je serai	*I shall be*
Tu seras	*thou wilt be*
Il sera	*he will be*
Nous serons	*we shall be*
Vous serez	*you will be*
Ils seront	*they will be*

FUTURE ANTERIOR.

J'aurai été	*I shall have been*
Tu auras été	*thou wilt have been*
Il aura été	*he will have been*
Nous aurons été	*we shall have been*
Vous aurez été	*you will have been*
Ils auront été	*they will have been*

CONDITIONAL MODE.

PRESENT.

Je serais	*I should be*
Tu serais	*thou wouldst be*
Il serait	*he would be*
Nous serions	*we should be*
Vous seriez	*you would be*
Ils seraient	*they would be*

PAST.

J'aurais été	*I should have been*
Tu aurais été	*thou wouldst have been*
Il aurait été	*he would have been*
Nous aurions été	*we should have been*
Vous auriez été	*you would have been*
Ils auraient été	*they would have been*

IMPERATIVE MODE.

Sois	*be (thou)*
Soyons	*let us be*
Soyez	*be (you)*

SUBJUNCTIVE MODE.

PRESENT.

Que je sois	*that I may be*
Que tu sois	*that thou mayst be*
Qu'il soit	*that he may be*
Que nous soyons	*that we may be*
Que vous soyez	*that you may be*
Qu'ils soient	*that they may be*

PAST.

Que j'aie été	*that I may have been*
Que tu aies été	*that thou mayst have been*
Qu'il ait été	*that he may have been*
Que nous ayons été	*that we may have been*
Que vous ayez été	*that you may have been*
Qu'ils aient été	*that they may have been*

IMPERFECT.		PLUPERFECT.	
Que je fusse	that I might be	Que j'eusse été	that I
Que tu fusses	that thou mightst be	Que tu eusses été	that thou
Qu'il fût	that he might be	Qu'il eût été	that he
Que nous fussions	that we might be	Que nous eussions été	that we
Que vous fussiez	that you might be	Que vous eussiez été	that you
Qu'ils fussent	that they might be	Qu'ils eussent été	that they

might have been

Vocabulary 23.

La campagne, the country; à la campagne, in the country; à la ville, in town.
Sage, wise; good (*of children*).
Économe, economical.
De retour, back.
Prêt (à),† ready.
Pressé (de),† in a hurry.
Obligé (de), obliged.
Étonné (de) (que),‡ astonished.
Fâché (de) (que), sorry.
Bien aise (de) (que), glad, very glad.
Il est bien (de) (que), it is well.
Il est temps (de) (que), it is time.
Quelle heure est-il? What o'clock is it?

À quelle heure? At what time?
À six heures, at six o'clock.
Il est une heure, it is one o'clock.
Il est deux heures, it is two o'clock.
Il est trois heures, it is three o'clock.
Il est quatre heures, it is four o'clock.
Il est cinq heures, it is five o'clock.
Il est onze heures, it is eleven o'clock.
Il est midi, it is twelve o'clock, noon.
Il est minuit, it is twelve o'clock, midnight.

---

† The preposition indicated in the vocabularies, after the adjectives and participles, is required before the infinitive which may follow, as; *Je suis prêt à partir*, I am ready to start; *Je suis pressé de partir*, I am in a hurry to start.

‡ The preposition *de* is required before the infinitive, and the conjunction *que* to introduce a subordinate clause, in which the verb is put in the subjunctive mode. The English construction may be different from the French: It would be well for you to be economical. *Il serait bien que vous fussiez économe.* (It would be well that you were economical.)

Exercise 23.

IMPERFECT TENSE. 1. Quand j'étais prêt, il était temps de partir. 2. Il était dix heures. 3. Tu n'étais pas ici. 4. Nous étions pressés. 5. Vous n'étiez pas de retour. 6. Mes parents étaient absents.

PAST DEFINITE TENSE. 7. Le mois passé, je fus obligé d'aller à Boston. 8. J'eus le plaisir d'y rencontrer votre ami. 9. Il fut étonné de m'y voir. 10. Nous fûmes contents d'être ensemble.

FUTURE TENSE. 11. Je serai chez moi à midi. 12. Tu ne seras pas ici demain. 13. Mon oncle sera de retour ce soir. 14. Quand nous serons à la campagne, nous aurons du plaisir. 15. Quand vous serez grands, vous serez obligés de travailler. 16. Nos amis seront ici dans deux heures.

CONDITIONAL MODE. 17. Je serais fâché de partir. 18. Tu serais bien aise d'être de retour. 19. Il serait ici, s'il n'était pas malade. 20. Nous serions contents, si vous l'étiez. 21. Vous seriez étonnés de les voir. 22. Ils seraient contents d'être ici.

IMPERATIVE MODE. 23. Sois sage et prudent. 24. Soyez studieux. 25. Soyons économes.

SUBJUNCTIVE MODE, PRESENT TENSE. 26. Il est bien que je sois ici. 27. Il est temps qu'il soit de retour. 28. Je suis fâché que vous soyez malade. 29. Je suis bien aise que nous soyons ici.

SUBJUNCTIVE MODE, IMPERFECT TENSE. 30. Il serait bien que je fusse de retour. 31. Je serais bien aise qu'il fût ici. 32. Je voudrais que vous fussiez studieux.

Theme 23.

IMPERFECT TENSE. 1. I was here at nine o'clock. 2. Thou wast not ready. 3. He was in a hurry to start. 4. We were obliged to wait. 5. You were not here. 6. They were in the country.

PAST DEFINITE TENSE. 7. Last Thurday, I was astonished to see my parents. 8. They were obliged to go to the city. 9. We were glad to see them.

FUTURE TENSE. 10. I shall be back at seven o'clock. 11. Wilt thou be absent to-morrow? 12. My aunt will be here in two hours. 13. We shall be glad to see her. 14. You will be astonished. 15. They will be satisfied, if we are (so).

CONDITIONAL MODE. 16. I should be very glad to be at home. 17. Thou wouldst be sorry to leave the country. 18. He would be sick, if he were in (à la) town. 19. We would be obliged to work. 20. You would not be satisfied, if you had nothing to do.

IMPERATIVE MODE. 21. Be (*sing.*) prudent and economical. 22. Be (*plur.*) satisfied with what you have. 23. Let us be good.

SUBJUNCTIVE MODE, PRESENT TENSE. 24. It is time that I were ready. 25. It is well that thou art here. 26. I am sorry that he is sick. 27. I am glad that you are back.

SUBJUNCTIVE MODE, IMPERFECT TENSE. 28. It would be well that I were ready. 29. I was astonished that he was back. 30. I wish (that) you were more economical.

TWENTY-FOURTH LESSON.

Regular Conjugations.—First Conjugation in ER.

1. **COUPER, To Cut.**—(Model Verb.)

INFINITIVE MODE.

Present.		Past.	
Couper	*to cut*	Avoir coupé	*to have cut*

PARTICIPLES.

Present.		Compound.	
Coupant	*cutting*	Ayant coupé	*having cut*

	Past.	
	Coupé *cut*	

INDICATIVE MODE.

Present.		Past Indefinite.	
Je coupe	*I cut*	J'ai coupé	*I have cut*
Tu coupes	*thou cuttest*	Tu as coupé	*thou hast cut*
Il coupe	*he cuts*	Il a coupé	*he has cut*
Nous coupons	*we cut*	Nous avons coupé	*we have cut*
Vous coupez	*you cut*	Vous avez coupé	*you have cut*
Ils coupent	*they cut*	Ils ont coupé	*they have cut*

Imperfect.		Pluperfect.	
Je coupais	*I was cutting*	J'avais coupé	*I had cut*
Tu coupais	*thou wast cutting*	Tu avais coupé	*thou hadst cut*
Il coupait	*he was cutting*	Il avait coupé	*he had cut*
Nous coupions	*we were cutting*	Nous avions coupé	*we had cut*
Vous coupiez	*you were cutting*	Vous aviez coupé	*you had cut*
Ils coupaient	*they were cutting*	Ils avaient coupé	*they had cut*

Past Definite.		Past Anterior.	
Je coupai	*I cut*	J'eus coupé	*I had cut*
Tu coupas	*thou cuttedst*	Tu eus coupé	*thou hadst cut*
Il coupa	*he cut*	Il eut coupé	*he had cut*
Nous coupâmes	*we cut*	Nous eûmes coupé	*we had cut*
Vous coupâtes	*you cut*	Vous eûtes coupé	*you had cut*
Ils coupèrent	*they cut*	Ils eurent coupé	*they had cut*

FUTURE.

Je couperai	I shall cut	J'aurai coupé	I shall have cut
Tu couperas	thou wilt cut	Tu auras coupé	thou wilt have cut
Il coupera	he will cut	Il aura coupé	he will have cut
Nous couperons	we shall cut	Nous aurons coupé	we shall have cut
Vous couperez	you will cut	Vous aurez coupé	you will have cut
Ils couperont	they will cut	Ils auront coupé	they will have cut

FUTURE ANTERIOR.

(included above)

CONDITIONAL MODE.

PRESENT.

Je couperais	I should cut	J'aurais coupé	I should have cut
Tu couperais	thou wouldst cut	Tu aurais coupé	thou wouldst have cut
Il couperait	he would cut	Il aurait coupé	he would have cut
Nous couperions	we should cut	Nous aurions coupé	we should have cut
Vous couperiez	you would cut	Vous auriez coupé	you would have cut
Ils couperaient	they would cut	Ils auraient coupé	they would have cut

PAST.

(included above)

IMPERATIVE MODE.

Coupe	cut (thou)
Coupons	let us cut
Coupez	cut (you)

SUBJUNCTIVE MODE.

PRESENT.

Que je coupe	that I may cut	Que j'aie coupé	that I may ⎫
Que tu coupes	that thou mayst cut	Que tu aies coupé	that thou mayst
Qu'il coupe	that he may cut	Qu'il ait coupé	that he may ⎬ have cut
Que nous coupions	that we may cut	Que nous ayons coupé	that we may
Que vous coupiez	that you may cut	Que vous ayez coupé	that you may
Qu'ils coupent	that they may cut	Qu'ils aient coupé	that they may ⎭

PAST.

(included above)

IMPERFECT.

Que je coupasse	that I ⎫	Que j'eusse coupé	that I ⎫
Que tu coupasses	that thou	Que tu eusses coupé	that thou
Qu'il coupât	that he ⎬ might cut	Qu'il eût coupé	that he ⎬ might have cut
Que nous coupassions	that we	Que nous eussions coupé	that we
Que vous coupassiez	that you	Que vous eussiez coupé	that you
Qu'ils coupassent	that they ⎭	Qu'ils eussent coupé	that they ⎭

PLUPERFECT.

(included above)

2. Remarks on the French and English Tense-Forms.

The several tenses of a French verb have each but one form; whereas the corresponding English tenses have two, three, or even more, forms.

Je coupe is equivalent to *I cut, I am cutting, I do cut,* and so forth, throughout the present tense.

Je coupais is equivalent to *I cut, I was cutting, I did cut,* or *I used to cut,* etc.

Je couperai is equivalent to *I shall,* or *will cut.*

In translating from English into French, the learner will bear in mind that the auxiliary verbs *am, do; was, did, used to; shall, will,* are only signs that indicate whether the verb is to be in the *present, imperfect,* or *future tense.*

The verb *will* is sometimes a sign of the future tense, and sometimes a part of the verb *to be willing.* When *will* has the meaning of *to be willing,* it is to be expressed, in French by a part of the verb *vouloir.*

Vocabulary 24.

Aimer, to love; to like; to be fond of.
Arriver, to arrive.
Casser, to break.
Chanter, to sing.
Danser, to dance.
Demander, to ask for.
Demeurer, to live, to dwell.
Jouer, to play.
Oublier, to forget.
Parler, to speak.
Penser (à), to think (of).
Quitter, to leave; to quit.
Rester, to remain; to stay.
Tranquille, quiet; still.
Maintenant, now.
Quelquefois, sometimes.
Autant que, as much as.
Le travail, work; working.
L'étude, *f.,* study; studying.

Exercise 24.

PRESENT TENSE. 1. Je travaille maintenant. 2. Tu ne travailles pas beaucoup. 3. Il étudie trop peu. 4. Nous étudions autant que vous. 5. Vous n'aimez pas l'étude. 6. Ils aiment à jouer.

IMPERFECT TENSE. 7. J'étudiais quand tu jouais. 8. Ma sœur chantait et nous dansions. 9. Vous ne travailliez pas. 10. Ils n'aimaient pas le travail ni l'étude.

PAST DEFINITE TENSE. 11. J'arrivai ici le même jour que mes parents arrivèrent à Paris. 12. Nous quittâmes la ville le quinze mai. 13. Quand je rencontrai Henri l'autre jour, il me demanda pourquoi j'avais quitté la classe.

FUTURE TENSE. 14. Je resterai ici. 15. Tu ne parleras pas de cela. 16. Il n'y pensera pas. 17. Nous étudierons demain. 18. Vous l'oublierez. 19. Nous quitterons la ville quand mes parents arriveront.

CONDITIONAL MODE. 20. Je resterais ici, si j'étais à (in) votre place. 21. Il ne travaillerait pas, s'il n'y était pas obligé. 22. Nous oublierions nos leçons, si nous ne les étudiions pas bien. 23. Vous casseriez cette montre, si vous l'aviez. 24. Ils danseraient, si vous chantiez.

IMPERATIVE MODE. 25. Reste tranquille. 26. Travaillez. 27. Parlons français.

SUBJUNCTIVE MODE, PRESENT TENSE. 28. Je veux que vous étudiiez vos leçons. 29. Il veut que nous parlions français.

SUBJUNCTIVE MODE, IMPERFECT TENSE. 30. Il serait bon que j'étudiasse un peu. 31. Je voudrais que vous parlassiez français. 32. Je voudrais qu'il quittât la classe.

Theme 24.

PRESENT TENSE. 1. I am studying. 2. Thou dost not study much. 3. Charles is playing, and Mary is singing. 4. We dance sometimes. 5. You do not work enough. 6. They do not like to work.

IMPERFECT TENSE. 7. I was working, and thou wast singing. 8. He was not fond of work or study. (In French: He liked neither work nor study.) 9. We studied as much as you. 10. You played *a great deal* (beaucoup). 11. They lived in the same street in which we lived.

PAST DEFINITE TENSE. 12. I left Paris on the same day that you arrived there. 13. We met your cousins yesterday. 14. They asked us for your address.

FUTURE TENSE. 15. I shall speak of that when I (shall) arrive there. 16. Thou wilt not think of it. 17. He will forget it. 18. Will you leave the city to-day? 19. We will stay here *till to-morrow* (jusqu'à demain). 20. They will arrive here this evening.

CONDITIONAL MODE. 21. I would take off my wet clothes, if I were *in* (à) your place. 22. Thou wouldst not forget thy lessons, if thou studiedst them well. 23. He would break the violin, if he had it. 24. We would stay, if you stayed. 25. They would not study, if they were not obliged *to* (y).

IMPERATIVE MODE. 26. Remain where thou art. 27. Keep (*plur.*) quiet. 28. Let us study.

SUBJUNCTIVE MODE, PRESENT TENSE. 29. He wants us to study our lesson. (In French: He will that we study our lesson.) 30. I want you to speak French. (In French: I will that you speak French.) 31. I am sorry that you leave the school.

SUBJUNCTIVE MODE, IMPERFECT TENSE. 32. It would be well for him to leave the city. (In French: It would be well that he should leave the city.) 33. I wish (that) you would speak to him about it (of it). 34. He was astonished that we spoke of it.

TWENTY-FIFTH LESSON.

VERBS OF THE FIRST CONJUGATION. — ORTHOGRAPHIC IRREGULARITIES.

Some classes of verbs in the first conjugation, though regularly varied throughout, undergo, in certain persons and tenses, slight changes, to make their orthography conformable to the pronunciation.

1. In verbs ending in **ger**, as **manger**, *to eat*, an **e** is inserted after **g**, before **a** and **o**, to make the **g** retain its soft sound, as: **mangeant, nous mangeons.**

2. In verbs ending in **cer**, as **commencer**, *to commence*, the letter **c**, to retain the sound of **s**, takes the cedilla before **a** and **o**, as: **commençant, nous commençons.**

3. In verbs ending in **yer**, as **nettoyer**, *to clean*, the **y** is changed into **i** before **e** mute, as: **je nettoie, tu nettoies, il nettoie, ils nettoient;** but **nous nettoyons, vous nettoyez.**

REM. Verbs ending in **ayer**, as **payer**, *to pay*, may either retain the **y** before e mute, or change it into **i**: **je paye,** or **je paie.**

4. In verbs having **é** (acute) or **e** (mute), before the consonant that precedes the ending **er**, as: **espérer**, *to hope*, and **mener**, *to lead*, the **é** or **e** is changed into **è** (grave),

before a mute syllable, as: **j'espère,** *I hope;* **je mène,** *I lead,* etc.

REM. Verbs in **éger,** as **abréger, protéger,** retain the **é** in the future and conditional: **j'abrégerai, il protégera.** (See also verbs in **eler** and **eter,** No. 5.)

5. Verbs ending in **eler,** as **appeler,** *to call,* double the **l,** and those in **eter,** as **jeter,** *to throw,* double the **t,** before **e** mute, as: **j'appelle, tu appelles, il appelle, ils appellent;** and **je jette, tu jettes, il jette, ils jettent.** But **nous appelons, vous appelez; nous jetons, vous jetez,** etc.

REM. The verbs **acheter,** *to buy;* **bourreler,** *to torment;* **déceler,** *to disclose;* **geler,** *to freeze;* **harceler,** *to harass;* **peler,** *to peel,* are exceptions to this last rule. They come under Rule 4.

Vocabulary 25.

Voyager, to travel.
Manger, to eat.
Protéger, to protect.
Commencer (à), to commence; to begin.
Placer, to place.
Menacer, to threaten.
***Envoyer,** to send.
Nettoyer, to clean.
Payer, to pay.
Mener, to lead; to take.
Espérer, to hope; to hope for.
Appeler, to call.
Jeter, to throw; to throw away.
Acheter, to buy.
Geler, to freeze.
Le libraire, the bookseller.
Le panier, the basket.
La voiture, the carriage.
La nuit, the night; **la nuit passée,** last night; **cette nuit,** to-night.
Bien des choses, many things.
Autrefois, formerly.
A intérêt, at interest.
A temps, in time.
Le soir, in the evening.

Exercise 25.

VERBS IN **ger.** 1. J'aime à voyager. 2. On voit bien des choses en voyageant. 3. Autrefois je voyageais beaucoup. 4. Je n'ai pas mangé de viande. 5. Nous mangeons peu de viande le soir.

Verbs in **cer**. 6. Je vais commencer mon travail. 7. Nous commençons à parler français. 8. Je commençais à le parler quand je quittai Paris. 9. Nous plaçons notre argent à intérêt. 10. Ils nous menaçaient.

Verbs in **yer**. 11. J'ai envoyé ma lettre à la poste. 12. J'envoie les journaux à mon oncle. 13. Il nous envoie un panier de pêches. 14. Je nettoierai mon pupitre quand j'aurai fini d'écrire. 15. Je vous payerai (*or* paierai) quand j'aurai de l'argent.

Verbs that change é or e into è. 16. Nous espérons vous voir ce soir. 17. J'espère que vous resterez avec nous jusqu'à demain. 18. Où voulez-vous nous mener? 19. Je vous mènerai aux Champs Élysées. 20. Nous vous protégerons.

Verbs in **eler** and **eter**. 21. Voulez-vous m'appeler quand tout sera prêt. 22. Je vous appellerai quand la voiture arrivera. 23. Vous ne m'avez pas appelé à temps. 24. Où jetterai-je ces papiers? 25. Jetez-les dans le panier.

Exceptions. 26. Où achetez-vous votre papier? 27. Je l'achète chez le libraire Dumont. 28. Je vous en achèterai, si vous voulez. 29. Il va geler. 30. Il gèle déjà. 31. Il a gelé, et il gèlera encore.

Theme 25.

Verbs in **ger**. 1. I have traveled much. 2. I have seen many things while traveling. 3. My uncle used to travel a great deal (formerly). 4. Are you still eating? 5. He was eating when I began (have begun) to write.

Verbs in **cer**. 6. I was beginning to write when some

one (has) called me. 7. We begin the lesson at nine o'clock. 8. Where will you place your money? 9. I will place it in the bank. 10. We do not threaten anybody.

Verbs in **yer**. 11. I have sent a letter to my cousins. 12. They send us the newspaper every week. 13. John is cleaning my clothes. 14. He will clean yours when he has (shall have) cleaned mine. 15. I will pay him when he is through (shall have finished).

Verbs that change é or e into è. 16. I have hoped, and I still hope, to see him. 17. Where do you lead us? 18. I lead you to the Elysian Fields. 19. Our courage will protect us. 20. I hope so.

Verbs in **eler** and **eter**. 21. Who has called us? 22. Our friends call us. 23. I will call you in time. 24. What do you throw into the basket? 25. I throw some papers into it.

Exceptions. 26. What do you buy? 27. I do not buy anything. 28. I would buy something, if I had money. 29. Did it freeze last night? 30. No, but it will freeze to-night.

TWENTY-SIXTH LESSON.

Regular Conjugations.—Second Conjugation in IR.

FINIR, To Finish.—(Model Verb.)

INFINITIVE MODE.

Present.		Past.	
Finir	*to finish*	Avoir fini	*to have finished*

PARTICIPLES.

Present.		Compound.	
Finissant	*finishing*	Ayant fini	*having finished*

Past.	
Fini	*finished*

INDICATIVE MODE.

Present.

Je finis	I finish
Tu finis	thou finishest
Il finit	he finishes
Nous finissons	we finish
Vous finissez	you finish
Ils finissent	they finish

Past Indefinite.

J'ai fini	I have finished
Tu as fini	thou hast finished
Il a fini	he has finished
Nous avons fini	we have finished
Vous avez fini	you have finished
Ils ont fini	they have finished

Imperfect.

Je finissais	I was finishing
Tu finissais	thou wast finishing
Il finissait	he was finishing
Nous finissions	we were finishing
Vous finissiez	you were finishing
Ils finissaient	they were finishing

Pluperfect.

J'avais fini	I had finished
Tu avais fini	thou hadst finished
Il avait fini	he had finished
Nous avions fini	we had finished
Vous aviez fini	you had finished
Ils avaient fini	they had finished

Past Definite.

Je finis	I finished
Tu finis	thou finishedst
Il finit	he finished
Nous finîmes	we finished
Vous finîtes	you finished
Ils finirent	they finished

Past Anterior.

J'eus fini	I had finished
Tu eus fini	thou hadst finished
Il eut fini	he had finished
Nous eûmes fini	we had finished
Vous eûtes fini	you had finished
Ils eurent fini	they had finished

Future.

Je finirai	I shall finish
Tu finiras	thou wilt finish
Il finira	he will finish
Nous finirons	we shall finish
Vous finirez	you will finish
Ils finiront	they will finish

Future Anterior.

J'aurai fini	I shall have finished
Tu auras fini	thou wilt have finished
Il aura fini	he will have finished
Nous aurons fini	we shall have finished
Vous aurez fini	you will have finished
Ils auront fini	they will have finished

CONDITIONAL MODE.

Present.

Je finirais	I should finish
Tu finirais	thou wouldst finish
Il finirait	he would finish
Nous finirions	we should finish
Vous finiriez	you would finish
Ils finiraient	they would finish

Past.

J'aurais fini	I should have ⎫
Tu aurais fini	thou wouldst have ⎪
Il aurait fini	he would have ⎬ finished
Nous aurions fini	we should have ⎪
Vous auriez fini	you would have ⎪
Ils auraient fini	they would have ⎭

REGULAR CONJUGATIONS. 113

IMPERATIVE MODE.

Finis — *finish (thou)*
Finissons — *let us finish*
Finissez — *finish (you)*

SUBJUNCTIVE MODE.

PRESENT.

Que je finisse	*that I may*
Que tu finisses	*that thou mayst*
Qu'il finisse	*that he may*
Que nous finissions	*that we may*
Que vous finissiez	*that you may*
Qu'ils finissent	*that they may*

} *finish*

PAST.

Que j'aie fini	*that I may*
Que tu aies fini	*that thou mayst*
Qu'il ait fini	*that he may*
Que nous ayons fini	*that we may*
Que vous ayez fini	*that you may*
Qu'ils aient fini	*that they may*

} *have finished*

IMPERFECT.

Que je finisse	*that I might*
Que tu finisses	*that thou mightst*
Qu'il finît	*that he might*
Que nous finissions	*that we might*
Que vous finissiez	*that you might*
Qu'ils finissent	*that they might*

} *finish*

PLUPERFECT.

Que j'eusse fini	*that I*
Que tu eusses fini	*that thou*
Qu'il eût fini	*that he*
Que nous eussions fini	*that we*
Que vous eussiez fini	*that you*
Qu'ils eussent fini	*that they*

} *might have finished*

Vocabulary 26.

Finir, to finish.
Choisir, to choose ; to select.
Remplir, to fill ; to fulfil.
Réussir, to succeed.
Bâtir, to build.
Punir, to punish.
Obéir† (à), to obey.
Avertir, to inform ; to give notice.
Il faut,‡ it is necessary; must.
Un ordre, an order.

Le devoir, the duty ; the task (at school).
Un encrier, an inkstand.
Le moment, the moment.
L'arrivée *f.*, the arrival.
L'hiver *m.*, winter.
Pendant, during.
Pendant que, while.
Avant, before.
Après, after.

---

† *Obéir* requires the preposition *à* before the noun, the same as if you said *to obey to* in English.

‡ *Il faut* is followed by a verb in the infinitive, or by *que* and a clause in which the verb is in the subjunctive mode. *Il faut obéir*, It is necessary to obey. *Il faut que j'obéisse*, I must obey.

Exercise 26.

Present Tense. 1. Je remplis mes devoirs. 2. Tu remplis les tiens, et il remplit les siens. 3. Nous obéissons à nos parents. 4. Vous obéissez aux vôtres. 5. Ils obéissent aux leurs.

Imperfect Tense. 6. Je finissais mon thème pendant que tu remplissais les encriers. 7. On bâtissait cette église quand j'étais ici pendant l'hiver. 8. Nous obéissions toujours à nos maîtres. 9. Vous réussissiez dans vos études. 10. Ils finissaient ce qu'ils avaient commencé.

Past Definite Tense. 11. Ce jour-là je finis mon devoir avant tous les autres. 12. Tu m'avertis de l'arrivée de mon père. 13. Nous choisîmes le bon moment pour réussir, et nous réussîmes. 14. Vous finîtes vos devoirs après moi. 15. Ils n'obéirent pas aux ordres, et ils furent punis.

Future Tense. 16. Je finirai mon thème après les classes. 17. Tu choisiras quelque chose de joli quand tu auras fini. 18. On bâtira une nouvelle école avant l'hiver. 19. Nous obéirons à vos ordres. 20. Vous nous avertirez quand la voiture arrivera. 21. Ils réussiront s'ils travaillent.

Conditional Mode. 22. Je remplirais les encriers, si je n'avais rien autre chose à faire. 23. Tu n'en finirais pas. 24. On vous punirait, si vous ne remplissiez pas vos devoirs. 25. Nous obéirions aux ordres du capitaine, si nous étions soldats. 26. S'ils avaient l'intention de partir, ils nous en avertiraient.

Imperative Mode. 27. Obéis, ou tu seras puni. 28. Finissez, je vous en prie. 29. Remplissons nos devoirs.

Subjunctive Mode, Present Tense. 30. Il faut que

j'obéisse. 31. Il faut que tu remplisses ton devoir. 32. Il faut qu'il finisse ce thème.

SUBJUNCTIVE MODE, IMPERFECT TENSE. 33. Je voudrais qu'il en finît. 34. Il serait bien que vous l'avertissiez de votre intention de partir.

Theme 26.

PRESENT TENSE. 1. I obey (to) my parents. 2. Thou obeyest thine, and he obeys his. 3. We fulfil our duties. 4. You fulfil yours. 5. They fulfil theirs.

IMPERFECT TENSE. 6. I was filling my inkstand, while thou wast finishing thy task. 7. We were building a stable last winter, when you were here. 8. You were finishing it. 9. They always obeyed their teachers.

PAST DEFINITE TENSE. 10. On that day I informed thee of the arrival of thy father. 11. Thou didst finish thy task before all the others. 12. You fulfilled your duty. 13. They chose the right (bon) moment, and they succeeded.

FUTURE TENSE. 14. I shall choose something pretty for Eliza. 15. You will finish this exercise after *school* (les classes). 16. He will succeed, if he works. 17. We shall inform you, when the carriage is (will be) here. 18. They will not finish what they have begun.

CONDITIONAL MODE. 19. I would finish this exercise before twelve o'clock, if I had *nothing else* (rien autre chose) to do. 20. He would succeed, if he worked. 21. We would obey (to the) orders, if we were in your place. 22. They would punish you, if you did not obey.

IMPERATIVE MODE. 23. Choose something for thyself. 24. Obey, or you will be punished. 25. Let us choose something pretty.

SUBJUNCTIVE MODE, PRESENT TENSE. 26. I must fulfil my duties. 27. He must finish his exercise. 28. We must obey orders.

SUBJUNCTIVE MODE, IMPERFECT TENSE. 29. It would be well for him to obey orders (It would be well that he should obey etc.). 30. I wish that you would finish (*with it*) (en).

TWENTY-SEVENTH LESSON.

REGULAR CONJUGATIONS.— THIRD CONJUGATION IN OIR.

RECEVOIR, TO RECEIVE.—(MODEL VERB.)

The third conjugation has only seven regular verbs; they have the letters **ev** before the infinitive-ending **oir**. The **ev** is syncopated in certain parts of the verb.

The **c** of the verbs in **cevoir** takes the cedilla before **o** and **u**.

INFINITIVE MODE.

PRESENT.		PAST.	
Recevoir	*to receive*	Avoir reçu	*to have received*

PARTICIPLES.

PRESENT.		COMPOUND.	
Recevant	*receiving*	Ayant reçu	*having received*

PAST.	
Reçu	*received*

INDICATIVE MODE.

PRESENT.		PAST INDEFINITE.	
Je reçois	*I receive*	J'ai reçu	*I have received*
Tu reçois	*thou receivest*	Tu as reçu	*thou hast received*
Il reçoit	*he receives*	Il a reçu	*he has received*
Nous recevons	*we receive*	Nous avons reçu	*we have received*
Vous recevez	*you receive*	Vous avez reçu	*you have received*
Ils reçoivent	*they receive*	Ils ont reçu	*they have received*

Imperfect.		Pluperfect.	
Je recevais	*I was receiving*	J'avais reçu	*I had received*
Tu recevais	*thou wast receiving*	Tu avais reçu	*thou hadst received*
Il recevait	*he was receiving*	Il avait reçu	*he had received*
Nous recevions	*we were receiving*	Nous avions reçu	*we had received*
Vous receviez	*you were receiving*	Vous aviez reçu	*you had received*
Ils recevaient	*they were receiving*	Ils avaient reçu	*they had received*

Past Definite.		Past Anterior.	
Je reçus	*I received*	J'eus reçu	*I had received*
Tu reçus	*thou receivedst*	Tu eus reçu	*thou hadst received*
Il reçut	*he received*	Il eut reçu	*he had received*
Nous reçûmes	*we received*	Nous eûmes reçu	*we had received*
Vous reçûtes	*you received*	Vous eûtes reçu	*you had received*
Ils reçurent	*they received*	Ils eurent reçu	*they had received*

Future.		Future Anterior.	
Je recevrai	*I shall receive*	J'aurai reçu	*I shall have received*
Tu recevras	*thou wilt receive*	Tu auras reçu	*thou wilt have received*
Il recevra	*he will receive*	Il aura reçu	*he will have received*
Nous recevrons	*we shall receive*	Nous aurons reçu	*we shall have received*
Vous recevrez	*you will receive*	Vous aurez reçu	*you will have received*
Ils recevront	*they will receive*	Ils auront reçu	*they will have received*

CONDITIONAL MODE.

Present.		Past.	
Je recevrais	*I should receive*	J'aurais reçu	*I should have*
Tu recevrais	*thou wouldst receive*	Tu aurais reçu	*thou wouldst have*
Il recevrait	*he would receive*	Il aurait reçu	*he would have*
Nous recevrions	*we should receive*	Nous aurions reçu	*we should have*
Vous recevriez	*you would receive*	Vous auriez reçu	*you would have*
Ils recevraient	*they would receive*	Ils auraient reçu	*they would have*

received

IMPERATIVE MODE.

Reçois	*receive (thou)*
Recevons	*let us receive*
Recevez	*receive (you)*

SUBJUNCTIVE MODE.

PRESENT.

Que je reçoive	that I may	
Que tu reçoives	that thou mayst	
Qu'il reçoive	that he may	*receive*
Que nous recevions	that we may	
Que vous receviez	that you may	
Qu'ils reçoivent	that they may	

PAST.

Que j'aie reçu	that I may	
Que tu aies reçu	that thou mayst	
Qu'il ait reçu	that he may	*have received*
Que nous ayons reçu	that we may	
Que vous ayez reçu	that you may	
Qu'ils aient reçu	that they may	

IMPERFECT.

Que je reçusse	that I might	
Que tu reçusses	that thou mightst	
Qu'il reçût	that he might	*receive*
Que nous reçussions	that we might	
Que vous reçussiez	that you might	
Qu'ils reçussent	that they might	

PLUPERFECT.

Que j'eusse reçu	that I	
Que tu eusses reçu	that thou	
Qu'il eût reçu	that he	*might have received*
Que nous eussions reçu	that we	
Que vous eussiez reçu	that you	
Qu'ils eussent reçu	that they	

Vocabulary 27.

Recevoir, to receive.
Devoir,† to owe; to be obliged; to be to; to have to.
Une nouvelle, a piece of news; intelligence.
Les nouvelles, the news; news.
Un cadeau, a present.
La paye, the pay.
La fin, the end.
Le départ, the departure.
La veille, the day before.
Le lendemain, the day after.
Une visite, a visit; a call.
La marque, the mark; the token.
Le respect, the respect.
La bienveillance, the good-will; the kindness.
La félicitation, the congratulation.
Triste, sad.
Sincère, sincere.
Bientôt, soon, very soon.
Par, through; by.
Par jour, a day, each day; **par semaine,** a week; **par mois,** a month.

---

† *Devoir*, to owe, has the meaning of *to be obliged, to have to, to be*, when it precedes the infinitive : *Je dois sortir*, I have to go out. *Il doit venir ici*, he is to come here. The conditional mode of *devoir* is rendered into English by *ought*.

The past participle of *devoir* and *redevoir* (to owe again), takes a circumflex accent over the *u*, in the masculine singular only, *dû*, owed, due; *redû*, owed again.

Exercise 27.

Present Tense. 1. Je reçois des cadeaux; tu en reçois aussi. 2. Pierre me doit de l'argent. 3. Il doit me l'apporter ce matin. 4. Nous devons aller chez notre tante. 5. Vous devez venir avec moi. 6. Ils doivent partir bientôt.

Imperfect Tense. 7. Je devais sortir. 8. Il devait aller à la poste. 9. Nous recevions toutes les semaines des nouvelles de chez nous. 10. Vous receviez dix dollars par jour. 11. Ils recevaient cent dollars par mois.

Past Definite Tense. 12. Je reçus votre lettre la veille de mon départ. 13. Nous reçûmes la visite de votre oncle le lendemain de notre arrivée. 14. Ils reçurent cette triste nouvelle avant leur départ de Paris.

Future Tense. 15. Je recevrai sa lettre demain. 16. Tu recevras une visite aujourd'hui. 17. Il recevra sa paye à la fin du mois. 18. Nous recevrons des nouvelles aujourd'hui. 19. Combien recevront-ils par mois ?

Conditional Mode. 20. Je devrais écrire à mon oncle. 21. Henri devrait aller voir sa tante. 22. Nous devrions faire cela. 23. Vous n'auriez pas dû parler de cela.

Imperative Mode. 24. Reçois ce cadeau, comme une marque de ma bienveillance. 25. Recevez mes sincères félicitations. 26. Recevons nos amis avec bienveillance.

Subjunctive Mode, Present Tense. 27. Il faut que je reçoive une lettre aujourd'hui. 28. Il est temps que nous en recevions une de nos amis. 29. Je n'aime pas qu'il reçoive ces visites.

Subjunctive Mode, Imperfect Tense. 30. Il serait bien que je reçusse des nouvelles avant mon départ. 31. Je voudrais que vous reçussiez votre paye, et que nous reçussions la nôtre.

Theme 27.

PRESENT TENSE. 1. I receive my pay at the end of the month. 2. He receives a hundred dollars a month. 3. He owes me fifty dollars. 4. He is to pay me to-day. 5. We often receive presents. 6. They receive their friends *on Thursday* (jeudi).

IMPERFECT TENSE. 7. I received news from home every week. 8. He received ten dollars a week from his father. 9. We had to go out. 10. They always received us with kindness.

PAST DEFINITE TENSE. 11. I received the sad news the day after my arrival. 12. We received your letter the day before we started (before our departure). 13. They received the news at the moment of their departure.

FUTURE TENSE. 14. I will receive no calls to-day. 15. He will receive his money soon. 16. We shall receive news from Paris to-morrow. 17. They will pay us when they (will) receive their pay.

CONDITIONAL MODE. 18. I ought† to receive a letter to-day. 19. Julius ought to be here; he was to (*imperfect tense*) be here at ten o'clock. 20. We would receive him with kindness. 21. If we sent a letter to-day, they would receive it to-morrow.

IMPERATIVE MODE. 22. Receive (*sing.*) my congratulations. 23. Receive (*plur.*) this token of my good-will; I owe it to you. 24. Let us receive our teachers with the respect which is due to them.‡

---

† See foot-note, p. 118.   ‡ *Qui leur est dû*

SUBJUNCTIVE MODE, PRESENT TENSE. 25. It is time that I receive a letter. 26. I like him to receive presents. 27. We must receive money to-day.

SUBJUNCTIVE MODE, IMPERFECT TENSE. 28. It would be well that he received our letter before he leaves (before his departure). 29. I wish that we received news from home.

TWENTY-EIGHTH LESSON.

REGULAR VERBS.—FOURTH CONJUGATION IN RE.

VENDRE, To SELL.—(MODEL VERB.)

INFINITIVE MODE.

PRESENT.		PAST.	
Vendre	to sell	Avoir vendu	to have sold

PARTICIPLES.

PRESENT.		COMPOUND.	
Vendant	selling	Ayant vendu	having sold

PAST.
Vendu   sold

INDICATIVE MODE.

PRESENT.		PAST INDEFINITE.	
Je vends	I sell	J'ai vendu	I have sold
Tu vends	thou sellest	Tu as vendu	thou hast sold
Il vend	he sells	Il a vendu	he has sold
Nous vendons	we sell	Nous avons vendu	we have sold
Vous vendez	you sell	Vous avez vendu	you have sold
Ils vendent	they sell	Ils ont vendu	they have sold

IMPERFECT.		PLUPERFECT.	
Je vendais	I was selling	J'avais vendu	I had sold
Tu vendais	thou wast selling	Tu avais vendu	thou hadst sold
Il vendait	he was selling	Il avait vendu	he had sold
Nous vendions	we were selling	Nous avions vendu	we had sold
Vous vendiez	you were selling	Vous aviez vendu	you had sold
Ils vendaient	they were selling	Ils avaient vendu	they had sold

Past Definite.

Je vendis	*I sold*
Tu vendis	*thou soldest*
Il vendit	*he sold*
Nous vendîmes	*we sold*
Vous vendîtes	*you sold*
Ils vendirent	*they sold*

Past Anterior.

J'eus vendu	*I had sold*
Tu eus vendu	*thou hadst sold*
Il eut vendu	*he had sold*
Nous eûmes vendu	*we had sold*
Vous eûtes vendu	*you had sold*
Ils eurent vendu	*they had sold*

Future.

Je vendrai	*I shall sell*
Tu vendras	*thou wilt sell*
Il vendra	*he will sell*
Nous vendrons	*we shall sell*
Vous vendrez	*you will sell*
Ils vendront	*they will sell*

Future Anterior.

J'aurai vendu	*I shall have sold*
Tu auras vendu	*thou wilt have sold*
Il aura vendu	*he will have sold*
Nous aurons vendu	*we shall have sold*
Vous aurez vendu	*you will have sold*
Ils auront vendu	*they will have sold*

CONDITIONAL MODE.

Present.

Je vendrais	*I should sell*
Tu vendrais	*thou wouldst sell*
Il vendrait	*he would sell*
Nous vendrions	*we should sell*
Vous vendriez	*you would sell*
Ils vendraient	*they would sell*

Past.

J'aurais vendu	*I should have sold*
Tu aurais vendu	*thou wouldst have sold*
Il aurait vendu	*he would have sold*
Nous aurions vendu	*we should have sold*
Vous auriez vendu	*you would have sold*
Ils auraient vendu	*they would have sold*

IMPERATIVE MODE.

Vends	*sell (thou)*
Vendons	*let us sell*
Vendez	*sell (you)*

SUBJUNCTIVE MODE.

Present.

Que je vende	*that I may sell*
Que tu vendes	*that thou mayst sell*
Qu'il vende	*that he may sell*
Que nous vendions	*that we may sell*
Que vous vendiez	*that you may sell*
Qu'ils vendent	*that they may sell*

Past.

Que j'aie vendu	*that I may* ⎫
Que tu aies vendu	*that thou mayst* ⎪
Qu'il ait vendu	*that he may* ⎬ *have sold*
Que nous ayons vendu	*that we may* ⎪
Que vous ayez vendu	*that you may* ⎪
Qu'ils aient vendu	*that they may* ⎭

REGULAR VERBS.

IMPERFECT.			PLUPERFECT.		
Que je vendisse	that I		Que j'eusse vendu	that I	
Que tu vendisses	that thou		Que tu eusses vendu	that thou	
Qu'il vendît	that he	*might sell*	Qu'il eût vendu	that he	*might have sold*
Que nous vendissions	that we		Que nous eussions vendu	that we	
Que vous vendissiez	that you		Que vous eussiez vendu	that you	
Qu'ils vendissent	that they		Qu'ils eussent vendu	that they	

Vocabulary 28.

Vendre, to sell.
Rendre, to return, to give back.
Attendre, to wait; to wait for; to expect.
Entendre, to hear; to understand.
Perdre, to lose.
Répondre† (à), to answer.
Une question, a question.
Une réponse, an answer.
Un vaisseau, a vessel; a ship.
Un navire, } a vessel.
Un bâtiment, }
La vapeur, the steam.
Un bâtiment à vapeur, a steamer.
Un bateau à vapeur, a steamboat.

Le naufrage, shipwreck.
Un pont, a bridge.
La marchandise, the merchandise.
Les marchandises, the goods.
La monnaie, the money; the change.
Cher, dear.
À bon marché, cheap.
Tout de suite, immediately.
Tout à l'heure,‡ presently; just now.
Tantôt,‡ by and by; a little while ago.
Aussitôt que, as soon as.

Exercise 28.

PRESENT TENSE. 1. J'attends ta réponse. 2. Tu ne réponds pas à ma question. 3. Il ne vous entend pas. 4. Nous ne vendons pas cher. 5. Pourquoi ne me rendez-vous pas ma monnaie? 6. Ils perdent leur temps.

---

† *Répondre* requires the preposition *à* before the noun which is the object of the verb; *répondre à quelqu'un*, to answer some one; *répondre à une question*, to answer a question.

‡ *Tout à l'heure* and *tantôt* may refer to past or future time: *Je l'ai vu tout à l'heure* (or *tantôt*). I have seen him just now (or a little while ago). *Je vais le voir tout à l'heure* (or *tantôt*). I am going to see him presently (or by and by).

IMPERFECT TENSE. 7. J'attendais l'arrivée du bâtiment à vapeur. 8. Il n'entendait pas qu'on l'appelait. 9. Nous vendions nos marchandises à bon marché. 10. Ils perdaient patience.

PAST DEFINITE TENSE. 11. Je répondis à sa lettre aussitôt que je l'eus reçue. 12. Il vendit son navire le lendemain de son arrivée. 13. Nous lui rendîmes sa visite la veille de notre départ. 14. Ils perdirent leur vaisseau par un naufrage.

FUTURE TENSE. 15. Je vous rendrai votre monnaie tout à l'heure. 16. Il ne répondra pas à votre question. 17. Nous vous attendrons au pont. 18. Ils perdront tout ce qu'ils ont.

CONDITIONAL MODE. 19. Je vendrais ce bateau à vapeur, si j'étais à votre place. 20. Il vous rendrait une réponse tantôt, si vous attendiez un peu. 21. Vous perdriez votre temps, si vous attendiez.

IMPERATIVE MODE. 22. Attends-moi au pont. 23. Répondez à mes questions, je vous en prie. 24. Ne perdons pas courage.

SUBJUNCTIVE MODE, PRESENT TENSE. 25. Il est temps que je lui rende sa visite. 26. Je veux que tu répondes à ma question. 27. Il est prudent que nous attendions un peu.

SUBJUNCTIVE MODE, IMPERFECT TENSE. 28. Il serait prudent que j'attendisse. 29. Il serait bien qu'il entendît cela. 30. Je voudrais que vous me répondissiez tout de suite.

Theme 28.

PRESENT TENSE. 1. I hear you. 2. Thou dost not answer (to) my question. 3. He is waiting for an answer.

4. You sell too dear. 5. We lose money on these goods. 6. They do not return us our change.

IMPERFECT TENSE. 7. I was losing my time. 8. He was waiting for the arrival of the steamer. 9. We used to hear the noise of the carriages during the night, when we lived in that street. 10. They did not sell cheap.

PAST DEFINITE TENSE. 11. I returned (to him) his visit the day before my departure. 12. He answered (to) my letter the next day. 13. We lost our goods by shipwreck.† 14. They sold their vessel as soon as they arrived.

FUTURE TENSE. 15. I shall wait for you at the bridge. 16. He will lose his cloak by and by. 17. We will answer you presently. 18. They will wait for us.

CONDITIONAL MODE. 19. Why do you not wait for me; I would wait for you. 20. If he were master of his *property* (bien, *m.*), he would lose *everything* (tout ce qu') he has. 21. They would not hear us, if we called them.

IMPERATIVE MODE. 22. Answer (*sing.*) me immediately. 23. Do not lose patience. 24. Let us wait for our comrades.

SUBJUNCTIVE MODE, PRESENT TENSE. 25. I must sell this boat. 26. He must answer (to) that question. 27. We must wait for him.

SUBJUNCTIVE MODE, IMPERFECT TENSE. 28. It would be well for him to answer (to) our question. 29. I wish that you would wait a little. 30. I wish that thou wouldst give me back my money.

---

† By shipwreck, *par un naufrage.*

TWENTY-NINTH LESSON.

INTERROGATIVE CONJUGATION.

1. The tenses of the indicative and conditional modes only are used interrogatively.

The interrogative conjugation is formed by placing the pronoun subject, with a hyphen, after the verb: **ai-je? coupez-vous?** etc.

The final silent **e** of the verb is changed into **é** (acute). when the pronoun subject of the first person is placed after the verb, as: **coupé-je?** *do I cut?*

When the verb, in the third person singular ends with a vowel, the letter **t**, between two hyphens, is placed. for the sake of euphony, before the pronouns **il, elle, on,** as : **a-t-il? coupe-t-elle? coupera-t-on?**

When the subject of an interrogative sentence is a noun, it is placed before the verb, and a personal pronoun of the same person, gender, and number, is placed after the verb, as:

Charles a-t-il la lettre ?	Has Charles the letter?
Louise est-elle en haut ?	Is Louisa up stairs?
Ces hommes coupent-ils nos arbres ?	Do those men cut our trees?

The noun subject is, however, generally placed after the verb in interrogative sentences that begin with an interrogative pronoun, or an adverb, such as: **que, comment, où.**

Que demandent ces hommes ?	What do those men ask for?
Savez-vous où demeure M. Ducrot ?	Do you know where Mr. Ducrot lives?
Comment va cette affaire ?	How is that business?

2.   **INTERROGATIVE FORM WITH EST-CE QUE.**

Interrogative sentences are also formed by placing **est-ce que** before the subject of the verb:

Est-ce que Charles a le journal ?   Has Charles the journal?
Est-ce que Marie est encore en haut ?   Is Mary still up stairs?
Est-ce que M. Ducrot a vendu son magasin ?   Has Mr. Ducrot sold his store?

The interrogative form with **est-ce que** is always used when the verb, in the first person singular, ends in **ge**, as: **est-ce que je mange ?** *do I eat?* not **mange-je ?**

The interrogative form with **est-ce que** is also used for the first person singular when the verb has only one syllable, as: **est-ce que je vends ?** *do I sell?* not **vends-je ?**

Eight verbs, which have only one syllable in the first person singular of the indicative present, may be used interrogatively either way: **ai-je?** *have I?* **suis-je?** *am I?* **vais-je?** *do I go?* **puis-je?** *can I?* **sais-je?** *do I know?* **vois-je?** *do I see?* **dois-je?** *do I owe?* and **dis-je?** *do I say?* or **est-ce que j'ai ?** etc.

3.   **NEGATIVE CONJUGATION.**

We have seen that the two words (**ne .... pas**) that accompany a verb to express negation, are separated by the verb (in compound tenses, by the auxiliary only), as: **Je n'ai pas ; je n'ai jamais été ; je n'ai rien dit.**

When the verb is in the infinitive, the two negative words are generally placed before the verb; they may, or may not, be separated by a personal pronoun.

Je vous conseille de ne pas le faire, *or* de ne le pas faire.   I advise you not to do it.
Je vous prie de n'en pas parler, de n'en rien dire.   I beg you not to speak of it, not to say anything about it.

Vocabulary 29.

Chercher, to seek ; to look for.
Désirer, to desire ; to wish for.
Demander, to ask for.
Écouter, to listen to.
Regarder, to look at.
Découper, to carve.
Conseiller (de), to advise.
Servir, to serve ; to help to.
Savez-vous? do you know?

Le poulet, the chicken.
Le canard, the duck.
Le dindon, the turkey.
Le jambon, the ham.
Le poisson, the fish.
Le potage, } the soup.
La soupe,
En haut, upstairs.
En bas, downstairs.

Exercise 29.

1. Votre sœur est-elle encore en haut ? 2. Marie est-elle en bas ? 3. Nos amis sont-ils à la campagne ? 4. Charles a-t-il perdu sa grammaire ? 5. M. votre père désire-t-il me parler ? 6. Va-t-on servir la soupe ? 7. Pierre va-t-il découper le poulet ? 8. Votre oncle achètera-t-il quelques canards ? 9. Nos voisins ont-ils plusieurs beaux dindons ? 10. Cette dame nous regarde-t-elle ? 11. Ces matelots écoutent-ils le capitaine, qui leur donne des ordres ? 12. Ces hommes nous ont-ils vendu du poisson ? 13. Est-ce que Henri a bien étudié sa leçon ? 14. Est-ce qu'il n'a pas eu de fautes dans son thème ? 15. Est-ce que le professeur me demande ? 16. Est-ce qu'il parle de moi ou de vous ? 17. Est-ce que je mange votre potage ? 18. Est-ce que je ne vous rends pas ce que vous m'avez prêté ? 19. Est-ce que je dis cela ? 20. Que sais-je ? 21. Où suis-je ? 22. Savez-

vous où demeure notre professeur de français? 23. Je vous conseille de ne pas le lui dire. 24. Je vous prie de n'en pas parler. 25. J'ai envie de ne pas y aller.

Theme 29.

1. Is mamma up stairs? 2. Is the professor down stairs? 3. Are your books at school? 4. Does your mother wish to see me in the parlor? 5. Is John carving the turkey? 6. Does Mary wish for some soup? 7. Does your aunt ask for some (un peu) of this duck? 8. Have our neighbors a great many chickens? 9. Why do those boys look at us? 10. Do the scholars listen to the teacher? 11. Have I had a good exercise? 12.† Has Louisa seen her aunt? 13.† Did the professor ask for anybody? 14.† What am I eating; is it fish? 15.‡ What can I help you to? 16.‡ Can I help you to some soup? 17.† Do I not sell cheap? 18.† Do I do my duty well? 19.§ What do those men ask for? 20. Where does Mr. Ducrot live? 21.‡ How much do I owe you? 22. I beg you not to say anything about it. 23. I advise you not to go there any more. 24. He has told me not to do it.

THIRTIETH LESSON.

The Passive Verb.

1. The passive verb is formed by joining the past participle of the active verb to the various forms of the auxiliary verb **être**, *to be,* as: **aimer**, *to love;* **être aimé**, *to be loved.*

---

† Follow the construction indicated in Sect. 2 of the Lesson.
‡ See last paragraph of Sect. 2, Exceptions.
§ Follow the construction indicated in last paragraph of Sect. 1.

The past participle agrees, in gender and number, with the subject of the verb.

CONJUGATION OF THE PASSIVE VERB.

ÊTRE AIMÉ, To Be Loved.—(Model Verb.)

INFINITIVE MODE.

PRESENT.

Être aimé *or* aimée, aimés *or* aimées } *to be loved*

PAST.

Avoir été aimé *or* aimée, aimés *or* aimées } *to have been loved*

PARTICIPLES.

PRESENT.

Étant aimé *or* aimée, aimés *or* aimées } *being loved*

COMPOUND.

Ayant été aimé *or* aimée, aimés *or* aimées } *having been loved*

PAST.

Été aimé *or* aimée, aimés *or* aimées   *been loved*

INDICATIVE MODE.

PRESENT.

Je suis aimé *or* aimée
Tu es aimé (ée)
Il *or* elle est aimé (ée)
Nous sommes aimés *or* aimées
Vous êtes aimés (ées)
Ils *or* elles sont aimés (ées)
} *I am loved, etc.*

PAST INDEFINITE.

J'ai été aimé *or* aimée
Tu as été aimé (ée)
Il *or* elle a été aimé (ée)
Nous avons été aimés *or* aimées
Vous avez été aimés (ées)
Ils *or* elles ont été aimés (ées)
} *I have been loved, etc.*

IMPERFECT.

J'étais aimé (ée)
Tu étais aimé (ée)
Il *or* elle était aimé (ée)
Nous étions aimés (ées)
Vous étiez aimés (ées)
Ils *or* elles étaient aimés (ées)
} *I was being loved, etc.*

PLUPERFECT.

J'avais été aimé (ée)
Tu avais été aimé (ée)
Il *or* elle avait été aimé (ée)
Nous avions été aimés (ées)
Vous aviez été aimés (ées)
Ils *or* elles avaient été aimés (ées)
} *I had been loved, etc.*

THE PASSIVE VERB.

PAST DEFINITE.		PAST ANTERIOR.	
Je fus aimé (ée)	*I was loved, etc.*	J'eus été aimé (ée)	*I had been loved, etc.*
Tu fus aimé (ée)		Tu eus été aimé (ée)	
Il *or* elle fut aimé (ée)		Il *or* elle eut été aimé (ée)	
Nous fûmes aimés (ées)		Nous eûmes été aimés (ées)	
Vous fûtes aimés (ées)		Vous eûtes été aimés (ées)	
Ils *or* elles furent aimés (ées)		Ils *or* elles eurent été aimés (ées)	

FUTURE.		FUTURE ANTERIOR.	
Je serai aimé (ée)	*I shall be loved, etc.*	J'aurai été aimé (ée)	*I shall have been loved, etc.*
Tu seras aimé (ée)		Tu auras été aimé (ée)	
Il *or* elle sera aimé (ée)		Il *or* elle aura été aimé (ée)	
Nous serons aimés (ées)		Nous aurons été aimés (ées)	
Vous serez aimés (ées)		Vous aurez été aimés (ées)	
Ils *or* elles seront aimés (ées)		Ils *or* elles auront été aimés (ées)	

CONDITIONAL MODE.

PRESENT.		PAST.	
Je serais aimé (ée)	*I should be loved, etc.*	J'aurais été aimé (ée)	*I should have been loved, etc.*
Tu serais aimé (ée)		Tu aurais été aimé (ée)	
Il *or* elle serait aimé (ée)		Il *or* elle aurait été aimé (ée)	
Nous serions aimés (ées)		Nous aurions été aimés (ées)	
Vous seriez aimés (ées)		Vous auriez été aimés (ées)	
Ils *or* elles seraient aimés (ées)		Ils *or* elles auraient été aimés (ées)	

IMPERATIVE MODE.

Sois aimé (ée)	*be (thou) loved*
Soyons aimés (ées)	*let us be loved*
Soyez aimés (ées)	*be (you) loved*

SUBJUNCTIVE MODE.

PRESENT.		PAST.	
Que je sois aimé (ée)	*that I may be loved, etc.*	Que j'aie été aimé (ée)	*that I may have been, etc.*
Que tu sois aimé (ée)		Que tu aies été aimé (ée)	
Qu'il *or* qu'elle soit aimé (ée)		Qu'il *or* qu'elle ait été aimé (ée)	
Que nous soyons aimés (ées)		Que nous ayons été aimés (ées)	
Que vous soyez aimés (ées)		Que vous ayez été aimés (ées)	
Qu'ils *or* elles soient aimés (ées)		Qu'ils *or* elles aient été aimés (ées)	

132 ELEMENTARY FRENCH GRAMMAR.

IMPERFECT.		PLUPERFECT.	
Que je fusse aimé (ée)	⎫ *that I might be loved, etc.*	Que j'eusse été aimé (ée)	⎫ *that I might have been, etc.*
Que tu fusses aimé (ée)		Que tu eusses été aimé (ée)	
Qu'il *or* qu'elle fût aimé (ée)		Qu'il *or* qu'elle eût été aimé (ée)	
Que nous fussions aimés (ées)		Que nous eussions été aimés (ées)	
Que vous fussiez aimés (ées)		Que vous eussiez été aimés (ées)	
Qu'ils *or* elles fussent aimés (ées)		Qu'ils *or* elles eussent été aimés	

BY, AFTER A PASSIVE VERB EXPRESSED BY PAR OR DE.

The agent of a passive verb is preceded by the preposition **par**, if the verb expresses action, and by the preposition **de**, if the verb expresses a sentiment.

Il est blâmé par ses amis.   He is blamed by his friends.
Elle est aimée de ses parents.   She is loved by her parents.
Il est puni de ses fautes.   He is punished for his faults.

REM. The passive form of the verb is less frequently used in French than in English. The French prefer the active form, with the pronoun on for subject, or the pronominal form of the verb:

On vous appelle.   You are called.
On l'a vu.   He has been seen.
Il s'appelle Henri.   He is called Henry.

Vocabulary 30.

Blâmer (de), to blame (for).   **L'obéissance,** *f.*, obedience.
Louer (de), to praise (for).   **Obéissant,** obedient.
Récompenser (de), to reward (for).   **La désobéissance,** disobedience.
Réprimander (de), to reprove (for).   **Désobéissant,** disobedient.
Estimer, to esteem.   **La diligence,** diligence.
Respecter, to respect.   **Diligent,** diligent.
Mépriser, to despise.   **La négligence,** carelessness.
Négliger, to neglect.   **Négligent,** careless; negligent.
Les bons, the good.   **Partout,** everywhere.
Les méchants, the wicked.   **Il est juste,** it is just *or* right.

Exercise 30.

1. Je suis aimé de mes parents. 2. Il est blâmé par ses amis, parce qu'il a été négligent. 3. Sa sœur est louée, parce qu'elle a été diligente. 4. Nous sommes récompensés quand nous sommes diligents. 5. Nous sommes réprimandés quand nous sommes négligents. 6. Les bons sont partout estimés et respectés. 7. Les méchants sont méprisés et punis. 8. Vous avez été récompensé de votre diligence. 9. Votre sœur a été louée de son obéissance. 10. Ces élèves ont été blâmés de leur négligence. 11. Jules était aimé de ses maîtres, parce qu'il était obéissant et diligent. 12. Nous étions réprimandés quand nous étions désobéissants. 13. La désobéissance était réprimandée et punie. 14. Vous serez récompensé, si vous êtes diligent. 15. Vous serez puni, si vous êtes désobéissant. 16. Ceux qui n'obéissent pas au maître, seront punis. 17. Vous seriez récompensé, si vous aviez été diligent. 18. Ils auraient été punis, s'ils avaient négligé leurs devoirs. 19. Je veux que tu sois puni, si tu négliges tes devoirs. 20. Il est juste qu'il soit récompensé, s'il est diligent. 21. Il serait juste que vous fussiez puni, si vous n'obéissiez pas à vos maîtres. 22. Il faut être obéissant et diligent pour être aimé et récompensé.

Theme 30.

1. You are blamed for your carelessness. 2. They are punished for their disobedience. 3. She is loved and respected by everybody. 4. He was rewarded by his teacher because he was diligent and obedient. 5. His obedience has been praised. 6. His diligence has been rewarded. 7. The

wicked shall be punished. 8. The good shall be rewarded. 9. He was often reproved for his carelessness. 10. Those who neglect their duties will be despised. 11. You would be rewarded, if you had been diligent. 12. They would be punished, if they had been disobedient. 13. It is just that you be (*subj.*) punished, if you are disobedient. 14. It would be right that he were (*subj., imp.*) rewarded, if he had been diligent and obedient. 15. In order to be loved and esteemed, one must *behave well* (se bien comporter). 16. He who *behaves well* (se comporte bien) is everywhere well received.

THIRTY-FIRST LESSON.

Neuter Verbs, Conjugated with Être.

1. Certain neuter verbs, principally those that express a change in the position or condition of the subject, are conjugated in the compound tenses with the auxiliary verb **être,** *to be.* The past participle agrees with the subject of the verb (p. 88–1). The verb **arriver,** *to arrive,* is given as the model verb of the class.

INFINITIVE MODE.

Present.		Past.	
Arriver	*to arrive*	Être arrivé *or* arrivée, arrivés *or* arrivées	*to have arrived*

PARTICIPLES.

Present.		Compound.	
Arrivant	*arriving*	Étant arrivé *or* arrivée, arrivés *or* arrivées	*having arrived*

Past.

Arrivé *or* arrivée, arrivés *or* arrivées   *arrived*

NEUTER VERBS.

INDICATIVE MODE.

PRESENT.

J'arrive	I arrive	Je suis arrivé or arrivée	
Tu arrives	thou arrivest	Tu es arrivé (ée)	
Il arrive	he arrives	Il or elle est arrivé (ée)	*I have arrived, etc.*
Nous arrivons	we arrive	Nous sommes arrivés (ées)	
Vous arrivez	you arrive	Vous êtes arrivés (ées)	
Ils arrivent	they arrive	Ils or elles sont arrivés (ées)	

PAST INDEFINITE.

IMPERFECT.

J'arrivais	I was arriving	J'étais arrivé (ée)	
Tu arrivais	thou wast arriving	Tu étais arrivé (ée)	
Il arrivait	he was arriving	Il or elle était arrivé (ée)	*I had arrived, etc.*
Nous arrivions	we were arriving	Nous étions arrivés (ées)	
Vous arriviez	you were arriving	Vous étiez arrivés (ées)	
Ils arrivaient	they were arriving	Ils or elles étaient arrivés (ées)	

PLUPERFECT.

PAST DEFINITE.

J'arrivai	I arrived	Je fus arrivé (ée)	
Tu arrivas	thou arrivedst	Tu fus arrivé (ée)	
Il arriva	he arrived	Il or elle fut arrivé (ée)	*I had arrived, etc.*
Nous arrivâmes	we arrived	Nous fûmes arrivés (ées)	
Vous arrivâtes	you arrived	Vous fûtes arrivés (ées)	
Ils arrivèrent	they arrived	Ils or elles furent arrivés (ées)	

PAST ANTERIOR.

FUTURE.

J'arriverai	I shall arrive	Je serai arrivé (ée)	
Tu arriveras	thou wilt arrive	Tu seras arrivé (ée)	
Il arrivera	he will arrive	Il or elle sera arrivé (ée)	*I shall have arrived, etc.*
Nous arriverons	we shall arrive	Nous serons arrivés (ées)	
Vous arriverez	you will arrive	Vous serez arrivés (ées)	
Ils arriveront	they will arrive	Ils or elles seront arrivés (ées)	

FUTURE ANTERIOR.

CONDITIONAL MODE.

PRESENT.

J'arriverais	I should arrive	Je serais arrivé (ée)	
Tu arriverais	thou wouldst arrive	Tu serais arrivé (ée)	
Il arriverait	he would arrive	Il or elle serait arrivé (ée)	*I should have arrived, etc.*
Nous arriverions	we should arrive	Nous serions arrivés (ées)	
Vous arriveriez	you would arrive	Vous seriez arrivés (ées)	
Ils arriveraient	they would arrive	Ils or elles seraient arrivés (ées)	

PAST.

IMPERATIVE MODE.

Arrive	*arrive (thou)*
Arrivons	*let us arrive*
Arrivez	*arrive (you)*

SUBJUNCTIVE MODE.

PRESENT.

Que j'arrive	*that I may*	⎫
Que tu arrives	*that thou mayst*	⎪
Qu'il arrive	*that he may*	⎬ *arrive.*
Que nous arrivions	*that we may*	⎪
Que vous arriviez	*that you may*	⎪
Qu'ils arrivent	*that they may*	⎭

PAST.

Que je sois arrivé (ée)		⎫
Que tu sois arrivé (ée)		⎪
Qu'il *or* qu'elle soit arrivé (ée)		⎬ *that I may have arrived, etc.*
Que nous soyons arrivés (ées)		⎪
Que vous soyez arrivés (ées)		⎪
Qu'ils *or* elles soient arrivés (ées)		⎭

IMPERFECT.

Que j'arrivasse	*that I*	⎫
Que tu arrivasses	*that thou*	⎪
Qu'il arrivât	*that he*	⎬ *might arrive*
Que nous arrivassions	*that we*	⎪
Que vous arrivassiez	*that you*	⎪
Qu'ils arrivassent	*that they*	⎭

PLUPERFECT.

Que je fusse arrivé (ée)		⎫
Que tu fusses arrivé (ée)		⎪
Qu'il *or* qu'elle fût arrivé (ée)		⎬ *that I might have arrived, etc.*
Que nous fussions arrivés (ées)		⎪
Que vous fussiez arrivés (ées)		⎪
Qu'ils *or* elles fussent arrivés (ées)		⎭

2. LIST OF NEUTER VERBS THAT ARE CONJUGATED WITH ÊTRE, TO BE.

Arriver, to arrive;	**être arrivé,** to have arrived.
Aller, to go;	**être allé,** to have gone.
Décéder, to decease;	**être décédé,** to have deceased.
Entrer, to enter; to go *or* come in;	**être entré,** to have entered.
Rentrer, to re-enter; to come home;	**être rentré,** to have come.
Retourner, to return; to go back;	**être retourné,** to have returned.
Rester, to remain, to stay;	**être resté,** to have remained.
Tomber, to fall;	**être tombé,** to have fallen.
***Mourir,** to die;	**être mort,** to have died.
***Naître,** to be born;	**être né,** to have been born.
***Partir,** to start; to leave;	**être parti,** to have started.
***Sortir,** to go out; to come out;	**être sorti,** to have gone out.

NEUTER VERBS. 137

*Venir, to come ; être venu, to have come.
*Devenir, to become ; être devenu, to have become.
*Parvenir, to reach; to succeed ; être parvenu, to have become.
*Revenir, to return; to come back ; être revenu, to have returned.

3. NEUTER VERBS THAT TAKE SOMETIMES AVOIR AND SOMETIMES ÊTRE.

Some neuter verbs take **avoir** for their auxiliary when they express action only, and **être** when they express rather the state resulting from the action, as:

Elle a grandi rapidement. She has grown rapidly.
Elle est grandie de deux pouces. She has grown (by) two inches.
La procession a passé ici. The procession passed here.
La procession est passée. The procession has passed.

The following are some of this class:

Cesser, to cease.
*Croître, to grow.
Grandir, to grow tall.
Vieillir, to grow old.

Descendre, to go or come down.
Monter, to go or come up.
Remonter, to reascend.
Passer, to pass.

REM. Several of the above verbs, under 2 and 3, are sometimes used as transitive verbs, in which case they are conjugated with **avoir**.

Vocabulary 31.

Le déjeuner, breakfast.
Le dîner, dinner.
Le souper, supper.
Le bal, the ball.
Le notaire, the notary.
La procession, the procession.
Le train, the train.

Une famille, a family.
Hier au matin, yesterday morning.
Hier au soir, last night.
De bonne heure, early.
Tard, late.
Jusque, till, until.
Jusqu'à samedi, until Saturday.

Exercise 31.

1. Je suis arrivé ce matin. 2. Ma tante est arrivée hier au soir. 3. Le train était parti quand nous sommes arrivés. 4. Mes cousines sont arrivées de bonne heure. 5. Jules est allé au bureau. 6. Mes sœurs sont allées à l'église. 7. Le marchand est entré dans son magasin. 8. Le médecin est rentré tard hier au soir. 9. Nos amis sont retournés chez eux. 10. Mes parents sont restés à la campagne jusqu'à samedi. 11. Ces pommes sont tombées de l'arbre. 12. La femme du notaire est morte hier au matin. 13. Notre voisine est née à Berlin. 14. Nous sommes partis de bonne heure. 15. Ils sont sortis après le déjeuner. 16. Mes cousines sont venues à la ville pour aller au bal. 17. Elles sont arrivées à temps pour le souper. 18. Cette famille est devenue très-pauvre. 19. Les fils de notre voisin sont devenus soldats. 20. Votre lettre m'est parvenue trop tard. 21. Mes parents ne sont pas encore revenus. 22. La procession est déjà passée ; elle a passé par ici.

Theme 31.

1.† We arrived in time for the train. 2.† My sister came with me. 3.† My father came alone last evening. 4.† Henry and William came together. 5. Mary went to see her aunt. 6. The children went for a walk. 7. The procession had entered the church when I came by† (passed). 8.† My sisters came in early. 9. My aunt has returned home. 10.† Those are pears that fell from the trees. 11.† We stayed in the country until Saturday. 12.† Our friend, the notary, died last night. 13. I was born in this city. 14.† They started

---

† Put the verb in the past indefinite tense.

after breakfast. 15.† We went out after supper. 16. That family has left *for Europe* (pour l'Europe). 17. Our neighbors have become very rich. 18.† Your letter did not reach me in time. 19. Our friends have not yet come back to town. 20.† The soldiers have passed; they passed by here.

THIRTY-SECOND LESSON.

Pronominal Verbs.

1. Pronominal verbs are conjugated with two pronouns of the same person; the one is the subject, the other the direct, or indirect, object, of the verb.

In the compound tenses of pronominal verbs the auxiliary verb **être** is used for the auxiliary verb **avoir**. The past participle is subject to the same rule of agreement as the past participle of transitive verbs; that is, it agrees with its direct object, when the direct object precedes the participle.

Conjugation of the Pronominal Verb.

SE COUPER, To Cut One's Self.—(Model Verb.)

INFINITIVE MODE.

Present.		Past.	
Se couper	*to cut one's self*	S'être coupé	*to have cut one's self*

PARTICIPLES.

Present.		Compound.	
Se coupant	*cutting one's self*	S'étant coupé	*having cut one's self*

Past.

Coupé   *cut*

---

† Put the verb in the past indefinite tense.

INDICATIVE MODE.

Present.

Je me coupe	*I cut myself, etc.*
Tu te coupes	
Il se coupe	
Nous nous coupons	
Vous vous coupez	
Ils se coupent	

Past Indefinite.

Je me suis coupé	*I have cut myself, etc.*
Tu t'es coupé	
Il s'est coupé	
Nous nous sommes coupés	
Vous vous êtes coupés	
Ils se sont coupés	

Imperfect.

Je me coupais	*I was cutting myself, etc.*
Tu te coupais	
Il se coupait	
Nous nous coupions	
Vous vous coupiez	
Ils se coupaient	

Pluperfect.

Je m'étais coupé	*I had cut myself, etc.*
Tu t'étais coupé	
Il s'était coupé	
Nous nous étions coupés	
Vous vous étiez coupés	
Ils s'étaient coupés	

Past Definite.

Je me coupai	*I cut myself, etc.*
Tu te coupas	
Il se coupa	
Nous nous coupâmes	
Vous vous coupâtes	
Ils se coupèrent	

Past Anterior.

Je me fus coupé	*I had cut myself, etc.*
Tu te fus coupé	
Il se fut coupé	
Nous nous fûmes coupés	
Vous vous fûtes coupés	
Ils se furent coupés.	

Future.

Je me couperai	*I shall cut myself, etc.*
Tu te couperas	
Il se coupera	
Nous nous couperons	
Vous vous couperez	
Ils se couperont	

Future Anterior.

Je me serai coupé	*I shall have cut my*
Tu te seras coupé	*[self, etc.*
Il se sera coupé	
Nous nous serons coupés	
Vous vous serez coupés	
Ils se seront coupés	

CONDITIONAL MODE.

Present.

Je me couperais	*I should cut myself,*
Tu te couperais	*[etc.*
Il se couperait	
Nous nous couperions	
Vous vous couperiez	
Ils se couperaient	

Past.

Je me serais coupé	*I should have cut*
Tu te serais coupé	*[myself, etc.*
Il se serait coupé	
Nous nous serions coupés	
Vous vous seriez coupés	
Ils se seraient coupés.	

IMPERATIVE MODE.

Coupe-toi   *cut thyself*
Coupons-nous   *let us cut ourselves*
Coupez-vous   *cut yourselves*

SUBJUNCTIVE MODE.

PRESENT.

Que je me coupe   *that I may cut myself,*
Que tu te coupes   [*etc.*
Qu'il se coupe
Que nous nous coupions
Que vous vous coupiez
Qu'ils se coupent

PAST.

Que je me sois coupé   *that I may have*
Que tu te sois coupé   [*cut myself, etc.*
Qu'il se soit coupé
Que nous nous soyons coupés
Que vous vous soyez coupés
Qu'ils se soient coupés

IMPERFECT.

Que je me coupasse,   *that I might cut*
Que tu te coupasses   [*myself, etc.*
Qu'il se coupât
Que nous nous coupassions
Que vous vous coupassiez
Qu'ils se coupassent

PLUPERFECT.

Que je me fusse coupé   *that I might have*
Que tu te fusses coupé   [*cut myself, etc.*
Qu'il se fût coupé
Que nous nous fussions coupés
Que vous vous fussiez coupés
Qu'ils se fussent coupés

2.   **REMARKS AND EXAMPLES.**

The pronominal form of the verb is often used in French, when, in English, the verb is intransitive or passive, as:

Se coucher,   To lie down.
Se lever,   To rise.
Se proméner,   To walk.
Se tromper,   To be mistaken; to deceive one's self.
Se porter,   To be; to do (*of one's health*).
S'appeler,   To be called.
Se rappeler,   To recollect (to recall to one's self).
Comment vous portez-vous?   How do you do?
Je me porte bien,   I am well.
Comment s'appelle votre ami?   What is your friend's name?
Il s'appelle Jules,   His name is Julius.
Je ne me rappelle pas cela,   I do not recollect that.

Pronominal verbs express either reflective or reciprocal action. Reflective action is confined to the subject; reciprocal action requires two or more persons; hence, in the latter case, the verb is always in the plural. **S'aimer** may mean *to love one's self,* or *to love each other,* or *one another.*

To distinguish between reflective and reciprocal action, it is sometimes necessary to make use of an additional pronoun, either a compound pronoun, to express reflective action; or an indefinite pronoun, to express reciprocal action.

S'aimer soi-même.	To love one's self.
S'aimer l'un l'autre.	To love each other.
S'aimer les uns les autres.	To love one another.

Vocabulary 32.

Se coucher, to lie down; to go to bed.
Se lever, to rise.
S'habiller, to dress (one's self).
Se déshabiller, to undress one's self.
Se promener, to walk; to take a walk.
Se tromper,† to be mistaken.
Se porter, to be; to do.
S'appeler, to be called.

Se rappeler, to recollect.
Le voyage, the voyage; the journey.
Le chemin, the road; the way.
Le boulevard, the boulevard.
Le nom, the name.
Jacques, James.
Le soir, in the evening.
Là-bas, yonder; there.
Lorsque,‡ when.
Ensuite, then.
Avant de,§ before.

---

† *Se tromper de,* to be mistaken in; *se tromper de chemin,* to be mistaken in the road; to take the wrong road.

‡ *Lorsque, quand,* when. *Lorsque* is a conjunction; *quand* is an adverb of time, often used interrogatively; it is also used as a conjunctive adverb.

§ *Avant de* is used before the infinitive, instead of *avant. Je me promène avant de me coucher,* I take a walk before I go to bed.

Exercise 32.

Simple Tenses. 1. Je me couche tard, et je me lève de bonne heure. 2. Je me promène pendant une heure avant de me coucher. 3. Comment vous portez-vous ? 4. Je me porte bien. 5. Il ne s'habille jamais avant midi. 6. Ami, tu te trompes. 7. Comment s'appelle votre ami ? 8. Il s'appelle Jacques. 9. Nous nous trompons quelquefois. 10. Les hommes se trompent les uns les autres. 11. C'est une histoire que je ne me rappelle pas. 12. Lorsque j'étais à Paris, je me portais bien. 13. Nous nous promenions tous les jours sur les boulevards. 14. Nous nous couchions tard, et nous nous levions de bonne heure. 15. Ma mère ne se portait pas bien pendant le voyage. 16. Elle se portera mieux quand elle sera à la campagne. 17. Je me lèverai demain matin à six heures. 18. Vous ne vous rappellerez pas cela. 19. Vous vous porteriez mieux, si vous vous couchiez de bonne heure. 20. Couche-toi de bonne heure, et ne te lève pas trop tard. 21. Promenez-vous pendant une heure avant de vous coucher. 22. Rappelons-nous ce que nous étions autrefois. 23. Ne nous trompons pas. 24. Il faut que je me lève de bonne heure. 25. Je voudrais que vous vous levassiez de bonne heure tous les jours.

Compound Tenses. 1. Je me suis levé à six heures ce matin. 2. Je me suis habillé, et ensuite je suis allé me promener. 3. Je me suis trompé de rue, en revenant, et je suis rentré très-tard. 4. Tu t'es couché de bonne heure hier au soir. 5. Vous étiez-vous habillés quand je suis venu ? 6. Nous nous sommes habillés de bonne heure. 7. Jacques s'était couché sans se déshabiller. 8. Nous nous étions trompés de chemin, et nous sommes arrivés à la maison après le dîner. 9. Il se sera couché quand vous arriverez là-bas. 10. Nous nous serions levés à six heures, si nous vous avions attendus avant le déjeuner. 11. Ils ne se seraient pas rappelé cette histoire, si je ne leur en avais pas parlé. 12. Il est bien que je me la sois rappelée. 13. Je voudrais que vous ne vous fussiez pas trompé.

Theme 32.

SIMPLE TENSES. 1. I am mistaken. 2. Thou art often mistaken. 3. In the evening, we walk for an hour before we go to bed. 4. You go to bed too late, and you rise too late. 5. We are in good health.† 6. What is that gentleman's name? 7. I do not recollect his name. 8. We were dressing when you came (have come). 9. I was not in good health when I was in Paris. 10. I used to walk every day on the boulevards. 11. I shall dress immediately, and then I shall breakfast. 12. We shall go to bed early, and we shall rise early. 13. They will not recollect what they have told you. 14. You would take the wrong road if you were alone. 15. He would be in better health, if he did not work so much. 16. Rise (*sing.*); it is nine o'clock. 17. Do not go to bed (*sing.*) too late. 18. Dress (*plur.*) immediately. 19. Recollect (*plur.*) what I have told you. 20. Let us take a walk before going to bed. 21. It is well that you recollect that. 22. It would be well that they should recollect it too.

COMPOUND TENSES. 1. went‡ to bed early last night; I was (*imp.*) tired. 2. He rose before six o'clock. 3. He dressed himself immediately, and then he went for a walk. 4. We took the wrong street. 5. I had dressed when you

---

† To be in good health, *se porter bien ;* to be in better health, *se porter mieux*,
‡ Past indefinite tense.

IMPERSONAL VERBS. 145

came (have come). 6. We had lain down without undressing (ourselves). 7. They had taken the wrong road, and arrived very late. 8. He will not have risen, when we (shall) arrive there. 9. They would not have gone to bed, if they had expected us. 10. You would not have recollected that, if I had not spoken of it. 11. I am glad that you recollected that. 12. I wish that we had dressed before breakfast.

THIRTY-THIRD LESSON.

IMPERSONAL VERBS.

1. An impersonal verb is only used in the third person singular, and is conjugated with the pronoun **il**, *it*, for subject.

Verbs are essentially impersonal when they cannot be used as personal verbs. Such verbs take, in the compound tenses, the auxiliary verb **avoir**.

CONJUGATION OF THE IMPERSONAL VERB.

TONNER, To Thunder.—(MODEL VERB.)

INFINITIVE.		PRESENT PARTICIPLE.		PAST PARTICIPLE.	
Tonner	*to thunder*	Tonnant	*thundering*	Tonné	*thundered*

INDICATIVE MODE.

PRESENT.		PAST INDEFINITE.	
Il tonne	*it thunders*	Il a tonné	*it has thundered*

IMPERFECT.		PLUPERFECT.	
Il tonnait	*it was thundering*	Il avait tonné	*it had thundered*

Past Definite.		**Past Anterior.**	
Il tonna	*it thundered*	Il eut tonné	*it had thundered*
Future.		**Future Anterior.**	
Il tonnera	*it will thunder*	Il aura tonné	*it will have thundered*

CONDITIONAL MODE.

Present.		**Past.**	
Il tonnerait	*it would thunder*	Il aurait tonné	*it would have thundered*

SUBJUNCTIVE MODE.

Present.		**Past.**	
Qu'il tonne	*that it may thunder*	Qu'il ait tonné	*that it may have [thundered*
Imperfect.		**Pluperfect.**	
Qu'il tonnât	*that it might thunder*	Qu'il eût tonné	*that it might have [thundered*

Rem. Verbs that express the condition of the atmosphere are impersonal.

2. Faire,† To Do, To Make, and Être, To Be, as Impersonal Verbs.

Faire is used as an impersonal verb, to express the state of the weather.

Quel temps fait-il?	How is the weather?
Il fait beau temps.	It is fine weather.
Il fait mauvais temps.	It is bad weather.
Il fait chaud; froid.	It is warm; cold.
Il fait de l'orage.	It is stormy.
Il fait des éclairs.	It lightens.

Être is used as an impersonal verb, to express the hour of the day.

Quelle heure est-il?	What time is it?
Il est trois heures.	It is three o'clock.

---

† *Faire* is conjugated page 185.

IMPERSONAL VERBS.

Etre is also used as an impersonal verb in connection with the noun **temps**, *time*, and with adjectives and adverbs: **il est temps**, *it is time;* **il est bon**, *it is good;* **il est bien,** *it is well.*

These and other impersonal phrases, if followed by a verb in the infinitive, require the preposition **de** before the verb.

Il est temps de partir.	It is time to start.
Il est bon de savoir cela.	It is good to know that.
Il est bien de faire cela.	It is well to do that.

3. Conjugation of the Irregular Impersonal Verbs.

Y AVOIR, To Be (in existence). — FALLOIR, To Be Necessary. — PLEUVOIR, To Rain.

(We give only the simple tenses, and omit the English, which the student can easily supply.)

Infinitive.	Y avoir	Falloir	Pleuvoir
Pres. Part.	Y ayant	(*wanting*)	Pleuvant
Past. Part.	Eu	Fallu	Plu
Ind. Pres.	Il y a (*there is, there are*)	Il faut	Il pleut
Ind. Imp.	Il y avait	Il fallait	Il pleuvait
Ind. Past Def.	Il y eut	Il fallut	Il plut.
Ind. Future.	Il y aura	Il faudra	Il pleuvra
Cond. Pres.	Il y aurait	Il faudrait	Il pleuvrait
Subj. Pres.	Qu'il y ait	Qu'il faille	Qu'il pleuve
Subj. Imp.	Qu'il y eût	Qu'il fallût	Qu'il plût

4. Falloir, To Be Necessary, Must.

Falloir is either followed by a verb in the infinitive, or by **que** and a verb in the subjunctive mode.

When **falloir** (*must*) is construed with the infinitive, the subject of the English verb *must*, is, in French, the indirect object of the verb **falloir**.

Que me faut-il faire ?	What must I do ?
Il vous faut rester tranquille.	You must keep quiet.

The subject is omitted when it is of a general character; and generally, also, when the meaning is sufficiently obvious without it.

Il faut travailler pour réussir.	It is necessary to work in order to to succeed.
Faut-il aller à la banque ?	Must I go to the bank ?
Il faut y aller.	You must go there.

Falloir is also used in the sense of *to want*.

Que lui faut-il ?	What does he want ?
Il lui faut de l'argent.	He wants money

Vocabulary 33.

Tonner, to thunder.	La pluie, the rain.
Neiger, to snow.	Il fait de la pluie, it rains.
Grêler, to hail.	La neige, the snow.
Geler, to freeze.	Le tonnerre, the thunder.
Dégeler, to thaw.	Un éclair, a flash of lightning; il
*Pleuvoir, to rain.	fait des éclairs, it lightens.
*Savoir, to know.	La langue, the language.
*Y avoir, to be.	Du monde, company; people.
*Falloir, to be necessary.	Chaud, warm.
Comme il faut, as it should be.	Froid, cold.
Se comporter, to behave.	Tranquille, quiet; still.

Exercise 33.

1. Quel temps fait-il ? 2. Il fait beau temps ; il fait chaud. 3. Il fait mauvais temps ; il pleut. 4. Il a neigé pendant la nuit ; il fait froid. 5. Il grêle à présent. 6. Il gèlera cette nuit. 7. Demain il dégèlera. 8. Il tonne et il fait des éclairs. 9. Il va pleuvoir. 10. Il pleuvra beaucoup. 11. Il a plu toute la nuit. 12. Il est temps de se lever.

13. Il est bon de savoir cela. 14. Il est utile de savoir plusieurs langues. 15. Il y avait beaucoup de monde à l'église. 16. Il y aura peu de fruit cette année. 17. Il y aurait beaucoup de monde ici, s'il ne pleuvait pas. 18. Que me faut-il faire ? 19. Il vous faut étudier. 20. Il faut rester tranquille. 21. Il faut se bien comporter pour être respecté. 22. Que faut-il à votre frère ? 23. Il lui faut de l'argent. 24. J'ai tout ce qu'il me faut. 25. C'est comme il faut.

Theme 33.

1. Is it raining ? 2. No, sir, it is fine weather. 3. It is warm. 4. It was (has been) cold during the night. 5. It froze (has frozen). 6. It snows now. 7. I like (the) snow better than (the) rain. 8. It hails. 9. It is going to thaw. 10 Is that thunder ? 11. Yes, it thunders and lightens. 12. It will rain soon. 13. It is time to go to bed. 14. It is well to know several languages. 15. In order to know them, it is necessary to study them. 16. There was company in the parlor, when I came in. 17. There will be many peaches this year. 18. There would not be anybody here, if it rained as it did (has done) yesterday. 19. James did not behave (has not behaved) well. 20. You must tell it to his father. 21. What do you want ? 22. I want some gloves.

THIRTY-FOURTH LESSON.

Irregular Verbs.

1. There are, besides the auxiliary verbs **avoir** and **être**, forty-four irregular forms of conjugation, and about two hundred and eighty irregular verbs, which are conjugated

according to some one of the irregular forms or model verbs. We give the irregular model verbs of the first (*two*), second (*ten*), third (*eleven*), and fourth (*twenty-three*) conjugations successively and in alphabetical order, and below each model, the verbs that follow its conjugation.

IRREGULAR MODEL VERBS. — FIRST CONJUGATION.

2. *ALLER, To Go. — (FIRST MODEL.)

Aller   Allant   Allé

Être allé†   *to have gone*

PRESENT.	Je vais	tu vas	il va
	Nous allons	vous allez	ils vont
IMPERF.	J'allais	tu allais	il allait
	Nous allions	vous alliez	ils allaient
PAST DEF.	J'allai	tu allas	il alla
	Nous allâmes	vous allâtes	ils allèrent
FUTURE.	J'irai	tu iras	il ira
	Nous irons	vous irez	ils iront
COND. PR.	J'irais	tu irais	il irait
	Nous irions	vous iriez	ils iraient
IMPER.		Va	
	Allons	allez	
SUBJ. PR.	Que j'aille	que tu ailles	qu'il aille
	Que nous allions	que vous alliez	qu'ils aillent
IMPERF.	Que j'allasse	que tu allasses	qu'il allât
	Que nous allassions	que vous allassiez	qu'ils allassent

2.   S'EN *ALLER, To Go Away.

S'en aller, *to go away*, follows the model verb **aller**; but its conjugation presents some additional difficulties, and is therefore given in full.

---

† Only the simple tenses of the verbs are given here; the auxiliary verb, which is to be used in the formation of the compound tenses, is indicated. The student can form the compound tenses himself, and also supply the English, which he will now have no difficulty in doing.

IRREGULAR VERBS. 151

	S'en aller	S'en allant	Allé
	S'en être allé	*to have gone away*	
PRESENT.	Je m'en vais	tu t'en vas	il s'en va
	Nous nous en allons	vous vous en allez	ils s'en vont
IMPERF.	Je m'en allais	tu t'en allais	il s'en allait
	Nous nous en allions	vous vous en alliez	ils s'en allaient
PAST DEF.	Je m'en allai	tu t'en allas	il s'en alla
	Nous nous en allâmes	vous vous en allâtes	ils s'en allèrent
FUTURE.	Je m'en irai	tu t'en iras	il s'en ira
	Nous nous en irons	vous vous en irez	ils s'en iront
COND. PR.	Je m'en irais	tu t'en irais	il s'en irait
	Nous nous en irions	vous vous en iriez	ils s'en iraient
IMPER.		Va-t'en	
	Allons-nous-en	allez-vous-en	
SUBJ. PR.	Que je m'en aille	que tu t'en ailles	qu'il s'en aille
	Que nous nous en allions	que vous vous en alliez	qu'ils s'en aillent
IMPERF.	Que je m'en allasse	que tu t'en allasses	qu'il s'en allât
	Que nous nous en allassions	que vous vous en allassiez	qu'il s'en allassent

*S'EN ALLER. (NEGATIVELY.)

Ne pas s'en aller   Ne s'en allant pas

Ne s'en être pas allé

PRESENT.	Je ne m'en vais pas	tu ne t'en vas pas	il ne s'en va pas
	Nous ne nous en allons pas	vous ne vous en allez pas	ils ne s'en vont pas
PAST IND.	Je ne m'en suis pas allé	tu ne t'en es pas allé	il ne s'en est pas allé
	Nous ne nous en sommes pas allés	vous ne vous en êtes pas allés	ils ne s'en sont pas allés

REM. The student will have no difficulty in forming the remaining tenses himself.

*S'EN ALLER. (INTERROGATIVELY.)

PRESENT.	M'en vais-je ?	T'en vas-tu ?	S'en va-t-il ?
	Nous en allons nous ?	Vous en allez-vous ?	S'en vont-ils ?
PAST IND.	M'en suis-je allé ?	T'en es-tu allé ?	S'en est-il allé ?
	Nous en sommes-nous allés ?	Vous en êtes-vous allés ?	S'en sont-ils allés ?

*S'EN ALLER. (INTERROGATIVELY AND NEGATIVELY.)

PRESENT. Ne m'en vais-je pas ?   Ne nous en allons-nous pas ?
PAST IND. Ne m'en suis-je pas allé ?   Ne nous en sommes-nous pas allés ?

*ENVOYER, To Send.—(Second Model.)

Envoyer   Envoyant   Envoyé

Avoir envoyé   to have sent

PRESENT.   J'envoie   tu envoies   il envoie
           Nous envoyons   vous envoyez   ils envoient
IMPERF.   J'envoyais   tu envoyais   il envoyait
           Nous envoyions   vous envoyiez   ils envoyaient
PAST DEF.   J'envoyai   tu envoyas   il envoya
           Nous envoyâmes   vous envoyâtes   ils envoyèrent
FUTURE.   J'enverrai   tu enverras   il enverra
           Nous enverrons   vous enverrez   ils enverront
COND. PR.   J'enverrais   tu enverrais   il enverrait
           Nous enverrions   vous enverriez   ils enverraient
IMPER.   Envoie
           Envoyons   envoyez
SUBJ. PR.   Que j'envoie   que tu envoies   qu'il envoie
           Que nous envoyions   que vous envoyiez   qu'ils envoient
IMPERF.   Que j'envoyasse   que tu envoyasses   qu'il envoyât
           Que nous envoyassions   que vous envoyassiez   qu'ils envoyassent

Conjugate in the same manner:

*Renvoyer, to send back ; to send away.

Vocabulary 34.

*Aller, to go.
*Aller chercher, to go for.
*S'en aller, to go away.
*Envoyer, to send.
*Envoyer chercher, to send for.
*Renvoyer, to send back ; to send away.
Rappeler, to call back.

Déjeuner, to breakfast.
Le cocher, the coachman.
Quelque part, somewhere.
Nulle part (ne), nowhere.
Vite, quick ; quickly ; fast ; bien vite, very quickly.
Lentement, slowly.
De là, from there.

Exercise 34.

1. Je vais au bureau. 2. Je m'en vais à présent. 3. Alexis va chercher de l'argent à la banque. 4. Nous nous en allons ensemble. 5. Vous en allez-vous déjà? 6. Ils vont partir. 7. J'allais partir quand on m'a rappelé. 8. Je m'en allais quand mon oncle est entré. 9. A quelle heure vous en êtes-vous allé? 10. Je m'en suis allé à dix heures. 11. Nous nous en sommes allés ensemble. 12. J'irai chercher les lettres quand j'aurai fini d'écrire. 13. Je m'en irai bien vite. 14. Irez-vous quelque part ce soir? 15. Je n'irai nulle part; je resterai chez moi. 16. J'irais au spectacle, s'il ne pleuvait pas. 17. Je m'en irais, si mon frère était de retour. 18. Va maintenant. 19. Va-t'en bien vite. 20. Allons-nous-en lentement. 21. Il faut que j'aille à la banque. 22. Il faut que je m'en aille tout à l'heure.† 23. J'enverrai chercher mes livres tantôt. 24. Vous nous renverrez la voiture quand vous serez arrivé. 25. Il renverra son cocher à la fin du mois.

Thème 34.

1. Are you going to your uncle's? 2. I am going there by and by.† 3. I am going away now. 4. We are going for our books. 5. They are going away. 6. Louis is going away with them. 7. He was going to leave when I called him back (*past indef.*). 8. They were going away when I came (*past indef.*). 9. Where were you going when I met (*past indef.*) you a little while ago?† 10. I was going to the post-office. 11. From there I went (*past indef.*) to the bank. 12. The children have gone to school. 13. They

---

† See Vocabulary 28, p. 123.

went away (*past indef.*) just now.† 14. I will go to the store when I have breakfasted. 15. I am not going anywhere this morning. 16. I would go somewhere, if it did not rain. 17. Go (*plur.*) quickly to the post-office. 18. Let us go slowly; it is so warm. 19. We must go to our aunt's; she is going to leave. 20. I will send you that book this afternoon. 21. You will send it back to me when you (shall) have read it. 22. We shall send our coachman away at the end of the month; he has become *so lazy* (si paresseux). 23. I will send for some paper presently.

THIRTY-FIFTH LESSON.

Irregular Verbs (Continued).— Second Conjugation.

1. *ACQUÉRIR, To Acquire. —(First Model.)

Acquérir   Acquérant   Acquis

Avoir acquis   *to have acquired*

Present.	J'acquiers	tu acquiers	il acquiert
	Nous acquérons	vous acquérez	ils acquièrent
Imperf.	J'acquérais	tu acquérais	il acquérait
	Nous acquérions	vous acquériez	ils acquéraient
Past Def.	J'acquis	tu acquis	il acquit
	Nous acquîmes	vous acquîtes	ils acquirent
Future.	J'acquerrai	tu acquerras	il acquerra
	Nous acquerrons	vous acquerrez	ils acquerront
Cond. Pr.	J'acquerrais	tu acquerrais	il acquerrait
	Nous acquerrions	vous acquerriez	ils acquerraient
Imper.		Acquiers	
	Acquérons	acquérez	
Subj. Pr.	Que j'acquière	que tu acquières	qu'il acquière
	Que nous acquérions	que vous acquériez	qu'ils acquièrent
Imperf.	Que j'acquisse	que tu acquisses	qu'il acquît
	Que nous acquissions	que vous acquissiez	qu'ils acquissent

† See Vocabulary 28, p. 123.

Conjugate in the same manner as *acquérir:
*Conquérir, to conquer.   *Reconquérir, to reconquer.
*S'enquérir, to inquire.

*BOUILLIR, To Boil.—(Second Model.)

Bouillir   Bouillant   Bouilli
Avoir bouilli   *to have boiled*

Present.	Je bous	tu bous	il bout
	Nous bouillons	vous bouillez	ils bouillent
Imperf.	Je bouillais	tu bouillais	il bouillait
	Nous bouillions	vous bouilliez	ils bouillaient
Past Def.	Je bouillis	tu bouillis	il bouillit
	Nous bouillîmes	vous bouillîtes	ils bouillirent
Future.	Je bouillirai	tu bouilliras	il bouillira
	Nous bouillirons	vous bouillirez	ils bouilliront
Cond. Pr.	Je bouillirais	tu bouillirais	il bouillirait
	Nous bouillirions	vous bouilliriez	ils bouilliraient
Imper.		Bous	
	Bouillons	bouillez	
Subj. Pr.	Que je bouille	que tu bouilles	qu'il bouille
	Que nous bouillions	que vous bouilliez	qu'ils bouillent
Imperf.	Que je bouillisse	que tu bouillisses	qu'il bouillît
	Que nous bouillissions	que vous bouillissiez	qu'ils bouillissent

*COURIR, To Run.—(Third Model.)

Courir   Courant   Couru
Avoir couru   *to have run*

Present.	Je cours	tu cours	il court
	Nous courons	vous courez	ils courent
Imperf.	Je courais	tu courais	il courait
	Nous courions	vous couriez	ils couraient
Past Def.	Je courus	tu courus	il courut
	Nous courûmes	vous courûtes	ils coururent
Future.	Je courrai	tu courras	il courra
	Nous courrons	vous courrez	ils courront
Cond. Pr.	Je courrais	tu courrais	il courrait
	Nous courrions	vous courriez	ils courraient
Imper.		Cours	
	Courons	courez	

Subj. Pr.	Que je coure	que tu coures	qu'il coure
	Que nous courions,	que vous couriez	qu'ils courent
Imperf.	Que je courusse	que tu courusses	qu'il courût
	Que nous courussions	que vous courussiez	qu'ils courussent

Conjugate in the same manner as *courir :

*Accourir, to run up.
*Concourir, to concur.
*Discourir, to discourse.
*Parcourir, to go over ; to look over.
*Secourir, to succor.

*CUEILLIR, To Gather.—(Fourth Model.)

	Cueillir	Cueillant	Cueilli
	Avoir cueilli	*to have gathered*	
Present.	Je cueille	tu cueilles	il cueille
	Nous cueillons	vous cueillez	ils cueillent
Imperf.	Je cueillais	tu cueillais	il cueillait
	Nous cueillions	vous cueilliez	ils cueillaient
Past Def.	Je cueillis	tu cueillis	il cueillit
	Nous cueillimes	vous cueillites	ils cueillirent
Future.	Je cueillerai	tu cueilleras	il cueillera
	Nous cueillerons	vous cueillerez	ils cueilleront
Cond. Pr.	Je cueillerais	tu cueillerais	il cueillerait
	Nous cueillerions	vous cueilleriez	ils cueilleraient
Imper.		Cueille	
	Cueillons	cueillez	
Subj. Pr.	Que je cueille	que tu cueilles	qu'il cueille
	Que nous cueillions	que vous cueilliez	qu'ils cueillent
Imperf.	Que je cueillisse	que tu cueillisses	qu'il cueillît
	Que nous cueillissions	que vous cueillissiez	qu'ils cueillissent

Conjugate in the same manner as *cueillir :

*Accueillir, to receive.
*Recueillir, to collect.
*Assaillir, to assail.
*Tressaillir, to start.

Rem. Assaillir and tressaillir have in the future tense **j'assaillirai, je tressaillirai,** etc., and in the conditional mode, **j'assaillirais, je tressaillirais,** etc., instead of **j'assaillerai, je tressaillerai,** etc.

*FUIR, To Flee.—(Fifth Model.)

Fuir	Fuyant	Fui
	Avoir fui *to have fled*	

Present.	Je fuis	tu fuis	il fuit
	Nous fuyons	vous fuyez	ils fuient
Imperf.	Je fuyais	tu fuyais	il fuyait
	Nous fuyions	vous fuyiez	ils fuyaient
Past Def.	Je fuis	tu fuis	il fuit
	Nous fuîmes	vous fuîtes	ils fuirent
Future.	Je fuirai	tu fuiras	il fuira
	Nous fuirons	vous fuirez	ils fuiront
Cond. Pr.	Je fuirais	tu fuirais	il fuirait
	Nous fuirions	vous fuiriez	ils fuiraient
Imper.		Fuis	
	Fuyons	fuyez	
Subj. Pr.	Que je fuie	que tu fuies	qu'il fuie
	Que nous fuyions	que vous fuyiez	qu'ils fuient
Imperf.	Que je fuisse	que tu fuisses	qu'il fuît
	Que nous fuissions	que vous fuissiez	qu'ils fuissent

Conjugate in the same manner as *fuir :

*S'enfuir (être), to run away.

Vocabulary 35.

*Acquérir, to acquire.
*Conquérir, to conquer ; to obtain.
*Bouillir, to boil.
*Courir, to run.
*Parcourir, to go over ; to look over.
*Cueillir, to gather.
*Recueillir, to reap ; to collect.
*Assaillir, to assail.
*Fuir, to flee ; to shun.
*S'enfuir, to run away.
Le bien, the property.
Le commerce, commerce.
La réputation, the reputation.
La connaissance, the knowledge.
Des connaissances, knowledge ; learning.
La liberté, liberty.
La bravoure, bravery.
La persévérance, perseverance.
L'industrie, *f.*, industry.
Le vice, vice.
La société, society.
Un créancier, a creditor.
De quoi, wherewith.
Honnête, honest.
Car, for (*a conj.*).
Les États-Unis, the United States.

Exercise 35.

MODEL ACQUÉRIR. 1. J'acquiers des connaissances utiles par l'étude. 2. Nous acquérons du bien par le travail. 3. Nos voisins ont acquis une grande fortune par le commerce. 4. Nous acquerrons la réputation d'honnête homme, si nous nous comportons bien. 5. Les États-Unis conquirent leur liberté par la bravoure et par la persévérance.

MODEL BOUILLIR. 6. Avez-vous de l'eau bouillie ? 7. L'eau ne bout pas, mais elle bouillira en peu de temps. 8. Elle a bouilli. 9. Pour faire de bon café, il faut de l'eau bouillante. 10. J'attendrai qu'elle bouille.

MODEL COURIR. 11. Je cours et ils courent aussi, car nous sommes pressés. 12. Je courrai aussi, si vous courez. 13. Si vous couriez, vous arriveriez à temps. 14. Vous courriez, si vous étiez pressé comme moi. 15. J'ai parcouru ce livre ; il est intéressant.

MODEL CUEILLIR. 16. Je cueille des fleurs, et j'en fais des bouquets. 17. J'en cueillerai avec vous, si vous voulez. 18. Cueillons-en ensemble ; ce sera amusant. 19. Il n'a point recueilli le fruit de ses travaux. 20. Ses créanciers l'assaillirent, parce qu'il n'avait pas de quoi les payer.

MODEL FUIR. 21. Je fuis la société des méchants. 22. Il me fuit, et je ne sais pas pourquoi. 23. Nous fuyons le vice, et nous l'avons toujours fui. 24. Il s'est enfui quand il m'a vu. 25. Si tu n'étais pas à blâmer, tu ne t'enfuirais pas.

Theme 35.

MODEL ACQUÉRIR. 1. Thou acquirest useful knowledge at school. 2. They acquire property by their industry. 3. You will acquire the reputation of an honest man, if you pay what you owe. 4. They have acquired a great fortune. 5. We obtained our liberty by our bravery and (by) our perseverance.

MODEL BOUILLIR. 6. Is there any boiling water? 7. The water will boil in a few minutes. 8. It has boiled, but it is not boiling now. 9. Wait *until* (qu') it boils (*subj.*). 10. I wish (that) it would boil (*subj. imp.*); I am in a hurry.

MODEL COURIR. 11. If you run, I shall run. 12. I would not run, if you did not run. 13. They were running, and I do not know why. 14. I will look over this book when I have time (*for it*, en). 15. We have run very fast.

MODEL CUEILLIR. 16. For whom are you gathering those flowers? 17. I am gathering them for my mother. 18. Have you not gathered enough? 19. I will gather a few more. 20. Pay your creditors, and they will not assail you.

MODEL FUIR. 21. I shun that man, because I do not like him. 22. We shun the society of those whom we do not like. 23. Flee from vice and the company of the wicked. 24. They were running away; I do not know why. 25. You would not have run away, if you were not *to* (à) blame.

THIRTY-SIXTH LESSON.

IRREGULAR VERBS (CONTINUED).— SECOND CONJUGATION.

MOURIR, TO DIE.— SIXTH MODEL.

	Mourir	Mourant	Mort
		Etre mort *to have died*	
PRESENT.	Je meurs	tu meurs	Il meurt
	Nous mourons	vous mourez	Ils meurent
IMPERF.	Je mourais	tu mourais	Il mourait
	Nous mourions	vous mouriez	Ils mouraient

Past Def.	Je mourus	tu mourus	il mourut
	Nous mourûmes	vous mourûtes	ils moururent
Future.	Je mourrai	tu mourras	il mourra
	Nous mourrons	vous mourrez	ils mourront
Cond. Pr.	Je mourrais	tu mourrais	il mourrait
	Nous mourrions	vous mourriez	ils mourraient
Imper.		Meurs	
	Mourons	mourez	
Subj. Pr.	Que je meure	que tu meures	qu'il meure
	Que nous mourions	que vous mouriez	qu'ils meurent
Imperf.	Que je mourusse	que tu mourusses	qu'il mourût
	Que nous mourussions	que vous mourussiez	qu'ils mourussent

*OUVRIR, To Open.—(Seventh Model.)

	Ouvrir	Ouvrant	Ouvert
	Avoir ouvert	*to have opened*	
Present.	J'ouvre	tu ouvres	il ouvre
	Nous ouvrons	vous ouvrez	ils ouvrent
Imperf.	J'ouvrais	tu ouvrais	il ouvrait
	Nous ouvrions	vous ouvriez	ils ouvraient
Past Def.	J'ouvris	tu ouvris	il ouvrit
	Nous ouvrîmes	vous ouvrîtes	ils ouvrirent
Future.	J'ouvrirai	tu ouvriras	il ouvrira
	Nous ouvrirons	vous ouvrirez	ils ouvriront
Cond. Pr.	J'ouvrirais	tu ouvrirais	il ouvrirait
	Nous ouvririons	vous ouvririez	ils ouvriraient
Imper.		Ouvre	
	Ouvrons	ouvrez	
Subj. Pr.	Que j'ouvre	que tu ouvres	qu'il ouvre
	Que nous ouvrions	que vous ouvriez	qu'ils ouvrent
Imperf.	Que j'ouvrisse	que tu ouvrisses	qu'il ouvrît
	Que nous ouvrissions	que vous ouvrissiez	qu'ils ouvrissent

Conjugate in the same manner as ***ouvrir** :

*Couvrir, to cover. ***Offrir**, to offer. ***Souffrir**, to suffer.

And the derivatives of ***ouvrir, *couvrir**, and ***offrir**.

*SENTIR, To Feel.—(Eighth Model.)

Sentir   Sentant   Senti

Avoir senti   *to have felt*

PRESENT.	Je sens	tu sens	il sent
	Nous sentons	vous sentez	ils sentent
IMPERF.	Je sentais	tu sentais	il sentait
	Nous sentions	vous sentiez	ils sentaient
PAST DEF.	Je sentis	tu sentis	il sentit
	Nous sentîmes	vous sentîtes	ils sentirent
FUTURE.	Je sentirai	tu sentiras	il sentira
	Nous sentirons	vous sentirez	ils sentiront
COND. PR.	Je sentirais	tu sentirais	il sentirait
	Nous sentirions	vous sentiriez	ils sentiraient
IMPER.		Sens	
	Sentons	sentez	
SUBJ. PR.	Que je sente	que tu sentes	qu'il sente
	Que nous sentions	que vous sentiez	qu'ils sentent
IMPERF.	Que je sentisse	que tu sentisses	qu'il sentît
	Que nous sentissions	que vous sentissiez	qu'ils sentissent

Conjugate in the same manner as ***sentir**:

*__Partir (être)__, to start.   *__Mentir__, to lie.
*__Sortir (être)__, to go out.   *__Dormir__, to sleep.
*__Se repentir__, to repent.   *__Servir__, to serve.

And the derivatives of these verbs.

REM. 1. The final radical letter of **dormir** (m) and of **servir** (v) disappears and reappears in the inflections of the verb, the same as the final radical t of the models **partir** and **sentir**. **Je dors, nous dormons; Je sers, nous servons,** etc.

*TENIR, To Hold.—(Ninth Model.)

Tenir   Tenant   Tenu

Avoir tenu   *to have held*

PRESENT.	Je tiens	tu tiens	Il tient
	Nous tenons	vous tenez	Ils tiennent

Imperf.	Je tenais	tu tenais	il tenait
	Nous tenions	vous teniez	ils tenaient
Past Def.	Je tins	tu tins	il tint
	Nous tînmes	vous tîntes	ils tinrent
Future.	Je tiendrai	tu tiendras	il tiendra
	Nous tiendrons	vous tiendrez	ils tiendront
Cond. Pr.	Je tiendrais	tu tiendrais	il tiendrait
	Nous tiendrions	vous tiendriez	ils tiendraient
Imper.		Tiens	
	Tenons	tenez	
Subj. Pr.	Que je tienne	que tu tiennes	qu'il tienne
	Que nous tenions	que vous teniez	qu'ils tiennent
Imperf.	Que je tinsse	que tu tinsses	qu'il tînt
	Que nous tinssions	que vous tinssiez	qu'ils tinssent

Conjugate in the same manner as *tenir:

*Venir (être), to come.

And the compounds of *venir and *tenir.

Rem. 2. The derivatives of venir, generally take the auxiliary verb être; the derivatives of tenir, the auxiliary avoir, except the pronominal verbs.

*VÊTIR, To Clothe.—(Tenth Model.)

Vêtir	Vêtant	Vêtu

Avoir vêtu   *to have clad*

Present.	Je vêts	tu vêts	il vêt
	Nous vêtons	vous vêtez	ils vêtent
Imperf.	Je vêtais	tu vêtais	il vêtait
	Nous vêtions	vous vêtiez	ils vêtaient
Past Def.	Je vêtis	tu vêtis	il vêtit
	Nous vêtîmes	vous vêtîtes	ils vêtirent
Future.	Je vêtirai	tu vêtiras	il vêtira
	Nous vêtirons	vous vêtirez	ils vêtiront
Cond. Pr.	Je vêtirais	tu vêtirais	il vêtirait
	Nous vêtirions	vous vêtiriez	ils vêtiraient
Imper.		Vêts	
	Vêtons	vêtez	

IRREGULAR VERBS.

Subj. Pr. Que je vête	que tu vêtes	qu'il vête
Que nous vêtions	que vous vêtiez	qu'ils vêtent
Imperf. Que je vêtisse	que tu vêtisses	qu'il vêtît
Que nous vêtissions	que vous vêtissiez	qu'ils vêtissent

Conjugate in the same manner as *vêtir:

*Devêtir, to undress.   Revêtir, to clothe; to invest.

Vocabulary 36.

*Mourir (de), to die (with).
*Ouvrir, to open.
*Couvrir, to cover.
*Découvrir, to discover.
*Offrir, to offer.
*Souffrir (de), to suffer.
*Sentir, to feel; to smell.
*Partir (être), to start; to depart.
*Sortir (être), to go out.
*Dormir, to sleep.
*Servir, to serve.
*Tenir, to hold; to keep.
*Retenir, to retain.
*Venir (être), to come.
*Revenir (être), to come back, to return.
*Devenir (être), to become.
*Parvenir (être), to succeed; to attain.

*Vêtir, to clothe.
*Revêtir, to clothe; to invest.
Dieu, God.
La prière, the prayer.
La promesse, the promise.
Le mot, the word.
Le plancher, the floor.
Le tapis, the carpet.
La fenêtre, the window.
Le grand-père, the grandfather.
La maladie, the sickness.
L'Amérique, America.
Le froid, the cold.
La saison, the season.
Un an, a year; en l'an, in the year.
Le pouvoir, the power.
Suprême, supreme.
Chaudement, warmly.

Exercise 36.

MODEL MOURIR. 1. Nous mourons de froid ici. 2. J'espère que nous ne mourrons pas encore. 3. On souffre et l'on meurt partout. 4. Le grand-père de Jacques est mort pendant la nuit. 5. Le Général Washington mourut à Mont Vernon en l'an mil sept cent quatre-vingt-dix-neuf.

MODEL OUVRIR. 6. J'ouvre la fenêtre pour regarder dans la rue. 7. Il souffrait beaucoup pendant sa maladie. 8. On a couvert le plancher d'un tapis. 9. Lui offrirai-je quelque chose? 10. Christophe Colomb découvrit l'Amérique en mil quatre cent quatre-vingt-douze.

MODEL SENTIR. 11. Je pars maintenant ; mes frères sont déjà partis. 12. Jules et son frère ne sortiront pas ce soir. 13. Je ne sentais pas le froid pendant le voyage. 14. Vous dormiez tout le temps. 15. Que vous servirai-je ?

MODEL TENIR. 16. Je tiendrai ma promesse, si vous tenez la vôtre. 17. Nous viendrons vous voir ce soir. 18. Vous retiendriez ces mots, si vous les copiiez deux ou trois fois. 19. Il faut que je revienne ici demain. 20. Vous êtes devenu grand. 21. Vous parviendrez, si vous vous comportez bien.

MODEL VÊTIR. 22. Il faut vous vêtir chaudement dans cette saison-ci. 23. Ces hommes étaient bien vêtus. 24. Le Président est revêtu du pouvoir suprême.

Exercise 36.

MODEL MOURIR. 1. I am dying with impatience. 2. We shall all die : the one to-day, the other to-morrow. 3. I would die, if I lost my friend. 4. My grandfather died last week (*past indef.*) 5. Napoléon died (*past def.*) *in* (en) eighteen hundred and twenty-one.

MODEL OUVRIR. 6. Open the door, if you please. 7. He has opened the windows of his room. 8. I will cover the floor of your room with a carpet. 9. I suffer to see him suffer. 10. Let us offer our prayers to God for those who suffer.

MODEL SENTIR. 11. I feel the cold here. 12. When will

you start? 13. We would go out, if it did not rain. 14. He sleeps, and it is well that he sleeps (*subj. pres.*) 15. They have always served us well.

MODEL TENIR. 16. If I keep my promise, will you keep yours? 17. I shall retain these words; I have copied them. 18. He has succeeded by his industry. 19. Those children have grown up (have become tall). 20. My father would come back to town, if my mother were not sick. 21. They would have returned last night.

MODEL VÊTIR. 22. You are not clad warmly enough for this season. 23. Would you be happy, if you were invested with the supreme power of the *state* (état)?

THIRTY-SEVENTH LESSON.

IRREGULAR VERBS (CONTINUED).—THIRD CONJUGATION.

The third conjugation has nine irregular forms or models. They are

*S'ASSEOIR, To Sit Down.—(FIRST MODEL.)

	S'asseoir	S'asseyant	Assis
	S'être assis	*to have sat down*	
PRESENT.	Je m'assieds	tu t'assieds	il s'assied
	Nous nous asseyons	vous vous asseyez	ils s'asseyent
IMPERF.	Je m'asseyais	tu t'asseyais	il s'asseyait
	Nous nous asseyions	vous vous asseyiez	ils s'asseyaient
PAST DEF.	Je m'assis	tu t'assis	il s'assit
	Nous nous assîmes	vous vous assîtes	ils s'assirent
FUTURE.	Je m'assiérai	tu t'assiéras	il s'assiéra
	Nous nous assiérons	vous vous assiérez	ils s'assiéront
COND. PR.	Je m'assiérais	tu t'assiérais	il s'assiérait
	Nous nous assiérions	vous vous assiériez	ils s'assiéraient
IMPER.		Assieds-toi	
	Asseyons-nous	asseyez-vous	

166 ELEMENTARY FRENCH GRAMMAR.

SUBJ. PR.	Que je m'asseye	que tu t'asseyes	qu'il s'asseye
	Que nous nous asseyions	que vous vous asseyiez	qu'ils s'asseyent
IMPERF.	Que je m'assise	que tu t'assisses	qu'il s'assît
	Que nous nous assissions	que vous vous assissiez	qu'ils s'assissent

The verb **s'asseoir* is also conjugated in the following manner:

	S'asseoir	S'assoyant	Assis
	S'être assis	*to have sat down*	
PRESENT.	Je m'assois	tu t'assois	il s'assoit
	Nous nous assoyons	vous vous assoyez	ils s'assoient
IMPERF.	Je m'assoyais	tu t'assoyais	il s'assoyait
	Nous nous assoyions	vous vous assoyiez	ils s'assoyaient
PAST DEF.	Je m'assis	tu t'assis	il s'assit
	Nous nous assîmes	vous vous assîtes	ils s'assirent
FUTURE.	Je m'assoirai	tu t'assoiras	il s'assoira
	Nous nous assoirons	vous vous assoirez	ils s'assoiront
COND. PR.	Je m'assoirais	tu t'assoirais	il s'assoirait
	Nous nous assoirions	vous vous assoiriez	ils s'assoiraient
IMPER.		Assois-toi	
	Assoyons-nous	assoyez-vous	
SUBJ. PR.	Que je m'assoie	que tu t'assoies	qu'il s'assoie
	Que nous nous assoyions	que vous vous assoyiez	qu'ils s'assoient
IMPERF.	Que je m'assisse	que tu t'assisses	qu'il s'assît
	Que nous nous assissions	que vous vous assissiez	qu'ils s'assissent

**FALLOIR, TO BE NECESSARY.—(SECOND MODEL.)*

See Lesson Thirty-third.

**MOUVOIR, TO MOVE.—(THIRD MODEL.)*

	Mouvoir	Mouvant	Mu
	Avoir mu	*to have moved*	
PRESENT.	Je meus	tu meus	il meut
	Nous mouvons	vous mouvez	ils meuvent

IRREGULAR VERBS.

Imperf.	Je mouvais	tu mouvais	il mouvait
	Nous mouvions	vous mouviez	ils mouvaient
Past Def.	Je mus	tu mus	il mut
	Nous mûmes	vous mûtes	ils murent
Future.	Je mouvrai	tu mouvras	il mouvra
	Nous mouvrons	vous mouvrez	ils mouvront
Cond Pr.	Je mouvrais	tu mouvrais	il mouvrait
	Nous mouvrions	vous mouvriez	ils mouvraient
Imper.		Meus	
	Mouvons	mouvez	
Subj. Pr.	Que je meuve	que tu meuves	qu'il meuve
	Que nous mouvions	que vous mouviez	qu'ils meuvent
Imperf.	Que je musse	que tu musses	qu'il mût
	Que nous mussions	que vous mussiez	qu'ils mussent

Conjugate in the same manner as *mouvoir:

*Émouvoir, to move; to affect.

*PLEUVOIR, To Rain.—(Fourth Model.)

See Lesson Thirty-third.

*POUVOIR, To Be Able.—(Fifth Model.)

	Pouvoir	Pouvant	Pu
	Avoir pu	*to have been able*	
Present.	Je puis, *or* je peux	tu peux	il peut
	Nous pouvons	vous pouvez	ils peuvent
Imperf.	Je pouvais	tu pouvais	il pouvait
	Nous pouvions	vous pouviez	ils pouvaient
Past Def.	Je pus	tu pus	il put
	Nous pûmes	vous pûtes	ils purent
Future.	Je pourrai	tu pourras	il pourra
	Nous pourrons	vous pourrez	ils pourront
Cond. Pr.	Je pourrais	tu pourrais	il pourrait
	Nous pourrions	vous pourriez	ils pourraient
Imper.		(*None*)	
Subj. Pr.	Que je puisse	que tu puisses	qu'il puisse
	Que nous puissions	que vous puissiez	qu'ils puissent
Imperf.	Que je pusse	que tu pusses	qu'il pût
	Que nous pussions	que vous pussiez	qu'ils pussent

Vocabulary 37.

*S'asseoir, to sit down.
*Etre assis, to be sitting.
*Mouvoir, to move.
*Émouvoir, to move; to affect.
*Pouvoir, to be able.
Bouger, to stir.
*Se servir, to use; to make use of.
*Aller trouver, to go to (find a person).

Un hôtel, an hotel.
Le banquier, the banker.
Le récit, the recital.
A côté de, by the side of.
Près de, near.
Autour de, around.
Longtemps, a long time.
Il y a longtemps, long ago.

Exercise 37.

MODEL S'ASSEOIR. 1. Je vais m'asseoir. 2. Je m'assieds parce que je suis fatigué. 3. Je m'assiérai à côté de vous. 4. Elle s'est assise à côté de sa mère. 5. Asseyez-vous. 6. Ne vous asseyez pas près de la fenêtre ouverte. 7. Ils étaient assis autour de la table quand je suis entré.

MODEL FALLOIR. 8. Il faut partir. 9. Il fallait quitter l'hôtel; nous ne pouvions plus y rester. 10. Il faudra aller trouver le banquier pour avoir de l'argent. 11. Il aurait fallu écrire chez nous il y a longtemps.

MODEL MOUVOIR. 12. Je ne peux pas mouvoir cette table. 13. Rien ne se meut; rien ne bouge ici. 14. Le récit de cette histoire nous a émus.

MODEL PLEUVOIR. 15. Il a plu, mais il ne pleut plus. 16. Il pleuvait quand je suis venu. 17. Il pleuvra encore. 18. Qu'il pleuve; nous avons besoin de pluie. 19. Il faudrait qu'il plût.

MODEL POUVOIR. 20. Je ne peux pas sortir dans ce moment. 21. Puis-je me servir de votre dictionnaire. 22. J'ai pu y aller hier. 23. Il ne pouvait pas venir; il ne pouvait pas quitter ses affaires. 24. Je pourrai vous donner cet argent demain. 25. Vous pourriez l'avoir aujourd'hui, si vous alliez trouver mon père.

Theme 37.

MODEL S'ASSEOIR. 1. I have no time to sit down. 2. She is sitting down by the side of her mother. 3. We will sit down near the door. 4. You were sitting around the table. 5. Let us sit down somewhere.

MODEL FALLOIR. 6. It is necessary to go to the banker. 7. We shall want money to-morrow. 8. It was necessary to speak of that. 9. It would be necessary to start, if they came. 10. It was necessary to wait for a long time.

MODEL MOUVOIR. 11. You cannot move that box. 12. Nothing was moving (*pronominal verb*) when we came (*past indef.*). 13. She was moved by the recital of that story.

MODEL PLEUVOIR. 14. If it rains, I shall not come. 15. If it did not rain, he would be here. 16. You will need your umbrella; it will rain. 17. It would be well that it should rain (*subj. imp.*).

MODEL POUVOIR. 18. I cannot leave my work. 19. May† I ask you something? 20. You may† use my dictionary, if you need it. 21. We have not been able to come. 22. He could not go out; he was sick. 23. I shall be able to tell you to-morrow. 24. You might‡ go and see him at the hotel. 25. I might have done that long since.

---

† Translate *may* by the present tense of the verb *pouvoir*.

‡ Translate *might* by the conditional mode of the verb *pouvoir*, and *might have* by the past tense of the conditional, and translate *done* by *faire*.

THIRTY-EIGHTH LESSON.

IRREGULAR VERBS (CONTINUED).—THIRD CONJUGATION.

*SAVOIR, To Know, To Know How.—(SIXTH MODEL.)

	Savoir	Sachant	Su
	Avoir su	*to have known*	
PRESENT.	Je sais	tu sais	il sait
	Nous savons	vous savez	ils savent
IMPERF.	Je savais	tu savais	il savait
	Nous savions	vous saviez	ils savaient
PAST DEF.	Je sus	tu sus	il sut
	Nous sûmes	vous sûtes	ils surent
FUTURE.	Je saurai	tu sauras	il saura
	Nous saurons	vous saurez	ils sauront
COND. PR.	Je saurais	tu saurais	il saurait
	Nous saurions	vous sauriez	ils sauraient
IMPER.		Sache	
	Sachons	sachez	
SUBJ. PR.	Que je sache	que tu saches	qu'il sache
	Que nous sachions	que vous sachiez	qu'ils sachent
IMPERF.	Que je susse	que tu susses	qu'il sût
	Que nous sussions	que vous sussiez	qu'ils sussent

*VALOIR, To Be Worth.—(SIXTH MODEL.)

	Valoir	Valant	Valu
	Avoir valu	*to have been worth*	
PRESENT.	Je vaux	tu vaux	il vaut
	Nous valons	vous valez	ils valent
IMPERF.	Je valais	tu valais	il valait
	Nous valions	vous valiez	ils valaient
PAST DEF.	Je valus	tu valus	il valut
	Nous valûmes	vous valûtes	ils valurent
FUTURE.	Je vaudrai	tu vaudras	il vaudra
	Nous vaudrons	vous vaudrez	ils vaudront
COND. PR.	Je vaudrais	tu vaudrais	il vaudrait
	Nous vaudrions	vous vaudriez	ils vaudraient
IMPER.		Vaux	
	Valons	valez	

Subj. Pr.	Que je vaille	que tu vailles	qu'il vaille
	Que nous valions	que vous valiez	qu'ils vaillent
Imperf.	Que je valusse	que tu valusses	qu'il valût
	Que nous valussions	que vous valussiez	qu'ils valussent

Conjugate in the same manner as *valoir :

Équivaloir, to be equivalent.

*VOIR, To See.—(Eighth Model.)

Voir   Voyant   Vu

Avoir vu   *to have seen*

Present.	Je vois	tu vois	il voit
	Nous voyons	vous voyez	ils voient
Imperf.	Je voyais	tu voyais	il voyait
	Nous voyions	vous voyiez	ils voyaient
Past Def.	Je vis	tu vis	il vit
	Nous vîmes	vous vîtes	ils virent
Future.	Je verrai	tu verras	il verra
	Nous verrons	vous verrez	ils verront
Cond. Pr.	Je verrais	tu verrais	il verrait
	Nous verrions	vous verriez	ils verraient
Imper.		Vois	
	Voyons	voyez	
Subj. Pr.	Que je voie	que tu voies	qu'il voie
	Que nous voyions	que vous voyiez	qu'ils voient
Imperf.	Que je visse	que tu visses	qu'il vît
	Que nous vissions	que vous vissiez	qu'ils vissent

Conjugate in the same manner as *voir:

*Revoir, to see again.   *Prévoir, to foresee.
*Entrevoir, to see imperfectly.   *Pourvoir, to provide.

Rem. *Prévoir and *pourvoir do not, in all respects, follow the model **voir**.

Prévoir has, in the future, **je prévoirai**, etc., and, in the conditional, **je prévoirais**, etc.

Pourvoir has, in the past definite, **je pourvus**, etc.; in the future, **je pourvoirai**, etc.; in the conditional, **je pourvoirais**, etc., and in the subjunctive imperfect, **que je pourvusse**, etc.

*VOULOIR, To Be Willing.—(Ninth Model.)

Vouloir   Voulant   Voulu

Avoir voulu   *to have been willing*

Present.	Je veux	tu veux	il veut
	Nous voulons	vous voulez	ils veulent
Imperf.	Je voulais	tu voulais	il voulait
	Nous voulions	vous vouliez	ils voulaient
Past Def.	Je voulus	tu voulus	il voulut
	Nous voulûmes	vous voulûtes	ils voulurent
Future.	Je voudrai	tu voudras	il voudra
	Nous voudrons	vous voudrez	ils voudront
Cond. Pr.	Je voudrais	tu voudrais	il voudrait
	Nous voudrions	vous voudriez	ils voudraient
Imper.		Veux	
	Voulons	voulez *or* veuillez	
Subj. Pr.	Que je veuille	que tu veuilles	qu'il veuille
	Que nous voulions	que vous vouliez	qu'ils veuillent
Imperf.	Que je voulusse	que tu voulusses	qu'il voulût
	Que nous voulussions	que vous voulussiez	qu'ils voulussent

Vocabulary 38.

*Savoir, to know; to know how; ne savoir que, not to know what.
*Valoir, to be worth; valoir mieux, to be better; il vaut mieux, it is better.
*Voir, to see.
*Revoir, to see again; au revoir, good-by.
*Vouloir, to be willing.
Je veux bien, I am willing.
*Vouloir *dire, to mean.

Le ciel, heaven; the sky.
La mer, the sea.
La terre, the land.
La montagne, the mountain.
Notre patrie, *f.*, our native land.
Le milieu, the middle; au milieu de, in the midst of.
Ces gens, those people.
Enfin, at last; finally.
A la fin, in the end.
Ne....que, only, but; nothing but.

Theme 38.

Model Savoir. 1. Vous savez ce que je veux dire. 2. Il n'a pas su me répondre. 3. Il ne savait que dire.

4. Nous ne savions que faire. 5. Je saurai demain, s'il viendra ou non. 6. Il faut que je le sache aujourd'hui. 7. Je voudrais que nous le sussions. 8. Sachez ce que vous avez à faire.

MODEL VALOIR. 9. Cela ne vaut rien, et n'a jamais rien valu. 10. Il vaudra mieux rester ici que de sortir. 11. Ces gens-là ne valent pas mieux que nous.

MODEL VOIR. 12. Vous voyez enfin ce que c'est. 13. Il voyait à la fin qu'on l'avait trompé. 14. Nous verrons ce que nous pourrons faire. 15. Quand vous reverrai-je ? 16. Hier je vis votre oncle ; il vint nous voir.

MODEL VOULOIR. 17. Nous voulons partir. 18. Que veulent ces hommes ? 19. Il n'a pas voulu me recevoir. 20. Henri ne voulait pas venir. 21. Il viendra quand il voudra. 22. Je voudrais bien le voir. 23. Je ne pense pas qu'il veuille partir. 24. Si je pensais qu'il voulût partir, j'irais le trouver.

Theme 38.

MODEL SAVOIR. 1. He does not know what I mean. 2. We do not know what to say. 3. I have not known that. 4. They knew (*imperf.*) that we were here. 5. Everybody will know it to-morrow. 6. I am willing that people should know it (*subj. pres.*). 7. I wish that they knew it (*subj. imperf.*).

MODEL VALOIR. 8. Those pictures are each worth one hundred dollars. 9. He gave them a house which was worth ten thousand dollars. 10. It is better not to say anything about it. 11. That would be better.

MODEL VOIR. 12. We see, at last, what it is. 13. You will see in the end that they will deceive you. 14. We were in the midst of the sea, we saw (*imperf.*) nothing but the sky and the water. 15. I thought that I never should see land again. 16. We saw (*past def.*), at last, the mountains of our native country.

MODEL VOULOIR. 17. What does he want? 18. What do you mean? 19. He was not willing (*past indef.*) to wait. 20. He wanted (*imperf.*) to start the next day. 21. He may start (*fut.*) when he wishes (*fut.*). 22. You would not wish to see him leave.

THIRTY-NINTH LESSON.

IRREGULAR VERBS (CONTINUED). — FOURTH CONJUGATION.

The Fourth Conjugation has twenty-three irregular forms or models.

*BATTRE, TO BEAT. — (FIRST MODEL.)

	Battre	Battant	Battu
	Avoir battu	*to have beaten*	
PRESENT.	Je bats	tu bats	il bat
	Nous battons	vous battez	ils battent
IMPERF.	Je battais	tu battais	il battait
	Nous battions	vous battiez	ils battaient
PAST DEF.	Je battis	tu battis	il battit
	Nous battîmes	vous battîtes	ils battirent
FUTURE.	Je battrai	tu battras	il battra
	Nous battrons	vous battrez	ils battront
COND. PR.	Je battrais	tu battrais	il battrait
	Nous battrions	vous battriez	ils battraient
IMPER.		Bats	
	Battons	battez	
SUBJ. PR.	Que je batte	que tu battes	qu'il batte
	Que nous battions	que vous battiez	qu'ils battent
IMPERF.	Que je battisse	que tu battisses	qu'il battît
	Que nous battissions	que vous battissiez	qu'ils battissent

Conjugate in the same manner as *__battre__, the derivatives of __battre__:

*__Abattre__, to beat down, etc.   *__Combattre__, to fight, etc.

*BOIRE, To Drink.—(Second Model.)

	Boire	Buvant	Bu
	Avoir bu	*to have drunk*	
Present.	Je bois	tu bois	il boit
	Nous buvons	vous buvez	ils boivent
Imperf.	Je buvais	tu buvais	il buvait
	Nous buvions	vous buviez	ils buvaient
Past Def.	Je bus	tu bus	il but
	Nous bûmes	vous bûtes	ils burent
Future.	Je boirai	tu boiras	il boira
	Nous boirons	vous boirez	ils boiront
Cond. Pr.	Je boirais	tu boirais	il boirait
	Nous boirions	vous boiriez	ils boiraient
Imper.		Bois	
	Buvons	buvez	
Subj. Pr.	Que je boive	que tu boives	qu'il boive
	Que nous buvions	que vous buviez	qu'ils boivent
Imperf.	Que je busse	que tu busses	qu'il bût
	Que nous bussions	que vous bussiez	qu'ils bussent

*CONCLURE, To Conclude.—(Third Model.)

	Conclure	Concluant	Conclu
	Avoir conclu	*to have concluded*	
Present.	Je conclus	tu conclus	il conclut
	Nous concluons	vous concluez	ils concluent
Imperf.	Je concluais	tu concluais	il concluait
	Nous concluions	vous concluiez	ils concluaient
Past Def.	Je conclus	tu conclus	il conclut
	Nous conclûmes	vous conclûtes	ils conclurent
Future.	Je conclurai	tu concluras	il conclura
	Nous conclurons	vous conclurez	ils concluront
Cond. Pr.	Je conclurais	tu conclurais	il conclurait
	Nous conclurions	vous concluriez	ils concluraient

176 ELEMENTARY FRENCH GRAMMAR.

IMPER.		Conclus	
	Concluons	concluez	
SUBJ. PR.	Que je conclue	que tu conclues	qu'il conclue
	Que nous concluions	que vous concluiez	qu'ils concluent
IMPERF.	Que je conclusse	que tu conclusses	qu'il conclût
	Que nous conclussions	que vous conclussiez	qu'ils conclussent

CONDUIRE, To Conduct.—(Fourth Model.)

Conduire   Conduisant   Conduit

Avoir conduit   *to have conducted*

PRESENT.	Je conduis	tu conduis	il conduit
	Nous conduisons	vous conduisez	ils conduisent
IMPERF.	Je conduisais	tu conduisais	il conduisait
	Nous conduisions	vous conduisiez	ils conduisaient
PAST DEF.	Je conduisis	tu conduisis	il conduisit
	Nous conduisîmes	vous conduisîtes	ils conduisirent
FUTURE.	Je conduirai	tu conduiras	il conduira
	Nous conduirons	vous conduirez	ils conduiront
COND. PR.	Je conduirais	tu conduirais	il conduirait
	Nous conduirions	vous conduiriez	ils conduiraient
IMPER.		Conduis	
	Conduisons	conduisez	
SUBJ. PR.	Que je conduise	que tu conduises	qu'il conduise
	Que nous conduisions	que vous conduisiez	qu'il conduisent
IMPERF.	Que je conduisisse	que tu conduisisses	qu'il conduisît
	Que nous conduisissions	que vous conduisissiez	qu'ils conduisissent

Conjugate in the same manner as *__conduire__:

*Instruire, to instruct.   *Traduire, to translate.

And all the verbs that end in **uire**.

REM. *__Nuire__, *to injure;* *__luire__, *to shine,* and *__reluire__, *to shine,* deviate from the model verb **conduire** in the past participle, which ends in **i**, as: nui, lui, relui.

IRREGULAR VERBS.

*CONNAITRE, To Be Acquainted With, To Know.—
(Fifth Model.)

	Connaître	Connaissant	Connu
	Avoir connu	*to have been acquainted with*	
Present.	Je connais	tu connais	il connait
	Nous connaissons	vous connaissez	ils connaissent
Imperf.	Je connaissais	tu connaissais	il connaissait
	Nous connaissions	vous connaissiez	ils connaissaient
Past Def.	Je connus	tu connus	il connut
	Nous connûmes	vous connûtes	ils connurent
Future.	Je connaîtrai	tu connaîtras	il connaîtra
	Nous connaîtrons	vous connaîtrez	ils connaîtront
Cond. Pr.	Je connaîtrais	tu connaîtrais	il connaîtrait
	Nous connaîtrions	vous connaîtriez	ils connaîtraient
Imper.		Connais	
	Connaissons	connaissez	
Subj. Pr.	Que je connaisse	que tu connaisses	qu'il connaisse
	Que nous connaissions	que vous connaissiez	qu'ils connaissent
Imperf.	Que je connusse	que tu connusses	qu'il connût
	Que nous connussions	que vous connussiez	qu'ils connussent

Conjugate in the same manner as ***connaître** :

*Paraître, to appear.   ***Croître**, to grow.

And all the verbs that end in **aître** and **oître**, except ***naître**, *to be born*, and ***renaître**, *to be born again*.

Rem. 1. The i of the verbs in **aître** and **oître**, when it is immediately followed by t, has the circumflex accent.

Rem. 2. Croître and its derivatives have the circumflex accent over the u of the past participle and in all the persons of the past definite tense.

Vocabulary 39.

*Battre, to beat.
*Se battre, to fight.
*Boire, to drink.
*Conclure, to conclude.
*Conduire, to conduct.
*Se conduire, to conduct one's self.

*Traduire, to translate.
*Connaitre, to be acquainted with.
*Reconnaître, to recognize.
*Paraître, to appear; to seem.
Bien des fois, many times.
La soif, thirst; avoir soif,† to be thirsty.
Le vin, the wine.
Le marché, the bargain.
Une phrase, a sentence.

Depuis, since.
L'anglais, English.
De l'anglais en français, from English into French.
Un inconnu, an unknown; a stranger.
Un étranger, a stranger; a foreigner.
Étrange, strange.
Seulement, only.

Exercise 39.

MODEL BATTRE. 1. Si tu bats les autres, on te battra aussi. 2. On se battait dans les rues de Paris. 3. On s'y est battu bien des fois, et l'on s'y battra encore. 4. Je ne veux me battre avec personne. 5. Je fuis ceux qui se battent.

MODEL BOIRE. 6. Je bois seulement quand j'ai soif. 7. Ils boivent de l'eau. 8. Nous ne buvons jamais de vin. 9. Si vous buviez du vin, vous seriez malade. 10. Si j'avais du lait, j'en boirais un verre.

MODEL CONCLURE. 11. Nous concluons le marché maintenant. 12. Nous avons conclu cette affaire. 13. Enfin, c'est une affaire conclue.

MODEL CONDUIRE. 14. Nous vous conduisons chez vous. 15. Il m'a conduit jusqu'au dépôt du chemin de fer. 16. Ils se conduisaient bien. 17. Ils se sont toujours bien conduits. 18. Nous traduirons cette histoire en anglais. 19. Traduisez cette phrase en français pour moi.

---

† *Avoir soif*, literally *to have thirst*; in English, *to be thirsty*. See Lesson Forty-seventh.

Model Connaître. 20. C'est un étranger que nous ne connaissons pas. 21. Je ne vous ai pas reconnu. 22. Cela paraît étrange. 23. Cet inconnu paraissait nous regarder, comme s'il nous connaissait. 24. Il vous reconnaîtrait, si vous parliez.

Theme 39.

Model Battre. 1. I beat nobody. 2. I have never beaten anybody; and I will not beat anybody. 3. I do not like those who fight. 4. I would not fight for any one. 5. I do not like to fight.

Model Boire. 6. I do not drink any wine. 7. I do not wish to drink, for I am not thirsty. 8. I will drink a glass of water. 9. I have not drunk anything since this morning. 10. Do not drink if you are not thirsty.

Model Conclure. 11. Let us conclude that affair. 12. We cannot conclude it. 13. The bargain is concluded.

Model Conduire. 14. He conducts himself well. 15. I will conduct you to the dépôt. 16. If you conduct yourself well, you will succeed. 17. We have translated this history from French into English. 18. They were translating from English into French. 19. How will you translate this sentence?

Model Connaître. 20. I do not know that gentleman; he is a stranger to me.† 21. That stranger seems to know us. 22. Do you not recognize him? 23. He did not recognize me. 24. It would appear strange, if he did not recognize us.

---

† He is a stranger to me, *il m'est inconnu.*

FORTIETH LESSON.

IRREGULAR VERBS (CONTINUED).— FOURTH CONJUGATION

*COUDRE, To Sew.—(Sixth Model.)

	Coudre	Cousant	Cousu
	Avoir cousu	*to have sewed*	
PRESENT.	Je couds	tu couds	il cond
	Nous cousons	vous cousez	ils cousent
IMPERF.	Je cousais	tu cousais	il cousait
	Nous cousions	vous cousiez	ils cousaient
PAST DEF.	Je cousis	tu cousis	il cousit
	Nous cousîmes	vous cousîtes	ils cousirent
FUTURE.	Je coudrai	tu coudras	il coudra
	Nous coudrons	vous coudrez	ils coudront
COND. PR.	Je coudrais	tu coudrais	il coudrait
	Nous coudrions	vous coudriez	ils coudraient
IMPER.		Couds	
	Cousons	cousez	
SUBJ. PR.	Que je couse	que tu couses	qu'il couse
	Que nous cousions	que vous cousiez	qu'ils cousent
IMPERF.	Que je cousisse	que tu cousisses	qu'il cousît
	Que nous cousissions	que vous cousissiez	qu'ils cousissent

Conjugate in the same manner as *coudre :

*Découdre, to unsew.   *Recoudre, to sew again.

*CRAINDRE, To Fear.—(Seventh Model.)

	Craindre	Craignant	Craint
	Avoir craint	*to have feared*	
PRESENT.	Je crains	tu crains	il craint
	Nous craignons	vous craignez	ils craignent
IMPERF.	Je craignais	tu craignais	il craignait
	Nous craignions	vous craigniez	ils craignaient
PAST DEF.	Je craignis	tu craignis	il craignit
	Nous craignîmes	vous craignîtes	ils craignirent

IRREGULAR VERBS.

Future.	Je craindrai	tu craindras	il craindra
	Nous craindrons	vous craindrez	ils craindront
Cond. Pr.	Je craindrais	tu craindrais	il craindrait
	Nous craindrions	vous craindriez	ils craindraient
Imper.		Crains	
	Craignons	craignez	
Subj. Pr.	Que je craigne	que tu craignes	qu'il craigne
	Que nous craignions	que vous craigniez	qu'ils craignent
Imperf.	Que je craignisse	que tu craignisses	qu'il craignît
	Que nous craignissions	que vous craignissiez	qu'ils craignissent

Conjugate in the same manner as *craindre, all the verbs that end in indre:

*Plaindre, to pity. *Teindre, to dye.
*Peindre, to paint. *Joindre, to join.

And many others.

*CROIRE, To Believe.—(Eighth Model.)

	Croire	Croyant	Cru
	Avoir cru	*to have believed*	
Present.	Je crois	tu crois	il croit
	Nous croyons	vous croyez	ils croient
Imperf.	Je croyais	tu croyais	il croyait
	Nous croyions	vous croyiez	ils croyaient
Past Def.	Je crus	tu crus	il crut
	Nous crûmes	vous crûtes	ils crurent
Future.	Je croirai	tu croiras	il croira
	Nous croirons	vous croirez	ils croiront
Cond. Pr.	Je croirais	tu croirais	il croirait
	Nous croirions	vous croiriez	ils croiraient
Imper.		Crois	
	Croyons	croyez	
Subj. Pr.	Que je croie	que tu croies	qu'il croie
	Que nous croyions	que vous croyiez	qu'ils croient
Imperf.	Que je crusse	que tu crusses	qu'il crût
	Que nous crussions	que vous crussiez	qu'ils crussent

*DIRE, To Say, To Tell.—(Ninth Model.)

Dire　　　　Disant　　　　Dit

Avoir dit　　*to have said*

Present.	Je dis	tu dis	il dit
	Nous disons	vous dites	ils disent
Imperf.	Je disais	tu disais	il disait
	Nous disions	vous disiez	ils disaient
Past Def.	Je dis	tu dis	il dit
	Nous dîmes	vous dîtes	ils dirent
Future.	Je dirai	tu diras	il dira
	Nous dirons	vous direz	ils diront
Cond. Pr.	Je dirais	tu dirais	il dirait
	Nous dirions	vous diriez	ils diraient
Imper.		Dis	
	Disons	dites	
Subj. Pr.	Que je dise	que tu dises	qu'il dise
	Que nous disions	que vous disiez	qu'ils disent
Imperf.	Que je disse	que tu disses	qu'il dît
	Que nous dissions	que vous dissiez	qu'ils dissent

Conjugate in the same manner as **dire**:

*Redire, to say again.

The other derivatives of **dire**: *dédire, *to unsay;* *interdire, *to forbid;* *médire, *to slander;* *prédire, *to foretell;* have, in the second person plural of the present tense of the indicative, and in the second person plural of the imperative, **dédisez, interdisez,** etc., instead of **dédites, interdites,** etc. *Maudire, *to curse,* has, in the present participle, **maudissant,** doubling the **s**. The double **s** is retained in all the parts derived from the present participle.

Vocabulary 40.

*Coudre, to sew.　　　*Plaindre, to pity.
*Craindre, to fear.　　*Se plaindre, to complain.

*Croire, to believe.
*Dire, to say; to tell; dire la vérité, to speak the truth.
Avoir raison,† to be right.
Avoir tort,† to be wrong.

La conduite, the conduct.
La loi, the law.
Mal, badly.
Nécessaire, necessary.
Fou, fol, *f.* folle, mad.

Exercise 40.

MODEL COUDRE. 1. Cousez ceci pour moi, s'il vous plaît. 2. Je le coudrai tantôt. 3. Qui a cousu cela? 4. Si vous cousiez tous les jours, vous coudriez mieux. 5. Il n'est pas nécessaire que je couse tous les jours.

MODEL CRAINDRE. 6. Je crains les méchants, et je les plains. 7. Nous ne plaignons pas ceux que nous craignons. 8. Elle s'est plainte de votre conduite. 9. On le craignait, mais on ne l'aimait pas. 10. Je me plaindrai de vous, si vous vous comportez mal. 11. On ne se plaindrait pas de vous, si vous vous comportiez bien.

MODEL CROIRE. 12. Je crois que vous avez raison. 13. Personne n'a cru cette nouvelle. 14. Vous ici! Je vous croyais à Boston depuis hier. 15. On ne croira pas cela. 16. Vous le croiriez, si vous le voyiez. 17. Nous ne croyons pas pouvoir faire cela.

MODEL DIRE. 18. Je crois ce que vous dites. 19. Nous disons que vous avez raison. 20. Ils disent que nous avons tort. 21. Qu'en dit-on? 22. On en dira ce que l'on voudra. 23. Je dirai la vérité. 24. Si nous disions cela, on dirait que nous sommes fous.

Theme 40.

MODEL COUDRE. 1. I sew and Mary sews. 2. We sew together. 3. I was sewing when you came in. 4. I have

---

† *Avoir raison; avoir tort,* literally, *to have right; to have wrong;* in English, *to be right; to be wrong.* See Lesson Forty-seventh.

sewn this. 5. I will sew that by and by. 6. I wish you would sew (*subj. imperf.*) it now.

MODEL CRAINDRE. 7. I fear him and I pity him. 8. The wicked fear the law, which protects the good. 9. He feared everybody, and pitied nobody. 10. You are always complaining. 11. They have complained of your conduct. 12. If you behave badly, people will complain of you.

MODEL CROIRE. 13. You believe what I say; do you not? 14. We believe that you are right. 15. They believe that we are wrong. 16. They did not believe what we said (*past indef.*). 17. I would believe it, if I saw it.

MODEL DIRE. 18. What you say is true. 19. We say the same thing, and they say so too. 20. Do you know what he has told me? 21. What will people say of it? 22. We will speak the truth. 23. You would not say that, if you knew what I know.

FORTY-FIRST LESSON.

IRREGULAR VERBS (CONTINUED).—FOURTH CONJUGATION.

*ÉCRIRE, TO WRITE.—(TENTH MODEL.)

	Écrire	Écrivant	Écrit
	Avoir écrit	*to have written*	
PRESENT.	J'écris	tu écris	il écrit
	Nous écrivons	vous écrivez	ils écrivent
IMPERF.	J'écrivais	tu écrivais	il écrivait
	Nous écrivions	vous écriviez	ils écrivaient
PAST DEF.	J'écrivis	tu écrivis	il écrivit
	Nous écrivîmes	vous écrivîtes	ils écrivirent
FUTURE.	J'écrirai	tu écriras	il écrira
	Nous écrirons	vous écrirez	ils écriront
COND PR.	J'écrirais	tu écrirais	il écrirait
	Nous écririons	vous écririez	ils écriraient

		Écris	
IMPER.	Écrivons	écrivez	
SUBJ. PR.	Que j'écrive	que tu écrives	qu'il écrive
	Que nous écrivions	que vous écriviez	qu'ils écrivent
IMPERF.	Que j'écrivisse	que tu écrivisses	qu'il écrivît
	Que nous écrivissions	que vous écrivissiez	qu'ils écrivissent

Conjugate in the same manner as *écrire:

*Décrire, to describe.   *Prescrire, to prescribe.
*Inscrire, to inscribe.   *Transcrire, to transcribe.

And other derivatives of *écrire.

*FAIRE, To Do, To Make.—(Eleventh Model.)

	Faire	Faisant	Fait

		Avoir fait	*to have made*	
PRESENT.	Je fais	tu fais	il fait	
	Nous faisons	vous faites	ils font	
IMPERF.	Je faisais	tu faisais	il faisait	
	Nous faisions	vous faisiez	ils faisaient	
PAST DEF.	Je fis	tu fis	il fit	
	Nous fîmes	vous fîtes	ils firent	
FUTURE.	Je ferai	tu feras	il fera	
	Nous ferons	vous ferez	ils feront	
COND. PR.	Je ferais	tu ferais	il ferait	
	Nous ferions	vous feriez	ils feraient	
IMPER.		Fais		
	Faisons	faites		
SUBJ. PR.	Que je fasse	que tu fasses	qu'il fasse	
	Que nous fassions	que vous fassiez	qu'ils fassent	
IMPERF.	Que je fisse	que tu fisses	qu'il fît	
	Que nous fissions	que vous fissiez	qu'ils fissent	

Conjugate in the same manner as *faire:

*Contrefaire, to counterfeit.   *Surfaire, to overcharge.
*Défaire, to undo.   *Satisfaire, to satisfy.
   *Refaire, to do again.

*LIRE, To Read.—(Twelfth Model.)

	Lire	Lisant	Lu
		Avoir lu	*to have read*
Present.	Je lis	tu lis	il lit
	Nous lisons	vous lisez	ils lisent
Imperf.	Je lisais	tu lisais	il lisait
	Nous lisions	vous lisiez	ils lisaient
Past Def.	Je lus	tu lus	il lut
	Nous lûmes	vous lûtes	ils lurent
Future.	Je lirai	tu liras	il lira
	Nous lirons	vous lirez	ils liront
Cond. Pr.	Je lirais	tu lirais	il lirait
	Nous lirions	vous liriez	ils liraient
Imper.		Lis	
	Lisons	lisez	
Subj. Pr.	Que je lise	que tu lises	qu'il lise
	Que nous lisions	que vous lisiez	qu'ils lisent
Imperf.	Que je lusse	que tu lusses	qu'il lût
	Que nous lussions	que vous lussiez	qu'ils lussent

Conjugate in the same manner as *lire:

*Élire, to elect.   *Relire, to read again.
                *Réélire, to re-elect.

*METTRE, To Put, To Put On.—(Thirteenth Model.)

	Mettre	Mettant	Mis
		Avoir mis	*to have put*
Present.	Je mets	tu mets	il met
	Nous mettons	vous mettez	ils mettent
Imperf.	Je mettais	tu mettais	il mettait
	Nous mettions	vous mettiez	ils mettaient
Past Def.	Je mis	tu mis	il mit
	Nous mîmes	vous mîtes	ils mirent
Future.	Je mettrai	tu mettras	il mettra
	Nous mettrons	vous mettrez	ils mettront
Cond. Pr.	Je mettrais	tu mettrais	il mettrait
	Nous mettrions	vous mettriez	ils mettraient

IMPER.		Mets	
	Mettons	mettez	
SUBJ. PR.	Que je mette	que tu mettes	qu'il mette
	Que nous mettions	que vous mettiez	qu'ils mettent
IMPERF.	Que je misse	que tu misses	qu'il mît
	Que nous missions	que vous missiez	qu'ils missent

Conjugate in the same manner as *mettre:

*Admettre, to admit.
*Commettre, to commit.
*Permettre, to permit.
*Promettre, to promise.

And all the derivatives of *mettre.

Vocabulary 41.

*Écrire, to write.
*Faire, to make; to do; *faire attention, to pay attention; *faire une question, to ask a question; *faire un plaisir, to do a favor; *faire *faire,† to have or get made; *faire *venir, to send for.
*Lire, to read.
*Mettre, to put; to put on; mettre en ordre, to put in order.
*Se mettre, to sit down.
*Remettre, to put back; to deliver, to hand; to put off.
Raccommoder, to mend.
Remarquer, to observe, to remark.
Le pupitre, the desk.
Le banc, the bench.
La boîte, the box; la boîte aux lettres, the letter box.
Un cahier, a copy-book.
La musique, the music.
Un cahier de musique, a music-book.
Quinze jours, a fortnight.
Prochain, next.
Ancien, f. ancienne, ancient; former.
Au lieu de, instead of.

Exercise 41.

MODEL ÉCRIRE. 1. J'écris mon thème, et il écrit le sien. 2. Nous écrivons tous les jours. 3. Il écrivait à son père

---

† *Faire faire*, *to have* or *get made*. *Faire* is used before the infinitive of almost any verb, in the sense of *to have* or *to get*. *Faire* and the infinitive are equivalent to a transitive verb.

pendant que j'écrivais mon thème. 4. J'écrivis chez moi le lendemain de mon arrivée à Paris. 5. Je n'ai pas écrit chez moi depuis lundi. 6. Vous m'écrirez aussitôt que vous serez arrivé.

MODEL FAIRE. 7. Je fais ce que vous m'avez dit de faire. 8. Vous faites bien. 9. Nous faisons la même chose. 10. Ils font venir le médecin. 11. Il me faisait mille questions auxquelles je ne pouvais répondre. 12. Nous lui fîmes remarquer cela. 13. Faites raccommoder ce fauteuil. 14. Je ferai faire des pupitres comme ceux-là. 15. Il faut que je fasse nettoyer cet habit.

MODEL LIRE. 16. Lisez ceci. 17. Je l'ai lu. 18. Il lisait le journal au lieu d'étudier. 19. Je lus hier que notre ancien professeur est mort. 20. Je lirai ce livre quand vous l'aurez lu.

MODEL METTRE. 21. Je mets votre dictionnaire dans votre pupitre. 22. Mettez votre manteau, si vous allez sortir. 23. Nous avons mis votre lettre dans la boîte. 24. Elle se mettait toujours à côté de lui. 25. Remettons chaque chose à sa place. 26. Je remettrai votre lettre à mon père. 27. Nous remettrons la leçon à demain.

Theme 41.

MODEL ÉCRIRE. 1. Are you writing your exercise? 2. I have written it. 3. I was writing a letter to my father. 4. He wishes (desires) me to write to him every week (that I write) (*subj. pres.*). 5. He wrote to me (*past def.*) last week that he would be here in a fortnight. 6. I will write to you as soon as I reach (shall arrive) home.

MODEL FAIRE. 7. What are you doing? 8. I am not doing anything. 9. Will you do me a favor? 10. I will do it as soon as I can (shall be able). 11. He asked (*past indef.*) me a question (to) which I did not wish (*past indef.*) to answer. 12. You were not paying attention to what I was saying. 13. We shall have those old benches mended. 14. I must send for the notary, *he said* (dit-il). 15. I made (*past def.*) him observe that the notary was present.

Model Lire. 16. I am reading a very interesting book. 17. Have you read it? 18. I will read it when you have (shall have) read it. 19. They were reading instead of writing. 20. We read (*past def.*) that news when we were in the country.

Model Mettre. 21. I put everything in order before I go out. 22. Where did you put (*past indef.*) my music book? 23. I will put your letter in the box. 24. She was putting on her gloves to (in order to) go out. 25. I have handed your letter to my father. 26. We will put everything back in its place. 27. I will put off that journey till next week. 28. Let us sit down on this bench.

FORTY-SECOND LESSON.

Irregular Verbs (Continued). — Fourth Conjugation.

*MOUDRE, To Grind. — (Fourteenth Model.)

	Moudre	Moulant	Moulu
	Avoir moulu	*to have ground*	
Present.	Je mouds	tu mouds	il moud
	Nous moulons	vous moulez	ils moulent
Imperf.	Je moulais	tu moulais	il moulait
	Nous moulions	vous mouliez	ils moulaient
Past Def.	Je moulus	tu moulus	il moulut
	Nous moulûmes	vous moulûtes	ils moulurent

Future.	Je moudrai	tu moudras	il moudra
	Nous moudrons	vous moudrez	ils moudront
Cond. Pr.	Je moudrais	tu moudrais	il moudrait
	Nous moudrions	vous moudriez	ils moudraient
Imper.		Mouds	
	Moulons	moulez	
Subj. Pr.	Que je moule	que tu moules	qu'il moule
	Que nous moulions	que vous mouliez	qu'ils moulent
Imperf.	Que je moulusse	que tu moulusses	qu'il moulût
	Que nous moulussions	que vous moulussiez	qu'ils moulussent

Conjugate in the same manner as *moudre :

*Émoudre, to grind.   *Remoudre, to grind again.

*NAÎTRE, To Be Born.—(Fifteenth Model.)

Naître   Naissant   Né

Être né   *to have been born*

Present.	Je nais	tu nais	il naît
	Nous naissons	vous naissez	ils naissent
Imperf.	Je naissais	tu naissais	il naissait
	Nous naissions	vous naissiez	ils naissaient
Past Def.	Je naquis	tu naquis	il naquit
	Nous naquîmes	vous naquîtes	ils naquirent
Future.	Je naîtrai	tu naîtras	il naîtra
	Nous naîtrons	vous naîtrez	ils naîtront
Cond. Pr.	Je naîtrais	tu naîtrais	il naîtrait
	Nous naîtrions	vous naîtriez	ils naîtraient
Imper.		Nais	
	Naissons	naissez	
Subj. Pr.	Que je naisse	que tu naisses	qu'il naisse
	Que nous naissions	que vous naissiez	qu'ils naissent
Imperf.	Que je naquisse	que tu naquisses	qu'il naquît
	Que nous naquissions	que vous naquissiez	qu'ils naquissent

Conjugate in the same manner as *naître:

*Renaître, to be born again.

*PLAIRE, To Please.—(Sixteenth Model.)

Plaire	Plaisant	Plu
Avoir plu	*to have pleased*	

Present.	Je plais	tu plais	il plaît
	Nous plaisons	vous plaisez	ils plaisent
Imperf.	Je plaisais	tu plaisais	il plaisait
	Nous plaisions	vous plaisiez	ils plaisaient
Past Def.	Je plus	tu plus	il plut
	Nous plûmes	vous plûtes	ils plurent
Future.	Je plairai	tu plairas	il plaira
	Nous plairons	vous plairez	ils plairont
Cond. Pr.	Je plairais	tu plairais	il plairait
	Nous plairions	vous plairiez	ils plairaient
Imper.		Plais	
	Plaisons	plaisez	
Subj. Pr.	Que je plaise	que tu plaises	qu'il plaise
	Que nous plaisions	que vous plaisiez	qu'ils plaisent
Imperf.	Que je plusse	que tu plusses	qu'il plût
	Que nous plussions	que vous plussiez	qu'ils plussent.

Conjugate in the same manner as *plaire :

*Se plaire (être), to be pleased.
*Complaire, to humor.
*Taire, not to say.
*Se taire, to be silent.

*PRENDRE, To Take.—(Seventeenth Model.)

Prendre	Prenant	Pris
Avoir pris	*to have taken*	

Present.	Je prends	tu prends	il prend
	Nous prenons	vous prenez	ils prennent
Imperf.	Je prenais	tu prenais	il prenait
	Nous prenions	vous preniez	ils prenaient
Past Def.	Je pris	tu pris	il prit
	Nous prîmes	vous prîtes	ils prirent
Future.	Je prendrai	tu prendras	il prendra
	Nous prendrons	vous prendrez	ils prendront
Cond. Pr.	Je prendrais	tu prendrais	il prendrait
	Nous prendrions	vous prendriez	ils prendraient

IMPER.	Prends	
	Prenons	
	prenez	
SUBJ. PR.	Que je prenne	que tu prennes	qu'il prenne
	Que nous prenions	que vous preniez	qu'ils prennent
IMPERF.	Que je prisse	que tu prisses	qu'il prit
	Que nous prissions	que vous prissiez	qu'ils prissent

Conjugate in the same manner as ***prendre**:

*Apprendre, to learn ; to hear.   ***Reprendre**, to take back ; to resume.
*Comprendre, to comprehend.
*Entreprendre, to undertake.

And the other derivatives of ***prendre**.

***RÉSOUDRE, To Resolve.**—(Eighteenth Model.)

Résoudre   Résolvant   Résolu *or* Résous

Avoir résolu   *to have resolved*

PRESENT.	Je résous	tu résous	il résout
	Nous résolvons	vous résolvez	ils résolvent
IMPERF.	Je résolvais	tu résolvais	il résolvait
	Nous résolvions	vous résolviez	ils résolvaient
PAST DEF.	Je résolus	tu résolus	il résolut
	Nous résolûmes	vous résolûtes	ils résolurent
FUTURE.	Je résoudrai	tu résoudras	il résoudra
	Nous résoudrons	vous résoudrez	ils résoudront
COND. PR.	Je résoudrais	tu résoudrais	il résoudrait
	Nous résoudrions	vous résoudriez	ils résoudraient
IMPER.		Résous	
	Résolvons	résolvez	
SUBJ. PR.	Que je résolve	que tu résolves	qu'il résolve
	Que nous résolvions	que vous résolviez	qu'ils résolvent
IMPERF.	Que je résolusse	que tu résolusses	qu'il résolût
	Que nous résolussions	que vous résolussiez	qu'ils résolussent

Conjugate in the same manner as ***résoudre**:

*Absoudre, to absolve (*past part.*); absous, *f.* absoute.

Vocabulary 42.

*Moudre, to grind.
*Naître (être), to be born.
*Plaire,† to please; il plaît (de),† it pleases.
*Se plaire, to like to be.
*Se taire, to be silent.
*Prendre, to take; *prendre congé, to take leave.
*Apprendre, to learn; to hear (news).
*Comprendre, to comprehend; to understand.
*Entreprendre, to undertake.
*Reprendre, to take back; to resume.
Le meunier, the miller.
Le moulin, the mill.
Le grain, the grain.
Une partie, a part.
Le reste, the rest.
Le tout, the whole.
Un instant, an instant.
Un pas, a step.
La mort, death.
La peine, the trouble.
À la fois, at once.
Tant (de), so many.
Vers, towards.
Ne .... guère, but little; not much.
Donc, then.
S'il vous plaît, if you please.

Exercise 42.

MODEL MOUDRE. 1. Il faut moudre le grain avant de pouvoir faire le pain. 2. Le meunier le moud aujourd'hui. 3. On le moulait lorsque j'étais au moulin. 4. On en avait moulu une partie. 5. On moudra le reste demain.

MODEL NAÎTRE. 6. On naît et l'on meurt sans le savoir. 7. L'instant où nous naissons est un pas vers la mort. 8. Où êtes-vous né? 9. Ces enfants sont nés dans ce pays-ci. 10. Le Président Lincoln naquit à Springfield, Ill., et mourut à Washington.

MODEL PLAIRE. 11. Comment ce dessin plaît-il à votre sœur? 12. Il ne lui plaît guère. 13. Il ne plaira pas à

---

† *Plaire à quelqu'un* to please somebody. The impersonal verb *il plaît* requires *de* before the infinitive. *Il ne lui plaît pas d'attendre*, It does not please him to wait.

mon père de revenir ici demain. 14. Ces dames ne se plaisaient pas à la campagne. 15. Taisez-vous donc. 16. Il s'est tu quand je lui ai dit cela.

MODEL PRENDRE. 17. Je prends du café le matin et du thé le soir. 18. Nous prenons ces gants-ci, et nos sœurs prennent ceux-là. 19. Avez-vous pris la peine de lire cela ? 20. Je ne vous ai pas compris. 21. Il apprenait lentement. 22. N'entreprenez pas tant de choses à la fois. 23. Reprenez votre argent. 24. Nous reprendrons notre histoire. 25. Il prit congé de nous à Paris, et partit le même jour pour Berlin.

MODEL RÉSOUDRE. 26. La question a été enfin résolue. 27. Nous avons résolu de quitter la ville.

Theme 42.

MODEL MOUDRE. 1. They were not grinding at the mill; the miller was not there. 2. They will grind a part of our grain to-morrow, and the rest the day after to-morrow. 3. The whole will be ground *by Saturday* (samedi).

MODEL NAÎTRE. 4. We are born without knowing it. 5. I was born† in this country. 6. My grandfather, who died last spring, was born† in Paris.

MODEL PLAIRE. 7. This book pleases my mother. 8. What pleases the one, does not please the other. 9. Will it please you to wait until to-morrow? 10. That does not please me. 11. My sisters do not like to be in the country. 12. I did not like to be there, because my friends were not there. 13. When they began‡ to speak of that, she kept silent.‡

---

† *Was born* is rendered in French by the past indefinite tense of the verb if the person is still alive, and by the pluperfect, if the person is dead.

‡ Past definite tense.

Model Prendre. 14. I take coffee, my sisters take tea. 15. She was taking her music lesson when I was there. 16. Have you taken my fan ? 17. Will you take the trouble to read this. 18. I understand you. 19. I have heard (learned) all. 20. I shall not undertake that business. 21. I took leave of him yesterday. 22. Let us resume our story. 23. He wants me to take back my money.

Model Résoudre. 24. What have you resolved to do ? 25. We have resolved to start.

FORTY-THIRD LESSON.

Irregular Verbs (Continued).—Fourth Conjugation.

*RIRE, To Laugh.—(Nineteenth Model.)

	Rire	Riant	Ri
	Avoir ri	to have laughed	
Present.	Je ris	tu ris	il rit
	Nous rions	vous riez	ils rient
Imperf.	Je riais	tu riais	il riait
	Nous riions	vous riiez	ils riaient
Past Def.	Je ris	tu ris	il rit
	Nous rîmes	vous rîtes	ils rirent
Future.	Je rirai	tu riras	il rira
	Nous rirons	vous rirez	ils riront
Cond. Pr.	Je rirais	tu rirais	il rirait
	Nous ririons	vous ririez	ils riraient
Imper.		Ris	
	Rions	riez	
Subj. Pr.	Que je rie	que tu ries	qu'il rie
	Que nous riions	que vous riiez	qu'ils rient
Imperf	Que je risse	que tu risses	qu'il rît
	Que nous rissions	que vous rissiez	qu'ils rissent

Conjugate in the same manner as *rire :

*Sourire, to smile.

*SUIVRE, To Follow.—(Twentieth Model.)

	Suivre	Suivant	Suivi
	Avoir suivi	to have followed	

Present.	Je suis	tu suis	il suit
	Nous suivons	vous suivez	ils suivent
Imperf.	Je suivais	tu suivais	il suivait
	Nous suivions	vous suiviez	ils suivaient
Past Def.	Je suivis	tu suivis	il suivit
	Nous suivîmes	vous suivîtes	ils suivirent
Future.	Je suivrai	tu suivras	il suivra
	Nous suivrons	vous suivrez	ils suivront
Cond. Pr.	Je suivrais	tu suivrais	il suivrait
	Nous suivrions	vous suivriez	ils suivraient
Imper.		Suis	
	Suivons	suivez	
Subj. Pr.	Que je suive	que tu suives	qu'il suive
	Que nous suivions	que vous suiviez	qu'ils suivent
Imperf.	Que je suivisse	que tu suivisses	qu'il suivît
	Que nous suivissions	que vous suivissiez	qu'ils suivissent

Conjugate in the same manner as *suivre :

*Poursuivre, to pursue. *S'ensuivre, to follow from.

*TRAIRE, To Milk.—(Twenty-first Model.)

	Traire	Trayant	Trait
	Avoir trait	to have milked	

Present.	Je trais	tu trais	il trait
	Nous trayons	vous trayez	ils traient
Imperf.	Je trayais	tu trayais	il trayait
	Nous trayions	vous trayiez	ils trayaient
		(No Past Def.)	
Future.	Je trairai	tu trairas	il traira
	Nous trairons	vous trairez	ils trairont
Cond. Pr.	Je trairais	tu trairais	il trairait
	Nous trairions	vous trairiez	ils trairaient

IMPER.		Trais	
	Trayons	trayez	
SUBJ. PR.	Que je traie	que tu traies	qu'il traie
	Que nous trayions	que vous trayiez	qu'ils traient
		(*No Imperf. Subj.*)	

Conjugate in the same manner as *traire :

*Extraire, to extract.   *Soustraire, to take away.

*VAINCRE, To Vanquish.—(Twenty-second Model.)

Vaincre   Vainquant   Vaincu

Avoir vaincu   *to have vanquished*

PRESENT.	Je vaincs	tu vaincs	il vainc
	Nous vainquons	vous vainquez	ils vainquent
IMPERF.	Je vainquais	tu vainquais	il vainquait
	Nous vainquions	vous vainquiez	ils vainquaient
PAST DEF.	Je vainquis	tu vainquis	il vainquit
	Nous vainquîmes	vous vainquîtes	ils vainquirent
FUTURE.	Je vaincrai	tu vaincras	il vaincra
	Nous vaincrons	vous vaincrez	ils vaincront
COND. PR.	Je vaincrais	tu vaincrais	il vaincrait
	Nous vaincrions	vous vaincriez	ils vaincraient
IMPER.		Vaincs	
	Vainquons	vainquez	
SUBJ. PR.	Que je vainque	que tu vainques	qu'il vainque
	Que nous vainquions	que vous vainquiez	qu'ils vainquent
IMPERF.	Que je vainquisse	que tu vainquisses	qu'il vainquît
	Que nous vainquissions	que vous vainquissiez	qu'ils vainquissent

Conjugate in the same manner as *vaincre :

*Convaincre, to convince.

*VIVRE, To Live.—(Twenty-third Model.)

Vivre   Vivant   Vécu

Avoir vécu   *to have lived*

PRESENT.	Je vis	tu vis	il vit
	Nous vivons	vous vivez	ils vivent

IMPERF.	Je vivais	tu vivais	il vivait
	Nous vivions	vous viviez	ils vivaient
PAST DEF.	Je vécus	tu vécus	il vécut
	Nous vécûmes	vous vécûtes	ils vécurent
FUTURE.	Je vivrai	tu vivras	il vivra
	Nous vivrons	vous vivrez	ils vivront
COND. PR.	Je vivrais	tu vivrais	il vivrait
	Nous vivrions	vous vivriez	ils vivraient
IMPER.		Vis	
	Vivons	vivez	
SUBJ. PR.	Que je vive	que tu vives	qu'il vive
	Que nous vivions	que vous viviez	qu'ils vivent
IMPERF.	Que je vécusse	que tu vécusses	qu'il vécût
	Que nous vécussions	que vous vécussiez	qu'ils vécussent.

Conjugate in the same manner as *vivre:

*Survivre, to survive.

Vocabulary 43.

*Rire (de), to laugh (at).
*Suivre, to follow.
*Poursuivre, to pursue.
*Traire, to milk.
*Extraire, to extract; to take out.
*Vaincre, to vanquish.
*Convaincre, to convince.
*Vivre, to live.
*Survivre, to survive; to outlive.
Un Romain, a Roman.
L'Asie, f., Asia.
Un pays, a country.
Un roi, a king.
La nation, the nation.
À l'étranger, abroad.
En ma présence, in my presence.

L'intempérance, f., intemperance.
Une passion, a passion.
Un ennemi, an enemy.
La guerre, the war.
L'embarras, m., the embarrassment.
Le conseil, the advice; the counsel.
Un exemple, an example.
Le marbre, the marble.
La carrière, the quarry.
Une vache, a cow.
Le sort, the lot.
Loin, far.
Partout où, wherever.
Éternellement, eternally.
Tant que, as long as.
Tel, many a one.

Exercise 43.

MODEL RIRE. 1. Tel rit aujourd'hui qui pleurera demain. 2. Je ne ris pas. 3. Vous avez ri de mon embarras. 4. Vous riiez et elle riait aussi. 5. Ne riez pas des défauts d'autrui.

MODEL SUIVRE. 6. Je suis mon chemin, et vous suivez le vôtre. 7. Je vous suivrai partout où vous irez. 8. Vous avez suivi l'exemple d'un autre, au lieu de suivre mes conseils. 9. Il serait bien qu'il suivît les conseils de ses parents. 10. Si vous poursuiviez vos études, elles vous conduiraient loin. 11. Je ne savais pas, si vous poursuivriez cette affaire ou non.

MODEL TRAIRE. 12. On a trait les vaches en ma présence. 13. Le marbre qu'on extrait de cette carrière, est d'une belle qualité.

MODEL VAINCRE. 14. Alexandre vainquit les rois de l'Asie, mais il ne sut vaincre ses passions. 15. Après avoir vaincu ses ennemis à la guerre, il fut vaincu lui-même par l'intempérance. 16. Je vous convaincrai de la vérité de ce que je dis.

MODEL VIVRE. 17. Je vis comme je puis, sans me plaindre de mon sort. 18. Vous vivez comme si vous deviez toujours vivre. 19. Mon grand-père vivait du temps de Washington ; ils étaient amis. 20. Il vivra éternellement dans l'histoire. 21. Après avoir vécu longtemps dans l'abondance, il mourut pauvre. 22. Caton† ne survécut pas longtemps à la liberté de son pays.

Theme 43.

MODEL RIRE. 1. Do you laugh at me ? 2. I do not laugh at you. 3. I was laughing at that boy. 4. They

---

† Cato.

laughed (*past indef.*) at our embarrassment. 5. We shall laugh too when they (will) cry.

MODEL SUIVRE. 6. I follow your advice. 7. We do not follow that example. 8. Why did you not follow us? 9. My friends will follow me wherever I (will) go. 10. I wish that you would pursue (*subj. imp.*) your studies without paying attention to what they say.

MODEL TRAIRE. 11. *They* (On) milk the cows twice a day, in the morning and in the evening. 12. This is an example, taken out of an old history.

MODEL VAINCRE. 13. I will vanquish my passions; they are my greatest enemies. 14. I am convinced of the truth of what you say. 15. The Romans vanquished (*past def.*) all the nations of the earth.

MODEL VIVRE. 16. I will convince you of that, if I live long enough. 17. He lived (*past indef.*) a long time abroad, where he learned to speak French. 18. Henry Clay was living when I came (*past indef.*) to this country. 19. I saw him; I shall remember it (of it), as long as I (shall) live.

FORTY-FOURTH LESSON.

THE ADVERB.†

1. Adverbs may express time, place, manner, order, quantity, comparison, affirmation, negation, doubt, etc.

Many adverbs, which are of frequent use, have been introduced in the preceding lessons: **Aujourd'hui,** *to-day;* **aussi,** *also, too;* **autrefois,** *formerly;* **bien,** *well;* **bientôt,** *soon;* **comme,** *like, as;* **comment,** *how;* **déjà,** *already;* **demain,** *to-morrow;* **encore,** *still, yet;* **ensemble,** *together;*

---

† Introduction, pp. 17, 7 and 20, 30.

THE ADVERB.   201

ensuite, *afterwards;* hier, *yesterday;* loin, *far;* longtemps, *a long time;* maintenant, *now;* mal, *badly;* où, *where;* partout, *everywhere;* quand, *when;* quelque part, *somewhere;* quelquefois, *sometimes;* si, *so;* souvent, *often;* tantôt, *by and by; a little while ago;* tard, *late;* toujours, *always;* tout à l'heure, *presently, just now;* tout de suite, *immediately,* etc.

The following adverbs are also frequently used:

Ailleurs, elsewhere.
Ainsi, thus; so.
À la fois, at a time; at once.
Alors, then; at that time.
Auparavant, before; first.
Autrement, otherwise.
D'abord, at first; first.
Dedans, within; in it.
Dehors, outside; out of doors.
Dessous, below; under it.
Dessus, above; upon it.

Dorénavant, henceforth.
Exprès, purposely, on purpose.
Même, even; also.
Peut-être, perhaps.
Plutôt, rather.
Presque, almost.
Sans doute, undoubtedly.
Surtout, especially.
Tôt, soon.
Tôt ou tard, sooner or later.
Volontiers, willingly.

2.   ADVERBS OF QUANTITY.

Adverbs of quantity are used with verbs and with nouns. When they are used with nouns, they require the preposition **de** before the noun, and when the noun is not expressed, it is represented in the sentence by the pronoun **en**.

The adverbs of quantity are:

Assez, enough.
Autant, as much; as many.
Beaucoup, much; many.
Bien (Rem. 1), much; many.
Combien, how much; how many.
Davantage, (Rem. 2), more.

Guère (ne), but little; but few.
Moins, less.
Peu, little; few.
Plus, more.
Tant, so much; so many.
Trop, too much; too many.

REM. 1. **Bien** requires **de** and the article before the noun; that is: **du, de la, de l', or des.**

REM. 2. **Davantage** is never followed by **de** and a noun; it is used preferably to **plus** at the end of a sentence.

Il travaille autant que vous. — He works as much as you do.
J'ai autant de livres que vous. — I have as many books as you.
Vous en avez plus que moi. — You have more than I.
Il y a beaucoup de fautes (*or* bien des fautes) dans ce thème. — There are many mistakes in this exercise.

When two nouns are compared in regard to quantity, the preposition **de** is repeated before the second noun.

Vous avez plus de courage que de patience. — You have more courage than patience.

3. Formation of Adverbs in ment.

Many adverbs are formed from adjectives by the addition of the syllable **ment**. When the adjective ends with a vowel, **ment** is added to the masculine form; when it ends with a consonant, to the feminine form, as:

Poli, polite, — *adv.* poliment, politely.
Ordinaire, usual, — *adv.* ordinairement, usually.
Seul, *f.* seule, alone, — *adv.* seulement, only.
Heureux, *f.* heureuse, happy, — *adv.* heureusement, happily; luckily.
Doux, *f.* douce, soft, — *adv.* doucement, softly; gently.

Rem. Beau, *beautiful;* nouveau, *new;* fou, *foolish;* mou, *soft;* though ending in a vowel, add **ment**, to the feminine forms; bellement, *finely;* nouvellement, *newly;* follement, *foolishly;* mollement, *softly*.

Adjectives ending in **nt**, change **nt** into **mment**, as:

Prudent, prudent, — *adv.* prudemment, prudently.

Except:

Lent, slow, — *adv.* lentement, slowly.
Présent, present, — *adv.* présentement, presently.

4. ADJECTIVES USED AS ADVERBS.

A few adjectives are also used as adverbs.

ADJECTIVE.		ADVERB.	ADJECTIVE.		ADVERB.
Cher,	dear,	dear.	Bas,	low,	in a low voice.
Faux,	false,	out of tune.	Juste,	just,	correctly.
Haut,	high,	loud.	Fort,	strong,	very; very much.

Il vend cher. — He sells dear.
Elle chante faux. — She sings out of tune.
Nous parlons trop haut. — We speak too loud.
Elle joue juste. — She plays correctly.
Il gèle fort. — It freezes hard.

5. COMPARISON OF ADVERBS.

Adverbs are compared in the same manner as adjectives.

Tard, late; plus tard, later; le plus tard, latest.

The following are irregularly compared.

Bien,	well;	mieux,	better;	le mieux,	best.
Beaucoup,	much;	plus,	more;	le plus,	most.
Mal,	badly;	pis,	worse;	le pis,	worst.
Peu,	little;	moins,	less;	le moins,	least.

6. ADVERBS MODIFYING ADVERBS AND ADJECTIVES.

Certain adverbs when used to modify adjectives or other adverbs, assume in this connection a different meaning.

Bien fort *or* très-fort, very strong; Fort bien *or* très-bien, very well.
Assez bien, pretty well; Assez joli, rather pretty.
Un peu tard, rather late; Trop tard, too late.

REM. Très, bien, and fort may be used to strengthen the sense of adjectives and adverbs. Before nouns bien is used, and before participles, either bien or fort.

7. THE ADVERB TOUT.

Tout is used as an adverb in the sense of *quite*.

Tout doucement.	Quite gently.

Tout before an adjective that is feminine, takes the same gender and number as the adjective when the adjective begins with a consonant, but not when the adjective begins with a vowel.

Elle est toute surprise.	She is quite surprised.
Elle était tout étonnée.	She was quite astonished.

8. ADVERBS OF NEGATION.

The adverbs of negation are:

Ne, not.	Aucunement (ne), by no means.
Pas (ne), not.	Nullement (ne), by no means.
Point (ne), not (*with emphasis*).	Que (ne), only, but; nothing but.
Plus (ne), no longer.	Guère (ne), but little; but few.
Jamais (ne), never.	Non, no.

REM. 1. Adverbs of negation accompanying a verb, require **ne** before the verb.

REM. 2. The negative **pas** is generally omitted in the negative conjugation of the verbs **cesser,** *to cease;* **oser,** *to dare;* **pouvoir,** *to be able;* **savoir,** *to know.*

Elle ne cesse de pleurer.	She does not cease weeping.
Je n'ose parler de cela.	I dare not speak of that.
Je ne puis le faire.	I cannot do it.
Je ne le puis.	I cannot.
Je ne sais où il est.	I don't know where he is.

The adverbial phrase **du tout,** *at all,* is often added to negative adverbs, to strengthen their sense, as: **pas du tout, point du tout. Du tout** is also used alone with the force of a negative.

Vocabulary 44.

Avancer, to advance; to bring forward.
Oser, to dare.
Marcher, to walk; to march.
Agir, to act.
L'âge, *m.*, the age.

Un châle, a shawl.
Confiant, confiding; confident.
Fidèle (à), faithful; true to.
Extrêmement, extremely.
Vraiment, truly; indeed.
Autrement, otherwise.

Exercise 44.

ADVERBS. (See List 1.) 1. Autrefois je travaillais peu; j'étais malade alors. 2. Maintenant je travaille davantage, et je me porte bien. 3. Dorénavant je serai moins confiant. 4. Je veux bien que vous jouiez, mais faites votre devoir auparavant. 5. Mes frères sont dehors; ils vont rentrer bientôt. 6. Voici la lettre; l'argent est dedans. 7. Avancez la table, et mettez votre cahier dessus. 8. Voilà votre châle; vos gants sont dessous.

ADVERBS OF QUANTITY. 9. Vous n'étudiez pas autant que votre frère. 10. Il a plus de patience que vous. 11. Je n'ai pas moins de courage que lui. 12. Si vous aviez autant de patience que de courage, vous réussiriez mieux.

ADVERBS IN MENT. 13. Il arrive ordinairement après l'heure. 14. J'ai voulu seulement vous faire remarquer cela. 15. Parlez doucement, s'il vous plaît. 16. Il m'a dit poliment que j'avais agi follement.

ADJECTIVES AS ADVERBS. 17. Vous avez payé cela trop cher. 18. Elle joue faux. 19. Ne parlez pas si haut. 20. Parlons bas; il y a quelqu'un dans l'autre chambre.

MODIFICATION OF ADVERBS AND ADJECTIVES. 21. Elle est très-forte pour son âge, et fort avancée dans ses études. 22. Elle est très-aimable et assez jolie. 23. Elle joue assez bien. 24. Sa sœur est bien malade. 25. Elle était tout étonnée de nous voir.

ADVERBS OF NEGATION. 26. Je n'ose aller la voir. 27. Elle ne cesse de pleurer. 28. Je ne sais que faire. 29. Je n'ai qu'un frère, et je ne sais où il est. 30. Je le cherche partout, et je ne puis le trouver. 31. Vous n'avez guère de patience. 32. Je crois vraiment que je n'en ai point du tout.

Theme 44.

ADVERBS. (See List 1.) 1. Formerly I studied little; now I study more, and I am more contented. 2. You were sick then, now you are in good health, and you are strong. 3. Henceforth I will be true to my duties. 4. I am first going to the post-office, and then to the bank. 5. I have the box; there is nothing in it. 6. He was in the house, and I was outside. 7. Here is a bench; let us sit down upon it. 8. Put your books under it. 9. Wait for me; I have almost finished.

ADVERBS OF QUANTITY. 10. I work more than you. 11. You have more patience than I. 12. He has as much courage as patience. 13. You have less prudence than courage.

ADVERBS IN MENT. 14. We usually dine at five o'clock. 15. Walk slowly; we cannot follow you. 16. Tell him politely that he has not acted prudently in that affair. 17. I say that only because he thinks otherwise.

ADJECTIVES AS ADVERBS. 18. He sells too dear. 19. You sing out of tune. 20. You speak too loud. 21. She speaks so low that I cannot understand her. 22. She does not play correctly.

MODIFICATION OF ADVERBS AND ADJECTIVES. 23. She

is very tall. 24. He is extremely polite. 25. They were very much astonished to see us. 26. It was very warm. 27. I was very thirsty. 28. She is rather pretty and quite young.

ADVERBS OF NEGATION. 29. He dares not say it. 30. You do not cease speaking. 31. I cannot answer all your questions. 32. I do not know what to say. 33. It shall be so (thus); you have but to say so (it). 34. I have but one sister, and she is not well at all.

FORTY-FIFTH LESSON.

The Preposition.*

List of Prepositions that are frequently used.

Avant, before (*time or order*).
À cause de, on account of.
À côté de, by the side of, by.
À l'égard de, with regard to.
Au lieu de, instead of.
Auprès de, near, close by; with.
Autour de, around.
Contre, against.
Depuis, since.
Dès, from.
Derrière, behind.
Devant, before (*position*).
Durant, during.
Entre, between.
Envers, towards (*morally*).
Environ, about.
Excepté, except.
Faute de, for want of.
Hors, out.
Jusque, till, until; as far as.
Malgré, in spite of.
Parmi, among.
Pendant, during.
Près de, near by.
Quant à, as to.
Selon, } according to.
Suivant, }
Sur, upon.
Vers, towards (*physically*).
Vis-à-vis, opposite.

---

* Introduction, p. 17, 8.

Vocabulary 45.

L'examen, *m.*, the examination.
Les vacances, *f.*, the vacation.
L'été, *m.*, summer.
Un parent, *m.*, a relative.
Une parente, *f.*, a relative.
Une personne, a person.
Une circonstance, a circumstance.
Mon avis, *m.*, my advice; my opinion.
L'hôtel de ville, the city-hall.
L'ouest, *m.*, the west.
Etre fâché contre, to be angry with.
Etre fâché de, to be sorry for.
Tourner, to turn.
Aîné, oldest.
En vérité, indeed.
Eh bien! well!

Exercise 45.

1. Jules se plaint de moi, parce que je n'ai pas voulu sortir avec lui. 2. Depuis ce jour, il croit que je suis fâché contre lui. 3. À cause de cela, il ne vient plus me voir. 4. Entre nous, je n'en suis pas fâché. 5. Il s'est toujours bien comporté envers moi. 6. Il est venu passer quelques jours avec moi pendant les vacances. 7. Durant l'été nous étions presque toujours hors de la ville. 8. Autrefois mon cousin demeurait auprès de la banque. 9. Je l'ai rencontré ce matin près d'ici. 10. Son frère demeure vis-à-vis de l'hôtel de ville. 11. Nous demeurons à côté de l'église. 12. Ne sortez pas sans parapluie. 13. Le vent a tourné vers l'ouest; il va pleuvoir. 14. Suivant votre avis je ne devrais pas y aller. 15. Quant à cela je n'ai rien à vous dire. 16. À l'égard de cette affaire, il faut agir selon les circonstances.

Theme 45.

1. I started from home after (the) breakfast, and (1) arrived here before (the) dinner. 2. My father came with me, but my mother staid at home on account of the cold. 3. I do not know what to do with regard to that business. 4. As to

that, I cannot tell you anything. 5. You must act according to the advice of your father. 6. I will act according to circumstances. 7. I have not seen Louis since last Monday. 8. I believe that he is angry with me. 9. I should be sorry for it, for he has always acted well towards me. 10. I shall return here towards *evening* (le soir). 11. There were about two hundred persons at the examination. 12. All my relatives were there except my eldest† brother, who was out of town. 13. Your cousin was sitting by me. 14. Julia was behind me, and my mother was sitting before me. 15. Henry was sitting near the window, between his two sisters. 16. I did not recognize you among so many strangers.

FORTY-SIXTH LESSON.

The Conjunction.‡ — The Interjection.§

1. List of conjunctions that are frequently used:

Afin que,‖ in order that.
Ainsi, thus.
Ainsi que, } as well as.
Aussi bien que, }
À moins que,‖ unless.
Aussitôt que, as soon as.
Avant que,‖ before.
Bien que,‖ although.
Car, for.
Cependant, however.
Depuis que, since (*temporal*).

Dès que, as soon as.
Donc, then ; therefore.
Et, and.
Jusqu'à ce que,‖ until.
Lorsque, when.
Mais, but.
Néanmoins, nevertheless.
Ni, neither ; nor.
Ou, or.
Parce que, because.
Pendant que, while.

---

† Place the adjective after the noun.
‡ Introduction, p. 17, 9.
§ Introduction, p. 17, 10.
‖ These conjunctions require the verb in the subjunctive mode.

Pourquoi, why.
Pourtant, however.
Pour que,† in order that.
Pourvu que,† provided
Puisque, since (*causal*).
Quand, when.

Que, that.
Quoique,† although.
Sans que,† unless; without.
Si, if ; whether.
Tant que, as long as.
Tandis que, while.

2.   INTERJECTIONS.

The principal interjections are:

Ha! ha!
Ah! ah!
Aïe! oh!
Hélas! alas!
Oh! oh!
Fi! fy!

Bah! pshaw!
Paix! silence!
Chut! hist!
Holà! hallo!
Hé bien! hey then! now then!
Eh bien! well then!

Vocabulary 46.

Se dépêcher, to make haste.
Se livrer (à), to apply (to).
Compter (sur), to rely (upon).
Aider, to help.
Tirer, to pull; to draw; tirer quelqu'un d'embarras, to get one out of difficulty.
Réparer, to repair; to amend; to make amends for.

Une occasion, an opportunity.
Une situation, a situation.
Un avantage, an advantage.
Levé, risen.
Magnifique, magnificent.
À propos, seasonably; bien à propos, at the right time.
Puis, then; et puis, and next what next.

Exercise 46.

CONJUNCTIONS. 1. Vous savez aussi bien que moi qu'on nous attend, cependant vous ne vous dépêchez pas. 2. Aussitôt que je me serai habillé, nous partirons. 3. Nous arriverons avant que mon oncle soit levé. 4. Depuis que mon

---

† These conjunctions require the verb in the subjunctive mode.

ami est parti, plusieurs personnes sont venues le demander. 5. Puisque vous le désirez, je remettrai ce voyage à demain. 6. Je suis content, pourvu que vous le soyez. 7. Étudiez tandis que vous êtes jeunes; quand vous serez grands, vous n'aurez, peut-être, ni le temps, ni les mêmes occasions que vous avez à présent, de vous livrer à l'étude. 8. Bien que vous soyez jeunes et riches, ne comptez pas trop sur ces avantages. 9. Je ne parviendrai jamais à traduire ce thème sans que vous m'aidiez.

INTERJECTIONS. 10. Hélas! que vais-je faire? 11. Ha! vous voilà bien à propos; vous allez me tirer d'embarras. 12. Oh! que c'est beau! 13. Chut! on vient. 14. Hé bien! que fîtes-vous alors? 15. Eh bien! vous avez donc réussi à la fin.

Theme 46.

CONJUNCTIONS. 1. I was mistaken as well as you, however. I hope to make amends for my fault. 2. When one is young, one is too confiding. 3. I have not seen my uncle, since you spoke of that to me. 4. Since I am ready, I will start. 5. Nevertheless, if you wish it, I will wait till to-morrow. 6. I show you this letter, in order that you may understand my situation. 7. You do not make haste, although you know that I am in a hurry. 8. As soon as you are ready, we will start. 9. Let us read while we are waiting. 10. Let us study, if we wish to acquire useful knowledge, for (the) time *flies* (s'enfuit), and you know that it will not return *again* (plus).

INTERJECTIONS. 11. Alas! that is a great misfortune. 12. Hallo! is there nobody at home? 13. Hey then! what next? 14. Oh! that is magnificent. 15. Well then! that will be the end of the story.

SYNTAX.

FORTY-SEVENTH LESSON.

The Noun.

1. A noun in a sentence is either the subject of a verb, the object of a transitive verb, called direct object; or the object of a preposition, called indirect object. (See Introduction, p. 17; 2, 6, etc.)

A noun may also be used in close connection with another word, so as to express with it but one idea; as **avoir besoin**, *to have need* (*to need*); **avec politesse**, *with politeness* (*politely*).

A verb and a noun closely connected are equivalent to a neuter verb.

Avoir envie, to have a wish.	**Entendre raison,** to listen to reason.
Avoir soin, to take care.	
Avoir mal, to have pain.	**Prendre congé,** to take leave.
Faire mal, to hurt.	**Rendre justice,** to do justice.
Demander pardon, to beg pardon.	**Rendre service,** to oblige.

2.   Idioms with Avoir, To Have, and a Noun.

In some French expressions **avoir**, *to have*, is used with a noun; whereas in the equivalent English expressions *to be* is used with an adjective.

Avoir faim, to be hungry.	**Avoir peur,** to be afraid.
Avoir soif, to be thirsty.	**Avoir honte,** to be ashamed.
Avoir chaud, to be warm.	**Avoir raison,** to be right.
Avoir froid, to be cold.	**Avoir tort,** to be wrong.
Avoir sommeil, to be sleepy.	

Avoir, *to have*, is also used in the following expressions:

Qu'y a-t-il?	What is the matter?
Il n'y a rien.	Nothing is the matter.
Qu'avez-vous?	What is the matter with you?
Je n'ai rien.	Nothing is the matter with me.

A-t-il quelque chose ?	Is anything the matter with him ?
Quel âge avez-vous ?	How old are you ?
J'ai dix ans.	I am ten years old.

3. Nouns used Adjectively.

A noun is used adjectively

(1.) When it stands in apposition with another noun, as:

Télémaque, fils d'Ulysse.	Telemachus, the son of Ulysses.

(2.) After a neuter verb when it qualifies the subject of the verb.

Son père était médecin.	His father was a physician.
Il est devenu soldat.	He has become a soldier.

(3.) When it is an adjunct of another noun which it describes, as:

Un maître de danse.	A dancing-master.
Un chemin de fer.	A railroad.

(4.) When it is descriptive of the use or purpose of an object, or states the means by which the object is put in motion, as:

Du papier à lettre.	Letter paper.
Une chaise à bascule.	A rocking-chair.
Une machine à vapeur.	A steam-engine.
Un moulin à vent.	A wind-mill.

4. Plural of Compound Nouns and of Proper Nouns.

When two nouns, or a noun and an adjective, form a compound noun, both component parts take the plural ending, as:

Un chou-fleur, des choux-fleurs.	A cauliflower ; cauliflowers.
Un gentilhomme; des gentils-hommes.	A nobleman ; noblemen.
Un monsieur; des messieurs.	A gentleman ; gentlemen.

When a compound noun is formed of two nouns connected by a preposition, the first of the two nouns only takes the plural ending, as:

Un chef-d'œuvre; des chefs-d'œuvre.	A master-piece; master-pieces.
Un arc-en-ciel; des arcs-en-ciel.	A rainbow ; rainbows.

Verbs and invariable parts of speech used substantively, or forming a part of a compound noun, are the same in the plural as in the singular.

Un porte-crayon; des porte-crayons.   A pencil-case; pencil-cases.

Les si et les pourquoi.   The ifs and the wherefores.

Proper names of persons are the same in the plural as in the singular.

Les deux Corneille.   The two Corneilles.

5. AN, ANNÉE, YEAR; JOUR, JOURNÉE, DAY, ETC.

An, *year;* **jour,** *day;* **matin,** *morning,* and **soir,** *evening,* are masculine nouns, and **année,** *year;* **journée,** *day;* **matinée,** *morning,* and **soirée,** *evening,* are feminine nouns.

The masculine nouns express divisions of time, as a unit. They are used in counting and in adverbial expressions: **trois ans,** *three years;* **tous les ans,** *every year;* **tous les jours,** *every day;* **le matin,** *the morning* or *in the morning;* **le soir,** *the evening* or *in the evening.*

The feminine nouns express periods of time with reference to their duration: **toute l'année,** *the whole year;* **cette année,** *this year;* **toute une journée,** *a whole day;* **la matinée,** *the morning time;* **une soirée,** *an evening,* or *an evening party.*

6. REMARK ON THE PLURAL NOUN GENS, PEOPLE.

The plural noun **gens,** *people,* is of the masculine gender, but, by a singular rule, the adjectives which precede it, must be in the feminine, and those that follow it, in the masculine gender: **Les vieilles gens sont soupçonneux,** *old people are distrustful.*

The compound nouns, **gens de lettres,** *literary men;* **gens de bien,** *good people,* etc., are not subject to the above rule.

Vocabulary 47.

La tête, the head.
Une dent, a tooth.
La gorge, the throat.
Le mal, evil; pain; sore.

Le mal de tête, the headache.
Avoir mal (à), to have pain (in).
Mal à la tête, a headache.
Mal aux dents, toothache.

Mal à la gorge, sore throat.
Une salle à manger, a dining-room.
Une boîte à thé, a tea-canister.
Un tiroir, a drawer.
Le bureau, the office.
Le voisinage, the neighborhood.
Montrer, to show.
Passer, to spend (*of time*).
En société, in company.
En famille, with one's family
Vide, empty.
Au contraire, on the contrary.

Exercise 47.

A Verb and a Noun, 1 and 2. 1. Qu'y a-t-il? 2. Vous me faites mal. 3. Je vous demande pardon. 4. Charles dit qu'on ne lui rend pas justice. 5. Il a tort de dire cela. 6. C'est un jeune homme qui ne veut pas entendre raison. 7. Avez-vous froid? 8. Au contraire, j'ai bien chaud. 9. Nous avons faim. 10. On va servir le dîner. 11. Qu'as-tu, Jules? as-tu peur de venir auprès de moi? 12. Il a pleuré; il a honte de se montrer. 13. Quel âge a-t-il? 14. Il a presque neuf ans. 15. Avez-vous sommeil? 16. Du tout; j'ai mal à la tête. 17. Henriette a mal aux dents. 18. La petite Élise a mal à la gorge. 19. Tout le monde est malade ici; il faudra faire venir le médecin.

Nouns used Adjectively, 3. 20. Le père de notre professeur de français est notaire. 21. Il y a deux chaises à bascule dans la salle à manger. 22. Il n'y a pas de moulin à vent dans ce voisinage. 23. La boîte à thé est vide. 24. Vous trouverez du papier à lettre dans ce tiroir.

An, année; jour, journée, etc., 4. 25. Mon frère Charles a douze ans. 26. Mon grand-père est dans sa quatre-vingtième année. 27. Il sort encore tous les jours. 28. Mon père est toute la journée au bureau. 29. Je ne le vois que le matin et le soir. 30. Moi, je suis toute la matinée dehors. 31. Je passe la soirée en famille.

Theme 47.

A Verb and a Noun, 1 and 2. 1. What is the matter with you? 2. I have a headache. 3. Mary has the toothache. 4. Henry has a sore throat. 5. The children are hungry and thirsty. 6. Little William is very sleepy. 7. John is afraid. 8. He is ashamed to say so. 9. What is the matter now? 10. Charles will not listen to reason. 11. I beg your (you) pardon. 12. You do not do me justice.

Nouns used Adjectively, 3. 13. We are translating the history of

Telemachus, *the* son of Ulysses. 14. Our dancing-master was *a* soldier formerly. 15. Have you bought letter paper? 16. Is there a rocking-chair in your room? 17. The tea-canister is in the dining-room. 18. There is a steam-mill in this neighborhood.

An, année; jour, journée, etc., 4. 19. I was a whole year in Paris. 20. I go there almost every year. 21. I see you pass here twice a day. 22. You did not see me pass here yesterday; for I stayed the whole day at home. 23. I never† go out in the morning; I study the whole morning. 24. I go out almost every evening. 25. I usually† spend the evening in company.

FORTY-EIGHTH LESSON.

THE ARTICLE.—USE OF THE ARTICLE BEFORE COMMON NOUNS.

1. The article is used before a common noun that denotes a particular person, place or thing, as:

Le livre que je lis.	The book which I am reading.
Le mois dernier.	Last month.
La semaine prochaine.	Next week.

The article is used before nouns taken in a general sense, as:

L'homme est mortel.	Man is mortal.
Nous admirons le courage.	We admire courage.
L'or est précieux.	Gold is precious.

The article, combined with the preposition **de**, is used before nouns that are taken in a partitive sense, as:

J'ai du papier.	I have paper.
Il possède du courage.	He possesses courage.

To this rule there are three exceptions. (See Fourth Lesson.)

(1.) The article is omitted after **pas**, or any other negative word, as:

Je n'ai pas de pain.	I have no bread.

---

† Put the adverb after the verb.

REM. The article is, however, used after a negative word, when the sense of the noun is restricted by some other words, as:

Je n'ai pas du pain comme le vôtre.   I have no bread like yours.

(2.) The article is omitted when the noun is preceded by an adjective, as:

J'ai de bon papier.   I have good paper.

REM. The article is not omitted when the adjective stands after the noun: **du papier blanc,** *white paper*. When the noun is omitted, the rule for the suppression or use of the article is the same as if the noun were expressed: **Avez-vous** *de* **bon papier? J'en ai** *de* **bon. Avez-vous** *du* **papier blanc? J'en ai** *du* **blanc.**

(3.) The article is omitted when the noun is governed by the preposition **de**, as the indirect object of a preceding word, as:

J'ai besoin de livres.   I have need of books.
Beaucoup de courage.   Much courage.

REM. The article is, however, used after **bien**, *much; many;* and after **la plupart**, *most*.

Bien de la peine.   Much trouble.
La plupart des hommes.   Most men.

The article is used before the noun that denotes the unit of weight, or measure, by which anything is bought or sold, and before nouns expressing fractional quantities when their sense is limited.

Vingt sous la livre.   Twenty cents a pound.
Deux dollars le mètre.   Two dollars a meter.
La moitié des marchandises.   One half of the goods.

The article is used, instead of the possessive adjective, before the parts of the body and the qualities of the mind. The construction of the sentence is so arranged that the part refers to the subject of the verb.

Il m'a donné la main.   He gave me his hand.
Elle a la bouche petite.   Her mouth is small.

When an operation is performed upon a person, the part acted upon is the direct, and the person the indirect, object of the verb.

Vous leur avez ouvert les yeux. You opened their eyes.

When a person performs an act upon a part of himself, the pronominal form of the verb is used.

Il s'est fait mal à la main. He hurts his hand.

The article is not used before nouns placed in apposition with, or explanatory of, preceding nouns.

Télémaque, fils d'Ulysse. Telemachus, the son of Ulysses.

The article is not used before nouns that qualify, or describe preceding nouns.

Un maître de danse. A dancing-master.
Un homme à cheveux blancs. A man with white hair.

The article is, however, used before a descriptive noun, and before a noun that expresses the use or destination of an object, when the sense is definite.

L'homme aux cheveux blancs. The man with the white hair.
La boîte aux lettres. The letter-box.
Le pot au lait. The milk-pot.

The article is not used after the preposition en, nor after the conjunction ni, before a noun that is taken in an indefinite or partitive sense.

En automne. In autumn.
Il est venu en voiture. He came in a carriage.
Il n'a ni argent ni amis. He has neither money nor friends.

2. USE OF THE ARTICLE BEFORE PROPER NOUNS.

The article is used before proper names of countries, provinces, seas, rivers, and mountains.

La France est un beau pays. France is a beautiful country.

The article is not used before the name of a country, when it is preceded by the preposition en, *in, to.*

Il est en France. He is in France.
Il va en Angleterre. He goes to England.

SYNTAX OF THE ARTICLE.

The article is not used before the name of a country of the feminine gender when it is preceded by the preposition de, in the sense of *from*.

Il vient d'Allemagne.   He comes from Germany.

But:

Il vient du Mexique.   He comes from Mexico.

The article is not used in connection with the preposition de, when the name of a country forms part of a title, or serves to qualify a preceding noun, as:

Le roi de Prusse.   The king of Prussia.
Du fromage d'Angleterre.   English cheese.

In other cases the article is used with the preposition de, as:

Le climat de la France.   The climate of France.

The article is used before proper names of persons, when they are preceded by a title or an adjective.

Le Président Jackson.   President Jackson.
Le petit Henri.   Little Henry.

The article is not used before the names of the months and of the days of the week. [See Ninth Lesson (*bis*).]

Vocabulary 48.

L'Europe, *f.*, Europe.
La France, France.
L'Angleterre, *f.*, England.
L'Allemagne, *f.*, Germany.
Un empereur, an emperor.
Un monarque, a monarch.
Le printemps, spring; au printemps, in spring.
L'été, summer; en été, in summer.
L'automne, autumn; en automne, in autumn.
L'hiver, winter; en hiver, in winter.
Le climat, the climate.
La gelée, the frost.
Le succès, success.
L'oisiveté, *f.* idleness.
L'amitié, *f.* friendship.
Un signe, a sign; en signe de, as a sign of.
Le sort, the lot.
Un cheveu, a hair; **les cheveux,** the hair.

Un œil, an eye; **les yeux,** the eyes.
La main, the hand.
Le bras, the arm.
Le pied, the foot.
La moitié, the half.
Le quart, the quarter.
Créer, to create.
Proclamer, to proclaim.
Flâner, to loiter.

S'approcher (de), to come near.
Blanc, *fem.* **blanche,** white.
Noir, black.
Vert, green.
Bleu, blue.
Brun, brown.
Blond, fair; light; flaxen.
Mécontent (de), dissatisfied (with).
Puissant, powerful.
Uni, united.

Exercise 48.

The Article before Common Nouns, 1 and 2. 1. Mon père est allé à Boston le mois dernier. 2. Il reviendra la semaine prochaine. 3. Dieu a créé le ciel et la terre en six jours. 4. L'automne est une saison plus agréable que l'hiver. 5. On admire le courage, mais la prudence est tout aussi nécessaire au succès. 6. Avez-vous du satin blanc comme celui-ci? 7. Nous n'avons pas de satin comme celui-là. 8. Nous en avons du blanc et du noir, mais d'une qualité différente. 9. Bien des gens passent leur temps dans l'oisiveté. 10. La plupart des hommes se plaignent de la fortune. 11. Nous payons la viande vingt sous la livre. 12. Cette soie blanche coûte trois dollars le mètre. 13. J'ai perdu le quart de mes plantes par la gelée. 14. Il m'a offert la main en signe d'amitié. 15. Elle a les cheveux blonds. 16. J'ai froid aux pieds. 17. Vous m'avez ouvert les yeux. 18. Je me suis fait mal au bras. 19. Un vieillard à cheveux blancs, qui tenait un livre à la main, s'est approché de nous. 20. Ce monsieur aux cheveux blancs est le grand-père de la petite Henriette.

The Article before Proper Names, 3. 21. La France est plus grande que l'Angleterre. 22. Le climat de la France est préférable à celui de l'Angleterre. 23. Le roi de Prusse fut proclamé empereur d'Allemagne. 24. Mon frère est en France, et j'irai en Angleterre au printemps. 25. Le Président Grant était en ville hier. 26. Je n'étudie pas beaucoup en été. 27. Nous reviendrons à la ville en automne. 28. Il fait bien froid ici en hiver.

Theme 48.

The Article before Common Nouns, 1 and 2. 1. We shall go to the country next month. 2. Last week I received a letter from my brother. 3. Spring is a beautiful season. 4. I like autumn better. 5. Prudence is as necessary to *a* (the) general* as courage. 6. Have you green velvet like this? 7. We have no velvet of that quality. 8. We have beautiful velvet, green, black and blue. 9. Many young people spend their time *in* (à) loitering in the streets. 10. Most men are dissatisfied with their lot. 11. This white *cloth* (étoffe) costs fifty cents a meter. 12. We pay *for* (le)* coffee forty cents a pound. 13. He has lost one-half of his books. 14. Give me your hand, and let us be friends. 15. My cousin Alice has blue eyes and brown hair. 16. You have hurt my foot? 17. I have a pain in my arm.

The Article before Proper Names, 3. 18. I do not like the climate of England. 19. Germany is now united and very powerful. 20. The emperor of Germany is the oldest monarch of Europe. 21. I was in Germany when the war began between Germany and France. 22. Do you speak French?† 23. I will study it next winter. 24. I will begin in autumn. 25. We intend to go to Europe in the spring.

FORTY-NINTH LESSON.

THE ADJECTIVE.—AGREEMENT.

1. An adjective qualifying two nouns in the singular, is put in the plural; if the nouns are of different genders the adjective is put in the masculine plural.

L'homme et la femme sont âgés. The man and the woman are old.

An adjective following two nouns connected by **ou**, agrees with the last.

Un homme ou une femme âgée. An old man or an old woman.

---

* General sense.

† *Parlez vous français?* After the verb *parler* the article is usually omitted before *français*, French, *anglais*, English, and other national names denoting languages.

The adjectives **demi,** *half,* and **nu,** *bare,* are invariable when they precede the noun, and agree with the noun when they follow it; **demi** in gender only; **une demi-heure,** *half an hour;* **deux heures et demie,** *two hours and a half:* **nu-pieds,** or **les pieds nus,** *barefooted.*

The adjective **feu,** *late, deceased,* placed immediately before the noun, agrees with it; when separated from it by the article or a possessive adjective, it is invariable; **la feue reine,** *the late queen;* **feu la reine,** *the deceased queen.*

2. ADJECTIVES USED AS NOUNS.

An adjective may be used as a noun to designate an individual, a class, or an abstract quality.

Le Français; la Française.	The Frenchman; the French woman.
Le français.	The French language.
Le (*or* la) malade va bien.	The patient is doing well.
L'ambitieux n'est jamais content.	The ambitious man is never satisfied.
Je préfère l'utile à l'agréable.	I prefer the useful to the agreeable.

3. PLACE OF THE ADJECTIVE.

Adjectives, as a rule, are placed after the noun, but the following generally precede it:

Beau, beautiful.	**Jeune,** young.	**Moindre,** least.
Bon, good.	**Joli,** pretty.	**Nouveau,** new.
Grand, great; large.	**Mauvais,** bad.	**Petit,** small.
Gros, large.	**Meilleur,** better.	**Vieux,** old.

Adjectives derived from proper names, those that denote color, form or shape, those that express physical or mental qualities, and past participles used as adjectives, always follow the noun.

La langue française.	The French language.
Une table ronde.	A round table.
Du drap noir.	Black cloth.
Un homme aveugle.	A blind man.
Des plats cassés.	Broken dishes.

SYNTAX OF THE ADJECTIVE. 223

Some adjectives have a different meaning, according as they precede or follow the noun. The following are a few of them:

Un brave homme, a worthy man.   **Un homme brave,** a brave man.
Mon cher ami, my dear friend.   **Une robe chère,** a costly dress.
Un grand homme, a great man.   **Un homme grand,** a tall man.
La dernière année, the last year   **L'année dernière,** last year (*the*
(*of a series*).   *preceding year*).

4.   GOVERNMENT.

Adjectives may be followed by a preposition and a noun, or a verb in the infinitive.

Adjectives that express our feelings, and those generally that are followed in English by *of, from, with,* require the preposition **de** before the noun or infinitive.

Je suis content de ce travail.   I am satisfied with this work.
Je suis heureux de vous voir.   I am happy to see you.

Adjectives that express advantage, likeness, fitness, or the opposite qualities, require the preposition **à.**

C'est utile à savoir.   That is useful to know.
C'est une chose difficile à faire.   That is a difficult thing to do.

Adjectives joined in construction with the impersonal verb **il est,** require, however, **de** before the infinitive.

Il est utile de savoir cela.   It is useful to know that.

5.   NUMERAL ADJECTIVES.

The numeral adjective **un** is used for the English indefinite article *a* or *an ;* but the indefinite article is used, in English, in cases in which its equivalent is not used in French.

The numeral **un** is not used before nouns placed in apposition with, or explanatory of, preceding nouns.

Athalie, tragédie de Racine.   Athaly, a tragedy of Racine.
Il est français.   He is a Frenchman.
Son père était notaire.   His father was a notary.

REM. The numeral un is, however, used before the explanatory noun, when it is qualified or restricted by other words, as:

Son père était un riche négociant. His father was a rich merchant.

The cardinal numbers are used for the ordinal after the names of sovereigns, and also to state the day of the month, and the chapter or page of a book, except for the first.

Henri quatre. Henry the Fourth.
Le deux janvier. The second of January.
Chapitre premier, page huit. Chapter the First, page eight.

Vocabulary 49.

Un bottier, a bootmaker.
Un cordonnier, a shoemaker.
Un tailleur, a tailor.
Un boulanger, a baker.
Un boucher, a butcher.
Une feuille, a leaf; a sheet.
Une livre, a pound.
Le lit, the bed.
La langue, the language.
Français, French.
Anglais, English.
Allemand, German.
Rond, round.
Carré, square.
Égal, equal; alike.
Avare, avaricious; miserly.
Mort, dead.
Aimable (de), amiable; kind.
Fatigué (de), tired.
Impossible (à), impossible.
Inutile (à), useless.
Difficile (à), difficult.
Prononcer, to pronounce.
Contenter, to satisfy.

Exercise 49.

1. Le père et la mère de ces enfants sont morts. 2. Le petit et sa sœur sortent ensemble. 3. Hier ils sont venus demander du pain; ils étaient nu-pieds. 4. Vous me donnez une demi-livre de café, et je vous en ai demandé une livre et demie. 5. La malade n'a pas quitté le lit aujourd'hui. 6. L'avare meurt de faim au milieu de l'abondance. 7. La langue française et la langue anglaise sont utiles à celui qui va voyager en Europe. 8. J'ai étudié l'allemand, mais je ne le parle pas. 9. J'aime mieux une table ronde qu'une table carrée. 10. Coupez-moi, s'il vous plaît, un mètre et demi de ce drap noir. 11. Je suis content de mon sort; l'êtes-vous du vôtre? 12. Nous sommes fatigués

d'entendre parler de cela. 13. Il est inutile de me le dire. 14. Mon bottier est français. 15. Son frère est boulanger. 16. Notre boucher est anglais et mon tailleur est allemand. 17. Henri quatre, roi de France, était le père du peuple. 18. Vous trouverez cela dans votre histoire, livre premier, chapitre deux, page soixante.

Theme 49.

1. That gentleman and lady are our neighbors. 2. The children of the poor often go barefooted in the midst of winter. 3. Lend me half a sheet of letter paper. 4. I have studied this lesson *for* (pendant) an hour and a half. 5. The patient *is* (va) better; he has gone out. 6. The rich and the poor are alike before God. 7. The French language is more difficult than the German. 8. I like French better than German. 9. Here is a round table and a square table, which one do you wish? 10. That general is a great man, and his son is a tall man. 11. Our teacher is a worthy man. 12. The brave man does his duty, and fears *none but* (que) God. 13. My shoemaker is a Frenchman. 14. That German is a baker. 15. I am glad to see you. 16. You are very kind to have thought of me. 17. These words are difficult to pronounce. 18. It is difficult to satisfy everybody. 19. It is impossible to do it.

FIFTIETH LESSON.

The Pronoun.

(See Lesson Eleventh to Lesson Nineteenth. We here add only what is necessary to complete the subject.)

A pronoun stands in the place of a noun. But the pronouns **ce, ceci, cela, en, y,** and the invariable pronoun **le,** may stand in the place of a sentence.

Je sais ce qui le désole.	I know what grieves him.
Savez-vous ce qu'il a dit?	Do you know what he said?
Cela est vrai.	That is true.
Tout le monde en parle.	Everybody speaks of it.
Je le sais.	I know it.

When a relative clause refers to a preceding sentence, the demonstrative pronoun ce is used as the antecedent of the relative pronoun.

Elle est fort mécontente, ce qui me désole.   She is very much displeased, which grieves me.

We have seen (Lesson Eleventh) that the objective personal pronouns are placed after the verb when the verb is in the imperative mode and used affirmatively. The pronouns moi and toi are then used for me and te, except before en.

Donnez-moi du papier.   Give me some paper.
Donnez-m'en.   Give me some.

When the objective pronouns stand after the verb, le, la, les precede moi, toi, lui, nous, vous, leur.

Donnez-le-moi.   Give it to me.
Envoyez-le-lui.   Send it to him.

The personal pronouns are generally repeated with each verb.

The pronoun subject may, however, be omitted before the second and succeeding verbs, when the verbs are connected by et, ou, or ni, are all in the same tense, and all used either affirmatively or negatively. We may say : **Il étudie et fait des progrès;** or **Il étudie et il fait des progrès.** *He studies and makes progress.*

The relative pronouns **qui, que, dont**, are placed immediately after their antecedent.

Le monsieur qui doit nous accompagner, est venu.   The gentleman, who is to accompany us, has come.

The relative pronoun dont must be followed by the subject of the next verb.

Je vais trouver l'agent dont vous m'avez donné l'adresse.   I am going to the agent whose address you gave me.

The pronoun *whose*, standing after a preposition and before a noun, is rendered by **duquel, delaquelle,** etc.

Le monsieur dans la maison duquel nous demeurons.   The gentleman in whose house we live.

SYNTAX OF THE PRONOUN.

The personal pronouns *he, she, him, her*, followed by a relative pronoun, are rendered by a demonstrative pronoun.

Celui qui travaille est plus heureux que celui qui est oisif.	He who works is happier than he who is idle.
Je connais celle dont vous parlez.	I know her of whom you speak.

REM. The relative pronouns are not omitted in the French sentence, though they may be omitted in the English sentence.

Vocabulary 50.

La beauté, beauty.
L'esprit, *m*., the mind; the intellect; the wit.
Le cœur, the heart.
La barbe, the beard.
Le chagrin, the grief; the trouble.
La flatterie, flattery.
Un agent, an agent.
Un appartement, an apartment.
Au premier, on the first floor.
Inquiéter, to trouble; to make uneasy.
S'intéresser (à), to be interested (in).
Consoler, to console; to comfort.
Louer, to hire; to rent; to let out.
Faire cas de, to value; to set a value upon.
Sans réserve, without reserve.
Avec égard, respectfully.
Gris, gray.

Exercise 50.

1. Je sais ce qui vous inquiète. 2. Votre ami me l'a dit. 3. Nous en avons parlé. 4. J'y ai beaucoup pensé, mais je n'y puis rien faire. 5. Vos amis s'intéressent à votre sort, ce qui doit vous consoler. 6. Donnez-moi du papier à lettre. 7. Donnez-m'en une demi-douzaine de feuilles. 8. Prêtez-lui votre grammaire, si vous n'en avez pas besoin. 9. Prêtez-la-lui; il vous la rendra tantôt. 10. On a tort de ne penser qu'à soi. 11. On a souvent besoin d'un plus petit que soi. 12. Le monsieur qui a loué l'appartement au premier, est ici. 13. C'est un monsieur à barbe grise, d'environ soixante ans. 14. Recevez-le avec égard, et donnez-lui la clef. 15. J'ai vu le peintre dont vous m'avez donné l'adresse. 16. C'est un homme dont tout le monde admire le talent. 17. Celui qui n'a jamais souffert, ne peut comprendre les maux d'autrui. 18. Je n'estime point celle qui fait plus de cas de sa beauté que de son esprit. 19. Prenez ce gâteau; coupez-le en quatre parties égales, et donnez-en un morceau à chacun de vos frères.

Theme 50.

1. You do not know what troubles me. 2. I cannot tell it to you. 3. I think of it all the time. 4. I cannot speak of it with any one. 5. I know that you have trouble, which grieves me. 6. If I can be useful to you, tell me of it (it to me). 7. Speak to me of your trouble. 8. Speak of it to me without reserve. 9. Every one is master in his own house. 10. The gentleman is here who sold you the horse. 11. Tell him to come back next week. 12. I know the lady of whom you speak. 13. She is a person, whose qualities of heart and mind we admire. 14. There is the agent whose address you ask for. 15. It is the same who rented us the house in which we live. 16. We do not pity him who pities nobody. 17. I do not esteem her who loves flattery better than truth.

FIFTY-FIRST LESSON.

THE VERB.—AGREEMENT OF THE VERB AND ITS SUBJECT.

1. A verb agrees in person and number with its subject. When the subject is composed of two or more nouns or pronouns in the singular, the verb is put in the plural; and when the nouns or pronouns are of different persons, the verb agrees with the first person in preference to the second, and with the second in preference to the third.

Mon frère et moi (nous) viendrons.   My brother and I will come.

When the words forming the subject are connected by *ou*, and are of the third person, the verb agrees with the last; but when they are of different persons, the verb is put in the plural and agrees with the person who has the precedence.

Lui ou son frère viendra.   He or his brother will come.
Lui ou moi viendrons.   He or I will come.

A verb having a collective noun in the singular for its subject, is put in the singular.

Le peuple était mécontent.   The people were dissatisfied.

SYNTAX OF THE VERB.   229

When the collective noun is followed by de and another noun, the verb agrees with the noun to which the action refers.

Une foule d'enfants encombrait la rue.	A crowd of children obstructed the street.
Une foule d'enfants couraient dans la rue.	A crowd of children ran through the street.

The verb être having ce for its subject, is put in the plural only when it is followed by a noun or pronoun in the third person plural: Ce sont eux. *It is they.* C'est nous. *It is we.*

A verb having a relative pronoun for its subject, agrees with the antecedent of the relative pronoun.

Moi, qui suis votre ami.	I, who am your friend.

2.   USE OF THE TENSES OF THE INDICATIVE.

The *present* tense is used to express what exists or takes place at the present time.

Je lis.	I am reading.
Je lis tous les jours.	I read every day.

The *present* tense may be used to express a proximate future.

Je pars demain.	I leave to-morrow.

The *present* tense is used to express a state or action which has been going on for some time, and is still continuing in the present. In this case the perfect tense is used in English.

Je suis ici depuis lundi.	I have been here since Monday.
Combien de temps y a-t-il que vous demeurez ici?	How long have you lived here?
Il y a trois ans que je demeure ici.	I have lived here three years.

The *imperfect* tense is used to express what existed, or what was going on, in past time.

Je lisais quand vous êtes entré.	I was reading when you came in.
Je lisais beaucoup autrefois.	I used to read a great deal.

The *past indefinite* tense represents the state or action as completed, either now or long since.

J'ai vu votre oncle.   I saw (*or* have seen) your uncle.
Je l'ai vu il y a un an.   I saw him a year ago.

The *past definite* tense is used to express what occurred in a time entirely elapsed, and of which the present day forms no part.

Je vis votre oncle l'an dernier.   I saw your uncle last year.

Rem. It is equally correct in such cases to use the past indefinite tense, and to say: **J'ai vu votre oncle l'an dernier.** In conversation, this tense is almost always preferred to the past definite.

The *pluperfect* tense denotes that an action or event had taken place at, or before, some past time mentioned.

Vous étiez parti quand je suis arrivé.   You had started when I arrived.

The *past anterior* tense is used to express the earlier of two actions immediately succeeding each other, when the latter action is expressed by a verb in the past definite tense.

Je partis aussitôt que je me fus levé.   I started as soon as I had risen.

The *future* tenses are used to express what will take place in future time.

The *future* tenses are used in French, though not in English, after adverbs of time, when the action is placed in the future.

Je partirai quand j'aurai fini mes affaires.   I will start when I have finished my business.

Rem. The *future* tenses are not used after the conjunction si, *if;* but they may be used after si, *whether.*

Je partirai, s'il vient.   I will leave, if he comes.
Je ne sais s'il viendra ou non.   I do not know whether he will come or not.

SYNTAX OF THE VERB.

3. USE OF THE CONDITIONAL MODE.

The conditional mode is used to express what would take place, or would have taken place, if a certain condition were, or had been, fulfilled. The condition, when expressed, is introduced by the conjunction **si**, *if*, with a verb in the imperfect or pluperfect tense of the indicative mood.

Je le ferais, si je pouvais.	I would do it, if I could.
Je l'aurais fait, si j'avais pu.	I would have done it, if I had been able.
Il aurait pu le faire, s'il avait voulu.	He could have done it, if he would.

REM. The conditional mode is not used after **si**, *if;* but may be used after si, *whether.*

Je ne sais s'il viendrait, si je l'invitais.	I do not know whether he would come, if I should invite him.

4. USE OF THE IMPERATIVE MODE.

The imperative mode is used in French, as in English, to exhort or to command.

Rendez-moi heureux.	Make me happy.
Ne me rendez pas malheureux.	Do not make me unhappy.
Rendons-nous utiles aux autres.	Let us render ourselves useful to others.

The third person of the imperative is supplied by the third person of the present tense of the subjunctive mode.

Qu'il le fasse, et qu'ils en rient.   Let him do it, and let them laugh.

Verbs ending in the second person singular of the imperative in **e**, as parle, pense, offre, and also the imperative **va**, add, for the sake of euphony, the letter s before en and y.

Parle de cela.	**Parles-en.**	Speak of that.	Speak of it.
Pense à cela.	**Penses-y.**	Think of that.	Think of it.
Va à la maison.	**Vas-y.**	Go home.	Go there.

5. USE OF THE SUBJUNCTIVE MODE.

The subjunctive mode is used in dependent sentences:

(1.) After verbs and phrases that express pleasure, pain, surprise, will, desire, command, doubt, fear, etc.

Je suis bien aise que vous ayez réussi.	I am glad that you succeeded.
Il s'étonne que nous soyons ici.	He wonders that we are here.
Il désire que nous partions.	He wishes us to leave.
Je doute qu'il le sache.	I doubt his knowing it.

(2.) After interrogative and negative sentences which imply doubt.

Croyez-vous qu'il le sache?	Do you believe that he knows it?
Je ne pense pas qu'il le sache.	I do not think that he knows it.

(3.) After impersonal verbs.

Il est temps que vous partiez.	It is time for you to leave.
Il faut qu'il le fasse.	He must do it.

(4.) In a relative sentence that limits one of the following words: le plus, le moins, le mieux, le meilleur, le pire, le moindre, le seul, le premier, le dernier, etc.

Vous êtes le premier qui l'ait su.	You are the first who knew it.
Le seul qui puisse le faire.	The only one who can do it.

(5.) In a relative sentence limiting a word of an indefinite sense.

Je cherche quelqu'un qui le sache.	I seek some one who knows it.
Il y a peu d'hommes qui le sachent.	There are few men who know it.

(6.) After certain conjunctions. (See Fifty-second Lesson.)

The tense of the verb, when it is in the subjunctive mode, depends on the tense of the governing verb.

The present and future tenses require the present or past tense of the subjunctive.

Je doute	qu'il le fasse.	I doubt	his doing it.
Je douterai	qu'il l'ait fait.	I shall doubt	his having done it.

SYNTAX OF THE VERB.

The past tenses and the tenses of the conditional require the imperfect or pluperfect of the subjunctive.

J'ai douté	qu'il le fit.	I doubted	his doing it.
Je douterais	qu'il l'eût fait.	I would doubt	his having done it.

6. USE OF THE INFINITIVE.

The infinitive may be used as subject or as object.

Parler trop est imprudent.	To speak too much is imprudent.
Je veux vous rendre ce service.	I will render you that service.
Je le ferai pour vous obliger.	I will do it to oblige you.

The past tense of the infinitive is used after the preposition **après**, whereas, in English, the present or compound participle is used.

Après avoir dit cela il sortit.	After saying that he went out.

7. GOVERNMENT OF VERBS.

Some verbs are transitive in English and intransitive or neuter in French; and again, some verbs are transitive or active in French, which are intransitive in English.

User de quelque chose.	To use a thing.
Abuser de quelque chose.	To abuse a thing.
Douter de quelque chose.	To doubt a thing.
Jouir de quelque chose.	To enjoy a thing.
Convenir à quelqu'un.	To suit somebody.
Obéir à quelqu'un.	To obey somebody.
Plaire à quelqu'un.	To please somebody.
Répondre à quelqu'un.	To answer somebody.
Ressembler à quelqu'un.	To resemble somebody.

And

Demander quelque chose.	To ask for something.
Désirer quelque chose.	To wish for something.
Payer quelque chose.	To pay for something.
Devoir quelque chose.	To owe for something.
Écouter quelqu'un.	To listen to somebody
Regarder quelqu'un.	To look at somebody.

Some verbs require a different preposition in French than they do in English.

Penser à, to think of. **Rire de,** to laugh at.

The following are some of the verbs which govern the infinitive directly (see Twentieth Lesson, 2):

Aimer mieux, to like better.
Compter, to intend.
Croire, to believe.
Entendre, to hear.
Faire, to get.
Pouvoir, to be able.
Savoir, to know how.
Voir, to see.
Vouloir, to be willing.

The following are some of the verbs which require à before the dependent infinitive (see Twenty-second Lesson):

Aimer, to like.
S'amuser, to amuse one's self.
Apprendre, to learn.
Chercher, to seek.
Donner, to give.
Employer, to employ.
Inviter, to invite.
Mettre, to put.
Parvenir, to succeed (in).
Penser, to think.
Perdre, to lose.
Se plaire, to delight (in).

The following are some of the verbs which require de before the dependent infinitive (see Twenty-second Lesson):

Cesser, to cease.
Conseiller, to advise.
Se dépêcher, to make haste.
Dire, to tell.
Finir, to finish.
Négliger, to neglect.
Oublier, to forget.
Permettre, to permit.
Promettre, to promise.
Refuser, to refuse.
Rire, to laugh.
Tâcher, to endeavor.

Some verbs require different prepositions, according to the sense in which they are used, **tarder à,** *to delay;* **tarder de,** (impers.) *to long;* **venir,** *to come;* **venir à,** *to happen;* **venir de,** *to come from, to have just...*

Il tarde bien à venir.	He is long in coming.
Il me tarde de le voir.	I long to see him.
Je viens travailler.	I come to work.
S'il vient à mourir.	If he happens to die.
Je viens de le voir.	I have just seen him.

*Appartenir, To Belong. Être à, To Belong.

À qui appartient cette maison? To whom does that house belong?

Être à is used in the sense of **appartenir**.

SYNTAX OF THE VERB. 235

À qui est cela ? — Whose is that?
C'est à moi. — That is mine.
À qui sont ces gants ? — Whose gloves are these?
Ils sont à ma tante ; *or*
Ce sont les gants de ma tante. } They are my aunt's.

Vocabulary 51.

Le peuple, the people.
Le palais, the palace.
Une troupe, a band.
Les troupes (*plur.*), the troops.
La bataille, the battle.
Un service, a service.
Garder, to keep ; to guard.
Tuer, to kill.
Retrouver, to find (*what was lost*).
Faire attendre, to keep waiting.
S'étonner, to wonder.
Vouloir du bien (à), to wish well.

Theme 51.

Agreement. 1. My friend and I shall start to-morrow. 2. You or Henry will come with us. 3. The people were complaining of the conduct of the troops. 4. A band of soldiers kept the door of the palace. 5. A great many soldiers were killed in the last battle. 6. They are our friends, who invited us. 7. It is you, gentlemen, who refused to come.

Use of the Tenses. 8. How long have you been here? 9. I have been here since Saturday. 10. I have been waiting two hours for my brother. 11. I have lost my grammar. 12. Yesterday I found it among the books which you returned to me. 13. Last winter we were in Paris. 14. One day I received a letter which called me back to New York ; my father was sick. 15. As soon as I had learned this news, I came back to the United States. 16. I shall start when my brother comes. 17. I will start to-day, if he comes. 18. I do not know whether he will come.

Conditional Mode. 19. He would come, if he could. 20. He would have come yesterday, if it had not rained. 21. I would render you that service, if *it* (ce) were *in* (en) my power. 22. I would have done so already.

Imperative Mode. 23. Do not keep me waiting long. 24. Let us render ourselves agreeable to those of whom we have need.

Subjunctive Mode. 25. I am glad that you have come. 26. I am sorry that your brother is sick. 27. I wonder that he has not written to me. 28. I doubt *whether* (que) he knows that you are here. 29. I do not think that he knows it. 30. It is time for us to go (away). 31. I must first finish what I am doing. 32. The professor wished me to write my exercise before I left.

Government. 33. Do you doubt that? 34. I do not doubt it. 35. You enjoy great advantages; do not abuse them. 36. Try to please your teachers; they wish you well. 37. I owe you for these boots; I will pay you for them as soon as I receive my money. 38. Whose penknife is this? 39. It is mine. 40. That store belongs to my uncle. 41. He is long in coming. 42. I long to see him. 43. He has just arrived. 44. I knew that it was he, because he resembles your father.

FIFTY-SECOND LESSON.

THE PARTICIPLE.

The principal uses of the participles, present and past, have been explained in the Twenty-first Lesson.

The present participle may be used without en:

1. To state a determinative or explanatory circumstance, with reference to the subject or object of the verb.

Un jeune homme connaissant ses intérêts, ne négligera pas ses études.	A young man knowing his own interest, will not neglect his studies.
J'ai vu cet homme tenant un livre à la main.	I have seen that man holding a book in his hand.

2. To state a conclusive circumstance, in an absolute manner.

La paix étant conclue, les armées se retirèrent.	Peace being concluded, the armies withdrew.

THE ADVERB.

Davantage, plus, *more*. **Davantage** can have no dependent words following it; but is preferable to **plus** at the end of a sentence.

Si, *so;* **tant,** *so much,* denote extension; **aussi,** *as, so;* **autant,** *as much, so much,* denote comparison.

SYNTAX OF THE PREPOSITION.

Rem. **Si** may be used for **aussi**, and **tant** for **autant**, in negative sentences.

Plutôt, plus tôt. Plutôt means *rather;* and plus tôt, *sooner.*

Tout à coup, means *suddenly;* and **tout d'un coup,** *all in one stroke.*

De suite means *in succession;* and **tout de suite,** *immediately.*

Adverbs are generally placed immediately after the verb. When the verb is in a compound tense, the adverb is placed between the auxiliary verb and the past participle. Adverbs of several syllables and adverbial phrases are placed after the participle. Adverbs denoting time absolute, as: **hier, aujourd'hui, demain,** etc, may be placed before the subject; but no adverb can be placed between the subject and the verb.

Adverbs of comparison are repeated with each word which they modify. Adverbs of quantity need not be repeated; but the preposition **de** must precede each noun which the adverb limits.

THE NEGATIVE PARTICLE NE.

The particle **ne** is required before a verb in the subjunctive mode:

1. After verbs that express fear or apprehension, when they are used affirmatively.

2. After the verbs **empêcher,** *to prevent, to hinder,* and **prendre garde,** *to beware; to take care* (*not*).

3. After **désespérer,** *to despair;* **disconvenir,** *to disown. to deny;* **douter,** *to doubt;* **nier,** *to deny,* when they are used negatively.

4. After the conjunctions **à moins que,** *unless;* **de crainte que, de peur que,** *for fear that.*

5. **Ne** is also required before the verb in the second member of a comparative sentence, when the first member is affirmative.

Il est plus riche qu'on ne le pense. He is richer than people think.

Il parle autrement qu'il ne pense. He speaks otherwise than he thinks.

THE PREPOSITION.

À, dans, en, *in.* À directs the mind to the locality; **dans,** points to the inside of it; **en** and the noun which it precedes, form a kind of adverbial phrase. **Il est au magasin,** *he is at the store.* **Il est dans le magasin,** *he is in the store.* **Le café est en magasin,** *the coffee is stored.*

En, à, *to* or *in*. The preposition **en** is used before the names of countries of the feminine gender; and the preposition **à** and the article, before the names of countries of the masculine gender. **En France,** *to* or *in France*. **Au Mexique,** *to* or *in Mexico*.

When **dans** and **en** are used with reference to time, **dans** precedes the epoch at which, and **en** the period in which, anything is to be, or can be, done. **Je pars dans deux heures,** *I start in two hours*. **Je peux finir cet ouvrage en deux heures,** *I can finish that work in two hours*.

De, avec, chez, *with*. **De** expresses result or consequence; **avec** has the meaning of *together with, by means of;* **chez** has reference to one's country, one's home. **Qu'avez-vous fait de mon canif?** *What have you done with my penknife?* (*Where is it?*) **Qu'avez-vous fait avec mon canif?** *What have you done with my penknife?* (*What use have you made of it?*) **Chez les Romains c'était la coutume.** *Among the Romans it was the custom.*

De, *than*. After **plus** and **moins, de** is used before a numeral adjective, and not **que**: **plus de vingt,** *more than twenty;* **moins de dix,** *less than ten*.

Avant, devant, *before*. **Avant** denotes priority, **devant,** position. **Il est venu avant moi. Il s'est placé devant moi.**

Entre, parmi, *among*. **Entre** is used distributively; **parmi** means *in the middle of*. **Entre nous,** *among us*. **Parmi le peuple,** *among the people*.

Vers, envers, *towards*. **Vers** is used to express physical direction, and **envers** to express moral direction. **Vers le nord,** *towards the north*. **Poli envers tout le monde,** *polite towards everybody*.

The prepositions **à, de, en, sans,** are repeated before each word.

The Conjunction.

Certain conjunctions are always followed by the subjunctive mode. The following are some of them, which are of frequent use.

Afin que, in order that.
À moins que, (Rem.) unless.
Avant que, before.
Bien que, although.

De crainte que, } for fear; lest
De peur que, } (Rem.)
Au cas *or* **en cas que,** in case.
Pour que, in order that.

SYNTAX OF THE CONJUNCTION.

Pourvu que, provided.
Quoique, although.
Sans que, without.
Supposé que, suppose.

REM. À moins que, de crainte que, de peur que, require ne before the verb.

After the conjunction que, the verb is put in the indicative or the subjunctive, according as the preceding proposition may require.

The conjunction cannot be omitted; but instead of repeating any of the compound conjunctions, que is used in their place, and governs the verb in the same manner as the conjunction for which it stands.

Que, used to avoid the conjunction si, *if,* governs the subjunctive mode, although si requires the verb in the indicative. **Si vous venez et que je ne sois pas au logis, attendez-moi.** *If you come and (if) I am not in, wait for me.*

Que, in exclamatory sentences, is used for comme and for combien.

Que c'est beau!	How beautiful that is!
Que vous êtes bon!	How good you are!
Que de bonté vous avez!	How much kindness you have!

Et is used to join similar parts of an affirmative proposition; ni to join similar parts of a negative proposition.

Il ressemble à son frère, et de visage et de caractère.	He resembles his brother, both in face and disposition.
Il ne ressemble pas à son frère, ni de visage ni de caractère.	He does not resemble his brother, either in face or disposition.

Ni is used in connection with non plus (*either,* in a negative sense). **Il ne veut pas le faire, ni moi non plus.** *He will not do it, nor I either.* **Mon frère ne veut pas le faire non plus.** *My brother will not do it either.*

Vocabulary 52.

La parole, the word.	Inviter, to invite.
La difficulté, the difficulty.	*Secourir quelqu'un, to come to one's assistance.
Un principe, a principle.	
Le Canada, Canada.	*Offrir (de), to offer (for).
En voiture, in a carriage.	Renoncer (à), to renounce.
Dans l'embarras, in difficulty.	Je vous en prie, pray.

Theme 52.

Present Part. 1. Our friends seeing that we were in difficulty, came promptly to our assistance. 2. On coming in, I saw the professor holding your copy-book in his hand. 3. He read your exercise, and having read it he said, this is the best exercise I have seen to-day.

Adverbs. 4. I offered you fifty dollars for your boat; and I will not give any more *for it* (en). 5. Do not laugh so loud. 6. Do not speak so much. 7. I would rather die than renounce my principles. 8. He had no sooner pronounced these words than he went out. 9. Your friend has been absent three days in succession. 10. I will go to him immediately. 11. I often see him, but I seldom speak to him. 12. I never had any difficulties with him.

The Particle Ne. 13. I fear that he may be sick. 14. I will prevent his going out. 15. Take care that he does not hear you. 16. I do not doubt his being sick. 17. I shall not go there, unless he invites me *personally* (lui-même). 18. His conduct is much better than it was formerly.

Prepositions. 19. My father is in his office; my mother is in her room; and my sister has gone out in a carriage. 20. My uncle was in France last year, and he has gone to Mexico now. 21. I will go to Canada in a fortnight. 22. I wrote this exercise in forty minutes. 23. What have you done with my grammar; I cannot find it anywhere? 24. What have you done with my gold pen; it is quite spoiled? 25. I have more than ten pens; but not one is good. 26. I shall not go out before noon. 27. There is a carriage before the door. 28. I will come towards evening. 29. Pray, be polite towards everybody.

Conjunctions. 30. If you see my brother before he goes to the office, give him this letter. 31. I send it to him (in order) that he may comprehend the situation of that business. 32. Provided you do your duty, all will be well. 33. If you have to leave, and cannot come to see me, write to me. 34. How kind you are! 35. How many fine things one sees in Paris! 36. He will never believe that story. 37. I cannot believe it either. 38. My father does not believe that he has done it, or that he ever will do it.

APPENDIX.

ADDITIONAL VOCABULARIES

I.

Une famille, a family.
Le père, *the father.*
La mère, *the mother.*
Les enfants, *the children.*
Un fils, *a son.*
Une fille, *a daughter.*
Un frère, *a brother.*
Une sœur, *a sister.*
Un frère jumeau, *a twin-brother.*
Une sœur jumelle, *a twin sister.*
Le grand-père, *the grand-father.*
La grand'mère, *the grand-mother.*
Un petit-fils, *a grandson.*
Une petite-fille, *a grand-daughter.*
Un oncle, *an uncle.*
Une tante, *an aunt.*
Un neveu, *a nephew.*
Une nièce, *a niece.*
Un cousin, *a cousin, m.*
Une cousine, *a cousin, f.*
Un parrain, *a godfather.*
Une marraine, *a godmother.*
Un filleul, *a godson.*
Une filleule, *a goddaughter.*
Un époux, }
Un mari,   } *a husband.*
Une épouse, }
Une femme, } *a wife.*
Un beau-père, *a father-in-law.*
Une belle-mère, *a mother-in-law.*
Un beau-fils, }
Un gendre,   } *a son-in-law.*
Une belle-fille, }
Une bru,   } *a daughter-in-law.*
Un beau-frère, *a brother-in-law.*
Une belle-sœur, *a sister-in-law.*
Un parent, *a relation, m.*
Une parente, *a relation, f.*
Un proche parent, *a near relation.*
Un parent éloigné, *a distant relation.*
Un cousin germain, *a first-cousin, m.*
Une cousine germaine, *a first-cousin, f.*
Un tuteur, *a guardian.*
Un pupille, *a ward, m.*
Une pupille, *a ward, f.*

II.

Le corps, the body.
La tête, *the head.*
Le front, *the forehead.*
La figure, *the face.*
Le visage, *the face.*
La peau, *the skin.*
Le teint, *the complexion.*
La barbe, *the beard.*
Les traits, *the features.*
Un œil, *an eye.*
Les yeux, *the eyes.*
La prunelle, *the eyeball.*
Les sourcils, *the eyebrows.*
Les paupières, *the eyelids.*
Le nez, *the nose.*
La bouche, *the mouth.*
Les lèvres, *the lips.*
Une dent, *a tooth.*
Les gencives, *the gums.*
Le palais, *the palate.*
La langue, *the tongue.*
Le gosier, *the throat.*
Les joues, *the cheeks.*
Les favoris, *the whiskers.*
Le menton, *the chin.*
Les oreilles, *the ears.*
Le cou, *the neck.*
Les épaules, *the shoulders.*
Le dos, *the back.*
La taille, *the waist.*
Les membres, *the limbs.*
Le bras, *the arm.*
Le coude, *the elbow.*
La main, *the hand.*
Les doigts, *the fingers.*
Le pouce, *the thumb.*
Les ongles, *the finger-nails.*
La jambe, *the leg.*
Le genou, *the knee.*
Le pied, *the foot.*

242 ADDITIONAL VOCABULARIES.

La cheville, *the ankle.*
Le talon, *the heel.*
La plante, *the sole.*
Un orteil, *a toe.*
La poitrine, *the breast.*
Les poumons, *the lungs.*
L'haleine, *the breath.*
Le cœur, *the heart.*
L'estomac, *the stomach.*
Le foie, *the liver.*
Le sang, *the blood.*
Un os, *a bone.*
Une artère, *an artery.*
Une veine, *a vein.*
Le pouls, *the pulse.*
Les nerfs, *the nerves.*
Les cheveux, *the hair.*
Une boucle, *a curl.*

III.

Un métier, a trade.
Un architecte, *an architect.*
Un fermier, *a farmer.*
Un jardinier, *a gardener.*
Un arpenteur, *a surveyor.*
Un avoué, *a lawyer.*
Un avocat, *a barrister.*
Un médecin, *a physician.*
Un chirurgien, *a surgeon.*
Un dentiste, *a dentist.*
Un pharmacien, *an apothecary.*
Un banquier, *a banker.*
Un négociant, *a merchant.*
Un commerçant, *a tradesman.*
Un marchand, *a shop-keeper.*
Un joaillier, }
Un bijoutier, } *a jeweler.*
Un orfèvre, *a goldsmith.*
Un éditeur, *a publisher.*
Un rédacteur, *an editor.*
Un imprimeur, *a printer.*
Un agent de change, *a stock-broker.*
Un courtier, *a broker.*
Un boulanger, *a baker.*
Un boucher, *a butcher.*
Un épicier, *a grocer.*
Un charpentier, *a carpenter.*
Un menuisier, *a joiner.*
Un ébéniste, *a cabinet-maker.*
Un tailleur, *a tailor.*
Un cordonnier, *a shoemaker.*
Un bottier, *a bootmaker.*
Un chapelier, *a hat-maker.*
Un vitrier, *a glazier.*
Un horloger, *a watchmaker.*
Un coiffeur, *a hair-dresser.*
Un peintre, *a painter.*
Un teinturier, *a dyer.*
Un papetier, *a stationer.*
Un tapissier, *an upholsterer.*
Un carossier, *a coach-maker.*
Un coutelier, *a cutler.*

Un serrurier, *a locksmith.*
Un forgeron, *a blacksmith.*
Un patissier, *a pastry-cook.*
Un confiseur, *a confectioner.*
Un couvreur, *a slater.*
Un maçon, *a mason.*
Un sellier, *a saddler.*
Un plombier, *a plumber.*
Un manufacturier, *a manufacturer.*
Un tisserand, *a weaver.*
Un artisan, *a mechanic.*
Un ouvrier, *a workman.*
Un ramoneur, *a chimney-sweeper.*
Un balayeur, *a sweeper.*
Une marchande de modes, *a milliner.*
Une couturière, *a dress-maker.*
Une lingère, *a seamstress.*
Une blanchisseuse, *a washer-woman.*
Une laitière, *a milk-woman.*
Une bonne, *a child's nurse.*
Une nourrice, *a wet-nurse.*
Une garde, *a nurse for the sick.*

IV.

Les sens, the senses.
Un sens, *a sense.*
La vue, *sight.*
L'ouïe, *hearing.*
L'odorat, *smelling.*
Le goût, *taste.*
Le toucher, *feeling.*
Une sensation, *a sensation.*
Une douleur, *a pain.*
Des élancements, *throbbings.*
Une maladie, *a sickness.*
Un rhume, *a cold.*
Un rhume de cerveau, *a cold in the head.*
Un rhume de poitrine, *a cold on the lungs.*
La toux, *the cough.*
La fièvre, *the fever.*
Un accès de fièvre, *a fit of ague.*
Le frisson, *shivering, cold chills.*
Le mal de gorge, *sore-throat.*
Le mal de tête, *the headache.*
Le mal de dents, *the toothache.*
Le mal de cœur, *sickness, nausea.*
La fièvre scarlatine, *the scarlet fever.*
La petite vérole, *the smallpox.*
La rougeole, *the measles.*
La coqueluche, *the whooping-cough.*
Une fluxion de poitrine, *an inflammation in the chest.*
La névralgie, *neuralgia.*
La gourme, *the mumps.*
Un compère loriot, *a sty.*
Des engelures, *chilblains.*
Un point de côté, *a stitch in the side.*
Le mal de mer, *sea-sickness.*
Le mal du pays, *home-sickness.*
La migraine, *the sick headache.*
Une démangeaison, *an itching.*

ADDITIONAL VOCABULARIES.

La goutte, *the gout.*
Une entorse, *a sprain.*
Une coupure, *a cut.*
Une égratignure, *a scratch.*
Une brûlure, *a burn.*
Une piqûre, *a prick.*
Une cicatrice, *a scar.*
Un remède, *a remedy.*
Une pillule, *a pill.*
Des pastilles, *lozenges.*
Une médecine, *physic.*
Une potion, *a mixture.*
Un gargarisme, *a gargle.*
Un cataplasme, *a poultice.*
Un vésicatoire, *a blister.*
Une saignée, *bleeding.*
Une incision, *cupping.*
Un emplâtre, *a plaster.*
Du taffetas d'Angleterre, *court-plaster.*
De la charpie, *lint.*
De l'onguent, *ointment.*
Une sangsue, *a leech.*
Du soulagement, *relief.*
Une guérison, *a cure.*
Une rechute, *a relapse.*
L'agonie, *the death-pangs.*
Le râle, *the death-rattle.*

V.

Un trousseau, a set of clothes.

La toilette, *the dress.*
La coiffure, *the head-dress.*
Un nécessaire, *a dressing-case.*
Un peigne, *a comb.*
Une brosse, *a brush.*
Des ciseaux, *scissors.*
Un rasoir, *a razor.*
Du savon, *soap.*
De la pommade, *pomatum.*
Un chapeau, *a hat, a bonnet.*
La forme, *the crown.*
Le bord, *the brim.*
La coiffe, *the lining.*
Une casquette, *a cap.*
Des habits, *clothes.*
Un habit, *a coat.*
Une redingote, }
Un paletôt, } *a greatcoat.*
Un gilet, *a waistcoat.*
Une veste, *a vest, a jacket.*
Le collet, *the collar.*
Les manches, *the sleeves.*
Les pans, *the skirts.*
Une couture, *a seam.*
La doublure, *the lining.*
Les revers, *the facings.*
Un pli, *a wrinkle.*
Une poche, *a pocket.*
Un bouton, *a button.*
Une boutonnière, *a button-hole.*
Des manchettes, *cuffs.*
Un pantalon, *a pair of pantaloons.*

Un caleçon, *a pair of drawers.*
Des bretelles, *suspenders.*
Le linge, *the linen.*
Une chemise, *a shirt.*
Une chemisette, *a shirt-bosom.*
Un col, *a collar, a stock.*
Une cravate, *a cravat.*
Une robe, *a dress.*
Une robe de chambre, *a dressing-gown.*
Une robe de bal, *a party-dress.*
Une robe de ville, *a walking-dress.*
Un jupon, *a petticoat.*
Un corset, *a corset.*
Les œillets, *the holes.*
Le lacet, *the lacing.*
Un fichu, *a neckerchief.*
Un tablier, *an apron.*
Une ceinture, *a belt.*
Un ruban, *a ribbon.*
Un cordon, *a string.*
Un nœud, *a knot.*
Une boucle, *a buckle.*
Une agrafe, *a clasp.*
Un crochet, *a hook.*
Une parure, *a set of jewels.*
Un collier, *a necklace.*
Un bracelet, *a bracelet.*
Une bague, *a ring.*
Une boucle d'oreille, *an ear-ring.*
Une écharpe, *a scarf.*
Un châle, *a shawl.*
Un manteau, *a cloak.*
Un manchon, *a muff.*
Un voile, *a veil.*
Des bottes, *boots.*
Des bottines, *ladies' boots.*
Des souliers, *shoes.*
Des guêtres, *gaiters.*
Des brodequins, *laced boots.*
Des pantoufles, *slippers.*
Des bas, *stockings.*
Une jarretière, *a garter.*
Un mouchoir, *a handkerchief.*
Des gants, *gloves.*
Un éventail, *a fan.*
Une lorgnette, *an opera-glass.*
Une ombrelle, *a parasol.*
Un flacon d'odeurs, *a smelling-bottle.*

VI.

Une maison, a house.

La façade, *the front.*
Le perron, *the flight of steps.*
La porte, *the door.*
Le numéro, *the number.*
Le marteau, *the knocker.*
La sonnette, *the bell.*
La clef, *the key.*
Un loquet, *a latch.*
Le décrottoir, *the scraper.*
Le vestibule, *the hall, the entry.*
Le rez-de-chaussée, *the ground-floor.*

La salle, *the parlor.*
Un mur, *a wall.*
Une cloison, *a partition.*
L'escalier, *the stairs.*
La rampe, *the banisters.*
Les marches, *the steps.*
Un étage, *a story.*
Un appartement, *an appartment.*
Une chambre, *a room.*
La chambre de devant, *the front room.*
La chambre du fond, *the back room.*
Une serrure, *a lock.*
Le trou de serrure, *the key-hole.*
Un verrou, *a bolt.*
Un gond, *a hinge.*
La fenêtre, *the window.*
Le chassis, *the sash.*
Un carreau de vitre, *a pane of glass.*
Un rideau, *a curtain.*
Une marquise, *an awning.*
Un gland, *a tassel.*
Un volet, *a shutter.*
Une jalousie, *a blind.*
Un balcon, *a balcony.*
Le salon, *the drawing-room.*
Le plafond, *the ceiling.*
La tenture, *the paper.*
La cheminée, *the chimney.*
L'âtre, *the hearth.*
Le plancher, *the floor.*
Une chambre à coucher, *a bed-room.*
Un cabinet de toilette, *a dressing-room.*
Une armoire, *a closet.*
La salle à manger, *the dining room.*
La chambre des enfants, *the nursery.*
Une bibliothèque, *a library.*
Un grenier, *a garret.*
Une mansarde, *an attic.*
Le toit, *the roof.*
Une poutre, *a beam.*
Une solive, *a joist.*
Une plate-forme, *a platform.*
Une gouttière, *a spout.*
Un tuyau, *a pipe.*
Un égout, *a drain.*
Une pierre, *a stone.*
Une brique, *a brick.*
Une ardoise, *a slate.*
De la chaux, *lime.*
Du mortier, *mortar.*
Du ciment, *cement.*
Du plâtre, *plaster.*
Le propriétaire, *the landlord.*
Le loyer, *the rent.*
Un locataire, *a tenant.*

VII.

Le mobilier, the furniture.
Un meuble, *a piece of furniture.*
Les pincettes, *the tongs.*
La pelle, *the shovel.*
Le tisonnier, *the poker.*
Le soufflet, *the bellows.*
Le garde-cendre, *the fender.*
La grille, *the grate.*
Les chenets, *the andirons.*
Le seau à charbon, *the coal-scuttle.*
Le coin du feu, *the fireside.*
Un écran, *a screen.*
Un calorifère, *a furnace.*
La bouche de chaleur, *the register.*
Une table, *a table.*
Une chaise, *a chair.*
Un fauteuil, *an arm-chair.*
Un sofa, *a sofa.*
Un coussin, *a cushion.*
Un tabouret, *a stool.*
Une armoire, *a cupboard.*
Les tablettes, *the shelves.*
Une commode, *a chest of drawers.*
Un tiroir, *a drawer.*
Une bibliothèque, *a book-case.*
Les rayons, *the shelves.*
Une toilette, *a toilet-table.*
Un lavabo, *a wash-stand.*
Un pot à l'eau, *a pitcher.*
La cuvette, *the wash-basin.*
Une serviette, *a napkin ; a towel.*
Un essuie-main, *a towel.*
Un miroir, *a looking-glass.*
Un lit, *a bed.*
Le bois de lit, *the bedstead.*
Une paillasse, *a straw bed.*
Un matelas, *a mattrass.*
Un lit de plume, *a feather bed.*
Un oreiller, *a pillow.*
Une taie d'oreiller, *a pillow-case.*
Un traversin, *a bolster.*
Un drap, *a sheet.*
Une couverture, *a blanket.*
Le couvre-pied, *the coverlet.*
Les rideaux, *the curtains.*
Une cousinière, *a mosquito net.*
Un tableau, *a picture.*
Le cadre, *the frame.*
Le verre, *the glass.*
La gravure, *the engraving.*
Une pendule, *a time-piece.*
Un vase, *a vase.*
Un chandelier, *a candlestick.*
Une chandelle, *a candle.*
Une bougie, *a wax-candle.*
La mèche, *the wick.*
Une allumette, *a match.*
Un lustre, *a chandelier.*
Le gaz, *the gas.*
Un bec-de-gaz, *a burner.*
Une lampe, *a lamp.*
De la porcelaine, *china.*
Une service de porcelaine, *a set of china*
Une statue, *a statue.*
Le piédestal, *the pedestal.*
Un ornement, *an ornament.*
La dorure, *the gilding.*
Un tapis, *a carpet.*

ADDITIONAL VOCABULARIES.

Un buffet, *a sideboard.*
Un plateau, *a waiter.*
Une tasse et la soucoupe, *a cup and saucer.*
Un bol, *a bowl.*
Un sucrier, *a sugar-bowl.*
Les pinces à sucre, *the sugar-tongs.*
Un théière, *a tea-pot.*
Une cafetière, *a coffee-pot.*
L'argenterie, *the silver.*
L'huilier, *the cruet-stand.*
La burette à l'huile, *the oil cruet.*
La salière, *the salt-cellar.*
La poivrière, *the pepper-box.*
Le moutardier, *the mustard-pot.*
Le saladier, *the salad dish.*
Une carafe, *a decanter.*
La cuisine, *the kitchen.*
La batterie de cuisine, *kitchen utensils.*
Un four, *an oven.*
Un fourneau, *a range.*
Une bouilloire, *a kettle.*
Une casserole, *a saucepan.*
La cave, *the cellar.*
Un baril, *a barrel.*
Un baquet, *a tub.*
Un seau, *a pail.*
Un balai, *a broom.*
Un trépied, *a trivet.*
Un fer à repasser, *a flat-iron.*
Un gril, *a gridiron.*
Un séchoir, *a clothes horse.*
Un hachoir, *a chopping knife.*

VIII.

Un repas, a meal.
Le déjeuner, *breakfast.*
Le dîner, *dinner.*
Le souper, *supper.*
Une collation, *a collation.*
Un goûter, *a luncheon.*
Un service, *a course (at dinner).*
Le dessert, *the dessert.*
La nappe, *the table-cloth.*
Une serviette, *a napkin.*
Une cuiller, or cuillère, *a spoon.*
Une fourchette, *a fork.*
Un couteau, *a knife.*
Du pain tendre, or frais, *new bread.*
Du pain rassis, *stale bread.*
Du pain de ménage, *home-made bread.*
Un pain, *a loaf.*
L'entame, *the first cut.*
De la croûte, *crust.*
De la mie, *crumb.*
Une tartine, *a slice of bread and butter.*
Des petits pains, *rolls.*
Du café, *coffee.*
Du thé, *tea.*
Du chocolat, *chocolate.*
Du lait, *milk.*
De la crême, *cream.*

Du beurre, *butter.*
Du fromage, *cheese.*
Du vermicelle, *vermicelli.*
Du riz, *rice.*
Un œuf, *an egg.*
La coque, *the shell.*
Le blanc, *the white.*
Le jaune, *the yolk.*
Un œuf à la coque, *a boiled egg.*
Des œufs brouillés, *scrambled eggs.*
Des œufs pochés, *poached eggs.*
Des œufs frits, *fried eggs.*
Une omelette, *an omelet.*
Du flan, *custard.*
Un plat, *a dish.*
Une assiette, *a plate.*
Un coquetier, *an egg-cup.*
Une soupière, *a soup tureen.*
De la soupe, *soup.*
Du bouillon, *broth, beef-soup.*
De la viande, *meat.*
Du bœuf, *beef.*
Du rôti, *roast beef.*
Du bouilli, *boiled beef.*
Du bifteck, *beefsteak.*
Du veau, *veal.*
Une côtelette de veau, *a veal-cutlet.*
De la viande bien cuite, *well-done meat.*
De la viande peu cuite, *rare meat.*
Du hachis, *mince meat.*
Du mouton, *mutton.*
Une côtelette de mouton, *a mutton-chop.*
Un gigot de mouton, *a leg of mutton.*
De l'agneau, *lamb.*
Du porc, *pork.*
Du saindoux, *lard.*
Du lard, *bacon.*
Du jambon, *ham.*
Une tranche de jambon, *a slice of ham.*
Du gras, *fat.*
Du maigre, *lean.*
Du jus, *gravy.*
De la sauce, *made-gravy.*
Un ragoût, *a stew.*
Des légumes, *vegetables.*
Un chou, *a cabbage.*
Un navet, *a turnip.*
Une carrotte, *a carrot.*
Un chou-fleur, *a cauliflower.*
Un artichaut, *an artichoke.*
Des asperges, *asparagus.*
Des épinards, *spinach.*
Des haricots verts, *string-beans.*
Des pois, *peas.*
Des petits pois, *green peas.*
Une betterave, *a beet.*
Du sel, *salt.*
Du poivre, *pepper.*
De la moutarde, *mustard.*
Des épices, *spices.*
Des cornichons, *pickles.*
Une bouteille, *a bottle.*
Le bouchon, *the cork.*

Un tire-bouchon, *a corkscrew.*
Une salade, *a salad.*
De la laitue, *lettuce.*
Du céléri, *celery.*
Un oignon, *an onion.*
Du persil, *parsley.*
De l'oseille, *sorrel.*
Une volaille, *a fowl.*
Du gibier, *game.*
Du poisson, *fish.*
Un pâté, *a meat-pie.*
Un tourte, *a pie.*
Une tarte, *a tart.*
Une pomme, *an apple.*
Une poire, *a pear.*
Des cerises, *cherries.*
Des groseilles, *currants.*
Des groseilles à maquereau, *gooseberries.*
Une pêche, *a peach.*
Un abricot, *an apricot.*
Une prune, *a plum.*
Des fraises, *strawberries.*
Des framboises, *raspberries.*
Des noix, *walnuts.*
Des noisettes, *hazelnuts.*
Du raisin, *grapes.*
Des bonbons, *sweetmeats.*
Des dragées, *sugar-plums.*
Une amande, *an almond.*
Une praline, *a burnt almond.*
Du miel, *honey.*
Des compotes, *stewed fruit.*
Des confitures, *preserves.*
Une gelée, *a jelly.*
Une glace, *an ice.*
Des beignets, *fritters.*
Des crêpes, *pancakes.*
Purée de pommes de terre, *mashed potatoes.*
Des patates, *sweet potatoes.*
De la sauce, *sauce.*
Compote de pommes, *apple-sauce.*

IX.

Un animal, an animal.
Une bête, *a beast.*
Un taureau, *a bull.*
Un bœuf, *an ox.*
Une vache, *a cow.*
Un veau, *a calf.*
Un bélier, *a ram.*
Un mouton, *a sheep.*
Une brebis, *a ewe, a sheep.*
Un agneau, *a lamb.*
Un bouc, *a he-goat.*
Une chèvre, *a she goat.*
Un cheval, *a horse.*
Une jument, *a mare.*
Un poulain, *a colt.*
Un âne, *an ass.*
Un chien, *a dog.*
Un chat, *a cat.*

Un renard, *a fox.*
Un cerf, *a stag.*
Un daim, *a deer.*
Une biche, *a kid.*
Un faon, *a fawn.*
Un loup, *a wolf.*
Un sanglier, *a wild boar.*
Un cochon, *a hog.*
Un lièvre, *a hare.*
Un lapin, *a rabbit.*
Un chien de chasse, *a hound.*
Un épagneul, *a spaniel.*
Un basset, *a terrier.*
Un chien d'arrêt, *a setter.*
Un terre-neuve, *a Newfoundland.*
Un lion, *a lion.*
Une lionne, *a lioness.*
Un tigre, *a tiger.*
Une tigresse, *a tigress.*
Un léopard, *a leopard.*
Un éléphant, *an elephant.*
Un chameau, *a camel.*
Une girafe, *a giraffe.*
Un ours, *a bear.*
Un singe, *a monkey.*
Un castor, *a beaver.*
Un oiseau, *a bird.*
Un moineau, *a sparrow.*
Une alouette, *a lark.*
Une hirondelle, *a swallow.*
Un rossignol, *a nightingale.*
Un serin, *a canary.*
Un rouge-gorge, *a robin.*
Un merle, *a blackbird.*
Un perroquet, *a parrot.*
Un paon, *a peacock.*
Un corbeau, *a raven.*
Une corneille, *a crow.*
Un hibou, *an owl.*
Une chauve-souris, *a bat.*
Un coq, *a cock.*
Une poule, *a hen.*
Un poulet, *a chicken.*
Un pigeon, *a pigeon.*
Une colombe, *a dove.*
Un dindon ⎫
Une dinde ⎭ *a turkey.*
Un canard, *a duck.*
Un cygne, *a swan.*
Une perdrix, *a partridge.*
Une bécasse, *a woodcock.*
Une bécassine, *a snipe.*
Une caille, *a quail.*
Une autruche, *an ostrich.*
Une mouette, *a gull.*
Un aigle, *an eagle.*
Une oie, *a goose.*
Un poisson, *a fish.*
Une baleine, *a whale.*
Un requin, *a shark.*
Une morue, *a cod.*
Une raie, *a skate.*
Un saumon, *a salmon.*

Un brochet, *a pike*.
Une merluche, *a haddock*.
Un éperlan, *a smelt*.
Une truite, *a trout*.
Une perche, *a perch*.
Une anguille, *an eel*.
Un maquereau, *a mackerel*.
Un hareng, *a herring*.
Une alose, *a shad*.
Un homard, *a lobster*.
Une crevette, *a shrimp*.
Une huître, *an oyster*.
Des insectes, *insects*.
Des reptiles, *reptiles*.
Une mouche, *a fly*.
Une abeille, *a bee*.
Une guêpe, *a wasp*.
Une sauterelle, *a grasshopper*.
Une couturière, *a lady bird*.
Un papillon, *a butterfly*.
Une demoiselle, *a dragon-fly*.
Un moustique, *a mosquito*.
Un cousin, *a gnat ; a mosquito*.
Une teigne, *a moth*.
Un escarbot, *a beetle*.
Un limaçon, *a snail*.
Un serpent, *a snake*.
Une chenille, *a caterpillar*.
Un ver, *a worm*.
Un lézard, *a lizard*.
Une souris, *a mouse*.
Une taupe, *a mole*.
Un crapaud, *a toad*.
Une grenouille, *a frog*.
Une araignée, *a spider*.
Une punaise, *a bedbug*.
Une puce, *a flea*.
Un perce-oreille, *an earwig*.
Une fourmi, *an ant*.
Un grillon, *a cricket*.
Une sangsue, *a leech*.

X.

Les arbres, the trees.
Un chêne, *an oak*.
Un orme, *an elm*.
Un tilleul, *a linden*.
Un frêne, *an ash*.
Un pin, *a pine*.
Un sapin, *a fir*.
Un noyer, *a walnut*.
Un châtaignier, } *a chestnut tree*.
Un marronnier, }
Un bouleau, *a birch*.
Un peuplier, *a poplar*.
Un saule, *a willow*.
Un saule pleureur, *a weeping willow*.
Un hêtre, *a beech*.
Un aune, *an alder*.
Un érable, *a maple*.
Un pommier, *an apple-tree*.
Un poirier, *a pear-tree*.

Un pêcher, *a peach-tree*.
Un prunier, *a plum-tree*.
Un cerisier, *a cherry-tree*.
Un mûrier, *a mulberry-tree*.
Des arbrisseaux, *shrubs*.
Un sureau, *an elder*.
Une aubépine, *a hawthorne*.
Un groseiller, *a currant-bush*.
Un figuier, *a fig-tree*.
Un oranger, *an orange-tree*.
Un fraisier, *a strawberry-vine*.
Un framboisier, *a raspberry-bush*.
De la fougère, *fern*.
Mauvaises herbes, *weeds*.
Un chardon, *a thistle*.
Des orties, *nettles*.
Une épine, *a thorn*.
Une liane, *a creeper*.
Du lierre, *ivy*.
De l'herbe, *grass*.
De la mousse, *moss*.
Des fruits, *fruits*.
Des melons d'eau, *water-melons*.
Du cassis, *black currants*.
Des ananas, *pineapples*.
Des mûres, *mulberries*.
Une orange, *an orange*.
Un citron, *a lemon*.
Une figue, *a fig*.
Une châtaigne, } *a chestnut*.
Un marron, }
Une amande, *an almond*.
Des fleurs, *flowers*.
Une rose, *a rose*.
Un œillet, *a pink*.
Un œillet de poète, *a sweet-william*.
Un soleil, *a sunflower*.
Un myrte, *a myrtle*.
Une jacinthe, *a hyacinth*.
Une tulipe, *a tulip*.
Un lis, *a lily*.
Un muguet, *a lily of the valley*.
Du lilac, *a lilac*.
Un géranium, *a geranium*.
Un pavot, *a poppy*.
Un souci, *a marigold*.
Une violette, *a violet*.
Un chèvrefeuille, *a honeysuckle*.
Des pois de senteur, *sweet peas*.
Un bouton d'or, *a buttercup*.
Une belle de jour, *a morning-glory*.
Une campanule, *a blue-bell*.
Un églantier odorant, *a sweetbrier*.
Une pivoine, *a peony*.
Une rose mousseuse, *a moss-rose*.
Une rose des quatre saisons, *a monthly rose*.
Une rose trémière, *a hollyhock*.
Une reine marguerite, *a china aster*.
Un héliotrope, *a heliotrope*.
Une citrouille, *a pumpkin*.
Des tomates, *tomatoes*.
Des champignons, *mushrooms*.

XI.

Le temps, the weather.
La chaleur, *the heat.*
Le froid, *the cold.*
Le ciel, *the sky.*
Le soleil, *the sun.*
Un rayon de soleil, *a sunbeam.*
La lune, *the moon.*
Le clair de lune, *the moonlight.*
Une étoile, *a star.*
L'air, *the air.*
Le vent, *the wind.*
Un nuage, *a cloud.*
La pluie, *the rain.*
Une averse, *a shower.*
Une goutte d'eau, *a drop of rain.*
La neige, *the snow.*
Un flocon de neige, *a flake of snow.*
La grêle, *the hail.*
Un grêlon, *a hailstone.*
Un orage, *a storm.*
Un ouragan, *a hurricane.*
Un coup de vent, *a gust of wind.*
Un éclair, *a flash of lightning.*
Le tonnerre, *the thunder.*
Un coup de tonnerre, *a clap of thunder.*
Un arc-en-ciel, *a rainbow.*
La gelée, *the frost.*
La glace, *the ice.*
Un glaçon, *an icicle.*
Une gelée blanche, *a hoar-frost.*
Le dégel, *the thaw.*
Le brouillard, *the fog.*
La brume, *the mist.*
La rosée, *the dew.*
L'aurore, *the dawn.*
Le point du jour, *the break of day.*
Le lever du soleil, *the sunrise.*
Le coucher du soleil, *the sunset.*
La lumière, *the light.*
L'horizon, *the horizon.*
L'atmosphère, *the atmosphere.*
L'obscurité, *the darkness.*
La sécheresse, *the drought.*
L'humidité, *the dampness.*
De la boue, *mud.*
De la poussière, *dust.*
Une girouette, *a vane.*
Les points cardinaux, *the cardinal points.*
L'est, *east.*
L'ouest, *west.*
Le sud, *south.*
Le nord, *north.*

XII.

Un collége, a college.
Une école, *a school.*
Un externat, *a day-school.*
Un pensionnat, *a boarding-school.*
Le maître de pension, *the schoolmaster.*
La maîtresse, *the schoolmistress.*
Un instituteur, *a teacher, m.*
Une institutrice, *a teacher, f.*
Un or une élève, *a pupil.*
Un écolier, *a scholar, m.*
Une écolière, *a scholar, f.*
La classe (salle de), *the schoolroom.*
Un pupitre, *a desk.*
Un banc, *a bench.*
Une carte, *a map.*
Un globe, *a globe.*
Un tableau, *a blackboard.*
Un dictionnaire, *a dictionary.*
Une grammaire, *a grammar.*
Une leçon, *a lesson.*
La lecture, *reading.*
L'orthographe, *spelling.*
Une dictée, *a dictation.*
Une version, } *a translation.*
Une traduction, }
Une faute, *a mistake.*
Un brouillon, *a rough copy.*
Le calcul, *ciphering.*
Une règle, *a sum or problem.*
La somme, *the sum.*
Une erreur, *a mistake (in calculation).*
Un chiffre, *a figure; a number.*
Un zéro, *a nought.*
Une main de papier, *a quire of paper.*
Une feuille de papier, *a sheet of paper.*
Du papier à lettre, *letter-paper.*
Du papier brouillard or buvard, *blotting paper.*
De l'encre, *ink.*
Un encrier, *an inkstand.*
Une plume, *a pen.*
Une plume métallique, *a steel-pen.*
Un canif, *a penknife.*
De la gomme élastique, *India-rubber.*
Un crayon, *a pencil.*
Un porte-crayon, *a pencil-case.*
Une règle, *a ruler.*
Une ardoise, *a slate.*
Un crayon d'ardoise, *a slate pencil.*
De la cire à cacheter, *sealing-wax.*
Un pain à cacheter, *a wafer.*
Un carton, *a portfolio.*
Un pinceau, *a paint-brush.*
Des crayons, *crayons.*
Des couleurs, *paints.*
L'écriture, *writing.*
Une ligne, *a line.*
Un trait, *a stroke.*
Un plein, *a down-stroke.*
Un délié, *an up-stroke.*
La ponctuation, *punctuation.*
Un chapitre, *a chapter.*
Une page, *a page.*
Un paragraphe, *a paragraph.*
Une phrase, *a sentence.*
Un mot, *a word.*
Une syllabe, *a syllable.*
Une lettre, *a letter.*
Une voyelle, *a vowel.*

ADDITIONAL VOCABULARIES.   249

Une consonne, *a consonant.*
Un point, *a point.*
Deux points, *a colon.*
Point et virgule, *a semicolon.*
Une virgule, *a comma.*
Point d'interrogation, *a note of interrogation.*
Point d'exclamation, *a note of exclamation.*
Des guillemets, *quotation marks.*
Un trait d'union, *a hyphen.*
Une parenthèse, *a bracket.*
Un tréma, *a diæresis.*
Un trait or tiret, *a dash.*

XIII.
Un outil, a tool.
Un marteau, *a hammer.*
Un maillet, *a mallet.*
Une vrille, *a gimlet.*
Un rabot, *a plane.*
Des tenailles, *pincers.*
Un ciseau, *a chisel.*
Une vis, *a screw.*
Un tourne-vis, *a screw-driver.*
Un clou, *a nail.*
Une cheville, *a peg.*
Une enclume, *an anvil.*
Une boîte à ouvrage, *a work box.*
Le couvercle, *the lid.*
Le dedans, *the inside.*
Le fond, *the bottom.*
Une pelote, *a pincushion.*
Une épingle, *a pin.*
Un étui, *a needle-case.*
Une aiguille, *a needle.*
Une aiguille à tapisserie, *a worsted-needle.*
Une aiguille à repriser, *a darning-needle.*
Un paquet d'aiguilles, *a paper of needles.*
Du fil, *thread.*
Un peloton de fil, *a ball of thread.*
Un écheveau de fil, *a skein of thread.*
Une bobine de fil, *a spool of thread.*
Une aiguillée, *a needleful.*
Un dé, *a thimble.*
Une paire de ciseaux, *a pair of scissors.*
Un passe-lacet, *a bodkin.*
Du ganse, *cord.*
Du ruban de fil, *tape.*
Du galon, *braid.*
Des agrafes et portes, *hooks and eyes.*
Des boutons, *buttons.*
Un peloton de laine, *a ball of yarn.*
Un cure-dent, *a tooth-pick.*
Une tabatière, *a snuff-box.*
Un pied, *a foot.*
Un pouce, *an inch.*
Une toise, *a fathom.*
Un mètre, *a meter.*
Un mille, *a mile.*
Une lieue, *a league.*
Une livre, *a pound.*

Une once, *an ounce.*
Un boisseau, *a bushel.*
Un gallon, *a gallon.*
Une pinte, *a pint.*
Une table à jouer, *a card-table.*
Un jeu de cartes, *a pack of cards.*
L'as, *the ace.*
Le roi, *the king.*
La reine, *the queen.*
Le valet, *the knave.*
Un cœur, *a heart.*
Un carreau, *a diamond.*
Un trèfle, *a club.*
Un pique, *a spade.*
Un atout, *a trump.*
Une partie de cartes, *a game of cards.*

XIV.
La campagne, the country.
Un champ, *a field.*
Une prairie, *a meadow.*
Une haie, *a hedge.*
Une clôture, *a fence.*
Un fossé, *a ditch.*
Un marais, *a marsh.*
Un étang, *a pond.*
Un ruisseau, *a brook.*
Une fontaine, *a fountain.*
Un puits, *a well.*
Un abreuvoir, *a watering-trough.*
Une colline, *a hill.*
Un village, *a village.*
Un paysan, *a peasant.*
Une paysanne, *a peasant woman.*
Un fermier, *a farmer.*
La fermière, *the farmer's wife.*
Une ferme, *a farm.*
Une charrue, *a plough.*
Le soc, *the ploughshare.*
Un moulin, *a mill.*
La meule, *the mill-stone.*
Une grange, *a barn.*
Une écurie, *a stable (for horses).*
Une étable, *a stable (for cattle).*
La cour, *the yard.*
La basse-cour, *the poultry-yard.*
La laiterie, *the dairy.*
La serre-chaude, *the hot-house.*
Le bétail, *the cattle.*
La paille, *the straw.*
Du foin, *hay.*
Du blé, *corn; wheat; grain.*
Du maïs, *Indian-corn.*
Une gerbe, *a sheaf.*
Une meule de foin, *a stack of hay.*
De l'orge, *barley.*
De l'avoine, *oats.*
Du froment, *wheat.*
Du seigle, *rye.*
Du houblon, *hops.*
Une faux, *a scythe.*
Une faucille, *a sickle.*

Un arrosoir, *a watering-pot.*
Une bêche, *a spade.*
Un râteau, *a rake.*
Une houe, *a hoe.*
Un fléau, *a flail.*
Un moissonneur, *a reaper.*
Un faucheur, *a mower.*
Un hangar, *a shed.*
Un cheval, *a horse.*
Le harnais, *the harness.*
Le mors, *the bit.*
Le collier, *the collar.*
Les rênes, or guides, *the reins.*
Une selle, *a saddle.*
Un fouet, *a whip.*
Une cravache, *a riding-whip.*
Des éperons, *spurs.*
La moisson, La récolte, } *the harvest.*
La vendange, *the vintage.*
Une maison de campagne, *a country seat.*
Un pavillon, *a summer-house.*
Un berceau, *an arbor.*

XV.

Un théâtre, a theatre.

La salle, *the house.*
Le parquet, *the orchestra-seats.*
Le parterre, *the pit.*
Une loge, *a box.*
Les avant-scènes, *the stage-boxes.*
La galerie, *the gallery.*
Le foyer, *the green-room.*
L'orchestre, *the orchestra.*
Le chef d'orchestre, *the leader.*
La scène, *the stage.*
Les décorations, *the scenery.*
Les coulisses, *the wings.*
La toile, *the curtain.*
Le spectacle, *the play.*
Un acteur, *an actor.*
Une actrice, *an actress.*
Le directeur, *the manager.*
Le souffleur, *the prompter.*
Une pièce, *a play.*
Une tragédie, *a tragedy.*
Une comédie, *a comedy.*
Un opéra, *an opera.*
Un ballet, *a ballet.*
Un drame, *a drama.*
Un mélodrame, *a melodrama.*
Une farce, *a farce.*
Un acte, *an act.*
Une scène, *a scene.*
Un entr'acte, *an interlude.*
Une répétition, *a rehearsal.*
Une représentation, *a performance.*
Un rôle, *a part.*
Le public, *the audience.*
Les applaudissements, *the applause.*
Bis; bisser, *encore; to encore.*
Les sifflets, *the hissing.*

Une affiche, *a bill.*
Un billet, *a ticket.*
Une contre-marque, *a check.*

XVI.

Un voyage, a journey.

La voiture, *the coach.*
Le dehors, *the outside.*
L'intérieur, *the inside.*
De la place, *room.*
Une place, *a place.*
Un siége, *a seat.*
Un voyageur, *a traveler.*
Une malle, *a trunk.*
Un sac, *a bag.*
Un paquet, *a parcel.*
Le départ, *the departure.*
Adieu, *farewell.*
La route, *the road.*
La halte, *the stopping; the stopping place.*
L'arrivée, *the arrival.*
La réception, *the reception.*
La ville, *the city; the town.*
Un faubourg, *a suburb.*
Une rue, *a street.*
Une place, *a square.*
Le pavé, *the pavement.*
Un trottoir, *a sidewalk.*
Une boutique, *a shop.*
Le comptoir, *the counter.*
Une pratique, *a customer.*
La vente, *the sale.*
Un acheteur, *a purchaser.*
Un achat, *a purchase (large).*
Une emplette, *a purchase (small).*
Un marché, *a bargain.*
La grande poste, *the general post-office.*
La petite poste, *the penny post.*
Un hôtel, *an hotel.*
Un restaurant, *an eating-house.*
Un café, *a coffee-room.*
Le garçon, *the waiter.*
La carte, *the bill of fare.*
Un bureau, *an office.*
Un commis, *a clerk.*
Un musée, *a museum.*
Un pont, *a bridge.*
Un quai, *a quay.*
La douane, *the custom-house.*
Une caserne, *a barrack.*
Une cour, *a court.*
Une ruelle, *a lane.*
Un coin, *a corner.*
Une borne, *a spur-post; a spur-stone.*
Une voiture, *a carriage.*
La portière, *the door.*
Les stores, *the blinds.*
Les roues, *the wheels.*
L'essieu, *the axle-tree.*
Le timon, *the pole.*
Un fiacre, *a hackney-coach.*

Un cabriolet, *a cab.*
Le cocher, *the coachman.*
Un chariot, *a cart or wagon.*
Une charrette, *a cart.*
Un wagon, *a wagon.*
Le chemin de fer, *the railway.*
La station, *the station.*
Un train *or* convoi, *a train.*
La locomotive, *the engine.*
L'embarcadère, } *the terminus.*
Le débarcadère, } *the depot.*
La gare, } *the platform.*

XVII.

L'âme, the soul.
L'esprit, *the mind.*
L'entendement, *the understanding.*
Le jugement, *the judgment.*
La raison, *the reason.*
La mémoire, *the memory.*
Une faculté, *a faculty.*
Le caractère, *the temper.*
L'humeur, *the humor.*
La douceur, *mildness.*
La sensibilité, *sensibility.*
La bonté, *kindness.*
La gaieté, *gayety.*
L'étourderie, *giddiness.*
La politesse, *politeness.*
La colère, *anger.*
L'amour, *love.*
La haine, *hatred.*
La jalousie, *jealousy.*
L'amitié, *friendship.*
La tendresse, *tenderness.*
La reconnaissance, *gratitude.*
Un raisonnement, *an argument.*
Un souhait, *a wish.*
Un désire, *a desire.*
Une vertu, *a virtue.*
Un vice, *a vice.*
La folie, *madness.*
La sottise, *foolishness.*
L'orgueil, *pride.*
La hauteur, } *haughtiness.*
La fierté, }
La timidité, *bashfulness.*
L'égoïsme, *selfishness.*
Un sentiment, *a sentiment.*
Une pensée, *a thought.*
L'humanité, *humanity.*
La charité, *charity.*
La pitié, *pity.*
Un présent, *a present.*
Un don, } *a gift.*
Un cadeau, }
L'aumône, *alms.*
La simplicité, *simplicity.*
La droiture, *uprightness.*
Une bassesse, *a baseness.*
Un mensonge, *a falsehood.*
Un souvenir, *a recollection.*

L'oubli, *forgetfulness.*
Un aveu, *an avowal.*
Un secret, *a secret.*
Un regret, *a regret.*
La repentir, *repentance.*
Un cri, *a cry.*
Un soupir, *a sigh.*
Une larme, *a tear.*
Un sanglot, *a sob.*
Un signe, *a nod.*
Une habitude, *a habit.*

XVIII.

Un coup, a blow; a stroke; a clap; a hit.
Un coup de main, *a blow with the hand.* (*fig.*) *assistance ;* (*mil.*) *a surprise.*
——— de poing, *a blow with the fist.*
——— de revers, *a back blow.*
——— de pied, *a kick.*
——— de dents, *a bite.*
——— de langue, *a reflection (censure).*
——— d'œil, *a glance.*
——— de bâton, *a blow with a stick.*
——— de fouet, *a blow with a whip.*
——— de couteau, *a cut.*
——— de sabre, *a sabre cut.*
——— d'épée, *a sword thrust.*
——— de canon, *a cannon shot.*
——— de fusil, *a gun shot.*
——— de pistolet, *a pistol shot.*
——— de vent, *a gust of wind.*
——— de soleil, *a sunstroke.*
——— de tonnerre, } *a clap of thunder.*
——— de foudre, }
——— d'état, *a stroke of policy.*
A grands coups, *with great blows.*
A coups de bâton, *with a stick.*
D'un seul coup, *at a single blow.*
Du premier coup, *at the first blow.*
Pour le coup, *for once.*
À coup sûr, *for a certainty.*
Faire son coup, *to succeed.*

XIX.

Une couleur, a color.
Rouge, *red.*
Orange, *orange.*
Jaune, *yellow.*
Vert, *green.*
Bleu, *blue.*
Indigo, *indigo.*
Violet, te, *violet.*
Noir, *black.*
Blanc, he, *white.*
Brun, *brown.*
Pourpre, *purple.*
Rose, *rose-colored.*
Rose tendre, *pink.*
Foncé, *deep (colored).*
Clair, *light.*

XX.

Un défaut, a defect.
Aveugle, *blind.*
Borgne, *one-eyed.*
Sourd, *deaf.*
Muet, te, *dumb.*
Boiteux, se, *lame.*
Bossu, *hunch-backed.*
Estropié, *crippled.*
Difforme, *deformed.*
Chauve, *bald.*
Chevelu, *hairy.*
Camus, *flat-nosed.*
Balafré, *covered with scars.*
Marqué de la petite vérole, *pock-marked.*

XXI.

Une qualité, a quality.
Sensé, *sensible.*
Spirituel, le, *witty.*
Intellectuel, le, *intellectual.*
Vif, ve, *lively; sprightly.*
Aimable, *amiable.*
Affable, *affable.*
Modeste, *modest.*
Réservé, *reserved.*
Bavard, *talkative.*
Adroit, *dexterous.*
Habile, *able; skillful.*
Maladroit, } *awkward.*
Gauche,
Stupide, *stupid.*
Vain, *vain.*
Orgueilleux, *proud.*
Egoïste, *selfish.*

Intéressé, *interested.*
Officieux, se, *officious.*
Rusé, *artful; crafty.*
Grand, *tall; large.*
Gros, se, *large; big; stout.*
Petit, *small; little.*
Haut, *high.*
Profound, *deep.*
Large, *wide; broad.*
Etroit, *narrow.*
Long, ue, *long.*
Court, *short.*
Epais, se, *thick.*
Mince, *thin.*
Pointu, *pointed.*
Tranchant, } *sharp.*
Affilé,
Aigu, ë, *acute.*
Effilé, *slender; tapering.*
Emoussé, *blunt.*
Aigre, *sour.*
Doux, ce, *sweet.*
Amer, *bitter.*
Insipide, *insipid.*
Savoureux, se, *savory.*
Exquis, *exquisite.*
Délicieux, se, *delicious.*
Délicat, *delicate.*
Astringent, *astringent.*
Piquant, *pungent.*
Moelleux, *mellow.*
Mou, mol, molle, *soft (yielding).*
Dur, *hard.*
Doux, ce, *soft (velvety).*
Tendre, *tender.*
Ferme, *firm.*
Solide, *solid.*
Fixe, *stable.*

VERBS OF THE FIRST CONJUGATION.*
(See model verb Couper, *to cut*; p. 102.)

Abandonner, *to abandon.*
Abîmer, *to spoil.*
Accepter, *to accept.*
Accompagner, *to accompany.*
Accorder, *to grant.*
——— (un piano), *to tune.*
S'accorder avec, *to agree with.*
Accoutumer, *to accustom.*
S'accoutumer à, *to get accustomed to.*
Accrocher, *to hook; to hang.*
Acheter, *to buy.*
Achever, *to finish.*
Acquitter, *to acquit.*
Admirer, *to admire.*

Adresser, *to address.†*
S'adresser à, *to apply to.*
Affliger, *to afflict.*
Agrafer, *to hook; to fasten.*
Aider, *to help.*
Aimer, *to love; to like; to be fond of.*
Altérer, *to make thirsty.*
Ajouter, *to add.*
Allumer, *to light; to kindle.*
Amener, *to bring (leading).*
Amuser, *to amuse.*
S'amuser, *to amuse or enjoy one's self.*
Annoncer, *to announce.*
Appeler, *to call.*

---
* *The first conjugation comprises more than three-fourths of all the French verbs We give only some of them, which are frequently used.*
† *To address, to speak to a person, is, adresser la parole à qqn.*

VERBS OF THE FIRST CONJUGATION.

Apporter, *to bring (carrying).*
Apprécier, *to appreciate.*
Approcher, *to approach.*
S'approcher de, *to come or go near.*
Appuyer, *to lean ; to dwell upon.*
Arracher, *to root up ; to pluck out.*
—— (une dent), *to pull (a tooth).*
Assister à, *to be present at ; to attend.*
Assurer, *to assure.*
Attacher, *to attach.*
Attaquer, *to attack.*
Attraper, *to catch.*
Avaler, *to swallow.*
Avancer, *to advance.*
Augmenter, *to increase ; to rise* (in price).
Avouer, *to own ; to acknowledge.*
Baigner, *to bathe.*
Bâiller, *to gape ; to yawn.*
Baiser, *to kiss.*
Baisser, *to lower.*
Balayer, *to sweep.*
Baptiser, *to christen.*
Bavarder, *to chatter.*
Boutonner, *to button.*
Briller, *to shine ; to glitter.*
Brûler, *to burn.*
Cacher, *to hide ; to conceal.*
Cacheter, *to seal.*
Casser, *to break.*
Causer, *to talk ; to chat.*
Causer, *to cause ; to occasion.*
Céder, *to yield.*
Chanter, *to sing.*
Charmer, *to charm.*
Chasser, *to chase ; to drive away.*
Chatouiller, *to tickle.*
Chauffer, *to warm ; to heat.*
Chercher, *to seek ; to look for.*
   aller chercher, *to go for.*
   venir chercher, *to come for.*
   envoyer chercher, *to send for.*
Commander, *to command.*
Commencer, *to begin.*
Compter, *to count ; to reckon ; to expect.**
Conseiller, *to advise.*
Contenter, *to satisfy.*
Conter, *to relate.*
Continuer, *to continue.*
Converser, *to converse.*
Copier, *to copy.*
Corriger, *to correct.*
Coucher,† *to lie down ; to sleep.*
Se coucher, *to go to bed.*
Coûter, *to cost.*
Créer, *to create.*
Crier, *to cry.*
Cultiver, *to cultivate.*
Danser, *to dance.*

Déchirer, *to tear.*
Décider, *to decide.*
Déclarer, *to declare.*
Dégrafer, *to unhook.*
Déjeuner, *to breakfast.*
Délier, *to untie.*
Déménager, *to remove (one's household).*
Demeurer, *to dwell ; to live.*
Dépenser, *to spend.*
Déranger, *to disturb.*
Désaltérer, *to quench the thirst.*
Déshabiller, *to undress.*
Désirer, *to desire.*
Dessiner, *to draw.*
Détacher, *to untie.*
Détromper, *to undeceive.*
Dicter, *to dictate.*
Digérer, *to digest.*
Dîner, *to dine.*
Douter de, *to doubt.*
Se douter de, *to suspect.*
Donner, *to give.*
Durer, *to last.*
Éclairer, *to light ; to enlighten.*
Économiser, *to save.*
Écouter, *to listen to.*
Effacer, *to efface.*
Effrayer, *to frighten.*
Égarer, *to mislay ; to mislead.*
S'égarer, *to stray ; to lose one's way.*
Embarrasser, *to embarrass.*
Emmener, *to take away (leading).*
Empêcher de, *to prevent ; to hinder.*
Employer, *to employ ; to use.*
Emporter, *to carry away.*
Emprunter, *to borrow.*
Enfermer, *to shut up.*
Enlever, *to take away.*
Ennuyer, *to annoy ; to weary.*
Enrhumer, *to give a cold.*
S'enrhumer, *to take or catch cold.*
Enseigner, *to teach.*
Entrer, *to enter.*
Envelopper, *to wrap up.*
Environner, *to surround.*
Épargner, *to spare.*
Épeler, *to spell.*
Épouser, *to marry.*
Espérer, *to hope.*
Essayer, *to try.*
Essuyer, *to wipe.*
Estimer, *to esteem.*
Étonner, *to astonish.*
S'étonner, *to be astonished.*
Étudier, *to study.*
Éveiller, *to wake ; to awake.*
S'éveiller, *to awake.*
Éviter, *to avoid.*
Excuser, *to excuse.*

---

* Compter, before a verb in the infinite mode, means, *to expect, to intend.*
† Coucher, *to sleep, to pass the night.* Dormir, *to sleep, to be asleep.*

VERBS OF THE FIRST CONJUGATION.

S'excuser, *to apologise.*
Féliciter, *to congratulate.*
Fermer, *to close ; to shut.*
Flatter, *to flatter.*
Frapper, *to strike ; to knock.*
Fumer, *to smoke.*
Gagner, *to gain.*
Garder, *to keep.*
Gâter, *to spoil.*
Gêner, *to be in the way ; to pinch (of boots) ; to be tight (of clothes).*
Goûter, *to taste.*
Gronder, *to scold.*
Habiller, *to dress.*
Honorer, *to honor.*
Imprimer, *to print.*
Insulter, *to insult.*
Inventer, *to invent.*
Jeter, *to throw ; to cast.*
Jouer, *to play.*
Laisser, *to let ; to leave ; to allow.*
Se lasser, *to get tired.*
Laver, *to wash.*
Se lever, *to get up.*
Lier, *to tie ; to fasten.*
Louer, *to hire ; to let.*
Louer, *to praise.*
Manquer, *to fail.*
Marcher, *to walk ; to march.*
Menacer, *to threaten.*
Mendier, *to beg.*
Mener, *to lead.*
Mépriser, *to despise.*
Mériter, *to merit ; to deserve.*
Meubler, *to furnish (a house).*
Monter, *to ascend ; to go or come up.*
Montrer, *to show.*
Négliger, *to neglect.*
Nettoyer, *to clean.*
Nommer, *to name.*
Nouer, *to tie in a knot.*
Noyer, *to drown.*
Nager, *to swim.*
Obliger, *to oblige.*
Observer, *to observe ; to notice.*
Occuper, *to occupy.*
Offenser, *to offend.*
Oser, *to dare.*
Ôter, *to take off ; to remove.*
Oublier, *to forget.*
Pardonner, *to pardon.*
Parier, *to bet ; to wager.*
Partager, *to share ; to divide.*
Passer, *to pass ; to spend (time).*
Passer à, chez. *to call at, upon.*
Patiner, *to skate.*
Pêcher, *to fish.*
Penser, *to think.*
Pleurer, *to weep.*
Porter, *to carry ; to bear, to wear.*
Pousser, *to push.*
Préférer, *to prefer.*

Préparer, *to prepare.*
Présenter, *to present.*
Presser, *to press ; to hurry.*
Prêter, *to lend.*
Prier, *to pray ; to beg.*
Prononcer, *to pronounce.*
Proposer, *to propose.*
Quereller, *to quarrel.*
Quitter, *to quit.*
Raccommoder, *to mend.*
Raconter, *to relate.*
Ramasser, *to pick up.*
Ramener, *to bring, or lead back.*
Rappeler, *to call back.*
Se rappeler, *to recollect.*
Rapporter, *to bring or carry back.*
Réciter, *to recite.*
Récompenser, *to reward.*
Refuser, *to refuse.*
Regarder, *to look at.*
Regretter, *to regret.*
Relier, *to bind.*
Remercier, *to thank.*
Remonter, *to wind up (a watch).*
Rencontrer, *to meet.*
Respecter, *to respect.*
Rester, *to remain.*
Rêver, *to dream.*
Ruiner, *to ruin.*
Saigner, *to bleed.*
Saler, *to salt.*
Saluer, *to bow to.*
Sauver, *to save.*
Serrer, *to press ; to squeeze ; to put away.*
Siffler, *to whistle ; to hiss.*
Soigner, *to attend ; to nurse (a patient).*
Sonner, *to ring.*
Souhaiter, *to wish.*
Soupçonner, *to suspect.*
Songer à, *to think of ; to dream.*
Souper, *to eat supper.*
Tâcher, *to endeavor.*
Tacher, *to stain.*
Tailler, *to cut.*
Tarder à, *to be long.*
Tirer, *to draw ; to pull ; to fire.*
Tirer un coup de fusil, *to fire off a gun.*
Tomber, *to fall.*
Tousser, *to cough.*
Tourner, *to turn.*
Travailler, *to work.*
Tromper, *to deceive.*
Se tromper, *to be mistaken.*
Trouver, *to find.*
User, *to use ; to wear out.*
Veiller, *to watch ; to sit up.*
Verser, *to pour.*
Vider, *to empty.*
Visiter, *to visit.*
Voler, *to fly ; to steal.*
Voyager, *to travel.*

CONVERSATIONAL PHRASES.

Bonjour,* monsieur.	*Good morning, sir.*
Bonsoir.	*Good evening,* or *Good night.*
Bonne nuit, maman.	*Good night, mamma.*
Adieu.	*Good-bye,* or *Farewell.*
Sans adieu.	*I will see you again.*
Au revoir,† or Au plaisir.	*Good-bye.*

Je suis charmé de vous voir.	*I am glad to see you.*
Comment vous portez-vous ?	*How do you do ?*
Je me porte bien, je vous remercie ; et vous-même ?	*I am well, I thank you. How are you ?*
Très-bien.	*Very well.*
Comment se porte-t on chez vous ?	*How are they at home ?*
Tout le monde se porte bien.	*They are all well.*
J'en suis bien aise.	*I am glad to hear it.*

Comment se porte Madame —— ?	*How is Mrs. ——?*
Elle se porte bien, je vous remercie.	*She is well, I thank you.*
Comment se porte monsieur votre frère ?	*How is your brother ?*
Comment se porte mademoiselle votre sœur ?	*How is your sister ?*
Elle ne se porte pas bien.	*She is not well.*
J'en suis fâché.	*I am sorry to hear it.*
De quoi se plaint-elle ?	*What does she complain of ?*
Elle souffre de la poitrine.	*She has pains in her chest.*
Elle s'est enrhumée au sortir de l'église dimanche dernier.	*She caught cold in coming from church last Sunday.*
Lundi elle était bien souffrante.	*On Monday she was very unwell.*
Hier nous avons fait venir le médecin.	*Yesterday we sent for the doctor.*
Aujourd'hui elle va beaucoup mieux.	*To-day she is a great deal better.*
Je pense qu'elle sortira demain, s'il fait beau.	*I think she will go out to-morrow, if the weather is fine.*
Le médecin dit que c'est peu de chose, et qu'elle sera bientôt rétablie.	*The doctor says that it is not serious, and that she will soon be well again.*
Je le souhaite de tout mon cœur.	*I wish it with all my heart.*

Comment va la santé ?	*How is your health ?*
Assez bien ; et la vôtre ?	*Pretty good ; and yours ?*
Comme toujours.	*As usual.*
Je viens vous dire le bonjour.	*I look in to say good morning.*
Vous êtes bien aimable.	*You are very kind.*
Veuillez vous asseoir ; or, Asseyez-vous, je vous en prie.	*Please be seated ;* or, *Sit down, pray.*
Il fait froid dehors.	*It is cold out of doors.*
Approchez-vous du calorifère.	*Come near the register.*

* Bonjour, *Good day,* is also used for *Good morning.*
† Au revoir, *or* Au plaisir, means Adieu, jusqu'au revoir, *or* jusqu'au plaisir de vous revoir, *Farewell until we meet again.*

CONVERSATIONAL PHRASES.

Il y a long temps que je ne vous ai vu.	I have not seen you for some time.
J'ai été très-occupé.	I have been very busy.
Mon père a été absent pendant quelque temps.	My father was absent for some time.
Voulez-vous me faire le plaisir de dîner avec moi.	Will you take dinner with me?
Vraiment, je ne pourrai.	Indeed, I cannot.
Je vous prie de m'excuser.	I beg you will excuse me.
Il faut que je sois chez moi dans une demi-heure.	I must be at home in half an hour.
Je serai obligé de vous quitter.	I shall be obliged to leave you.
J'en suis fâché.	I am sorry for it.
J'ai des affaires pressantes.	I have urgent business.
Les affaires avant tout ; n'est-ce pas ?	Business before everything; is that not so?
Voulez-vous venir passer la soirée chez moi.	Will you come and spend the evening at my house.
Vous y verrez quelques-uns de vos anciens camarades de classe.	You will meet some of your old classmates.
Vous êtes bien bon. Je ne manquerai pas de m'y trouver.	You are very kind. I shall not fail to be there.
Mes enfants, il est temps d'aller à l'école.	Children, it is time to go to school.
Oui, maman, nous y allons.	Yes, mamma, we are going.
Votre ami Albert est à la porte à vous attendre.	Your friend Albert is at the door waiting for you.
Partons, Charles, si tu es prêt.	Let us be off, Charles, if you are ready.
Oui, à l'instant.	Yes, in a moment.
As-tu fait ton thème ?	Have you written your exercise?
Je ne l'ai pas tout-à-fait fini.	I have not quite finished it.
J'étais à l'avant dernière phrase quand on m'a appelé.	I was at the last sentence but one, when some one called me.
Je le finirai à l'école.	I will finish it at school.
Sais-tu la leçon ?	Do you know the lesson?
Je crois que oui.	I think I do.
Je l'ai étudiée pendant trois quarts-d'heure.	I studied it for three quarters of an hour.
L'as-tu trouvée difficile ?	Did you find it difficult?
Non pas.	No.
Dépêchons-nous ; j'entends la clochette.	Let us make haste; I hear the bell.
Ne cours pas ; nous arriverons à temps.	Do not run; we shall arrive in time.
Tu sais que le maître n'aime pas qu'on arrive après l'appel.	You know that the teacher does not like us to come after roll-call.
Non, vraiment ; il veut qu'on soit en place avant que l'appel commence.	No, indeed; he wants us to be in our seats before the roll is called.
Il est strict, mais c'est un bon maître.	He is severe, but he is a good teacher.

Que vas-tu faire maintenant ?	What are you going to do now?
Je vais m'habiller, puis je vais sortir.	I am going to dress, and then I am going out.
Où veux-tu aller ?	Where are you going?
Je vais faire des emplettes.	I am going shopping.
Veux-tu m'accompagner ?	Will you go with me?
Je veux bien ; mais il faut que je finisse mon devoir premièrement.	I will, but I must first finish my task.
Tu en auras le temps.	You will have time for that.
Appelle-moi quand tu seras prêt.	Call me when you are ready.
Henri, me voici prêt à sortir.	Henry, here I am, ready to go out.
Un instant ; je vais dire à maman que nous sortons.	One moment; I am going to tell mamma that we are going.
Que vas-tu acheter ?	What are you going to buy?

CONVERSATIONAL PHRASES. 257

D'abord une grammaire française.	First, a French grammar.
Tu sais que nous avons fini la petite, la Grammaire Elémentaire.	You know that we have finished the small one, the Elementary Grammar.
Eh bien, le professeur veut que nous étudions maintenant la grande, par le même auteur, sa grammaire Analytique.	Well, the professor wishes us now to study the large one of the same author, his Analytical Grammar.
Où achètes-tu tes livres?	Where do you buy your books?
Chez Monsieur Christern, Place de l'Université, No. 77.	At Mr. Christern's, No. 77 University Place.

Monsieur, donnez-moi, s'il vous plaît, un exemplaire de la grammaire française par ——.	Sir, please give me a copy of the French grammar by ——.
Voici, monsieur, la grammaire que vous demandez.	Here is the grammar you asked for, sir.
Y a-t-il autre chose que vous désirez, monsieur?	Is there anything else that you wish, sir?
Il me faut du papier à lettre, des enveloppes et des timbres-poste.	I want some letter paper, envelopes, and postage stamps.
Je prendrai aussi quelques feuilles de papier buvard.	I will also take a few sheets of blotting paper.
Combien cela fait-il ensemble?	How much is that altogether?
C'est quatre dollars et demi.	It is four dollars and a half.
Faut-il envoyer ces choses chez vous, monsieur?	Shall I send these things to your house, sir?
Je ne vous donnerai pas cette peine-là. Faites-en un petit paquet, et je l'y porterai moi-même.	I will not trouble you. Make a small bundle of them, and I will carry it myself.

Je voudrais qu'on sonnât pour le dîner.	I wish the bell would ring for dinner.
La promenade m'a donné de l'appétit.	The walk has given me an appetite.
On va servir le dîner à l'instant.	Dinner will be served presently.
Le dîner est servi.	Dinner is served.
Mettons-nous à table.	Let us sit down to dinner.
Antoine, servez la soupe.	Anthony, serve the soup.
Cette julienne est bonne.	That (vegetable) soup is good.
Aimez-vous le poisson?	Are you fond of fish?
Assez bien.	Yes, rather.
Voici du turbot et voilà du saumon.	Here is turbot and there is salmon.
Je mangerai un peu de saumon.	I will eat some of the salmon.
Passez la sauce à monsieur.	Hand the sauce to the gentleman.
Antoine, avez-vous glacé le vin?	Anthony, have you iced the wine?
Voulez-vous du Sauterne, ou du vin du Rhin?	Will you drink a glass of Sauterne, or a glass of Rhine wine?
A votre santé.	I drink to your health.
A la vôtre.	Here is yours.
Changez d'assiettes, Antoine.	Change plates, Anthony.
Voici un gigot de mouton bouilli; en voulez-vous?	Here is a leg of boiled mutton; do you wish some of it?
Je prendrai de préférence un petit morceau de ce rôti de bœuf.	I would rather take a little piece of that roast beef.
L'aimez-vous bien cuit ou peu cuit?	Do you like it well done, or under done?
Donnez du jus à monsieur.	Give the gentleman some of the gravy.
Passez les petits pois, Antoine.	Pass the peas, Tony.
Versez-moi de l'eau.	Pour me out some water.
Découpez le poulet et faites la salade.	Carve the fowl and make the salad.
Voulez-vous boire du Bourdeaux ou du Bourgogne?	Will you drink claret or Burgundy?

Enlevez, Antoine, et apportez le dessert.	Remove the dishes, Anthony, and bring in the desert.
Mangez-vous de l'ananas ?	Do you eat pineapple ?
Je ne l'aime pas beaucoup.	I am not very fond of it.
J'aime mieux les fraises.	I prefer strawberries.
Les fraises ne sont pas assez sucrées.	The strawberries are not sweet enough.
Passez le sucre, Antoine.	Pass the sugar, Tony.
Prenez-vous du café et le petit verre ?	Do you take coffee and a glass of cognac ?
Pour moi du café avec un peu de lait.	I will take coffee with a little milk in it.
Un cigare ?	Will you have a cigar ?
Merci, je ne fume pas.	Thank you, I do not smoke.
Allons nous asseoir dans la bibliothèque; nous y causerons à notre aise.	Let us go and sit in the library, we may chat there at our ease.
Où irez-vous ce soir ?	Where will you go to-night ?
J'irai voir ma tante.	I will go to my aunt's.
Elle partira pour la campagne dans quelques jours.	She is going to leave for the country in a few days.
Où est votre oncle ?	Where is your uncle ?
Il est en Europe.	He is in Europe.
Il est parti il y a un mois.	He left a month ago.
Il doit être à Paris maintenant.	He must be in Paris now.
Il devait s'arrêter dix jours à Londres.	He was to stay ten days in London.
Ma tante a reçu une lettre de lui il y a trois ou quatre jours.	My aunt received a letter from him three or four days ago.
Il se portait bien.	He was in good health.
Quand partirez-vous pour la campagne ?	When will you leave for the country ?
Nous partirons vers la fin du mois.	We will start towards the end of the month.
Nous reviendrons à la ville au commencement du mois d'octobre.	We shall return to town in the beginning of October.
Venez passer quelques jours avec nous pendant l'été.	Come and spend a few days with us during summer.
Je ne puis vous le promettre.	I cannot promise you.
Nous aurons du monde pendant tout l'été.	We shall have company all the summer.
Mes deux cousines vont arriver de Paris.	My two cousins are coming from Paris.
Elles resteront chez nous jusqu'en automne.	They will stay with us until autumn.
Mon oncle dit qu'elles parlent français comme des Parisiennes.	My uncle says that they speak French like Parisian ladies.
Je suis bien curieux de les voir.	I am very desirous of seeing them.
Ce sera une belle occasion pour vous de vous exercer à la conversation française.	That will be a fine opportunity for you to practice French conversation.
J'en profiterai, je vous assure.	I will avail myself of it, I assure you.
Je crois qu'il est temps de nous séparer.	I believe it is time to part.
Il n'est que dix heures.	It is not more than ten.
J'ai l'habitude de me retirer de bonne heure.	It is my habit to retire early.
Ne vous dérangez pas.	Do not disturb yourself.
Pardonnez-moi, je vais vous conduire jusqu'à la porte.	I beg your pardon ; I am going with you as far as the door.
Au revoir.	Good-bye.
Bonsoir.	Good night to you.

VOCABULARY

TO THE

ENGLISH EXERCISES FOR TRANSLATION.

A.

A, an, un (*m.*), une (*f.*).
able (to be), pouvoir.
about, environ.
above, dessus.
abroad, à l'étranger.
absent, absent.
according to, selon, suivant.
account; on account of, à cause de.
acquainted with (to be), connaître.
acquire (to), acquérir.
act (to), agir.
address, adresse (*f.*).
admire (to), admirer.
advance (to), avancer.
advantage, avantage (*m.*).
advice, conseil (*m.*), avis (*m.*); information (*f.*).
advise (to), conseiller.
affair, affaire (*f.*)
affect (to), émouvoir.
afraid (to be), craindre, avoir peur; *I am afraid of*, je crains de.
after, après.
against, contre.
age, âge (*m.*); *aged*, âgé.
agent, agent (*m.*).
ago, il y a; *a little while ago*, tantôt; *long ago*, Il y-a longtemps.
agreeable, agréable.
ah! ah!
air-hole, soupirail (*m.*).
alas! hélas!
Alexis, Alexis.
alike, égal (*m.*), égale (*f.*).

all, tout (*m.*), tous (*m. pl.*), toute (*f.*)
almost, presque.
alone, seul.
already, déjà.
also, aussi.
although, bien que, quoique.
always, toujours.
amend (to), to make amends for, réparer.
America, l'Amérique
amiable, aimable (de).
among, parmi, entre.
amuse (to), amuser.
amusing, amusant.
ancestor, aïeul, *pl.* aïeux (*m.*).
ancient, ancien (*m.*), ancienne (*f.*).
and, et.
angry with (to be), être fâché contre.
answer, réponse (*f.*).
answer (to), répondre (à).
anything, quelque chose.
apartment, appartement (*m.*).
appear (to), paraître.
apple, pomme (*f.*).
apply one's self to (to), se livrer (à).
April, avril.
are, sont.
arm, bras (*m.*).
arm-chair, fauteuil (*m.*).
around, autour de.
arrival, arrivée (*f.*).
arrive (to,) arriver.
artist, artiste (*m.* and *f.*).
as, que, comme.
as far as, jusque.
as long as, tant que.

as much, as many, autant.
as soon as, aussitôt que.
as to, quant à.
as well as, ainsi que, aussi bien que.
ashamed (to be), avoir honte.
Asia, l'Asie (*f.*).
ask for (to), demander ; *I ask for,* je prie (de).
ask a question (to), faire une question.
assail (to), assaillir.
assistance, to come to one's assistance, secourir quelqu'un.
astonish (to), étonner.
at, à.
at present, à présent.
attached, attaché.
attain (to), parvenir.
attention (to pay), faire attention.
attentive, appliqué, attentif.
August, août.
aunt, tante (*f.*).
author, auteur (*m.*).

B.

back (returned), de retour.
bad, mauvais (*m.*), mauvaise (*f.*).
badly, mal.
baker, boulanger (*m.*).
ball, bal (*m.*).
band, troupe (*f.*).
bank, banque (*f.*).
banker, banquier (*m.*).
bargain, marché (*m.*).
basket, panier (*m.*).
battle, bataille (*f.*).
be (to), être ; *as it should be,* comme il faut.
be (to), (of health), se porter.
be called (to), s'appeler.
be there (to), y être.
beard, barbe (*f.*).
beat (to), battre.
beautiful, beau, bel (*m.*), belle (*f.*).
beauty, beauté (*f.*).
because, parce que.
become (to), devenir (être) ; *to have become,* être devenu.

been, été.
before (position), devant.
before (first), auparavant.
before (time, order), avant de ; *conj.* avant que.
beg (to), prier (de), demander.
begin (to), commencer.
behave (to), se comporter.
behind, derrière.
believe (to), croire.
bell, cloche (*f.*) ; *the bell rings,* on sonne.
below, au-dessous, en bas.
bench, banc (*m.*).
benign, bénin (*m.*). bénigne (*f.*).
best, le mieux.
better, meilleur (*adj.*), mieux (*adv.*); *to be better,* valoir mieux ; *it is better,* il vaut mieux.
between, entre.
big, gros (*m.*), grosse (*f.*).
bird, oiseau (*m.*).
black, noir.
blame (to), blâmer.
blue, bleu.
boarding house, boarding school, pension (*f.*).
boat, bateau (*m.*).
boil (to), bouillir.
bonnet, chapeau (*m.*).
book, livre (*m.*).
bookseller, libraire (*m.*).
boot, botte (*f.*).
bootmaker, bottier.
born (to be), naître, (être).
both, tous les deux, l'un et l'autre.
boulevard, boulevard (*m.*).
bouquet, bouquet (*m.*).
bow (to), saluer.
box, caisse (*f.*).
boy, garçon (*m.*).
bravery, bravoure (*f.*).
bread, pain (*m.*).
break (to), casser.
breakfast, déjeuner (*m.*).
breakfast (to), déjeuner.
bridge, pont (*m.*).

bring (to), apporter.
bring forward (to), avancer.
broken, cassé.
brother, frère (*m.*).
build (to), bâtir.
bundle, paquet (*m.*).
business, affaire (*f.*).
but, mais.
but (only), ne—que.
but little, ne—guère.
butcher, boucher (*m.*).
butter, beurre.
buy (to), acheter.
by, par.
by and by, tantôt ; *good bye,* au revoir.

C.

cabbage, chou (*m.*).
cage, cage (*f.*).
cake, gâteau (*m.*).
call (to), appeler.
call, visite (*f.*).
call back (to), rappeler.
callosity, cal (*m.*).
can, pouvoir.
Canada, le Canada (*m.*).
canister (tea), boîte à thé (*f.*).
captain, capitaine (*m.*).
care, to take care, avoir soin de.
careless, négligent.
carelessness, négligence (*f.*).
carnival, carnaval (*m.*).
carpet, tapis (*m.*).
carriage, voiture (*f.*); *in a carriage,* en voiture.
carry (to), porter, mener.
carve (to), découper.
case, caisse (*f.*) ; *in case,* en cas.
cat, chat (*m.*).
cease (to), cesser (de).
cent, sou (*m.*).
centime, centime (*m.*).
chain, chaîne (*f.*).
chair, chaise (*f.*).
change, monnaie (*f.*).
Charles, Charles.
charming, charmant.

cheap, à bon marché.
chicken, poulet (*m.*).
child, enfant (*m.* and *f.*).
choose (to), choisir.
church, église (*f.*) ; *at church,* à l'église.
circumstance, circonstance (*f.*).
city, ville (*f.*).
city hall, hôtel de ville (*m.*).
class, classe (*f.*).
class-mate, camarade de classe (*m.*).
clean (to), nettoyer.
climate, climat (*m.*).
cloak, manteau (*m.*).
clock, pendule, horloge (*f.*) ; *what o'clock is it ?* quelle heure est-il ?
cloth, drap (*m.*).
clothe (to), vêtir.
clothes, habits (*m. pl.*), vêtements (*m. pl.*).
coachman, cocher (*m.*).
coarse, gros (*m.*), grosse (*f.*).
coat, habit (*m.*).
coffee, café (*m.*).
cold, froid.
cold (to be), avoir froid.
cold (the), froid (*m.*).
collect (to), recueillir.
come (to), venir (être).
come in (to), entrer.
come home (to), revenir.
come back (to), revenir.
come out (to), sortir.
come near (to), s'approcher (de).
come down (to), descendre.
comrade, camarade (*m.*).
comfort (to), consoler.
commence (to), commencer (à).
commerce, commerce (*m.*).
company, compagnie (*f.*), du monde.
company (in), en société.
complain (to), se plaindre.
complete, complet (*m.*), complète (*f.*).
composition, composition (*f.*).
comprehend (to), comprendre.
concert, concert (*m.*).
conclude (to), conclure.

concrete, concret (*m.*), concrète (*f.*).
conduct, conduite (*f.*); *to conduct one's self*, se conduire.
confident, confiant.
confiding, confiant.
congratulation, félicitation (*f.*).
conquer (*to*), conquérir.
console (*to*), consoler.
contented, content.
contrary (*on the*), au contraire.
convince (*to*), convaincre.
copy (*to*), copier.
copy book, cahier (*m.*).
coral, corail (*m.*).
correctly, juste; *she plays correctly*, elle joue juste.
corpulent, replet (*m.*), replète (*f.*).
cotton, coton (*m.*).
counsel, conseil (*m.*).
country, campagne (*f.*); *in the country*, à la campagne; *my country*, mon pays.
courage, courage (*m.*).
cousin, cousin (*m.*), cousine (*f.*).
cover (*to*), couvrir.
cow, vache (*f.*).
create (*to*), créer.
cup, tasse (*f.*).
cut (*to*), couper.
cut up (*to*), découper.

D.

dance (*to*), danser.
dare (*to*), oser.
daughter, fille (*f.*).
day, jour (*m.*); *good day*, bon jour; *every day*, tous les jours; *to-day*, aujourd'hui; *a day, by the day*, par jour; *the day before*, la veille; *the day after*, le lendemain.
dead, mort.
dear, cher (*m.*), chère (*f.*).
death, mort (*f.*).
decease (*to*), décéder.
deceive (*to*), tromper.
December, décembre.
decrepit, caduc (*m.*), caduque (*f.*).

defeat (*to*), défaire, vaincre.
defect, défaut (*m.*).
deliver (*to*), délivrer.
delight in (*to*), se plaire.
dentist, dentiste (*m.*).
depart (*to*), partir (être).
departure, départ (*m.*).
depot, (*of railroad*) gare (*f.*).
desire, to have a desire, avoir envie de.
desire (*to*), désirer.
desk, pupitre (*m.*).
despise (*to*), mépriser.
dictionary, dictionnaire (*m.*).
die (*to*), mourir.
different, différent.
difficult, difficile.
difficulty, l'embarras (*m.*); *in difficulty*, dans l'embarras; *to get one out of difficulty*, tirer quelqu'un d'embarras.
diligence, diligence (*f.*).
diligent, diligent.
dine (*to*), dîner.
dinner, dîner.
dining-room, salle à manger (*f.*)
discover (*to*), découvrir.
discreet, discret (*m.*), discrète (*f.*)
dish, plat (*m.*).
disobedience, désobéissance.
disobedient, désobéissant.
dissatisfied (*with*), mécontent (*de*)
do (*to*), faire.
do a favor, faire un plaisir.
do (*to*) (*of health*), se porter.
doctor, médecin (*m.*).
dog, chien (*m.*).
dollar, dollar (*m.*), piastre (*f.*).
done, fait.
door, porte (*f.*).
doubt (*to*), douter.
down-stairs, en bas.
dozen, douzaine (*f.*).
draw (*to*), tirer.
drawer, tiroir (*m.*).
drawing, dessin (*m.*).
drawing-room, salon (*m.*).

dress, robe (*f.*).
dress (to) one's self, s'habiller.
dress goods, des étoffes.
dressing gown, robe de chambre (*f.*).
drink, boisson (*f.*), breuvage (*m.*).
drink (to), boire.
drunk, bu.
dry, sec (*m.*), sèche (*f.*).
duck, canard (*m.*).
durable, durable.
during, durant, pendant.
duty, devoir (*m.*).
dwell (to), demeurer.

E.

each, chaque.
each one, chacun.
each other, l'un l'autre.
early, de bonne heure.
easy, facile.
eat (to), manger.
eaten, mangé.
economical, économe.
either, l'un ou l'autre.
Eliza, Elise.
elsewhere, ailleurs.
embarassment, embarras (*m.*).
emperor, empereur (*m.*).
employ (to), employer.
empty, vide.
enamel, émail (*m.*).
end, fin (*f.*); *in the end*, à la fin.
endeavor, tâcher.
enemy, ennemi (*m.*).
England, l'Angleterre (*f.*).
English, l'anglais, anglais.
engraving, gravure (*f.*).
enough, assez (de).
enter (to), entrer.
equal, égal.
especially, surtout.
esteem (to), estimer.
eternally, éternellement.
even, also, même.
evening, soir (*m.*); *in the evening*, le soir.
every, tout (*m.*), toute (*f.*).

everybody, tout le monde.
everyone, chacun.
everything, tout.
everywhere, partout.
Europe, l'Europe (*f.*).
evil, mal (*m.*).
examination, examen (*m.*).
example, exemple (*m.*).
except, excepté.
excuse, excuse (*f.*).
exercise, exercice (*m.*).
expect (to await), attendre.
extract (to), extraire.
extremely, extrêmement.
eye, œil (*m.*), les yeux (*pl.*).

F.

fair, blond.
faithful, fidèle (à).
fall (to), tomber.
false, faux (*m.*), fausse (*f.*).
family, famille (*f.*); *with one's family*, en famille.
fan, éventail (*m.*).
far, loin.
fashion, mode (*f.*).
fashionable, à la mode.
fat, gras (*m.*), grasse (*f.*).
father, père (*m.*).
fatigued, fatigué.
fault, défaut (*m.*), faute (*f.*).
favor, faveur (*f.*); *to do a favor*, faire un plaisir.
favorite, favori (*m.*), favorite (*f.*).
fear (to), craindre.
fear, for fear, lest, de crainte que, de peur que.
feather, plume (*f.*).
February, février.
feel (to), sentir.
few, a few, quelques-uns.
fight (to), se battre.
fill (to), remplir.
finally, enfin.
find (to), trouver.
find again (to), retrouver.
fine, beau, bel (*m.*), belle (*f.*).

finger-ring, bague (*f.*).
finish (to), finir.
first, premier (*m.*), première (*f.*).
first, at first, d'abord.
firstly, premièrement.
fish, poisson (*m.*).
flash of lightning, éclair (*m.*).
flatter (to), flatter.
flattery, flatterie (*f.*).
flaxen, blond.
flee (to), fuir.
flint, caillou (*m.*).
floor, plancher (*m.*); *on the first floor,* au premier.
flower, fleur (*f.*).
follow (to), suivre.
fond of (to be), aimer.
foolish, fou, fol (*m.*), folle (*f.*).
foot, pied (*m.*).
for, pour, car (*conj.*).
foreigner, étranger (*m.*).
foresee (to), prévoir.
forget (to), oublier.
former, ancien (*m.*), ancienne (*f.*).
formerly, autrefois.
fork, fourchette (*f.*).
fortnight, quinze jours.
fortune, good fortune, bonheur (*m.*).
found, trouvé.
forward (to bring), avancer.
France, la France (*f.*).
frank, franc (*m.*), franche (*f.*).
freeze (to), geler.
French, français ; *from English to French,* de l'anglais en français.
fresh, frais (*m.*), fraîche (*f.*).
Friday, vendredi (*m.*).
friend, ami (*m.*), amie (*f.*).
friendship, amitié (*f.*).
from, de, dès.
frost, gelée (*f.*).
fruit, fruit (*m.*).
fulfill (to), remplir.

G.

garden, jardin (*m.*).
gate, porte (*f.*).
gather (to), cueillir.
general, général (*m.*).
gentleman, monsieur (*m.*).
German, allemand.
Germany, l'Allemagne.
get made (to), faire faire.
girl, fille (*f.*).
give (to), donner.
give back (to), rendre.
glad, very glad, bien aise (de, que).
glass, verre (*m.*).
glove, gant (*m.*).
go (to), aller.
go down (to), descendre.
go away (to), s'en aller.
go back (to), retourner.
go in (to), entrer.
go out (to), sortir.
go over (to), parcourir.
go to bed (to), se coucher.
go up (to), monter.
go and find (to), aller trouver.
God, Dieu.
gold, or (*m.*).
gold pen, plume d'or (*f.*).
good, bon (*m.*), bonne (*f.*); sage (*of children*).
good bye, au revoir.
good day, bon jour.
good morning, bon jour.
good (the), les bons (*pl.*).
goods, les marchandises (*pl.f.*).
grain, grain (*m.*).
grammar, grammaire (*f.*).
grandfather, grand-père (*m.*), aïeul (*m.*), aïeuls (*pl.*).
gray, gris.
Greek, grec (*m.*), grecque (*f.*).
green, vert.
grief, chagrin (*m.*).
grind (to), moudre.
grow (to), croître.
grow tall (to), grandir.
grow old (to), vieillir.
guard (to), garder.
guardian, gardien (*m.*).

H.

ha! ha!
hail (to), grêler.
hair, cheveu (m.); pl. cheveux.
hallo! holà.
ham, jambon (m.).
hand, main (f.).
hand (to), remettre.
handkerchief, mouchoir (m.).
handsome, beau, bel (m.), belle (f.).
hard, difficult, difficile.
happy, heureux (m.), heureuse (f.).
haste (to make), se dépêcher.
hat, chapeau (m.).
have (to), avoir.
have to (to), devoir.
head, tête (f.).
headache, mal de tête (m.).
hear (to), apprendre, entendre.
heart, cœur (m.).
heaven, ciel (m.).
help (to), aider.
help to (to), servir.
henceforth, dorénavant.
Henrietta, Henriette.
Henry, Henri.
her, son, sa; pl. ses.
herself, elle-même.
here, ici.
here is, here are, voici.
high, loud, haut.
himself, lui-même.
hire (to), louer.
his, son.
hist! chut!
history, histoire (f.).
hold (to), tenir.
holiday (to have a holiday), avoir congé.
home (at home), à la maison, chez soi.
honest, honnête.
hope (to), espérer.
horse, cheval (m.).
hour, heure (f.).
house, maison (f.).
how, comment.
however, cependant, pourtant.

how many, how much, combien (de).
hungry (to be), avoir faim.
hurry (in a), pressé.
hurt (to), faire mal.
husband, mari (m.).

I.

I, je.
idleness, oisiveté (f.).
if, si.
immediately, tout de suite.
impossible, impossible (à).
imprudent, imprudent.
in, dans.
indeed, vraiment; en vérité.
industry, industrie (f.).
inform (to), avertir.
injure (to), nuire.
ink, encre (f.).
inkstand, encrier (m.).
inquire for (to), demander.
instant, instant (..).
instead (of), au lieu (de).
instruct (to), instruire.
intellect, esprit (m.).
intelligence (news), nouvelle (f.).
intemperance, intempérance (f.).
intention, intention (f.).
intend (to), compter.
interest (at), à intérêt.
interested (to be), s'intéresser (à).
interesting, intéressant.
invest (with), revêtir (de).
invite (to), inviter.
is, est.
its, son; pl. ses.

J.

jackal, chacal (m.).
James, Jacques.
January, janvier (m.).
jewel, bijou (m.).
jeweler, bijoutier (m.).
John, Jean.
journey, voyage (m.).
Julia, Julie.
Julius, Jules.

July, juillet (*m.*).
June, juin (*m.*).
just, correctly, juste; *just now*, tout à l'heure.
justice (to do), rendre justice.

K.

keep (to), garder; *to keep waiting*, faire attendre.
kill (to), tuer.
kind, bon (*m.*), bonne (*f.*); aimable.
kindness, bonté (*f.*); bienveillance (*f.*).
king, roi (*m.*).
knee, genou (*m.*).
knife, couteau (*m.*).
knock (to), frapper.
know (to), to know how to, savoir.
knowledge, connaissance (*f.*).

L.

lace, dentelle (*f.*).
lady, dame (*f.*); *young lady*, demoiselle (*f.*).
land, terre (*f.*).
language, langue (*f.*).
large (big), gros (*m.*), grosse (*f.*).
large (great), grand (*m.*), grande (*f.*).
last, dernier (*m.*), dernière (*f.*); *at last*, enfin.
late, tard.
laugh (to), rire; *to laugh at*, rire de.
law, loi (*f.*).
lead (to), mener.
leaf, feuille (*f.*).
learn (to), apprendre.
lease, bail (*m.*).
least, moindre.
leave, quitter, partir; *leave of absence*, congé; *to take leave*, prendre congé.
lend (to), prêter.
less, moins.
lesson, leçon (*f.*).
let (to rent), louer.
letter, lettre (*f.*); *letter-box*, boîte aux lettres.

liberty, liberté (*f.*).
lie (to lie down), se coucher.
light (of hair), blond.
lighten (to), faire des éclairs; *it lightens*, il fait des éclairs.
lightning, éclair (*m.*).
like (to), aimer; *how do you like*, comment trouvez-vous; *I should like*, je voudrais; *I like better*, j'aime mieux.
like (as), comme.
listen to (to), écouter; *to listen to reason*, entendre raison.
little, peu (de); *a little*, un peu (de); *too little*, trop peu (de); *but little*, ne — guère.
live (to) (dwell), demeurer.
live (to), vivre.
lively, vif (*m.*), vive (*f.*).
loiter (to), flâner.
long, long (*m.*), longue (*f.*); *no longer*, ne plus.
look at (to), regarder; *look for (to)*, chercher.
looking-glass, miroir (*m.*).
lose (to), perdre; *lost*, perdu.
lot (fate), sort (*m.*).
loud, high, haut; *to speak too loud*, parler trop haut.
Louisa, Louise.
louse, pou (*m.*).
love (to), aimer.
low, bas (*m.*), basse (*f.*).
luck (good luck), bonheur (*m.*); *bad luck*, malheur (*m.*).

M.

mad, fou, fol (*m.*), folle (*f.*).
madam, madame (*f.*).
made, fait.
magnificent, magnifique.
make (to), faire.
mamma, maman (*f.*).
malicious, malin (*m.*), maligne (*f.*).
man, homme (*m.*).
man-servant, domestique (*m.*).

ENGLISH EXERCISES FOR TRANSLATION. 267

many, beaucoup, plusieurs ; *how many*, combien (de) ; *so many*, tant (de) ; *too many*, trop (de) ; *many a one*, maint, bien des.
marble, marbre (*m.*).
March, mars (*m.*).
march (to), marcher.
mark, marque (*f.*).
master, maître (*m.*).
May, mai (*m.*).
mean (to), vouloir dire ; *by no means*, aucunement (ne) ; nullement (ne).
meat, viande (*f.*).
meet (to), rencontrer.
mend (to), raccommoder.
merchandise, marchandise (*f.*).
merchant, négociant (*m.*).
meter, mètre (*m.*).
middle, milieu (*m.*).
midst (in the) (of), au milieu (de).
milk, lait (*m.*).
milk (to), traire.
mill, moulin (*m.*).
miller, meunier (*m.*).
mind, esprit (*m.*) ; *to have a mind (to)*, avoir envie (de).
minute, minute (*f.*).
miserly, avare.
misfortune, malheur (*m.*).
miss, mademoiselle (*f.*).
mistake, faute (*f.*).
mistaken (to be), se tromper.
Mister, monsieur (*m.*).
Mrs., madame (*f.*).
moment, moment (*m.*).
monarch, monarque (*m.*).
Monday, lundi (*m.*).
money, argent (*m*).
month, mois (*m.*) ; *monthly*, par mois.
more, plus, davantage ; *no more*, ne plus.
morning, matin (*m.*) ; *good-morning*, bonjour.
morrow, lendemain ; *to-morrow*, demain.

morsel, morceau (*m.*).
most, le plus, la plupart.
mother, mère (*f.*).
mountain, montagne (*f.*).
move (to) (affect), émouvoir.
much, many, beaucoup (de) ; *not much*, ne — guère, pas beaucoup ; *how much*, combien (de) ; *too much*, trop (de) ; *as much as*, autant que ; *so much, so many*, tant.
music, musique (*f.*).
music-book, cahier de musique (*m.*).
muslin, mousseline (*f.*).
must, devoir.
my, mon (*m.*), ma (*f.*).
myself, moi-même.

N.

name, nom (*m.*).
nation, nation (*f.*).
near (close by), près de, auprès de.
necessary, nécessaire ; *to be necessary*, falloir.
need, to have need of, avoir besoin de.
neglect (to), négliger.
negligent, négligent.
neighbor, voisin (*m.*).
neighborhood, voisinage (*m.*).
neither, ni l'un ni l'autre ; *neither — nor*, ni — ni.
nephew, neveu (*m.*).
never, jamais (ne).
nevertheless, néanmoins.
new, neuf (*m.*), neuve (*f.*).
new, nouveau, nouvel (*m.*), nouvelle (*f.*).
news, les nouvelles (*pl. f.*).
newspaper, journal (*m.*).
next, prochain.
nine, neuf.
night, nuit (*f.*) ; *to-night*, cette nuit ; *last night*, la nuit passée.
no, non ; nul (*m.*), nulle (*f.*).
no longer, no more, ne plus
no one, personne ; *none*, aucun (ne), nul (ne), pas un (ne).

nobody, personne (ne).
noise, bruit (*m*.).
noon (*at*), à midi.
nor, ni.
not, ne — pas ; ne point.
not one, nul (*m*.), nulle (*f*.).
notary, notaire (*m*.).
note, billet (*m*.).
nothing, rien (ne).
nothing but, only, ne — que.
notice (*to give*), avertir.
November, novembre (*m*.).
now, maintenant.
nowhere, nulle part (ne).

O.

obedience, obéissance (*f*.).
obedient, obéissant.
obey (*to*), obéir (à).
oblige (*to*), rendre service.
obliged, obligé (de) ; *to be obliged*, devoir.
oblong, oblong (*m*.), oblongue (*f*.).
observe (*to*), remarquer, observer.
obtain (*to*), obtenir.
October, octobre (*m*.).
of, de.
offend (*to*), offenser.
offer (*to*), offrir.
office, bureau (*m*.).
often, souvent.
oh! aïe! oh!
old, âgé ; vieux, vieil (*m*.), vieille (*f*.).
oldest, aîné.
oldish, vieillot (*m*.), vieillotte (*f*.).
on, sur.
once, une fois ; *at once*, à la fois.
one, un.
one's self, soi-même.
only, seulement.
only, ne — que.
open (*to*), ouvrir.
opinion, avis (*m*.).
opportunity, occasion (*f*.).
opposite, vis-à-vis.
or, ou.
orange, orange (*f*.).

order, ordre (*m*.) ; *to put in order*, mettre en ordre ; *in order that*, afin que, pour que.
other, autre.
others, autrui.
otherwise, autrement.
our, notre (*s*.), nos (*pl*.).
ourselves, nous-mêmes.
out, hors.
outlive (*to*), survivre.
outside, out of doors, dehors.
owe (*to*), devoir.
owl, hibou (*m*.).

P.

packet, paquet (*m*.).
pain, mal (*m*.) ; *to have pain*, avoir mal.
painter, peintre (*m*.).
painting, peinture (*f*.), tableau (*m*.).
palace, palais (*m*.).
paper, papier (*m*.).
parasol, ombrelle (*f*.).
pardon (*to beg*), demander pardon.
parents, parents (*pl. m*.).
parlor, salon (*m*.).
part, partie (*f*).
pass (*to*), passer.
passion, passion (*f*.).
patience, patience (*f*.).
pattern, dessin (*m*.).
Paul, Paul.
pay (*to*), payer ; *to pay attention*, faire attention.
peach, pêche (*f*.).
pear, poire (*f*.).
pen, plume (*f*.).
pencil, crayon (*m*.).
penknife, canif (*m*.).
people, du monde ; peuple (*m*.) ; gens (*pl. m*.).
perhaps, peut-être.
permission, permission (*f*.).
permit (*to*), permettre.
perseverance, persévérance (*f*.).
person, personne (*f*.).
physician, médecin (*m*.).

picture, tableau (*m.*), peinture (*f.*).
piece, morceau (*m.*), pièce (*f.*).
pine-apple, ananas (*m.*).
pity (*to*), plaindre.
place, place (*f.*).
place (*to*), placer.
plate, assiette (*f.*).
play (*to*), jouer.
plaything, joujou (*m.*).
please (*to*), plaire (à); *if you please*, s'il vous plaît.
pleased with, content de.
pleasure, plaisir (*m.*).
pocket, poche (*f.*).
pocket-handkerchief, mouchoir de poche (*m.*).
polite, poli.
poor, pauvre.
postman, facteur (*m.*).
post-office, poste (*f.*).
pound, livre (*f.*).
power, pouvoir (*m.*),
powerful, puissant.
praise (*to*), louer.
pray (*to*), prier (de).
prayer, prière (*f.*).
prefer (*to*), préférer.
preference, préférence (*f.*).
prefixed, préfix (*m.*), préfixe (*f.*).
presence (*in my*), en ma présence.
present, cadeau (*m.*); *at present*, à présent.
presently, tout à l'heure.
pretty, joli (*m.*), jolie (*f.*); gentil (*m.*), gentille (*f.*).
prevent, empêcher.
price, prix (*m.*).
principle, principe (*m.*).
prize, prix (*m.*).
procession, procession (*f.*).
proclaim (*to*), proclamer.
professor, professeur (*m.*).
professed, profès (*m.*), professe (*f.*).
promise, promesse (*f.*).
promise (*to*), promettre.
pronounce (*to*), prononcer.
property, bien (*m.*).

protect (*to*), protéger.
provide (*to*), pourvoir.
provided (*conjunction*), pourvu que.
prudence, prudence (*f.*).
prudent, prudent ; *prudently*, prudemment.
pshaw! bah !
public, public (*m.*), publique (*f.*).
pull (*to*), tirer.
punish (*to*), punir.
pupil, élève (*m.* and *f.*).
purposely, exprès (*m.*), expresse (*f.*)
pursue (*to*), poursuivre.
put on (*to*), mettre.
put back (*to*), *put off* (*to*), remettre.
put in order, mettre en ordre.

Q.

quality, qualité (*f.*).
quarry, carrière (*f.*).
quarter, quart (*m.*), quartier (*m.*).
question, question (*f.*) ; *to ask a question*, faire une question.
quick, *quickly*, vite.
quiet, tranquille.
quit (*to*), quitter.

R.

rain, pluie (*f.*).
rain (*to*), pleuvoir.
rather, plutôt.
reach (*to*), atteindre.
read (*to*), lire.
ready, prêt (à).
reap (*to*), recueillir.
reascend (*to*), remonter.
reason, raison (*f.*) ; *to listen to reason*, entendre raison.
receive (*to*), recevoir.
recital, récit (*m.*).
recognize (*to*), reconnaître.
recollect (*to*), se rappeler.
red, rouge.
reddish (*of hair*), roux (*m.*), rousse (*f.*).
re-enter (*to*), rentrer.
refuse (*to*), refuser.
regard, *with regard to*, à l'égard de.

relate (to), raconter.
relative, parent (*m.*), parente (*f.*).
rely upon (to), compter (sur).
remain (to), rester.
remember (to), se souvenir de.
renounce (to), renoncer (à).
rent (to), louer.
repair (to), réparer.
reprove (to) (for), réprimander de.
reputation, réputation (*f.*).
resemble (to), ressembler (à).
reserve (to), réserver.
respect, respect (*m.*).
respect (to), respecter.
respectfully, avec égard.
rest (remainder), reste (*m.*).
resume (to), reprendre.
retain (to), retenir.
return (to) (give back), rendre.
return (to) (come back), revenir
return (to) (go back), retourner.
reward (to) (for), récompenser (de).
ribbon, ruban (*m.*).
rich, riche.
right, juste.
right (to be), avoir raison.
ring, bague (*f.*), anneau (*m.*).
ring (to), sonner.
ripe, mûr.
rise (to), se lever.
road, chemin (*m.*).
robe, robe (*f.*).
room, chamber (*f.*).
round, rond.
run (to), courir.
run away (to), s'enfuir.

S.

sad, triste.
salt, sel (*m.*).
same, même.
satin, satin (*m.*).
satisfied, content.
satisfied (with), content (de).
satisfy (to), contenter.
Saturday, samedi (*m.*).
say (to), dire.

scholar, élève (*m.* and *f.*).
school, école (*f.*); *at school,* à l'école.
scissors, ciseaux (*m. pl.*).
sea, mer (*f.*).
season, saison (*f.*).
seasonable, à propos.
seat, place (*f.*).
secret, secret (*m.*), secrète (*f.*).
sedulous, appliqué.
see (to), voir.
see again (to), revoir.
seek (to), chercher.
select (to), choisir.
seem (to), paraître.
sell (to), vendre.
send (to), envoyer.
send away (to), send back (to), renvoyer.
send for (to), envoyer chercher, faire venir.
sentence, phrase (*f.*).
September, septembre (*m.*).
servant, domestique (*m.*), servante (*f.*).
serve (to), servir.
service, service (*m.*).
several, plusieurs.
sew (to), coudre.
shawl, châle (*m.*).
sheet, feuille (*f.*).
shine (to), luire.
ship, vaisseau (*m.*).
shipwreck, naufrage (*m.*)
shoe, soulier (*m.*).
shoemaker, cordonnier (*m.*).
shop (work-shop), atelier (*m.*).
show (to), montrer.
shun (to), fuir.
shut (to), fermer.
sick, malade.
sickness, maladie (*f.*).
side, côté; *by the side of,* à côté de.
sign, signe (*m.*).
silence! paix !
silent (to be), se taire.
silk, soie (*f.*).
silly, sot (*m.*), sotte (*f.*).

ENGLISH EXERCISES FOR TRANSLATION. 271

silver, argent (m.).
similar, pareil (m.), pareille (f.).
since (causal), puis que.
since (time), depuis.
since (conj.), depuis que.
sincere, sincère.
sing (to), chanter.
sister, sœur (f.).
sit down (to), s'asseoir; se mettre.
sitting (to be), être assis.
situation, situation (f.).
sky, ciel (m.).
sleep (to), dormir.
sleepy (to be), avoir sommeil.
slow, slowly, lent, lentement.
small, petit (m.), petite (f.).
smell (to), sentir.
snow, neige (f.).
snow (to), neiger.
so, si.
so, thus, ainsi.
soap, savon (m.).
society, société (f.).
soft, mou, mol (m.), molle (f.).
soft, doux (m.), douce (f.).
softly, gently, doucement.
soldier, soldat (m.).
some, quelque; quelques-uns.
somebody, quelqu'un.
something, quelque chose.
sometimes, quelquefois.
somewhere, quelque part.
son, fils (m.).
soon, bientôt, tôt; *sooner or later*, tôt ou tard ; *as soon as*, aussitôt que.
sore, mal (m.) ; *sore throat*, mal à la gorge.
sorry, fâché ; *to be sorry*, être fâché.
soup, potage (m.), soupe (f.).
speak (to), parler.
spend (to) (*of time*), passer.
spite, in spite of, malgré.
spoil (to), gâter.
spring, printemps (m.) ; *in the spring*, au printemps.
square, carré.
stable, écurie (f.).

start (to), partir (être).
stay (to), rester.
steam, vapeur (f.).
steamboat, bâteau à vapeur (m.).
steamer, bâtiment à vapeur (m.), steamer (m.).
step, pas (m.).
still (*again*), encore.
still (*snug*), coi (m.), coite (f.).
still (*quiet*), tranquille.
stir (to), bouger.
stocking, bas (m.).
store (*shop*), magasin (m.).
storekeeper, marchand (m.).
storm, orage (m.).
story, histoire (f.).
stout, fort, gros (m.), grosse (f.).
strange, étrange.
stranger, étranger (m.).
street, rue (f.).
strike (to), frapper.
strong, fort.
student, étudiant (m.).
studious, studieux (m.), studieuse (f.).
study (to), étudier.
study, étude (f.).
stuff, étoffe (f.), matière (f.).
subject, sujet (m.), sujette (f.).
succeed (to), réussir, parvenir (être.)
success, succès (m.).
such, tel (m.), telle (f.).
suffer (to), souffrir (de).
sugar, sucre (m.).
summer, été (m.).
Sunday, dimanche (m.).
supper, souper (m.).
supreme, suprême.
surety (*for payment*), aval.
surprise (to), surprendre ; *she is quite surprised*, elle est toute surprise.
survive (to), survivre.
sweet, doux (m.), douce (f.).

T.

table, table (f.).
tailor, tailleur (m.).

take (to), prendre, mener.
take away (to). ôter, emporter.
take back (to). reprendre.
take leave (to), prendre congé.
take a walk (to), se promener.
take off (to), ôter.
take out (to), extraire.
talk (to), parler, causer.
tall, grand (*m.*), grande (*f.*).
task, devoir (*m.*).
taste, goût (*m.*).
tea, thé (*m.*).
tea canister, boîte à thé (*f.*).
teacher, maître (*m.*).
tear (to), déchirer.
tell (to), dire.
Temple street, rue du Temple (*f.*).
than, que.
that, que (*conj.*); ce, cet (*m.*), cette (*f.*) (*adj.*).
thaw (to), dégeler.
their, leur (*m.*), leur (*f.*), leurs (*pl.*).
theme, thème (*m.*).
themselves, eux-mêmes (*m.*), elles-mêmes (*f.*).
then, alors, ensuite, donc, puis.
there, là.
therefore (then), donc.
there is, there are, il y a; voilà.
thick, épais (*m.*), épaisse (*f.*).
thing, chose (*f.*); *everything,* tout; *many things,* bien des choses.
think (to) (of), penser (à).
third, tiers (*m.*), tierce (*f.*).
thirst, soif (*f.*).
thirsty (to be), avoir soif.
this, ce, cet (*m.*), cette (*f.*).
threaten (to), menacer.
throat, gorge (*f.*).
throw (to), jeter.
through (by), par, à travers.
thunder (to), tonner; *thunder,* tonnerre (*m.*).
Thursday, jeudi (*m.*).
thus, ainsi.
thyself, toi-même.
till, jusqu'à.

time, temps (*m.*); *in time,* à temps; *at the right time,* bien à propos; *it is time,* il est temps; *a long time,* longtemps; *many times,* bien des fois; *how many times,* combien de fois; *at a time, at once,* à la fois.
tired, fatigué (de), las (*m.*), lasse (*f.*).
to, à.
to (in order to), pour.
together, ensemble.
told, dit.
too (also), aussi.
too (too much), trop (de).
tool, outil (*m.*).
tooth, dent (*f.*).
toothache, mal aux dents.
towards, vers, envers.
town, ville (*f.*); *in town,* en ville.
train, train (*m.*).
translate (to), traduire.
travel (to), voyager.
traitor, traître (*m.*), traîtresse (*f.*).
tree, arbre (*m.*).
troops, les troupes (*pl.f.*).
trouble, chagrin (*m.*).
trouble (to), inquiéter.
true, vrai, fidèle (à).
truly, vraiment.
Tuesday, mardi (*m.*).
tumbler, verre (*m.*).
tune, ton; *out of tune,* faux (*m.*) fausse (*f.*).
turkey, dindon (*m.*).
Turkish, turc (*m.*), turque (*f.*).
turn (to), tourner.
twice, deux fois.
twin, jumeau (*m.*), jumelle (*f.*).

U.

umbrella, parapluie (*m.*).
uncle, oncle (*m.*).
under, sous.
understand (to), comprendre.
undertake (to), entreprendre.
undoubtedly, sans doute.
uneasy, inquiet (*m.*), inquiète (*f.*).

United States, les Etats-Unis.
unless, à moins que, sans que.
unknown, inconnu (*m.*).
until, jusque ; (*conj.*) jusqu'à ce que.
up, upon, sur.
up stairs, en haut.
use, to make use of, se servir.
useless, inutile (à).
usual, ordinaire.

V.

vacation, les vacances (*pl. f.*).
value (to), to set value upon, faire cas de.
vanquish (to), vaincre.
veil, voile (*m.*).
velvet, velours (*m.*).
very, très.
vessel, navire, bâtiment (*m.*).
vice, vice (*m.*).
violin, violon (*m.*).
visit, visite (*f.*).
voyage, voyage (*m.*).

W.

waistcoat, gilet (*m.*).
wait, attendre ; *to keep one waiting,* faire attendre.
walk, promenade (*f.*) ; *to take a walk,* se promener.
walk (to), marcher.
want, for want of, faute de.
war, guerre (*f.*).
warehouse, magasin (*m.*).
warm, chaud.
warm (to be), avoir chaud.
warmly, chaudement.
watch, montre (*f.*).
watch-chain, chaîne de montre.
watchmaker, horloger (*m.*).
water, eau (*f.*).
weather, temps (*m.*).
Wednesday, mercredi (*m*).
week, semaine (*f.*) ; *weekly,* par semaine.
well, bien ; *it is well,* il est bien ; *well then!* eh bien !

west, ouest (*m.*).
wet (to), mouiller.
what, que.
what (that which) as subject, ce qui; *as object,* ce que.
whatever, quelconque.
when, lorsque; quand.
where, où.
wherever, partout où.
wherewith, de quoi.
whether (if), si.
which (which one), qui, lequel (*m.*), laquelle (*f.*); *which ones,* lesquels (*m.*), lesquelles (*f.*); *in which,* où; *from which,* d'où; *through which,* par où.
while, pendant ; *a little while ago,* tantôt.
while (*conj.*), pendant que.
while, tandis que.
white, blanc (*m.*), blanche (*f.*).
who, whom, que ; *of whom, of which, whose,* dont.
whoever, quiconque.
whole, tout, toute ; *the whole,* le tout.
why, pourquoi.
wicked (the), les méchants (*pl.*).
wife, femme (*f.*).
William, Guillaume.
willing (to be), vouloir.
willingly, volontiers.
window, fenêtre (*f.*).
wine, vin (*m.*).
wise, sage.
wish (to), vouloir, désirer, avoir envie de.
wish well (to), vouloir du bien (à).
wit, esprit (*m.*).
with, avec.
within (in it), dedans.
without, sans, dehors.
woman, femme (*f.*).
wonder (to), s'étonner.
wool, laine (*f.*).
word, mot (*m.*) ; parole (*f.*).
work, ouvrage (*m.*).

work (to), travailler.
world, monde (*m.*); *everybody,* tout le monde.
worth (to be worth), valoir; *it is worth,* il vaut.
write (to), écrire.
wrong (to be wrong), avoir tort.

Y.

year, an (*m.*), année (*f.*); *in the year,* en l'an.

yes, oui.
yesterday, hier.
yesterday morning, hier matin.
yet, encore; *not yet,* pas encore.
yonder, là-bas.
young, jeune.
young lady, demoiselle (*f.*).
yourself, vous-même.
yourselves, vous-mêmes.

ENDINGS OF THE REGULAR CONJUGATIONS.

Infinitive Forms		INDICATIVE				CONDITIONAL	IMPERATIVE	SUBJUNCTIVE	
	Present. *A*	Present. *B*	Imperfect. *B*	Past Def. *C*	Future. *D*	Present. *E*	*F*	Present. *G*	Imperfect. *H*
First Conjugation. er; c, çe	e es e ons ez ent	ais ais ait ions iez aient	ai as a âmes âtes èrent	erai eras era erons erez eront	erais erais erait erions eriez eraient	e ons ez	e es e ions iez ent	asse asses ât assions assiez assent
Second Conjugation. ir; issant; i, ie	is is it issons issez issent	issais issais issait issions issiez issaient	is is it îmes îtes irent	irai iras ira irons irez iront	irais irais irait irions iriez iraient	is issons issez	isse isses isse issions issiez issent	isse isses ît issions issiez issent
Third Conjugation. evoir, evant; u, ue	ois ois oit evons evez oivent	evais evais evait evions eviez evaient	us us ut ûmes ûtes urent	evrai evras evra evrons evrez evront	evrais evrais evrait evrions evriez evraient	ois evons evez	oive oives oive evions eviez oivent	usse usses ût ussions ussiez ussent
Fourth Conjugation. re; ant; u, ue	s s — ons ez ent	ais ais ait ions iez aient	is is it îmes îtes irent	rai ras ra rons rez ront	rais rais rait rions riez raient	s ons ez	e es e ions iez ent	isse isses ît issions issiez issent

CONJUGATION OF VERBS.

REGULAR AND IRREGULAR.

AVOIR—to have. *(Auxiliary Verb.)*

INDICATIVE MODE.

PRESENT.* *A*		PAST INDEFINITE.* *A'*	
J'ai,	I have.	J'ai eu,	I have had.
Tu as,	thou hast.	Tu as eu,	thou hast had.
Il a,	he has.	Il a eu,	he has had.
Nous avons,	we have.	Nous avons eu,	we have had.
Vous avez,	you have.	Vous avez eu,	you have had.
Ils ont,	they have.	Ils ont eu,	they have had.

IMPERFECT. *B*		PLUPERFECT. *B'*	
J'avais,	I had.	J'avais eu,	I had had.
Tu avais,	thou hadst.	Tu avais eu,	thou hadst had.
Il avait,	he had.	Il avait eu,	he had had.
Nous avions,	we had.	Nous avions eu,	we had had.
Vous aviez,	you had.	Vous aviez eu,	you had had.
Ils avaient,	they had.	Ils avaient eu,	they had had.

PAST DEFINITE. *C*		PAST ANTERIOR. *C'*	
J'eus,	I had.	J'eus eu,	I had had.
Tu eus,	thou hadst.	Tu eus eu,	thou hadst had.
Il eut,	he had.	Il eut eu,	he had had.
Nous eûmes,	we had.	Nous eûmes eu,	we had had.
Vous eûtes,	you had.	Vous eûtes eu,	you had had.
Ils eurent,	they had.	Ils eurent eu,	they had had.

FUTURE. *D*		FUTURE ANTERIOR. *D'*	
J'aurai,	I shall have.	J'aurai eu,	I shall have had.
Tu auras,	thou will have.	Tu auras eu,	thou will have had.
Il aura,	he will have.	Il aura eu,	he will have had.
Nous aurons,	we shall have.	Nous aurons eu,	we shall have had.
Vous aurez,	you will have.	Vous aurez eu,	you will have had.
Ils auront,	they will have.	Ils auront eu,	they will have had.

---

* A letter is assigned to each tense as a convenient abbreviation to be used in correcting exercises.

CONDITIONAL MODE.

PRESENT. *E*		PAST.* *E'*	
J'aurais,	*I should have.*	J'aurais eu,	*I should* ⎫
Tu aurais,	*thou wouldst have.*	Tu aurais eu,	*thou wouldst*
Il aurait,	*he would have.*	Il aurait eu,	*he would*
Nous aurions,	*we should have.*	Nous aurions eu,	*we should* ⎬ *have had.*
Vous auriez,	*you would have.*	Vous auriez eu,	*you would*
Ils auraient,	*they would have.*	Ils auraient eu,	*they would* ⎭

IMPERATIVE MODE. *F*

Aie,	*have (thou).*
Ayons,	*let us have.*
Ayez,	*have (you).*

SUBJUNCTIVE MODE.

PRESENT. *G*		PAST. *G'*	
Que j'aie,	*that I may have.*	Que j'aie eu,	*that I may* ⎫
Que tu aies,	*that thou mayst have.*	Que tu aies eu,	*that thou mayst*
Qu'il ait,	*that he may have.*	Qu'il ait eu,	*that he may* ⎬ *have had.*
Que nous ayons,	*that we may have.*	Que nous ayons eu,	*that we may*
Que vous ayez,	*that you may have.*	Que vous ayez eu,	*that you may*
Qu'ils aient,	*that they may have.*	Qu'ils aient eu,	*that they may* ⎭

IMPERFECT. *H*		PLUPERFECT. *H'*	
Que j'eusse,	*that I* ⎫	Que j'eusse eu,	*that I* ⎫
Que tu eusses,	*that thou*	Que tu eusses eu,	*that thou*
Qu'il eût,	*that he* ⎬ *might have.*	Qu'il eût eu,	*that he* ⎬ *might have had.*
Que nous eussions,	*that we*	Que nous eussions eu,	*that we*
Que vous eussiez,	*that you*	Que vous eussiez eu,	*that you*
Qu'ils eussent,	*that they* ⎭	Qu'ils eussent eu,	*that they* ⎭

INFINITIVE MODE.

PRESENT. *I*		PAST. *I'*	
Avoir,	*to have.*	Avoir eu,	*to have had.*

PARTICIPLES.

PRESENT. *J*		PAST. *J'*	
Ayant,	*having.*	Ayant eu,	*having had.*

PAST PASSIVE. *K*

Eu, *m.*; eue, *f.*,   *had.*

---

* Second form of the cond. past: j'eusse eu, tu eusses eu, il eût eu, nous eussions eu, vous eussiez eu, ils eussent eu.

ÊTRE—to be. *(Auxiliary Verb.)*

INDICATIVE MODE.

PRESENT. *A*

Je suis,	I am.	J'ai été,	I have been.
Tu es,	thou art.	Tu as été,	thou hast been.
Il est,	he is.	Il a été,	he has been.
Nous sommes,	we are.	Nous avons été,	we have been.
Vous êtes,	you are.	Vous avez été,	you have been.
Ils sont,	they are.	Ils ont été,	they have been.

PAST INDEFINITE. *A'*

IMPERFECT. *B*

J'étais,	I was.	J'avais été,	I had been.
Tu étais,	thou wast.	Tu avais été,	thou hadst been.
Il était,	he was.	Il avait été,	he had been.
Nous étions,	we were.	Nous avions été,	we had been.
Vous étiez,	you were.	Vous aviez été,	you had been.
Ils étaient,	they were.	Ils avaient été,	they had been.

PLUPERFECT. *B'*

PAST DEFINITE. *C*

Je fus,	I was.	J'eus été,	I had been.
Tu fus,	thou wast.	Tu eus été,	thou hadst been.
Il fut,	he was.	Il eut été,	he had been.
Nous fûmes,	we were.	Nous eûmes été,	we had been.
Vous fûtes,	you were.	Vous eûtes été,	you had been.
Ils furent,	they were.	Ils eurent été,	they had been.

PAST ANTERIOR. *C'*

FUTURE. *D*

Je serai,	I shall be.	J'aurai été,	I shall ⎫
Tu seras,	thou will be.	Tu auras été,	thou will ⎪
Il sera,	he will be.	Il aura été,	he will ⎬ have been.
Nous serons,	we shall be.	Nous aurons été,	we shall ⎪
Vous serez,	you will be.	Vous aurez été,	you will ⎪
Ils seront,	they will be.	Ils auront été,	they will ⎭

FUTURE ANTERIOR. *D'*

CONDITIONAL MODE.

PRESENT. *E*

Je serais,	I should be.	J'aurais été,	I should ⎫
Tu serais,	thou wouldst be.	Tu aurais été,	thou wouldst ⎪
Il serait,	he would be.	Il aurait été,	he would ⎬ have been.
Nous serions,	we should be.	Nous aurions été,	we should ⎪
Vous seriez,	you would be.	Vous auriez été,	you would ⎪
Ils seraient,	they would be.	Ils auraient été,	they would ⎭

PAST.* *E'*

* Second form of the cond. past: j'eusse été, tu eusses été, il eût été, nous eussions été, vous eussiez été, ils eurent été.

IMPERATIVE MODE. *F*

Sois,	*be (thou).*
Soyons,	*let us be.*
Soyez,	*be (you).*

SUBJUNCTIVE MODE.

PRESENT. *G*

Que je sois,	*that I may be.*
Que tu sois,	*that thou mayst be.*
Qu'il soit,	*that he may be.*
Que nous soyons,	*that we may be.*
Que vous soyez,	*that you may be.*
Qu'ils soient,	*that they may be.*

PAST. *G'*

Que j'aie été,	*that I may* ⎫
Que tu aies été,	*that thou mayst*
Qu'il ait été,	*that he may* ⎬ *have been.*
Que nous ayons été,	*that we may*
Que vous ayez été,	*that you may*
Qu'ils aient été,	*that they may* ⎭

IMPERFECT. *H*

Que je fusse,	*that I* ⎫
Que tu fusses,	*that thou*
Qu'il fût,	*that he* ⎬ *might be.*
Que nous fussions,	*that we*
Que vous fussiez,	*that you*
Qu'ils fussent,	*that they* ⎭

PLUPERFECT. *H'*

Que j'eusse été,	*that I* ⎫
Que tu eusses été,	*that thou*
Qu'il eût été,	*that he* ⎬ *might have been.*
Que nous eussions été,	*that we*
Que vous eussiez été,	*that you*
Qu'ils eussent été,	*that they* ⎭

INFINITIVE MODE.

PRESENT. *I*

Être, *to be.*

PAST. *I'*

Avoir été, *to have been.*

PARTICIPLES.

PRESENT. *J*

Étant, *being.*

PAST. *J'*

Ayant été, *having been.*

PAST PASSIVE. *K*

Été, *been.*

FORMATION OF THE TENSES.

Tenses are primitive or derivative. The primitive tenses are the principal parts of the verb, and serve to form the derivative tenses. There are five primitive tenses in French verbs: the PRESENT INDICATIVE, the PAST DEFINITE, the PRESENT INFINITIVE and the two PARTICIPLES.

1. The PRESENT INDICATIVE, although itself a primitive tense, has its plural formed from the present participle by changing ant into ons, ez, ent.

aim ant	fin iss ant	rec ev ant	rend ant
nous aim ons	nous fin iss ons	nous rec ev ons	nous rend ons
vous aim ez	vous fin iss ez	vous rec ev ez	vous rend ez
ils aim ent	ils fin iss ent	ils reç oiv ent	ils rend ent

2. The IMPERFECT INDICATIVE is also formed from the present participle by changing ant into ais, ais, ait, ions, iez, aient.

The two verbs **avoir** and **savoir** are the only exceptions to this rule.

3. The PAST DEFINITE is a primitive tense and has four sets of endings.

ai, as, a, âmes, âtes, èrent, for the 1st conjugation;
is, is, it, îmes, îtes, irent, for the 2d and 4th conjugation;
us, us, ut, ûmes, ûtes, urent, for the 3d conjugation;
ins, ins, int, înmes, întes, inrent, for tenir, venir and compounds.

4. The FUTURE adds ai, as, a, ons, ez, ont, to the present infinitive. But, in the third and fourth conjugations, the endings oir and re lose respectively oi and e.

aim er	fin ir	rec evoir	rend re
j'aim erai	je fin irai	je rec evrai	je rend rai

FORMATION OF THE TENSES.

5. The CONDITIONAL follows the peculiarities of the future in all verbs—whether regular, or irregular—and adds ais, ais, ait, ions, iez, aient, to the r of the infinitive : **aimer, j'aimerais; recevoir, je recevrais,** etc.

6. The IMPERATIVE has its second person singular like the first person singular of the present indicative—except in **avoir, être, aller, savoir.** The first and second persons plural are as in the present indicative—except in **avoir, être, savoir.**

7. The SUBJUNCTIVE PRESENT is formed from the present participle by changing ant into e, es, e, ions, iez, ent. Only, for euphony, verbs in **evoir**, change e into oi in the singular and in the third person plural : **devant, que je doive; recevant, que je reçoive.**

8. The SUBJUNCTIVE IMPERFECT. The first person singular of this tense can always be obtained by adding se to the second person singular of the past definite. This rule is good even for irregular verbs :

tu aim as	tu fin is	tu reç us	tu rend is
que j'aim asse	que je fin isse,	que je reç usse,	que je rend isse

9. The compound tenses are all formed of the past participle and one of the auxiliary verbs **avoir** or **être.**

REM. 1. All verbs that more or less deviate from the above rules are given in the Alphabetical List, "page 302, and" referred to their respective models in the paradigms for irregular verbs.

REM. 2. In the following paradigms, each tense has a letter assigned to it, which letter may be used as a convenient abbreviation to indicate the proper tense in written exercises.

REM. 3. Throughout the models of the regular conjugations, every simple **tense is headed by its primitive part** printed in bold type.

REGULAR VERBS.

First Conjugation in **ER—COUPER**, to cut. *(Model Verb.)*

Couper, to cut.   *Coupant, cutting.*   *Coupé, cut.*

INDICATIVE MODE.

Present. *A*		Past Indefinite. *A'*	
Je **coup** e,*	*I cut.*	J'ai coupé,	*I have cut.*
Tu **coup** es,	*thou cuttest.*	Tu as coupé,	*thou hast cut.*
Il **coup** e,	*he cuts.*	Il a coupé,	*he has cut.*
(**coup** ant.)*			
N. **coup** ons,	*we cut.*	Nous avons coupé,	*we have cut.*
V. **coup** ez,	*you cut.*	Vous avez coupé,	*you have cut.*
Ils **coup** ent,	*they cut.*	Ils ont coupé,	*they have cut.*

Imperfect. *B*		Pluperfect. *B'*	
(**coup** ant.)			
Je **coup** ais,	*I was cutting.*	J'avais coupé,	*I had cut.*
Tu **coup** ais,	*thou wast cutting.*	Tu avais coupé,	*thou hadst cut.*
Il **coup** ait,	*he was cutting.*	Il avait coupé,	*he had cut.*
N. **coup** ions,	*we were cutting.*	Nous avions coupé,	*we had cut.*
V. **coup** iez.	*you were cutting.*	Vous aviez coupé,	*you had cut.*
Ils **coup** aient,	*they were cutting.*	Ils avaient coupé,	*they had cut.*

Past Definite. *C*		Past Anterior. *C'*	
Je **coup** ai,	*I cut.*	J'eus coupé,	*I had cut.*
Tu **coup** as,	*thou cuttedst.*	Tu eus coupé,	*thou hadst cut.*
Il **coup** a,	*he cut.*	Il eut coupé,	*he had cut.*
N. **coup** âmes,	*we cut.*	Nous eûmes coupé,	*we had cut.*
V. **coup** âtes,	*you cut.*	Vous eûtes coupé,	*you had cut.*
Ils **coup** èrent,	*they cut.*	Ils eurent coupé,	*they had cut.*

Future. *D*		Future Anterior. *D'*	
(**coup** er.)			
Je **coup** erai,	*I shall cut.*	J'aurai coupé,	*I shall* ⎫
Tu **coup** eras,	*thou will cut.*	Tu auras coupé,	*thou will* ⎪
Il **coup** era,	*he will cut.*	Il aura coupé,	*he will* ⎬ *have cut.*
N. **coup** erons,	*we shall cut.*	Nous aurons coupé,	*we shall* ⎪
V. **coup** erez,	*you will cut.*	Vous aurez coupé,	*you will* ⎪
Ils **coup** eront,	*they will cut.*	Ils auront coupé,	*they will* ⎭

*Throughout the four model verbs of the regular conjugations, every simple tense has its primitive part thus marked in bold type.

CONJUGATION OF VERBS.

CONDITIONAL MODE.

PRESENT. *E*
(*coup er.*)

Je coup erais,	*I should cut.*	J'aurais coupé,	*I should* ⎫
Tu coup erais,	*thou wouldst cut.*	Tu aurais coupé,	*thou wouldst* ⎪
Il coup erait,	*he would cut.*	Il aurait coupé,	*he would* ⎬ *have cut.*
N. coup erions,	*we should cut.*	Nous aurions coupé,	*we should* ⎪
V. coup eriez,	*you would cut.*	Vous auriez coupé,	*you would* ⎪
Ils coup eraient,	*they would cut.*	Ils auraient coupé,	*they would* ⎭

PAST.* *E'*

IMPERATIVE MODE. *F*

(Je coup e.) Coup e, *cut (thou).*
(coup ant.) Coup ons, *let us cut.*
  Coup ez, *cut (you).*

SUBJUNCTIVE MODE.

PRESENT. *G*
(*coup ant.*)

Que je coup e,	*that I may cut.*	Que j'aie coupé,	*that I* ⎫
Que tu coup es,	*that thou mayst cut.*	Que tu aies coupé,	*that thou* ⎪
Qu'il coup e,	*that he may cut.*	Qu'il ait coupé,	*that he* ⎬ *may have cut.*
Que n. coup ions,	*that we may cut.*	Que nous ayons coupé,	*that we* ⎪
Que v. coup iez,	*that you may cut.*	Que vous ayez coupé,	*that you* ⎪
Qu'ils coup ent,	*that they may cut.*	Qu'ils aient coupé,	*that they* ⎭

PAST. *G'*

IMPERFECT. *H*
(je coup ai.)

Que je coup asse,	*that I* ⎫	Que j'eusse coupé,	*that I* ⎫
Que tu coup asses,	*that thou* ⎪	Que tu eusses coupé,	*that thou* ⎪
Qu'il coup ât,	*that he* ⎬ *might cut.*	Qu'il eût coupé,	*that he* ⎬ *might have cut.*
Que n. coup assions,	*that we* ⎪	Que nous eussions coupé,	*that we* ⎪
Que v. coup assiez,	*that you* ⎪	Que vous eussiez coupé,	*that you* ⎪
Qu'ils coup assent,	*that they* ⎭	Qu'ils eussent coupé,	*that they* ⎭

PLUPERFECT. *H'*

INFINITIVE MODE.

PRESENT. *I*
Coup er, *to cut.*

PAST. *I'*
Avoir coupé, *to have cut.*

PARTICIPLES.

PRESENT. *J*
Coup ant, *cutting.*

PAST. *J'*
Ayant coupé, *having cut.*

PAST PASSIVE. *K*
Coup é, m.; coup ée, f., *cut.*

---

* Second form of the cond. past : j'eusse coupé, tu eusses coupé, il eût coupé, nous eussions coupé, vous eussiez coupé, ils eussent coupé.

Second Conjugation in **IR**—FINIR, to finish. *(Model Verb.)*

Finir, to finish.   *Finissant,* finishing.   *Fini,* finished.

INDICATIVE MODE.

Present. *A*

Je fin is,	I finish.
Tu fin is,	thou finishest.
Il fin it,	he finishes.
(fin issant.)	
N. fin issons,	we finish.
V. fin issez,	you finish.
Ils fin issent,	they finish.

Past Indefinite. *A'*

J'ai fini,	I have finished.
Tu as fini,	thou hast finished.
Il a fini,	he has finished.
Nous avons fini,	we have finished.
Vous avez fini,	you have finished.
Ils ont fini,	they have finished.

Imperfect. *B*

(fin issant.)

Je fin issais,	I was finishing.
Tu fin issais,	thou wast finishing.
Il fin issait,	he was finishing.
N. fin issions,	we were finishing.
V. fin issiez,	you were finishing.
Ils fin issaient,	they were finishing.

Pluperfect. *B'*

J'avais fini,	I had finished.
Tu avais fini,	thou hadst finished.
Il avait fini,	he had finished.
Nous avions fini,	we had finished.
Vous aviez fini,	you had finished.
Ils avaient fini,	they had finished.

Past Definite. *C*

Je fin is,	I finished.
Tu fin is,	thou finishedst.
Il fin it,	he finished.
N. fin îmes,	we finished.
V. fin îtes,	you finished.
Ils fin irent,	they finished.

Past Anterior. *C'*

J'eus fini,	I had finished.
Tu eus fini,	thou hadst finished.
Il eut fini,	he had finished.
Nous eûmes fini,	we had finished.
Vous eûtes fini,	you had finished.
Ils eurent fini,	they had finished.

Future. *D*

(fin ir.)

Je fin irai,	I shall finish.
Tu fin iras,	thou wilt finish.
Il fin ira,	he will finish.
N. fin irons,	we shall finish.
V. fin irez,	you will finish.
Ils fin iront,	they will finish.

Future Anterior. *D'*

J'aurai fini,	I shall
Tu auras fini,	thou wilt
Il aura fini,	he will
Nous aurons fini,	we shall
Vous aurez fini,	you will
Ils auront fini,	they will

} have finished.

CONJUGATION OF VERBS.

CONDITIONAL MODE.

PRESENT. *E*   PAST.* *L'*

(*fin ir.*)

Je fin irais,	I should		J'aurais fini,	I should
Tu fin irais,	thou wouldst		Tu aurais fini,	thou wouldst
Il fin irait,	he would	*finish.*	Il aurait fini,	he would
N. fin irions,	we should		Nous aurions fini,	we should
V. fin iriez,	you would		Vous auriez fini,	you would
Ils fin iraient,	they would		Ils auraient fini,	they would

have finished.

IMPERATIVE MODE. *F*

(je *fin is.*) Fin is,   *finish (thou).*

(*fin issant.*) { Fin issons,   *let us finish.*
          { Fin issez,   *finish (you).*

SUBJUNCTIVE MODE.

PRESENT. *G*   PAST. *G'*

(*fin issant.*)

Que je fin isse,	that I may		Que j'aie fini,	that I
Que tu fin isses,	that thou mayst		Que tu aies fini,	that thou
Qu'il fin isse,	that he may	*finish.*	Qu'il ait fini,	that he
Que n. fin issions,	that we may		Que nous ayons fini,	that we
Que v. fin issiez,	that you may		Que vous ayez fini,	that you
Qu'ils fin issent,	that they may		Qu'ils aient fini,	that they

may have finished.

IMPERFECT. *H*   PLUPERFECT. *H'*

(je *fin is.*)

Que je fin isse,	that I		Que j'eusse fini,	that I
Que tu fin isses,	that thou		Que tu eusses fini,	that thou
Qu'il fin it,	that he	*might finish.*	Qu'il eût fini,	that he
Que n. fin issions,	that we		Que nous eussions fini,	that we
Que v. fin issiez,	that you		Que vous eussiez fini,	that you
Qu'ils fin issent,	that they		Qu'ils eussent fini,	that they

might have finished.

INFINITIVE MODE.

PRESENT *I*   PAST. *I'*

Fin ir,   *to finish.*   *Avoir* fini, *to have finished.*

PARTICIPLES.

PRESENT. *J*   PAST. *J'*

Fin issant,   *finishing.*   Ayant fini, *having finished.*

PAST PASSIVE. *K*

Fin i,   *finished.*

---

* Second form of the cond. past: j'eusse fini, tu eusses fini, il eût fini, nous eussions fini, vous eussiez fini, ils eussent fini.

Third Conjugation in **OIR***—**RECEVOIR**, to receive.

Recevoir, to receive.   *Recevant, receiving.*   *Reçu, received.*

INDICATIVE MODE.

PRESENT. *A*		PAST INDEFINITE. *A'*	
Je reç ois,	I receive.	J'ai reçu,	I have received.
Tu reç ois,	thou receivest.	Tu as reçu,	thou hast received.
Il reç oit,	he receives.	Il a reçu,	he has received.
(rec ev ant.)			
N. rec ev ons,	we receive.	Nous avons reçu,	we have received.
V. rec ev ez,	you receive.	Vous avez reçu,	you have received.
Ils reç oivent,†	they receive.	Ils ont reçu,	they have received.

IMPERFECT. *B*		PLUPERFECT. *B'*	
(rec ev ant.)			
Je rec ev ais,	I was receiving.	J'avais reçu,	I had received.
Tu rec ev ais,	thou wast receiving.	Tu avais reçu,	thou hadst received.
Il rec ev ait,	he was receiving.	Il avait reçu,	he had received.
N. rec ev ions,	we were receiving.	Nous avions reçu,	we had received.
V. rec ev iez,	you were receiving.	Vous aviez reçu,	you had received.
Ils rec ev aient,	they were receiving.	Ils avaient reçu,	they had received.

PAST DEFINITE. *C*		PAST ANTERIOR. *C'*	
Je reç us,	I received.	J'eus reçu,	I had received.
Tu reç us,	thou receivedst.	Tu eus reçu,	thou hadst received.
Il reç ut,	he received.	Il eut reçu,	he had received.
N. reç ûmes,	we received.	Nous eûmes reçu,	we had received.
V. reç ûtes,	you received.	Vous eûtes reçu,	you had received.
Ils reç urent,	they received.	Ils eurent reçu,	they had received.

FUTURE. *D*		FUTURE ANTERIOR. *D'*	
(rec ev oir.)			
Je rec ev rai,	I shall receive.	J'aurai reçu,	I shall have ⎤
Tu rec ev ras,	thou will receive.	Tu auras reçu,	thou will have ⎥
Il rec ev ra,	he will receive.	Il aura reçu,	he will have ⎥ received.
N. rec ev rons,	we shall receive.	Nous aurons reçu,	we shall have ⎥
V. rec ev rez,	you will receive.	Vous aurez reçu,	you will have ⎥
Ils rec ev ront,	they will receive.	Ils auront reçu,	they will have ⎦

---

* Verbs in *oir*—about thirty in number—are all more or less irregular. Six only, ending in *evoir*, follow *recevoir* in all the tenses (see Note on next page). The others will be found in the list of irregular verbs

† Here, as in the pres. subj., *oi* takes the place of *e*, for euphony. Observe also ç (cedilla) before *o* and *u*.

CONDITIONAL MODE.

PRESENT. *E*   PAST.* *E'*

(rec ev oir.)

Je rec ev rais,	I should receive.	J'aurais reçu,	I should
Tu rec ev rais,	thou wouldst receive.	Tu aurais reçu,	thou wouldst
Il rec ev rait,	he would receive.	Il aurait reçu,	he would
N. rec ev rions,	we should receive.	Nous aurions reçu,	we should
V. rec ev riez,	you would receive.	Vous auriez reçu,	you would
Ils rec ev raient,	they would receive.	Ils auraient reçu,	they would

have received.

IMPERATIVE MODE. *F*

(je reç ois.) Reç ois,   receive (thou).
(rec ev ant.) { Rec ev ons,   let us receive.
                 { Rec ev ez,   receive (you).

SUBJUNCTIVE MODE.

PRESENT. *G*   PAST. *G'*

(rec ev ant.)

Que je reç oive,	that I	Que j'aie reçu,	that I
Que tu reç oives,	that thou	Que tu aies reçu,	that thou
Qu'il reç oive,	that he	Qu'il ait reçu,	that he
Que n. rec ev ions,	that we	Que nous ayons reçu,	that we
Que v. rec ev iez,	that you	Que vous ayez reçu,	that you
Qu'ils reç oivent,	that they	Qu'ils aient reçu,	that they

may receive.   *may have received.*

IMPERFECT. *H*   PLUPERFECT. *H'*

(je reç us.)

Que je reç usse,	that I	Que j'eusse reçu,	that I
Que tu reç usses,	that thou	Que tu eusses reçu,	that thou
Qu'il reç ût,	that he	Qu'il eût reçu,	that he
Que n. reç ussions,	that we	Que nous eussions reçu,	that we
Que v. reç ussiez,	that you	Que vous eussiez reçu,	that you
Qu'ils reç ussent,	that they	Qu'ils eussent reçu,	that they

might receive.   *might have received.*

INFINITIVE MODE.

PRESENT. *I*   PAST. *I'*

Rec ev oir,   to receive.   Avoir reçu,   to have received.

PARTICIPLES.

PRESENT. *J*   PAST. *J'*

Rec ev ant,   receiving.   Ayant reçu,   having received.

PAST PASSIVE. *K*

Reç u, *m.*; reç ue, *f.*, received.

NOTE.—Like *recevoir*, conjugate *apercevoir, to perceive ; concevoir, to conceite ; décevoir, to deceive ; devoir* (p p., *dû, due*), *to owe ; percevoir, to collect* (rents or taxes); *redevoir* (p. p., *redû, redue*), *to owe again.*

---

* Second form of the cond. past: j'eusse reçu, tu eusses reçu, il eût reçu, etc.

Fourth Conjugation in RE—VENDRE, to sell. *(Model Verb.)*

Vendre, to sell. *Vendant,* selling. *Vendu,* sold.

INDICATIVE MODE.

Present. *A*

Je vend s,	I sell.
Tu vend s,	thou sellest.
Il vend,	he sells.
(vend ant.)	
N. vend ons,	we sell.
V. vend ez,	you sell.
Ils vend ent,	they sell.

Past Indefinite. *A'*

J'ai vendu,	I have sold.
Tu as vendu,	thou hast sold.
Il a vendu,	he has sold.
Nous avons vendu,	we have sold.
Vous avez vendu,	you have sold.
Ils ont vendu,	they have sold.

Imperfect. *B*

(vend ant.)

Je vend ais,	I was selling.
Tu vend ais,	thou wast selling.
Il vend ait,	he was selling.
N. vend ions,	we were selling.
V. vend iez,	you were selling.
Ils vend aient,	they were selling.

Pluperfect. *B'*

J'avais vendu,	I had sold.
Tu avais vendu,	thou hadst sold.
Il avait vendu,	he had sold.
Nous avions vendu,	we had sold.
Vous aviez vendu,	you had sold.
Ils avaient vendu,	they had sold.

Past Definite. *C*

Je vend is,	I sold.
Tu vend is,	thou soldest.
Il vend it,	he sold.
N. vend imes,	we sold.
V. vend ites,	you sold.
Ils vend irent,	they sold.

Past Anterior. *C'*

J'eus vendu,	I had sold.
Tu eus vendu,	thou hadst sold.
Il eut vendu,	he had sold.
Nous eûmes vendu,	we had sold.
Vous eûtes vendu,	you had sold.
Ils eurent vendu,	they had sold.

Future. *D*

(vend re.)

Je vend rai,	I shall sell.
Tu vend ras,	thou will sell.
Il vend ra,	he will sell.
N. vend rons,	we shall sell.
V. vend rez,	you will sell.
Ils vend ront,	they will sell.

Future Anterior. *D'*

J'aurai vendu,	I shall ⎫
Tu auras vendu,	thou will ⎪
Il aura vendu,	he will ⎬ have sold.
Nous aurons vendu,	we shall ⎪
Vous aurez vendu,	you will ⎪
Ils auront vendu,	they will ⎭

CONJUGATION OF VERBS.

CONDITIONAL MODE.

PRESENT. *E*
(*vend re.*)

Je vend rais,	*I should sell.*	J'aurais vendu,	*I should*
Tu vend rais,	*thou wouldst sell.*	Tu aurais vendu,	*thou wouldst*
Il vend rait,	*he would sell.*	Il aurait vendu,	*he would*
N. vend rions,	*we should sell.*	Nous aurions vendu,	*we should*
V. vend riez,	*you would sell.*	Vous auriez vendu,	*you would*
Ils vend raient,	*they would sell.*	Ils auraient vendu,	*they would*

PAST.* *E'* ... *have sold.*

IMPERATIVE MODE. *F*

(je *vend s.*)
(*vend ant.*) { Vend s,   *sell (thou).*
             Vend ons,   *let us sell.*
             Vend ez,   *sell (you).*

SUBJUNCTIVE MODE.

PRESENT. *G*
(*vend ant.*)

Que je vend e,	*that I may sell.*	Que j'aie vendu,	*that I*
Que tu vend es,	*that thou mayst sell.*	Que tu aies vendu,	*that thou*
Qu'il vend e,	*that he may sell.*	Qu'il ait vendu,	*that he*
Que n. vend ions,	*that we may sell.*	Que nous ayons vendu,	*that we*
Que v. vend iez,	*that you may sell.*	Que vous ayez vendu,	*that you*
Qu'ils vend ent,	*that they may sell.*	Qu'ils aient vendu,	*that they*

PAST. *G'* ... *may have sold.*

IMPERFECT. *H*
(*vend is.*)

Que je vend isse,	*that I*	Que j'eusse vendu,	*that I*
Que tu vend isses,	*that thou*	Que tu eusses vendu,	*that thou*
Qu'il vend it,	*that he*	Qu'il eût vendu,	*that he*
Que n. vend issions,	*that we*	Que n. eussions vendu,	*that we*
Que v. vend issiez,	*that you*	Que v. eussiez vendu,	*that you*
Qu'ils vend issent,	*that they*	Qu'ils eussent vendu,	*that they*

... *might sell.*   PLUPERFECT. *H'* ... *might have sold.*

INFINITIVE MODE.

PRESENT. *I*   PAST. *I'*

Vend re,   *to sell.*   Avoir vendu,   *to have sold.*

PARTICIPLES.

PRESENT. *J*   PAST. *J'*

Vend ant,   *selling.*   Ayant vendu,   *having sold.*

PAST PASSIVE. *K*

Vend u,   *sold.*

---

* Second form of the cond. past: j'eusse vendu, tu eusses vendu, il eût vendu, nous eussions vendu, vous eussiez vendu. Ils eussent vendu.

CONJUGATION OF PASSIVE VERBS.

The passive verb is formed by joining the past participle of the active verb to the various forms of the auxiliary verb *être, to be;* as *aimer, to love; être aimé, to be loved.*

The past participle agrees, in gender and number, with the subject of the verb.

ÊTRE AIMÉ—to be loved. *(Model Verb.)*

INDICATIVE MODE.

Present. *A*

Je suis	} aimé *or* aimée,	} *I am loved, etc.*
Tu es		
Il *or* elle est		
Nous sommes	} aimés *or* aimées,	
Vous êtes		
Ils *or* elles sont		

Past Indefinite. *A'*

J'ai été	} aimé *or* aimée,	} *I have been loved, etc.*
Tu as été		
Il *or* elle a été		
Nous avons été	} aimés *or* aimées,	
Vous avez été		
Ils *or* elles ont été		

Imperfect. *B*

J'étais	} aimé *or* aimée,	} *I was being loved, etc.*
Tu étais		
Il *or* elle était		
Nous étions	} aimés *or* aimées,	
Vous étiez		
Ils *or* elles étaient		

Pluperfect. *B'*

J'avais été	} aimé *or* aimée,	} *I had been loved, etc.*
Tu avais été		
Il *or* elle avait été		
Nous avions été	} aimés *or* aimées,	
Vous aviez été		
Ils *or* elles avaient été		

Past Definite. *C*

Je fus	} aimé *or* aimée,	} *I was loved, etc.*
Tu fus		
Il *or* elle fut		
Nous fûmes	} aimés *or* aimées,	
Vous fûtes		
Ils *or* elles furent		

Past Anterior. *C'*

J'eus été	} aimé *or* aimée,	} *I had been loved, etc.*
Tu eus été		
Il *or* elle eut été		
Nous eûmes été	} aimés *or* aimées,	
Vous eûtes été		
Ils *or* elles eurent été		

Future. *D*

Je serai	} aimé *or* aimée,	} *I shall be loved, etc.*
Tu seras		
Il *or* elle sera		
Nous serons	} aimés *or* aimées,	
Vous serez		
Ils *or* elles seront		

Future Anterior. *D'*

J'aurai été	} aimé *or* aimée,	} *I shall have been loved, etc.*
Tu auras été		
Il *or* elle aura été		
Nous aurons été	} aimés *or* aimées,	
Vous aurez été		
Ils *or* elles auront été		

CONDITIONAL MODE.

PRESENT. *E*

Je serais	} aimé *or* aimée,	} *I should be loved, etc.*
Tu serais		
Il *or* elle serait		
Nous serions	} aimés *or* aimées,	
Vous seriez		
Ils *or* elles seraient		

PAST.* *E′*

J'aurais été	} aimé *or* aimée,	} *I should have been loved, etc.*
Tu aurais été		
Il *or* elle aurait été		
Nous aurions été	} aimés *or* aimées,	
Vous auriez été		
Ils *or* elles auraient été		

IMPERATIVE MODE. *F*

Sois aimé *or* aimée,   *be (thou) loved.*
Soyons } aimés *or* aimées, { *let us be loved.*
Soyez   { *be (you) loved.*

SUBJUNCTIVE MODE.

PRESENT. *G*

Que je sois	} aimé *or* aimée,	} *that I may be loved, etc.*
Que tu sois		
Qu'il *or* elle soit		
Que nous soyons	} aimés *or* aimées,	
Que vous soyez		
Qu'ils *or* elles soient		

PAST. *G′*

Que j'aie été	} aimé *or* aimée,	} *that I may have been loved*
Que tu aies été		
Qu'il *or* elle ait été		
Que nous ayons été	} aimés *or* aimées,	
Que vous ayez été		
Qu'ils *or* elles aient été		

IMPERFECT. *H*

Que je fusse	} aimé *or* aimée,	} *that I might be loved, etc.*
Que tu fusses		
Qu'il *or* elle fût		
Que nous fussions	} aimés *or* aimées,	
Que vous fussiez		
Qu'ils *or* elles fussent		

PLUPERFECT. *H′*

Que j'eusse été	} aimé *or* aimée,	} *that I might have been loved*
Que tu eusses été		
Qu'il *or* elle eût été		
Que nous eussions été	} aimés *or* aimées,	
Que vous eussiez été		
Qu'ils *or* elles eussent été		

INFINITIVE MODE.

PRESENT. *I*

Être aimé *or* aimée, aimés *or* aimées, } *to be loved.*

PAST. *I′*

Avoir été aimé *or* aimée, aimés *or* aimées, } *to have been loved.*

PARTICIPLES.

PRESENT. *J*

Étant aimé *or* aimée, aimés *or* aimées, } *being loved.*

PAST. *J′*

Ayant été aimé *or* aimée, aimés *or* aimées, } *having been loved.*

PAST PASSIVE. *K*

Été aimé *or* aimée, aimés *or* aimées, *been loved.*

---

* Second form of the cond. past: j'eusse été aimé, tu eusses été aimé, il eût été aimé, nous eussions été aimés, vous eussiez été aimés, ils eussent été aimés.

CONJUGATION OF A NEUTER VERB WITH ÊTRE.

Certain neuter verbs are conjugated in the compound tenses with the auxiliary verb *être, to be;* their past participle agrees with the subject of the verb. The verb *arriver, to arrive,* is given as the model verb of this class.

ARRIVER—to arrive. *(Model Verb.)*

INDICATIVE MODE.

PRESENT. *A*

J'arrive,	*I arrive.*
Tu arrives,	*thou arrivest.*
Il arrive,	*he arrives.*
Nous arrivons,	*we arrive.*
Vous arrivez,	*you arrive.*
Ils arrrivent,	*they arrive.*

PAST INDEFINITE. *A'*

Je suis	} arrivé *or* arrivée,	} *I have arrived, etc.*
Tu es		
Il *or* elle est		
Nous sommes	} arrivés *or* arrivées,	
Vous êtes		
Ils *or* elles sont		

IMPERFECT. *B*

J'arrivais,	*I was arriving.*
Tu arrivais,	*thou wast arriving.*
Il arrivait,	*he was arriving.*
Nous arrivions,	*we were arriving.*
Vous arriviez,	*you were arriving.*
Ils arrivaient,	*they were arriving.*

PLUPERFECT. *B'*

J'étais	} arrivé *or* arrivée,	} *I had arrived, etc.*
Tu étais		
Il *or* elle était		
Nous étions	} arrivés *or* arrivées,	
Vous étiez		
Ils *or* elles étaient		

PAST DEFINITE. *C*

J'arrivai,	*I arrived.*
Tu arrivas,	*thou arrivedst.*
Il arriva,	*he arrived.*
Nous arrivâmes,	*we arrived.*
Vous arrivâtes,	*you arrived.*
Ils arrivèrent,	*they arrived.*

PAST ANTERIOR. *C'*

Je fus	} arrivé *or* arrivée,	} *I had arrived, etc.*
Tu fus		
Il *or* elle fut		
Nous fûmes	} arrivés *or* arrivées,	
Vous fûtes		
Ils *or* elles furent		

FUTURE. *D*

J'arriverai,	*I shall arrive.*
Tu arriveras,	*thou will arrive.*
Il arrivera,	*he will arrive.*
Nous arriverons,	*we shall arrive.*
Vous arriverez,	*you will arrive.*
Ils arriveront,	*they will arrive.*

FUTURE ANTERIOR. *D'*

Je serai	} arrivé *or* arrivée,	} *I shall have arrived, etc.*
Tu seras		
Il *or* elle sera		
Nous serons	} arrivés *or* arrivées,	
Vous serez		
Ils *or* elles seront		

CONDITIONAL MODE.

PRESENT. *E*   **PAST.*** *E'*

J'arriverais,	*I should* ⎫		Je serais	{ arrivé ⎫
Tu arriverais,	*thou wouldst* ⎬		Tu serais	{ *or* ⎬ *I should have*
Il arriverait,	*he would* ⎭ *arrive.*		Il *or* elle serait	{ arrivée, ⎭ *arrived, etc.*
Nous arriverions,	*we should* ⎫		Nous serions	{ arrivés ⎫
Vous arriveriez,	*you would* ⎬		Vous seriez	{ *or* ⎬
Ils arriveraient,	*they would* ⎭		Ils *or* elles seraient	{ arrivées, ⎭

IMPERATIVE MODE. *F*

Arrive,	*arrive (thou).*
Arrivons,	*let us arrive.*
Arrivez,	*arrive (you).*

SUBJUNCTIVE MODE.

PRESENT. *G*   **PAST.** *G'*

Que j'arrive,	*that I* ⎫		Que je sois	{ arrivé ⎫
Que tu arrives,	*that thou* ⎬ *may arrive.*		Que tu sois	{ *or* ⎬ *that I may have arrived.*
Qu'il arrive,	*that he* ⎭		Qu'il *or* elle soit	{ arrivée, ⎭
Que nous arrivions,	*that we* ⎫		Que nous soyons	{ arrivés ⎫
Que vous arriviez,	*that you* ⎬		Que vous soyez	{ *or* ⎬
Qu'ils arrivent,	*that they* ⎭		Qu'ils *or* elles soient	{ arrivées, ⎭

IMPERFECT. *H*   **PLUPERFECT.** *H'*

Que j'arrivasse,	*that I* ⎫		Que je fusse	{ arrivé ⎫
Que tu arrivasses,	*that thou* ⎬ *might arrive.*		Que tu fusses	{ *or* ⎬ *that I might have arrived.*
Qu'il arrivât,	*that he* ⎭		Qu'il *or* elle fût	{ arrivée, ⎭
Que nous arrivassions,	*that we* ⎫		Que nous fussions	{ arrivés ⎫
Que vous arrivassiez,	*that you* ⎬		Que vous fussiez	{ *or* ⎬
Qu'ils arrivassent,	*that they* ⎭		Qu'ils *or* elles fussent	{ arrivées, ⎭

INFINITIVE MODE.

PRESENT. *I*   **PAST.** *I'*

Arriver,	*to arrive.*	Être arrivé *or* arrivée, ⎫ *to have*	
		arrivés *or* arrivées, ⎭ *arrived.*	

PARTICIPLES.

PRESENT. *J*   **PAST.** *J'*

Arrivant,	*arriving.*	Etant arrivé *or* arrivée, ⎫ *having*	
		arrivés *or* arrivées, ⎭ *arrived.*	

PAST. *K*

Arrivé *or* arrivée, arrivés *or* arrivées, *arrived.*

---

* Second form of the cond. past: je fusse arrivé, tu fusses arrivé, il fût arrivé, nous fussions arrivés, vous fussiez arrivés, ils furent arrivés.

CONJUGATION OF A PRONOMINAL VERB.

Pronominal verbs are conjugated with two pronouns of the same person, the one is the subject, the other the direct, or indirect, object of the verb.

In the compound tenses of pronominal verbs the auxiliary verb *être* is used for the auxiliary verb *avoir*. The past participle is subject to the same rule of agreement as the past participle of transitive verbs; that is, it agrees with its direct object, when the direct object precedes the participle.

SE COUPER—to cut one's self. *(Model Verb.)*

INDICATIVE MODE.

PRESENT. *A*

Je me coupe,   *I cut myself, etc.*
Tu te coupes,
Il se coupe,
Nous nous coupons,
Vous vous coupez,
Ils se coupent.

PAST INDEFINITE. *A'*

Je me suis coupé, *I have cut myself,*
Tu t'es coupé,   [*etc.*
Il s'est coupé,
Nous nous sommes coupés,
Vous vous êtes coupés,
Ils se sont coupés.

IMPERFECT. *B*

Je me coupais, *I was cutting myself,*
Tu te coupais,   [*etc.*
Il se coupait,
Nous nous coupions,
Vous vous coupiez,
Ils se coupaient.

PLUPERFECT. *B'*

Je m'étais coupé, *I had cut myself,*
Tu t'étais coupé,   [*etc.*
Il s'était coupé,
Nous nous étions coupés,
Vous vous étiez coupés,
Ils s'étaient coupés.

PAST DEFINITE. *C*

Je me coupai, *I cut myself, etc.*
Tu te coupas,
Il se coupa,
Nous nous coupâmes,
Vous vous coupâtes,
Ils se coupèrent.

PAST ANTERIOR. *C'*

Je me fus coupé, *I had cut myself,*
Tu te fus coupé,   [*etc.*
Il se fut coupé,
Nous nous fûmes coupés,
Vous vous fûtes coupés,
Ils se furent coupés.

FUTURE. *D*

Je me couperai, *I shall cut myself,*
Tu te couperas,   [*etc.*
Il se coupera,
Nous nous couperons,
Vous vous couperez,
Ils se couperont.

FUTURE ANTERIOR. *D'*

Je me serai coupé, *I shall have cut*
Tu te seras coupé,   [*myself, etc.*
Il se sera coupé,
Nous nous serons coupés,
Vous vous serez coupés,
Ils se seront coupés.

CONJUGATION OF VERBS.

CONDITIONAL MODE.

PRESENT. *E*

Je me couperais, *I should cut myself,*
Tu te couperais, *[etc.*
Il se couperait,
Nous nous couperions,
Vous vous couperiez,
Ils se couperaient.

PAST.* *E'*

Je me serais coupé, *I should have cut*
Tu te serais coupé, *[myself, etc.*
Il se serait coupé,
Nous nous serions coupés,
Vous vous seriez coupés,
Ils se seraient coupés.

IMPERATIVE MODE. *F*

Coupe-toi, *cut thyself.*
Coupons-nous, *let us cut ourselves.*
Coupez-vous, *cut yourselves.*

SUBJUNCTIVE MODE.

PRESENT. *G*

Que je me coupe, *that I may cut*
Que tu te coupes, *[myself, etc.*
Qu'il se coupe,
Que nous nous coupions,
Que vous vous coupiez,
Qu'ils se coupent.

PAST. *G'*

Que je me sois coupé, *that I may have*
Que tu te sois coupé, *[cut myself, etc.*
Qu'il se soit coupé,
Que nous nous soyons coupés,
Que vous vous soyez coupés,
Qu'ils se soient coupés.

IMPERFECT. *H*

Que je me coupasse, *that I might cut*
Que tu te coupasses, *[myself, etc.*
Qu'il se coupât,
Que nous nous coupassions,
Que vous vous coupassiez,
Qu'ils se coupassent.

PLUPERFECT. *H'*

Que je me fusse coupé, *that I might have*
Que tu te fusses coupé, *[cut myself, etc.*
Qu'il se fût coupé,
Que nous nous fussions coupés,
Que vous vous fussiez coupés,
Qu'ils se fussent coupés.

INFINITIVE MODE.

PRESENT. *I*

Se couper, *to cut one's self.*

PAST. *I'*

S'être coupé, *to have cut o. self*

PARTICIPLES.

PRESENT. *J*

Se coupant, *cutting one's self.*

PAST. *J'*

S'étant coupé, *having cut o. s.*

PAST. *K*

Coupé, *cut.*

---

* Second form of the cond. past: je me fusse coupé, tu te fusses coupé, il se fût coupé, nous nous fussions coupés, vous vous fussiez coupés, ils se fussent coupés.

CONJUGATION OF IMPERSONAL VERBS.

TONNER—to thunder. *(Model Verb.)*

INDICATIVE MODE.

A	Il tonne,	*it thunders.*	*A'*	Il a tonné,	*it has thundered*
B	Il tonnait,	*it was thundering.*	*B'*	Il avait tonné,	*it had thundered.*
C	Il tonna,	*it thundered.*	*C'*	Il eut tonné,	*it had thundered.*
D	Il tonnera,	*it will thunder.*	*D'*	Il aura tonné,	*it will have thundered.*

CONDITIONAL MODE.

E	Il tonnerait,	*it would thunder.*	*E'*	Il aurait tonné,	*it would have, etc.*

SUBJUNCTIVE MODE.

G	Qu'il tonne,	*that it may thunder.*	*G'*	Qu'il ait tonné,	*that it may have, etc.*
H	Qu'il tonnât,	*that it might thunder.*	*H'*	Qu'il eût tonné,	*that it might have thundered.*

INFINITIVE.

I   Tonner,   *to thunder.*

PARTICIPLES.

J	Tonnant,	*thundering.*	*K* Tonné,	*thundered.*

IRREGULAR IMPERSONAL VERBS

Y AVOIR—to be there.   FALLOIR—to be necessary.
PLEUVOIR—to rain.

INDICATIVE { PRES. *A*	Il y a *(there is, there are).*	Il faut.	Il pleut.
IMPERF. *B*	Il y avait.	Il fallait.	Il pleuvait.
P. DEF. *C*	Il y eut.	Il fallut.	Il plut.
FUT. *D*	Il y aura.	Il faudra.	Il pleuvra.
COND. PRES. *E*	Il y aurait.	Il faudrait.	Il pleuvrait.
SUBJ. { PRES. *G*	Qu'il y ait.	Qu'il faille.	Qu'il pleuve
IMPERF. *H*	Qu'il y eût.	Qu'il fallut.	Qu'il plût.
INFINITIVE. *I*	Y avoir.	Falloir.	Pleuvoir.
PRES. PART. *J*	Y ayant.	*(wanting.)*	Pleuvant.
PAST PART. *K*	Eu.	Fallu.	Plu

ORTHOGRAPHIC IRREGULARITIES

In the First Conjugation.

Some classes of verbs in the first conjugation, though regularly varied throughout, undergo, in certain persons and tenses, slight changes to make their orthography conformable to the pronunciation.

1. In verbs ending in *cer*, as *commencer, to commence*, the letter *c*, to retain the sound of *s*, takes the cedilla before *a* and *o*; as, *commençant, nous commençons*.

2. In verbs ending in *ger*, as *manger, to eat*, an *e* is inserted after *g*, before *a* and *o*, to make the *g* retain its soft sound; as *mangeant, nous mangeons*.

3. In verbs ending in *yer*, as *nettoyer, to clean*, the *y* is changed into *i* before *e* mute; as, *je nettoie, tu nettoies, il nettoie, ils nettoient*; but *nous nettoyons, vous nettoyez*.

Rem.—Verbs having an *a* before the ending *yer*, as *payer, to pay*, may either retain the *y* before *e* mute or change it into *i*: *je paye*, or *je paie*.

4. In verbs having é (acute) or e (mute) before the consonant that precedes the ending *er*, as *espérer, to hope*, and *mener, to lead*, the é or e is changed into è (grave) before a mute syllable; as, *j'espère, I hope ; je mène, I lead*, etc.

Rem. Verbs in *éger*, as *abréger, protéger*, retain the é in the future and conditional: j'abrégerai, tu protégeras. See also verbs in *eler* and *eter*, No. 5.

5. Verbs ending in *eler*, as *appeler, to call*, double the *l*; and those in *eter*, as *jeter, to throw*, double the *t* before *e* mute ; as, *j'appelle, tu appelles, il appelle, ils appellent*; and, *je jette, tu jettes, il jette, ils jettent*. But *nous appelons, vous appelez ; nous jetons, vous jetez*, etc.

Rem.—The verbs *acheter, to buy; bourreler, to torment ; déceler, to disclose; geler, to freeze ; harceler, to harass ; peler, to peel*, are exceptions to this last rule; they come under Rule No. 4.

CONJUGATION OF

INFINITIVE FORMS.	INDICATIVE MODE.			
	PRESENT. *A*	IMPERFECT. *B*	PAST DEF. *C*	FUTURE. *D*
1. *Aller,* *to go.* allant. allé. être allé. étant allé.	je vais, tu vas, il va, nous allons, vous allez, ils vont.	j'allais, tu allais, il allait, nous allions, vous alliez, ils allaient.	j'allai, tu allas, il alla, nous allâmes, vous allâtes, ils allèrent.	j'irai, tu iras, il ira, nous irons, vous irez, ils iront.
2. *Envoyer,* *to send.* envoyant. envoyé. avoir envoyé. ayant envoyé.	j'envoie (p. 251). tu envoies, il envoie, nous envoyons, vous envoyez, ils envoient.	j'envoyais, tu envoyais, il envoyait, nous envoyions, vous envoyiez, ils envoyaient.	j'envoyai, tu envoyas, il envoya, n. envoyâmes, v. envoyâtes, ils envoyèrent.	j'enverrai, tu enverras, il enverra, nous enverrons, vous enverrez, ils enverront.
3. *Acquérir,* *to acquire.* acquérant. acquis. avoir acquis. ayant acquis.	j'acquiers, tu acquiers, il acquiert, nous acquérons, vous acquérez, ils acquièrent.	j'acquérais, tu acquérais, il acquérait, nous acquérions, vous acquériez, ils acquéraient.	j'acquis, tu acquis, il acquit, nous acquîmes, vous acquîtes, ils acquirent.	j'acquerrai, tu acquerras, il acquerra, nous acquerrons, vous acquerrez, ils acquerront.
4. *Bouillir,* *to boil.* bouillant. bouilli. avoir bouilli. ayant bouilli.	je bous, tu bous, il bout, nous bouillons, vous bouillez, ils bouillent.	je bouillais, tu bouillais, il bouillait, nous bouillions, vous bouilliez, ils bouillaient.	je bouillis, tu bouillis, il bouillit, nous bouillîmes, vous bouillîtes, ils bouillirent.	je bouillirai, tu bouilliras, il bouillira, nous bouillirons, vous bouillirez, ils bouilliront.
5. *Courir,* *to run.* courant. couru. avoir couru. ayant couru.	je cours, tu cours, il court, nous courons, vous courez, ils courent.	je courais, tu courais, il courait, nous courions, vous couriez, ils couraient.	je courus, tu courus, il courut, nous courûmes, vous courûtes, ils coururent.	je courrai, tu courras, il courra, nous courrons, vous courrez, ils courront.
6. *Cueillir,* *to gather.* cueillant. cueilli. avoir cueilli. ayant cueilli.	je cueille, tu cueilles, il cueille, nous cueillons, vous cueillez, ils cueillent.	je cueillais, tu cueillais, il cueillait, nous cueillions, vous cueilliez, ils cueillaient.	je cueillis, tu cueillis, il cueillit, nous cueillîmes, vous cueillîtes, ils cueillirent.	je cueillerai, tu cueilleras, il cueillera, nous cueillerons, vous cueillerez, ils cueilleront.
7. *Dormir,* *to sleep.* dormant. dormi. avoir dormi. ayant dormi.	je dors, tu dors, il dort, nous dormons, vous dormez, ils dorment.	je dormais, tu dormais, il dormait, nous dormions, vous dormiez, ils dormaient.	je dormis, tu dormis, il dormit, nous dormîmes, vous dormîtes, ils dormirent.	je dormirai, tu dormiras, il dormira, nous dormirons, vous dormirez, ils dormiront.
8. *Fuir,* *to flee.* fuyant. fui. avoir fui. ayant fui.	je fuis, tu fuis, il fuit, nous fuyons, vous fuyez, ils fuient.	je fuyais, tu fuyais, il fuyait, nous fuyions, vous fuyiez, ils fuyaient.	je fuis, tu fuis, il fuit, nous fûmes, vous fuîtes, ils fuirent.	je fuirai, tu fuiras, il fuira, nous fuirons, vous fuirez, ils fuiront.

* In the compound tenses of pronominal verbs, the auxiliary verb *être* is used for the
† *S'en aller* follows the model. The reflective pronoun and the adverb *en* precede the
used affirmatively: *va-t'en; allons-nous-en.*
‡ *Assaillir* and *tressaillir* differ from the model in the future and in the conditi

IRREGULAR MODEL VERBS.

CONDITIONAL PRESENT. *E*	IMPERATIVE. *F*	SUBJUNCTIVE MODE. PRESENT. *G*	IMPERFECT. *H*	VERBS conjugated like the Model Verb.
j'irais, tu irais, il irait, nous irions, vous iriez, ils iraient,	va, allons, allez.	que j'aille, que tu ailles, qu'il aille, que nous allions, que vous alliez, qu'ils aillent.	que j'allasse, que tu allasses, qu'il allât, que nous allassions, que vous allassiez, qu'ils allassent.	s'en aller.*
j'enverrais, tu enverrais, il enverrait, nous enverrions, vous enverriez, ils enverraient.	envoie, envoyons, envoyez.	que j'envoie, que tu envoies, qu'il envoie, que nous envoyions, que vous envoyiez, qu'ils envoient.	que j'envoyasse, que tu envoyasses, qu'il envoyât, que n. envoyassions, que v. envoyassiez, qu'ils envoyassent.	renvoyer.
j'acquerrais, tu acquerrais, il acquerrait, nous acquerrions, vous acquerriez, ils acquerraient.	acquiers, acquérons, acquérez.	que j'acquière, que tu acquières, qu'il acquière, que n. acquérions, que v. acquériez, qu'ils acquièrent.	que j'acquisse, que tu acquisses, qu'il acquît, que n. acquissions, que v. acquissiez, qu'ils acquissent.	conquérir. s'enquérir.* reconquérir.
je bouillirais, tu bouillirais, il bouillirait, nous bouillirions, vous bouilliriez, ils bouilliraient.	bous, bouillons, bouillez.	que je bouille, que tu bouilles, qu'il bouille, que nous bouillions, que vous bouilliez, qu'ils bouillent.	que je bouillisse, que tu bouillisses, qu'il bouillît, que n. bouillissions, que v. bouillissiez, qu'ils bouillissent.	
je courrais, tu courrais, il courrait, nous courrions, vous courriez, ils courraient.	cours, courons, courez.	que je coure, que tu coures, qu'il coure, que nous courions, que vous couriez, qu'ils courent.	que je courusse, que tu courusses, qu'il courût, que n. courussions, que v. courussiez, qu'ils courussent.	accourir. concourir. discourir. parcourir. secourir.
je cueillerais, tu cueillerais, il cueillerait, nous cueillerions, vous cueilleriez, ils cueilleraient.	cueille, cueillons, cueillez.	que je cueille, que tu cueilles, qu'il cueille, que nous cueillions, que vous cueilliez, qu'ils cueillent.	que je cueillisse, que tu cueillisses, qu'il cueillît, que n. cueillissions, que v. cueillissiez, qu'ils cueillissent.	accueillir. recueillir. assaillir.‡ tressaillir.‡
je dormirais, tu dormirais, il dormirait, nous dormirions, vous dormiriez, ils dormiraient.	dors, dormons, dormez.	que je dorme, que tu dormes, qu'il dorme, que nous dormions, que vous dormiez, qu'ils dorment.	que je dormisse, que tu dormisses, qu'il dormît, que n. dormissions, que v. dormissiez, qu'ils dormissent.	endormir. s'endormir. rendormir. se rendormir.*
je fuirais, tu fuirais, il fuirait, nous fuirions, vous fuiriez, ils fuiraient.	fuis, fuyons, fuyez.	que je fuie, que tu fuies, qu'il fuie, que nous fuyions, que vous fuyiez, qu'ils fuient.	que je fuisse, que tu fuisses, qu'il fuît, que nous fuissions, que vous fuissiez, qu'ils fuissent.	s'enfuir.*

auxiliary verb *avoir*.
verb: *je m'en vais; je m'en suis allé; t'en vas-tu?* except in the imperative mode when
t: *j'assaillirai, j'assaillirais; je tressaillirai, je tressaillirais*.

CONJUGATION OF

INFINITIVE FORMS.	INDICATIVE MODE.			
	PRESENT. *A*	IMPERFECT. *B*	PAST DEF. *C*	FUTURE. *D*
9. *Mourir,* *to die.* mourant. mort. être mort. étant mort.	je meurs, tu meurs, il meurt, nous mourons, vous mourez, ils meurent.	je mourais, tu mourais, il mourait, nous mourions, vous mouriez, ils mouraient.	je mourus, tu mourus, il mourut, nous mourûmes, vous mourûtes, ils moururent.	je mourrai, tu mourras, il mourra, nous mourrons, vous mourrez, ils mourront.
10. *Ouvrir,* *to open.* ouvrant. ouvert. avoir ouvert. ayant ouvert.	j'ouvre, tu ouvres, il ouvre, nous ouvrons, vous ouvrez, ils ouvrent.	j'ouvrais, tu ouvrais, il ouvrait, nous ouvrions, vous ouvriez, ils ouvraient.	j'ouvris, tu ouvris, il ouvrit, nous ouvrîmes, vous ouvrîtes, ils ouvrirent.	j'ouvrirai, tu ouvriras, il ouvrira, nous ouvrirons, vous ouvrirez, ils ouvriront.
11. *Partir,* *to start.* partant, parti, être parti. étant parti.	je pars, tu pars, il part, nous partons, vous partez, ils partent.	je partais, tu partais, il partait, nous partions, vous partiez, ils partaient.	je partis, tu partis, il partit, nous partîmes, vous partîtes, ils partirent.	je partirai, tu partiras, il partira, nous partirons, vous partirez, ils partiront.
12. *Sentir,* *to feel.* sentant. senti. avoir senti. ayant senti.	je sens, tu sens, il sent, nous sentons, vous sentez, ils sentent.	je sentais, tu sentais, il sentait, nous sentions, vous sentiez, ils sentaient.	je sentis, tu sentis, il sentit, nous sentîmes, vous sentîtes, ils sentirent.	je sentirai, tu sentiras, il sentira, nous sentirons, vous sentirez, ils sentiront.
13. *Tenir,* *to hold; to keep.* tenant. tenu. avoir tenu. ayant tenu.	je tiens, tu tiens, il tient, nous tenons, vous tenez, ils tiennent.	je tenais, tu tenais, il tenait, nous tenions, vous teniez, ils tenaient.	je tins, tu tins, il tint, nous tînmes, vous tîntes, ils tinrent.	je tiendrai, tu tiendras, il tiendra, nous tiendrons, vous tiendrez, ils tiendront.
14. *Venir,* *to come.* venant. venu. être venu. étant venu.	je viens, tu viens, il vient, nous venons, vous venez, ils viennent.	je venais, tu venais, il venait, nous venions, vous veniez, ils venaient.	je vins, tu vins, il vint, nous vînmes, vous vîntes, ils vinrent.	je viendrai, tu viendras, il viendra, nous viendrons, vous viendrez, ils viendront.
15. *Vêtir,* *to clothe.* vêtant. vêtu. avoir vêtu. ayant vêtu.	je vêts, tu vêts, il vêt, nous vêtons, vous vêtez, ils vêtent.	je vêtais, tu vêtais, il vêtait, nous vêtions, vous vêtiez, ils vêtaient.	je vêtis, tu vêtis, il vêtit, nous vêtîmes, vous vêtîtes, ils vêtirent.	je vêtirai, tu vêtiras, il vêtira, nous vêtirons, vous vêtirez, ils vêtiront.
16. *Asseoir (s'),* *to sit down.* s'asseyant. assis. s'être assis. s'étant assis.	je m'assieds,‡ tu t'assieds, il s'assied, nous n. asseyons, vous v. asseyez, ils s'asseyent.	je m'asseyais, tu t'asseyais, il s'asseyait, n. n. asseyions, v. v. asseyiez, ils s'asseyaient.	je m'assis, tu t'assis, il s'assit, nous n. assîmes, vous v. assîtes, ils s'assirent.	je m'assiérai, tu t'assiéras, il s'assiéra, n. n. assiérons, v. v. assiérez, ils s'assiéront.

* In the compound tenses of pronominal verbs, the auxiliary verb *être* is used
† The compounds of *venir* are conjugated with the auxiliary verb *être*, except
‡ Also : *je m'assois, tu t'assois, il s'assoit ; j'assoyais ; j'assoirai,* etc. This form
§ *Seoir* and *messeoir* are defective verbs. (See p. 210.)

IRREGULAR MODEL VERBS.

CONDITIONAL PRESENT. *E*	IMPERATIVE. *F*	SUBJUNCTIVE MODE.		Verbs conjugated like the Model Verb.
		PRESENT. *G*	IMPERFECT. *H*	
je mourrais, tu mourrais, il mourrait, nous mourrions, vous mourriez, ils mourraient.	meurs, mourons, mourez.	que je meure, que tu meures, qu'il meure, que nous mourions, que vous mouriez, qu'ils meurent.	que je mourusse, que tu mourusses, qu'il mourût, que n. mourussions, que v. mourussiez, qu'ils mourussent.	
j'ouvrirais, tu ouvrirais, il ouvrirait, nous ouvririons, vous ouvririez, ils ouvriraient.	ouvre, ouvrons, ouvrez.	que j'ouvre, que tu ouvres, qu'il ouvre, que nous ouvrions, que vous ouvriez, qu'ils ouvrent.	que j'ouvrisse, que tu ouvrisses, qu'il ouvrît, que n. ouvrissions, que v. ouvrissiez, qu'ils ouvrissent.	couvrir. découvrir. offrir. souffrir, etc.
je partirais, tu partirais, il partirait, nous partirions, vous partiriez, ils partiraient.	pars, partons, partez.	que je parte, que tu partes, qu'il parte, que nous partions, que vous partiez, qu'ils partent.	que je partisse, que tu partisses, qu'il partît, que n. partissions, que v. partissiez, qu'ils partissent.	repartir. sortir. ressortir.
je sentirais, tu sentirais, il sentirait, nous sentirions, vous sentiriez, ils sentiraient.	sens, sentons, sentez.	que je sente, que tu sentes, qu'il sente, que nous sentions, que vous sentiez, qu'ils sentent.	que je sentisse, que tu sentisses, qu'il sentît, que n. sentissions, que v. sentissiez, qu'ils sentissent.	assentir. consentir. pressentir. ressentir. mentir, etc.
je tiendrais, tu tiendrais, il tiendrait, nous tiendrions, vous tiendriez, ils tiendraient.	tiens, tenons, tenez.	que je tienne, que tu tiennes, qu'il tienne, que nous tenions, que vous teniez, qu'ils tiennent.	que je tinsse, que tu tinsses, qu'il tînt, que nous tinssions, que vous tinssiez, qu'ils tinssent.	The compounds of *tenir* with prefixes.
je viendrais, tu viendrais, il viendrait, nous viendrions, vous viendriez, ils viendraient.	viens, venons, venez.	que je vienne, que tu viennes, qu'il vienne, que nous venions, que vous veniez, qu'ils viennent.	que je vinsse, que tu vinsses, qu'il vînt, que nous vinssions, que vous vinssiez, qu'ils vinssent.	The compounds of *venir*.†
je vêtirais, tu vêtirais, il vêtirait, nous vêtirions, vous vêtiriez, ils vêtiraient.	vêts, vêtons, vêtez.	que je vête, que tu vêtes, qu'il vête, que nous vêtions, que vous vêtiez, qu'ils vêtent.	que je vêtisse, que tu vêtisses, qu'il vêtît, que nous vêtissions, que vous vêtissiez, qu'ils vêtissent.	dévêtir. revêtir. se vêtir.* se revêtir.* se dévêtir.*
je m'assiérais, tu t'assiérais, il s'assiérait, n. n. assiérions, v. v. assiériez, ils s'assiéraient.	assieds-toi, asseyons-n., asseyez-vous	que je m'asseye, que tu t'asseyes, qu'il s'asseye, que n. n. asseyions, que v. v. asseyiez, qu'ils s'asseyent.	que je m'assisse, que tu t'assisses, qu'il s'assît, que n. n. assissions, que v. v. assissiez, qu'ils s'assissent.	asseoir. rasseoir. se rasseoir.* seoir.§ messeoir.§

for the auxiliary verb *avoir*.
convenir, which takes *avoir* in the sense of *to suit*, and *être* in the sense of *to agree*, is little used.

CONJUGATION OF

INFINITIVE FORMS.	INDICATIVE MODE.			
	Present. A	Imperfect. B	Past Def. C	Future. D
17. *Mouvoir*, *to move.* mouvant. mû. avoir mû. ayant mû.	je meus, tu meus, il meut, nous mouvons, vous mouvez, ils meuvent.	je mouvais, tu mouvais, il mouvait, nous mouvions, vous mouviez, ils mouvaient.	je mus, tu mus, il mut, nous mûmes, vous mûtes, ils murent.	je mouvrai, tu mouvras, il mouvra, nous mouvrons, vous mouvrez, ils mouvront.
18. *Pouvoir*, *to be able.* pouvant. pu. avoir pu. ayant pu.	je peux, *or* puis, tu peux, il peut, nous pouvons, vous pouvez, ils peuvent.	je pouvais, tu pouvais, il pouvait, nous pouvions, vous pouviez, ils pouvaient.	je pus, tu pus, il put, nous pûmes, vous pûtes, ils purent.	je pourrai, tu pourras, il pourra, nous pourrons, vous pourrez, ils pourront.
19. *Savoir*, *to know.* sachant. su. avoir su. ayant su.	je sais, tu sais, il sait, nous savons, vous savez, ils savent.	je savais, tu savais, il savait, nous savions, vous saviez, ils savaient.	je sus, tu sus, il sut, nous sûmes, vous sûtes, ils surent.	je saurai, tu sauras, il saura, nous saurons, vous saurez, ils sauront.
20. *Valoir*, *to be worth.* valant. valu. avoir valu. ayant valu.	je vaux, tu vaux, il vaut, nous valons, vous valez, ils valent.	je valais, tu valais, il valait, nous valions, vous valiez, ils valaient.	je valus, tu valus, il valut, nous valûmes, vous valûtes, ils valurent.	je vaudrai, tu vaudras, il vaudra, nous vaudrons, vous vaudrez, ils vaudront.
21. *Voir*, *to see.* voyant. vu. avoir vu. ayant vu.	je vois, tu vois, il voit, nous voyons, vous voyez, ils voient.	je voyais, tu voyais, il voyait, nous voyions, vous voyiez, ils voyaient.	je vis, tu vis, il vit, nous vîmes, vous vîtes, ils virent.	je verrai, tu verras, il verra, nous verrons, vous verrez, ils verront.
22. *Vouloir*, *to be willing.* voulant. voulu. avoir voulu. ayant voulu.	je veux, tu veux, il veut, nous voulons, vous voulez, ils veulent.	je voulais, tu voulais, il voulait, nous voulions, vous vouliez, ils voulaient.	je voulus, tu voulus, il voulut, nous voulûmes, vous voulûtes, ils voulurent.	je voudrai, tu voudras, il voudra, nous voudrons, vous voudrez, ils voudront.
23. *Battre*, *to beat.* battant. battu. avoir battu. ayant battu.	je bats, tu bats, il bat, nous battons, vous battez, ils battent.	je battais, tu battais, il battait, nous battions, vous battiez, ils battaient.	je battis, tu battis, il battit, nous battîmes, vous battîtes, ils battirent.	je battrai, tu battras, il battra, nous battrons, vous battrez, ils battront.
24. *Boire*, *to drink.* buvant. bu. avoir bu. ayant bu.	je bois, tu bois, il boit, nous buvons, vous buvez, ils boivent.	je buvais, tu buvais, il buvait, nous buvions, vous buviez, ils buvaient.	je bus, tu bus, il but, nous bûmes, vous bûtes, ils burent.	je boirai, tu boiras, il boira, nous boirons, vous boirez, ils boiront.

* In the compound tenses of pronominal verbs, the
† These verbs slightly deviate from the model.
‡ The imperative form *veuilles* is used only in the

IRREGULAR MODEL VERBS.

CONDITIONAL PRESENT. *E*	IMPERATIVE. *F*	SUBJUNCTIVE MODE. PRESENT. *G*	IMPERFECT. *H*	VERBS conjugated like the Model Verb.
je mouvrais, tu mouvrais, il mouvrait, nous mouvrions, vous mouvriez, ils mouvraient.	meus, mouvons, mouvez.	que je meuve, que tu meuves, qu'il meuve, que nous mouvions, que vous mouviez, qu'ils meuvent.	que je musse, que tu musses, qu'il mût, que nous mussions, que vous mussiez, qu'ils mussent.	démouvoir. émouvoir. s'émouvoir.* promouvoir.
je pourrais, tu pourrais, il pourrait, nous pourrions, vous pourriez, ils pourraient.	peux, pouvons, pouvez.	que je puisse, que tu puisses, qu'il puisse, que nous puissions, que vous puissiez, qu'ils puissent.	que je pusse, que tu pusses, qu'il pût, que nous pussions, que vous pussiez, qu'ils pussent.	
je saurais, tu saurais, il saurait, nous saurions, vous sauriez, ils sauraient.	sache, sachons, sachez.	que je sache, que tu saches, qu'il sache, que nous sachions, que vous sachiez, qu'ils sachent.	que je susse, que tu susses, qu'il sût, que nous sussions, que vous sussiez, qu'ils sussent.	
je vaudrais, tu vaudrais, il vaudrait, nous vaudrions, vous vaudriez, ils vaudraient.	vaux, valons, valez.	que je vaille, que tu vailles, qu'il vaille, que nous valions, que vous valiez, qu'ils vaillent.	que je valusse, que tu valusses, qu'il valût, que nous valussions, que vous valussiez, qu'ils valussent.	valoir mieux. équivaloir. prévaloir. revaloir.
je verrais, tu verrais, il verrait, nous verrions, vous verriez, ils verraient.	vois, voyons, voyez.	que je voie, que tu voies, qu'il voie, que nous voyions, que vous voyiez, qu'ils voient.	que je visse, que tu visses, qu'il vît, que nous vissions, que vous vissiez, qu'ils vissent.	revoir. entrevoir. déchoir.† échoir.† pourvoir.† prévoir.†
je voudrais, tu voudrais, il voudrait, nous voudrions, vous voudriez, ils voudraient.	veux, voulons, voulez and veuillez.‡	que je veuille, que tu veuilles, qu'il veuille, que nous voulions, que vous vouliez, qu'ils veuillent.	que je voulusse, que tu voulusses, qu'il voulût, que n. voulussions, que v. voulussiez, qu'ils voulussent.	
je battrais, tu battrais, il battrait, nous battrions, vous battriez, ils battraient.	bats, battons, battez.	que je batte, que tu battes, qu'il batte, que nous battions, que vous battiez, qu'ils battent.	que je battisse, que tu battisses, qu'il battît, que n. battissions, que v. battissiez, qu'ils battissent.	abattre. combattre. débattre. s'ébattre.* rabattre. rebattre.
je boirais, tu boirais, il boirait, nous boirions, vous boiriez, ils boiraient.	bois, buvons, buvez.	que je boive, que tu boives, qu'il boive, que nous buvions, que vous buviez, qu'ils boivent.	que je busse, que tu busses, qu'il bût, que nous bussions, que vous bussiez, qu'ils bussent.	emboire. s'emboire.* reboire.

auxiliary verb *être* is used for the auxiliary verb *avoir*.
(See p. 278.)
sense of *please* or *be so kind as*.

CONJUGATION OF

INFINITIVE FORMS.	INDICATIVE MODE.			
	PRESENT. *A*	IMPERFECT. *B*	PAST DEF. *C*	FUTURE. *D*
25. Conclure, *to conclude.* concluant. conclu. avoir conclu. ayant conclu.	je conclus, tu conclus, il conclut, nous concluons vous concluez ils concluent.	je concluais, tu concluais, il concluait, nous concluions, vous concluiez, ils concluaient.	je conclus, tu conclus, il conclut, nous conclûmes, vous conclûtes, ils conclurent.	je conclurai, tu concluras, il conclura, nous conclurons, vous conclurez, ils concluront.
26. Conduire, *to conduct.* conduisant. conduit. avoir conduit. ayant conduit.	je conduis, tu conduis, il conduit, n. conduisons, v. conduisez, ils conduisent.	je conduisais, tu conduisais, il conduisait, n. conduisions, v. conduisiez, ils conduisaient.	je conduisis, tu conduisis, il conduisit, n. conduisîmes, v. conduisîtes, ils conduisirent.	je conduirai, tu conduiras, il conduira, n. conduirons, v. conduirez, ils conduiront.
27. Connaître, *to know.* connaissant. connu. avoir connu. ayant connu.	je connais, tu connais, il connaît, n. connaissons v. connaissez, ils connaissent.	je connaissais, tu connaissais, il connaissait, n. connaissions, v. connaissiez, ils connaissaient.	je connus, tu connus, il connut, nous connûmes, vous connûtes, ils connurent.	je connaîtrai, tu connaîtras, il connaîtra, n. connaîtrons, v. connaîtrez, ils connaîtront.
28. Coudre, *to sew.* cousant. cousu. avoir cousu. ayant cousu.	je couds, tu couds, il coud, nous cousons, vous cousez, ils cousent.	je cousais, tu cousais, il cousait, nous cousions, vous cousiez, ils cousaient.	je cousis, tu cousis, il cousit, nous cousîmes, vous cousîtes, ils cousirent.	je coudrai, tu coudras, il coudra, nous coudrons, vous coudrez, ils coudront.
29. Craindre, *to fear.* craignant. craint. avoir craint. ayant craint.	je crains, tu crains, il craint, nous craignons vous craignez, ils craignent.	je craignais, tu craignais, il craignait, nous craignions, vous craigniez, ils craignaient.	je craignis, tu craignis, il craignit, nous craignîmes, vous craignîtes, ils craignirent.	je craindrai, tu craindras, il craindra, nous craindrons, vous craindrez, ils craindront.
30. Croire, *to believe.* croyant. cru. avoir cru. ayant cru.	je crois, tu crois, il croit, nous croyons, vous croyez, ils croient.	je croyais, tu croyais, il croyait, nous croyions, vous croyiez, ils croyaient.	je crus, tu crus, il crut, nous crûmes, vous crûtes, ils crurent.	je croirai, tu croiras, il croira, nous croirons, vous croirez, ils croiront.
31. Croître, *to grow.* croissant. crû, *f.* crue. avoir crû. ayant crû.	je croîs, tu croîs, il croît, nous croissons vous croissez, ils croissent.	je croissais, tu croissais, il croissait, nous croissions, vous croissiez, ils croissaient.	je crûs, tu crûs, il crût, nous crûmes, vous crûtes, ils crûrent.	je croîtrai, tu croîtras, il croîtra, nous croîtrons, vous croîtrez, ils croîtront.
32. Dire, *to say; to tell.* disant. dit. avoir dit. ayant dit.	je dis, tu dis, il dit, nous disons, vous dites, ils disent.	je disais, tu disais, il disait, nous disions, vous disiez, ils disaient.	je dis, tu dis, il dit, nous dîmes, vous dîtes, ils dirent.	je dirai, tu diras, il dira, nous dirons, vous direz, ils diront.

* *Luire*, to shine; *reluire*, to glitter; and *nuire*, to hurt, to injure, deviate from the
† The compounds of *dire* and *confire* deviate from the model in the second person
maudire, the *s* is doubled: *maudissez* (see b*)*

IRREGULAR MODEL VERBS.

CONDITIONAL. PRESENT. *E*	IMPERATIVE. *F*	SUBJUNCTIVE MODE.		VERBS conjugated like the Model Verb.
		PRESENT. *G*	IMPERFECT. *H*	
je conclurais, tu conclurais, il conclurait, nous conclurions, vous concluriez, ils concluraient.	conclus, concluons, concluez.	que je conclue, que tu conclues, qu'il conclue, que n. concluions, que v. concluiez, qu'ils concluent.	que je conclusse, que tu conclusses, qu'il conclût, que n. conclussions, que v. conclussiez, qu'ils conclussent.	exclure. reclure.
je conduirais, tu conduirais, il conduirait, nous conduirions, vous conduiriez, ils conduiraient.	conduis, conduisons, conduisez.	que je conduise, que tu conduises, qu'il conduise, que n. conduisions, que v. conduisiez, qu'ils conduisent.	que je conduisisse, que tu conduisisses, qu'il conduisît, q. n. conduisissions, que v. conduisissiez, qu'ils conduisissent.	All verbs ending in *uire*.*
je connaîtrais, tu connaîtrais, il connaîtrait, n. connaîtrions, v. connaîtriez, ils connaîtraient.	connais, connaissons, connaissez.	que je connaisse, que tu connaisses, qu'il connaisse, que n. connaissions, que v. connaissiez, qu'ils connaissent.	que je connusse, que tu connusses, qu'il connût, que n. connussions, que v. connussiez, qu'ils connussent.	paraître and compounds.
je coudrais, tu coudrais, il coudrait, nous coudrions, vous coudriez, ils coudraient.	couds, cousons, cousez.	que je couse, que tu couses, qu'il couse, que nous cousions, que vous cousiez, qu'ils cousent.	que je cousisse, que tu cousisses, qu'il cousît, que n. cousissions, que v. cousissiez, qu'ils cousissent.	
je craindrais, tu craindrais, il craindrait, nous craindrions, vous craindriez, ils craindraient.	crains, craignons, craignez.	que je craigne, que tu craignes, qu'il craigne, que nous craignions, que vous craigniez, qu'ils craignent.	que je craignisse, que tu craignisses, qu'il craignît, que n. craignissions, que v. craignissiez, qu'ils craignissent.	All verbs ending in *aindre*, *eindre* and *oindre*.
je croirais, tu croirais, il croirait, nous croirions, vous croiriez, ils croiraient.	crois, croyons, croyez.	que je croie, que tu croies, qu'il croie, que nous croyions, que vous croyiez, qu'ils croient.	que je crusse, que tu crusses, qu'il crût, que nous crussions, que vous crussiez, qu'ils crussent.	
je croîtrais, tu croîtrais, il croîtrait, nous croîtrions, vous croîtriez, ils croîtraient.	croîs, croissons, croissez.	que je croisse, que tu croisses, qu'il croisse, que nous croissions, que vous croissiez, qu'ils croissent.	que je crusse, que tu crusses, qu'il crût, que nous crussions, que vous crussiez, qu'ils crussent.	
je dirais, tu dirais, il dirait, nous dirions, vous diriez, ils diraient.	dis, disons, dites.	que je dise, que tu dises, qu'il dise, que nous disions, que vous disiez, qu'ils disent.	que je disse, que tu disses, qu'il dît, que nous dissions, que vous dissiez, qu'ils dissent.	The compounds of *dire*† and *confire*.†

model in the past participle, which ends in *i* instead of *it*; as: *lui, relui, nui.* plural of the present indicative and of the imperative, which is *disez, confisez* (see 78; in

CONJUGATION OF

INFINITIVE FORMS.	INDICATIVE MODE.			
	PRESENT. *A*	IMPERFECT. *B*	PAST DEF. *C*	FUTURE. *D*
33. *Écrire,* *to write.* écrivant. écrit. avoir écrit. ayant écrit.	j'écris, tu écris, il écrit, nous écrivons, vous écrivez, ils écrivent.	j'écrivais, tu écrivais, il écrivait, nous écrivions, vous écriviez, ils écrivaient.	j'écrivis, tu écrivis, il écrivit, nous écrivîmes, vous écrivîtes, ils écrivirent.	j'écrirai, tu écriras, il écrira, nous écrirons, vous écrirez, ils écriront.
34. *Faire,* *to do; to make.* faisant. fait. avoir fait. ayant fait.	je fais, tu fais, il fait, nous faisons, vous faites, ils font.	je faisais, tu faisais, il faisait, nous faisions, vous faisiez, ils faisaient.	je fis, tu fis, il fit, nous fîmes, vous fîtes, ils firent.	je ferai, tu feras, il fera, nous ferons, vous ferez, ils feront.
35. *Lire,* *to read.* lisant. lu. avoir lu. ayant lu.	je lis, tu lis, il lit, nous lisons, vous lisez, ils lisent.	je lisais, tu lisais, il lisait, nous lisions, vous lisiez, ils lisaient.	je lus, tu lus, il lut, nous lûmes, vous lûtes, ils lurent.	je lirai, tu liras, il lira, nous lirons, vous lirez, ils liront.
36. *Mettre,* *to put.* mettant. mis. avoir mis. ayant mis.	je mets, tu mets, il met, nous mettons, vous mettez, ils mettent.	je mettais, tu mettais, il mettait, nous mettions, vous mettiez, ils mettaient.	je mis, tu mis, il mit, nous mîmes, vous mîtes, ils mirent.	je mettrai, tu mettras, il mettra, nous mettrons, vous mettrez, ils mettront.
37. *Moudre,* *to grind.* moulant. moulu. avoir moulu. ayant moulu.	je mouds, tu mouds, il moud, nous moulons, vous moulez, ils moulent.	je moulais, tu moulais, il moulait, nous moulions, vous mouliez, ils moulaient.	je moulus, tu moulus, il moulut, nous moulûmes, vous moulûtes, ils moulurent.	je moudrai, tu moudras, il moudra, nous moudrons, vous moudrez, ils moudront.
38. *Naître,* *to be born* naissant. né. être né. étant né.	je nais, tu nais, il naît, nous naissons, vous naissez, ils naissent.	je naissais, tu naissais, il naissait, nous naissions, vous naissiez, ils naissaient.	je naquis, tu naquis, il naquit, nous naquîmes, vous naquîtes, ils naquirent.	je naîtrai, tu naîtras, il naîtra, nous naîtrons, vous naîtrez, ils naîtront.
39. *Plaire,* *to please.* plaisant. plu. avoir plu. ayant plu.	je plais, tu plais, il plaît, nous plaisons, vous plaisez, ils plaisent.	je plaisais, tu plaisais, il plaisait, nous plaisions, vous plaisiez, ils plaisaient.	je plus, tu plus, il plut, nous plûmes, vous plûtes, ils plurent.	je plairai, tu plairas, il plaira, nous plairons, vous plairez, ils plairont.
40. *Prendre,* *to take.* prenant. pris. avoir pris. ayant pris.	je prends, tu prends, il prend, nous prenons, vous prenez, ils prennent.	je prenais, tu prenais, il prenait, nous prenions, vous preniez, ils prenaient.	je pris, tu pris, il prit, nous prîmes, vous prîtes, ils prirent.	je prendrai, tu prendras, il prendra, nous prendrons, vous prendrez, ils prendront.

* In the compound tenses of pronominal verbs the

IRREGULAR MODEL VERBS.

CONDITIONAL PRESENT. *E*	IMPERATIVE. *F*	SUBJUNCTIVE MODE.		VERBS conjugated like the Model Verb.
		PRESENT. *G*	IMPERFECT. *H*	
j'écrirais, tu écrirais, il écrirait, nous écririons, vous écririez, ils écriraient.	écris, écrivons, écrivez.	que j'écrive, que tu écrives, qu'il écrive, que nous écrivions, que vous écriviez, qu'ils écrivent.	que j'écrivisse, que tu écrivisses, qu'il écrivît, que n. écrivissions, que v. écrivissiez, qu'ils écrivissent.	The compounds of *écrire*.
je ferais, tu ferais, il ferait, nous ferions, vous feriez, ils feraient.	fais, faisons, faites.	que je fasse, que tu fasses, qu'il fasse, que nous fassions, que vous fassiez, qu'ils fassent.	que je fisse, que tu fisses, qu'il fît, que nous fissions, que vous fissiez, qu'ils fissent.	The compounds of *faire*.
je lirais, tu lirais, il lirait, nous lirions, vous liriez, ils liraient.	lis, lisons, lisez.	que je lise, que tu lises, qu'il lise, que nous lisions, que vous lisiez, qu'ils lisent.	que je lusse, que tu lusses, qu'il lût, que nous lussions, que vous lussiez, qu'ils lussent.	élire. réélire. relire.
je mettrais, tu mettrais, il mettrait, nous mettrions, vous mettriez, ils mettraient.	mets, mettons, mettez.	que je mette, que tu mettes, qu'il mette, que nous mettions, que vous mettiez, qu'ils mettent.	que je misse, que tu misses, qu'il mît, que nous missions, que vous missiez, qu'ils missent.	The compounds of *mettre*.
je moudrais, tu moudrais, il moudrait, nous moudrions, vous moudriez, ils moudraient.	mouds, moulons, moulez.	que je moule, que tu moules, qu'il moule, que nous moulions, que vous mouliez, qu'ils moulent.	que je moulusse, que tu moulusses, qu'il moulût, que n. moulussions, que v. moulussiez, qu'ils moulussent.	émoudre. remoudre.
je naîtrais, tu naîtrais, il naîtrait, nous naîtrions, vous naîtriez, ils naîtraient.	nais, naissons, naissez.	que je naisse, que tu naisses, qu'il naisse, que nous naissions, que vous naissiez, qu'ils naissent.	que je naquisse, que tu naquisses, qu'il naquît, que n. naquissions, que v. naquissiez, qu'ils naquissent.	renaître.
je plairais, tu plairais, il plairait, nous plairions, vous plairiez, ils plairaient.	plais, plaisons, plaisez.	que je plaise, que tu plaises, qu'il plaise, que nous plaisions, que vous plaisiez, qu'ils plaisent.	que je plusse, que tu plusses, qu'il plût, que nous plussions, que vous plussiez, qu'ils plussent.	*plaire*. complaire. taire. se taire.*
je prendrais, tu prendrais, il prendrait, nous prendrions, vous prendriez, ils prendraient.	prends, prenons, prenez.	que je prenne, que tu prennes, qu'il prenne, que nous prenions, que vous preniez, qu'ils prennent.	que je prisse, que tu prisses, qu'il prît, que nous prissions, que vous prissiez, qu'ils prissent.	The compounds of *prendre*.

auxiliary verb *être* is used for the auxiliary verb *avoir*.

CONJUGATION OF

INFINITIVE FORMS.	INDICATIVE MODE.			
	PRESENT. *A*	IMPERFECT. *B*	PAST DEF. *C*	FUTURE. *D*
41. *Résoudre,* *to resolve.* résolvant. résolu. avoir résolu. ayant résolu.	je résous, tu résous, il résout, nous résolvons, vous résolvez, ils résolvent.	je résolvais, tu résolvais, ⁑ résolvait, nous résolvions, vous résolviez, ils résolvaient.	je résolus, tu résolus, il résolut, nous résolûmes, vous résolûtes, ils résolurent.	je résoudrai, tu résoudras, il résoudra, nous résoudrons, vous résoudrez, ils résoudront.
42. *Rire,* *to laugh.* riant. ri. avoir ri. ayant ri.	je ris, tu ris, il rit, nous rions, vous riez, ils rient.	je riais, tu riais, il riait, nous riions, vous riiez, ils riaient.	je ris, tu ris, il rit, nous rîmes, vous rîtes, ils rirent.	je rirai, tu riras, il rira, nous rirons, vous rirez, ils riront.
43. *Suffire,* *to be sufficient.* suffisant. suffi. avoir suffi. ayant suffi.	je suffis, tu suffis, il suffit, nous suffisons, vous suffisez, ils suffisent.	je suffisais, tu suffisais, il suffisait, nous suffisions, vous suffisiez, ils suffisaient.	je suffis, tu suffis, il suffit, nous suffîmes, vous suffîtes, ils suffirent.	je suffirai, tu suffiras, il suffira, nous suffirons, vous suffirez, ils suffiront.
44. *Suivre,* *to follow.* suivant. suivi. avoir suivi. ayant suivi.	je suis, tu suis, il suit, nous suivons, vous suivez, ils suivent.	je suivais, tu suivais, il suivait, nous suivions, vous suiviez, ils suivaient.	je suivis, tu suivis, il suivit, nous suivîmes, vous suivîtes, ils suivirent.	je suivrai, tu suivras, il suivra, nous suivrons, vous suivrez, ils suivront.
45. *Traire,* *to milk.* trayant. trait. avoir trait. ayant trait.	je trais, tu trais, il trait, nous trayons, vous trayez, ils traient.	je trayais, tu trayais, il trayait, nous trayions, vous trayiez, ils trayaient.	....	je trairai, tu trairas, il traira, nous trairons, vous trairez, ils trairont.
46. *Vaincre,* *to vanquish.* vainquant. vaincu. avoir vaincu. ayant vaincu. *	je vaincs, tu vaincs, il vainc, nous vainquons, vous vainquez, ils vainquent.	je vainquais, tu vainquais, il vainquait, nous vainquions, vous vainquiez, ils vainquaient.	je vainquis, tu vainquis, il vainquit, n. vainquîmes, v. vainquîtes, ils vainquirent.	je vaincrai, tu vaincras, il vaincra, nous vaincrons, vous vaincrez, ils vaincront.
47. *Vivre,* *to live.* vivant. vécu. avoir vécu. ayant vécu.	je vis, tu vis, il vit, nous vivons, vous vivez, ils vivent.	je vivais, tu vivais, il vivait, nous vivions, vous viviez, ils vivaient.	je vécus, tu vécus, il vécut, nous vécûmes, vous vécûtes, ils vécurent.	je vivrai, tu vivras, il vivra, nous vivrons, vous vivrez, ils vivront.

* In the compound tenses of pronominal verbs, the
† *Absoudre* deviates from the model in the past

IRREGULAR MODEL VERBS.

CONDITIONAL	IMPERATIVE.	SUBJUNCTIVE MODE.		VERBS
PRESENT. *E*	*F*	PRESENT. *G*	IMPERFECT. *H*	conjugated like the Model Verb.
je résoudrais, tu résoudrais, il résoudrait, nous résoudrions, vous résoudriez, ils résoudraient.	résous, résolvons, résolvez.	que je résolve, que tu résolves, qu'il résolve, que nous résolvions, que vous résolviez, qu'ils résolvent.	que je résolusse, que tu résolusses, qu'il résolût, que n. résolussions, que v. résolussiez, qu'ils résolussent.	absoudre.†
je rirais, tu rirais, il rirait, nous ririons, vous ririez, ils riraient.	ris, rions, riez.	que je rie, que tu ries, qu'il rie, que nous riions, que vous riiez, qu'ils rient.	que je risse, que tu risses, qu'il rît, que nous rissions, que vous rissiez, qu'ils rissent.	sourire.
je suffirais, tu suffirais, il suffirait, nous suffirions, vous suffiriez, ils suffiraient.	suffis, suffisons, suffisez.	que je suffise, que tu suffises, qu'il suffise, que nous suffisions, que vous suffisiez, qu'ils suffisent.	que je suffisse, que tu suffisses, qu'il suffît, que nous suffissions, que vous suffissiez, qu'ils suffissent.	
je suivrais, tu suivrais, il suivrait, nous suivrions, vous suivriez, ils suivraient.	suis, suivons, suivez.	que je suive, que tu suives, qu'il suive, que nous suivions, que vous suiviez, qu'ils suivent.	que je suivisse, que tu suivisses, qu'il suivît, que n. suivissions, que v. suivissiez, qu'ils suivissent.	s'ensuivre.* poursuivre.
je trairais, tu trairais, il trairait, nous trairions, vous trairiez, ils trairaient.	trais, trayons, trayez.	que je traie, que tu traies, qu'il traie, que nous trayions, que vous trayiez, qu'ils traient.	....	extraire. soustraire.
je vaincrais, tu vaincrais, il vaincrait, nous vaincrions, vous vaincriez, ils vaincraient.	vaincs, vainquons, vainquez.	que je vainque, que tu vainques, qu'il vainque, que n. vainquions, que v. vainquiez, qu'ils vainquent.	que je vainquisse, que tu vainquisses, qu'il vainquît, que n. vainquissions, que v. vainquissiez, qu'ils vainquissent.	convaincre.
je vivrais, tu vivrais, il vivrait, nous vivrions, vous vivriez, ils vivraient.	vis, vivons, vivez.	que je vive, que tu vives, qu'il vive, que nous vivions, que vous viviez, qu'ils vivent.	que je vécusse, que tu vécusses, qu'il vécût, que n. vécussions, que v. vécussiez, qu'ils vécussent.	survivre.

auxiliary verb *être* is used for the auxiliary verb *avoir*, participle, which is *absous*, fem. *absoute*.

DEFECTIVE AND SLIGHTLY IRREGULAR VERBS.

FIRST CONJUGATION.

See Orthographic Irregularities in the first conjugation, page 108.

SECOND CONJUGATION.

48. *Bénir, to bless; to consecrate*, has two past participles: *béni*, in the sense of *blessed*, and *bénit*, in the sense of *consecrated*; otherwise it is regular.

49. *Défaillir, to fail*, is used only in the plural of the indicative present: *nous défaillons;* in the imperfect: *je défaillais;* in the past definite: *je défaillis;* and in the infinitive.

50. *Faillir, to fail*, has *faillant, failli:* present: *je faux, tu faux, il faut, nous faillons, vous faillez, ils faillent;* imperfect: *je faillais;* past definite: *je faillis.* It is used principally in the infinitive, the past definite, and the compound tenses.

51. *Férir, to strike*, is used only in *sans coup férir, without striking a blow*, and in the past participle: *féru*.

52. *Fleurir, to blossom; to flourish*. In the sense of *to blossom, fleurir* is regular; in the sense of *to flourish*, it has the present participle *florissant,* and the imperfect tense *je florissais,* etc.

53. *Gésir, to lie ill or dead,* has only : *il gît, nous gisons, vous gisez, ils gisent;* imperfect: *je gisais;* present participle: *gisant.*

54. *Haïr, to hate*, has no diæresis on the *i* in the singular of the present indicative and of the imperative: *je hais, tu hais, il hait; hais.*

55. *Issir, to issue,* is used only in the past participle: *issu.*

56. *Ouïr, to hear.* Of this verb only the infinitive and the past participle, *ouï*, are used.

57. *Quérir, to fetch*, is used only in the infinitive.

58. *Saillir, to project, to jut out,* is conjugated like *cueillir;* the third person and the present participle only are used.

59. *Surgir, to arrive at, to start up,* is used only in the infinitive.

THIRD CONJUGATION.

60. *Apparoir, to be evident,* is used only in the infinitive and in the third person singular of the indicative present: *il appert.*

61. *Choir, to fall,* is used only in the infinitive and past participle: *chu.*

62. *Comparoir, to appear in justice,* is used only in the infinitive.

63. *Déchoir, to fall away,* follows the model *voir,* except in the past definite: *je déchus.* The present participle, imperfect, and imperative are wanting.

64. *Echoir, to chance to be; to become due,* is used only in the third person; it has the same forms as *déchoir,* and also the present participle: *échéant.*

65. *Messeoir, to be unbecoming,* is conjugated as *asseoir: je messieds,* etc. It is not used in the past definite, the compound tenses, and the present participle.

66. *Pourvoir, to provide,* follows *voir,* except the past definite: *je pourvus,* and the future: *je pourvoirai.*

67. *Prévoir, to foresee,* follows *voir,* except the future: *je prévoirai.*

68. *Ravoir, to get again,* follows *avoir,* but is used only in the future, the conditional present, and the infinitive.

69. *Seoir, to become,* is used only in the third person of the present: *il sied, ils siéent;* of the imperfect: *il seyait,* and of the future: *il siéra.*

70. *Seoir, to be seated,* has only the present participle: *séant,* and the past participle: *sis.*

71. *Souloir, to be accustomed,* is used only in the imperfect: *je soulais.*

72. *Surseoir, to suspend;* present participle: *sursoyant;* past participle: *sursis;* future: *je sursoirai.* In other respects it follows the model *voir.*

FOURTH CONJUGATION.

73. *Accroire* is used only in the infinitive: *faire accroire, to make believe.*

74. *Braire, to bray;* present: *il brait, ils braient;* future: *il braira.*

75. *Bruire, to roar;* present participle: *bruyant;* present: *il bruit;* imperfect: *il bruyait.*

76. *Circoncire, to circumcise,* follows *dire,* except the second person of the present: *vous circoncisez;* and the past participle: *circoncis.*

77. *Clore, to close;* present: *je clos, tu clos, il clôt;* future: *je clorai;* past participle: *clos.*

78. *Contredire, to contradict,* and the following compounds of *dire,* viz.: *dédire, to unsay; interdire, to forbid; médire, to slander; prédire, to foretell,* follow the model *dire,* except in the second person plural of the present indicative and of the imperative, which is *disez* instead of *dites.*

79. *Courre, to hunt,* is used only in the infinitive.

80. *Déconfire, to discomfit;* past participle: *déconfit.*

81. *Eclore, to be hatched,* follows *clore (77);* it is used only in the third person.

82. *Frire, to fry;* present: *je fris, tu fris, il frit;* future: *je frirai;* past participle: *frit.*

83. *Malfaire, to do wrong,* is used only in the infinitive, the compound tenses, and the past participle: *malfait.*

84. *Maudire, to curse;* present participle: *maudissant.* The double *s* is retained in the parts derived from the present participle; in other respects it follows *dire.*

85. *Rompre, to break,* is regular, except in the third person singular of the indicative present: *il rompt.*

86. *Soudre, to solve,* is used only in the infinitive.

87. *Sourdre, to spring forth,* is used only in the third person singular and plural: *il sourd, ils sourdent.* It has no present participle.

88. *Tistre, to weave;* past participle: *tissu.*

LIST OF IRREGULAR VERBS.

The Model Verbs are in Bold Faced Type.

Abattre (23), *to fell.*
Absoudre (41), *to absolve.*
Abstenir (s') (13), *to abstain.*
Abstraire (45), *to abstract.*
Accourir (5), *to run to.*
Accroire (73), *to believe.*
Accroître (31), *to increase.*
Accueillir (6), *to receive.*
Acquérir (3), *to acquire.*
Admettre (36), *to admit.*
Advenir (14), *to happen.*
Aller (1), *to go.*
Apparaître (28), *to appear.*
Apparoir (60), *to be evident.*
Appartenir (13), *to belong.*
Apprendre (40), *to learn.*
Assaillir (6), *to assail.*
Assentir (12), *to assent.*
Asseoir (16), *to set.*
Asseoir (s') (16), *to sit down.*
Astreindre (29), *to force.*
Atteindre (29), *to attain.*
Attraire (45), *to attract.*
Aveindre (29), *to fetch out.*
Avenir (14), *to happen.*
Avoir (p. 245), *to have.*
Battre (23), *to beat.*
Bénir (48), *to bless.*
Boire (24), *to drink.*
Bouillir (4), *to boil.*
Braire (74), *to bray.*
Bruire (75), *to make a noise.*
Ceindre (29), *to gird.*
Choir (61), *to fall.*
Circoncire (76), *to circumcise.*
Circonscrire (33), *to circumscribe.*
Circonvenir (14), *to circumvent.*
Clore (77), *to close.*
Combattre (23), *to fight.*
Commettre (36), *to commit.*
Comparaître (27), *to appear.* [justice.
Comparoir (62), *to appear in a court of*
Complaire (39), *to comply with.*
Comprendre (40), *to understand.*
Compromettre (36), *to compromise.*

Conclure (25), *to conclude.*
Concourir (5), *to concur.*
Conduire (26), *to conduct.*
Confire (32), *to preserve.*
Conjoindre (29), *to unite.*
Connaître (27), *to know.*
Conquérir (3), *to conquer.*
Consentir (12), *to consent.*
Construire (26), *to construct.*
Contenir (13), *to contain.*
Contraindre (29), *to compel.*
Contredire (32, 78), *to contradict.*
Contrefaire (34), *to counterfeit.*
Contrevenir (14), *to transgress.*
Convaincre (46), *to convince.*
Convenir (14), *to agree.*
Corrompre (85), *to corrupt.*
Coudre (28), *to sew.*
Courir (5), *to run.*
Courre (79), *to hunt.*
Couvrir (10), *to cover.*
Craindre (29), *to fear.*
Croire (30), *to believe.*
Croître (31), *to grow.*
Cueillir (6), *to pluck.*
Cuire (26), *to cook.*
Débattre (23), *to debate.*
Déchoir (63), *to fall off.*
Déclore (77), *to unclose.*
Déconfire (80), *to rout.*
Découdre (29), *to unsew.*
Découvrir (10), *to discover.*
Décrire (33), *to describe.*
Décroire (30), *to disbelieve.*
Décroître (31), *to decrease.*
Dédire (32, 78), *to disown.*
Dédire (se) (32, 78), *to retract.*
Déduire (26), *to deduct.*
Défaillir (58), *to fail.*
Défaire (34), *to undo.*
Déjoindre (29), *to disjoin.*
Démentir (12), *to contradict.*
Démettre (36), *to dislocate.*
Démettre (se) (36), *to resign.*
Démouvoir (17), *to make one desist.*

LIST OF IRREGULAR VERBS.

Départir (11), *to distribute.*
Départir (se) (11), *to desist.*
Dépeindre (29), *to describe*
Déplaire (39), *to displease.*
Dépourvoir (21, 66), *to deprive.*
Désapprendre (40), *to unlearn.*
Desservir (7), *to disoblige.*
Déteindre (29), *to discolor.*
Détenir (13), *to detain.*
Détruire (26), *to destroy.*
Devenir (14), *to become.*
Dévêtir (15), *to strip.*
Dévêtir (se) (15), *to undress one's self.*
Dire (32), *to say.*
Disconvenir (14), *to disagree.*
Discourir (5), *to discourse.*
Disparaître (27), *to disappear.*
Dissoudre (41, 86), *to dissolve.*
Distraire (45), *to divert from.*
Distraire (se) (45), *to divert one's mind.*
Dormir (7), *to sleep.*
Duire (26), *to suit.*
Ébattre (s') (23), *to be merry.*
Ébouillir (4), *to boil down.*
Échoir (64), *to expire.*
Éclore (81), *to be hatched.*
Éconduire (26), *to put off.*
Écrire (33), *to write.*
Élire (35), *to elect.*
Emboire (24), *to imbibe.*
Émettre (36), *to emit.*
Émoudre (37), *to grind.*
Émouvoir (17), *to move.*
Empreindre (29), *to imprint.*
Enceindre (29), *to surround.*
Enclore (77), *to inclose.*
Encourir (5), *to incur.*
Endormir (7), *to make sleep.*
Enduire (26), *to do over with.*
Enfreindre (29), *to infringe.*
Enfuir (s') (8), *to run away.*
Enjoindre (29), *to enjoin.*
Enquérir (s') (3), *to inquire.*
Ensuivre (s') (44), *to result.*
Entremettre (s') (36), *to intermeddle.*
Entr'ouvrir (10), *to open a little.*
Entreprendre (40), *to undertake.*
Entretenir (13), *to keep up.*
Entrevoir (21), *to have a glimpse of.*
Envoyer (2), *to send.*
Épreindre (29), *to squeeze out.*
Éprendre (s') (40), *to be smitten.*
Équivaloir (20), *to be equivalent.*
Éteindre (29), *to extinguish.*
Être (p. 247), *to be.*
Étreindre (29), *to twist.*
Exclure (25), *to exclude.*
Extraire (45), *to extract.*
Faillir (50), *to fail.*

Faire (34), *to do.*
Falloir, *to be necessary.*
Feindre (29), *to feign.*
Férir (51), *to strike.*
Fleurir (52), *to bloom.*
Forfaire (34), *to forfeit.*
Frire (82), *to fry.*
Fuir (8), *to flee.*
Geindre (29), *to whine.*
Gésir (53), *to lay.*
Haïr (54), *to hate.*
Induire (26), *to induce.*
Inscrire (33), *to inscribe.*
Instruire (26), *to instruct.*
Interdire (32), *to forbid.*
Interrompre (85), *to interrupt.*
Intervenir (14), *to meddle.*
Introduire (26), *to introduce.*
Issir (55), *to come out.*
Joindre (29), *to join.*
Lire (35), *to read.*
Luire (26), *to shine.*
Maintenir (13), *to maintain.*
Malfaire (34, 83), *to do harm.*
Maudire (32, 84), *to curse.*
Méconnaître (27), *to disown.*
Médire (32), *to slander.*
Méfaire (34), *to do wrong.*
Mentir (12), *to lie.*
Méprendre (se) (40), *to mistake.*
Messeoir (65), *to be unbecoming*
Mettre (36), *to put.*
Moudre (37), *to grind.*
Mourir (9), *to die.*
Mouvoir (17), *to remove.*
Naître (38), *to be born.*
Nuire (26), *to harm.*
Obtenir (13), *to obtain.*
Offrir (10), *to offer.*
Oindre (29), *to anoint.*
Omettre (36), *to omit.*
Ouïr (56), *to hear.*
Ouvrir (10), *to open.*
Paître (27), *to graze.*
Paraître (27), *to appear.*
Parcourir (5), *to run over.*
Parfaire (34), *to complete.*
Partir (11), *to start.*
Parvenir (14), *to reach.*
Peindre (29), *to paint.*
Permettre (36), *to allow.*
Plaindre (29), *to pity.*
Plaire (39), *to please.*
Pleuvoir, *to rain.*
Poindre (29), *to dawn.*
Poursuivre (44), *to pursue.*
Pourvoir (21, 66), *to provide.*
Pouvoir (18), *to be able.*
Prédire (32, 78), *to foretell.*

CONJUGATION OF VERBS.

Prendre (40), *to take.*
Prescrire (33), *to prescribe.*
Pressentir (12), *to forebode.*
Prévaloir (20), *to prevail.*
Prévenir (14), *to prevent.*
Prévoir (21, 67), *to foresee.*
Produire (26), *to produce.*
Promettre (36), *to promise.*
Promouvoir (17), *to promote.*
Proscrire (33), *to proscribe.*
Provenir (14), *to proceed.*
Rabattre (23), *to pull down.*
Rapprendre (40), *to learn again.*
Rasseoir (16), *to replace.*
Rasseoir (se) (16), *to sit down again.*
Ratteindre (29), *to catch again.*
Ravoir (68), *to get again.*
Rebattre (23), *to beat again.*
Reboire (24), *to drink again.*
Rebouillir (4), *to boil again.*
Reclure (25), *to shut up.*
Reconduire (26), *to reconduct.*
Reconnaître (27), *to recognize.*
Reconquérir (3), *to reconquer.*
Reconstruire (26), *to reconstruct.*
Recoudre (28), *to sew again.*
Recourir (5), *to have recourse to.*
Recouvrir (10), *to cover.*
Récrire (33), *to write again.*
Recroître (31), *to grow again.*
Recueillir (6), *to gather.*
Recuire (26), *to cook again.*
Redéfaire (34), *to undo again.*
Redevenir (14), *to become again.*
Redire (32, 78), *to say again.*
Redormir (7), *to sleep again.*
Réduire (26), *to reduce.*
Réélire (25), *to reelect.*
Refaire (34), *to do again.*
Refleurir (52), *to bloom again.*
Rejoindre (29), *to overtake.*
Relire (35), *to read again.*
Reluire (26), *to glitter.*
Remettre (36), *to put again.*
Remoudre (37), *to grind again.*
Renaître (38), *to revive.*
Rendormir (7), *to lull to sleep again.*
Rentraire (45), *to fine-draw; to join on.*
Repaître (27), *to feed.*
Reparaître (27), *to reappear.*
Repartir (11), *to start again.*
Repeindre (29), *to paint again.*
Repentir (se) (12), *to repent.*
Reprendre (40), *to take again.*
Reproduire (26), *to reproduce.*
Requérir (3), *to request.*
Résoudre (41), *to resolve.*
Ressentir (12), *to resent.*
Ressortir (11), *to go out again.*
Ressouvenir (se) (14), *to remember.*
Restreindre (29), *to restrain.*
Reteindre (29), *to dye again.*
Retenir (13), *to retain.*
Retraire (45), *to milk again.*
Revaloir (20), *to give an equivalent.*
Revenir (14), *to come back.*
Revêtir (15), *to clothe.*
Revivre (47), *to revive.*
Revoir (21), *to see again.*
Rire (42), *to laugh.*
Rompre (85), *to break.*
Rouvrir (10), *to open again.*
Saillir (58), *to jut out.*
Satisfaire (34), *to satisfy.*
Savoir (19), *to know.*
Secourir (5), *to help.*
Séduire (26), *to seduce.*
Sentir (12), *to feel.*
Seoir (69), *to become.*
Seoir (70), *to be seated.*
Servir (7), *to serve.*
Sortir (11), *to go out.*
Soudre (86), *to solve.*
Souffrir (10), *to suffer.*
Souloir (71), *to be accustomed.*
Soumettre (36), *to submit.*
Sourire (42), *to smile.*
Sourdre (87), *to spring.*
Souscrire (33), *to subscribe.*
Soustraire (45), *to subtract.*
Soutenir (13), *to sustain.*
Souvenir (se) (14), *to remember.*
Subvenir (14), *to assist.*
Suffire (43), *to suffice.*
Suivre (44), *to follow.*
Surgir (59), *to land.*
Surfaire (34), *to overdo.*
Surprendre (40), *to surprise.*
Surseoir (72), *to put off.*
Survenir (14), *to survene.*
Survivre (47), *to survive.*
Taire (39), *to conceal.*
Taire (se) (39), *to keep silent.*
Teindre (29), *to dye.*
Tenir (13), *to hold.*
Tistre (88), *to weave.*
Traduire (26), *to translate.*
Traire (45), *to milk.*
Transcrire (33), *to copy.*
Transmettre (36), *to transmit.*
Tressaillir (6), *to start.*
Vaincre (46), *to vanquish.*
Valoir (20), *to be worth.*
Venir (14), *to come.*
Vêtir (15), *to dress.*
Vivre (47), *to live.*
Voir (21), *to see.*
Vouloir (22), *to will.*

IDIOMS AND PROVERBS.

PART FIRST.—ENGLISH INTO FRENCH.

The principal word in each expression, or the word on which the idiom turns is placed at the head of the division in which the expression is given.

About.
I have no money about me.
What is it about?
Go about your business.
Look about you (mind).

Environ; alentour.
Je n'ai pas d'argent sur moi.
De quoi s'agit-il?
Allez-vous-en.
Prenez garde à vous.

Account.
A man of no account.
On my account.
On no account.
Even accounts make lasting friends.

Compte, *m.*
Un homme de rien.
À cause de moi.
En aucune manière.
Les bons comptes font les bons amis.

Afford, to.
I cannot afford to do it.
I cannot afford it.
That affords me great pleasure.
What can you afford to give?
I cannot afford more.
Give as much as you can afford.

Avoir les moyens.
Je n'ai pas les moyens de le faire.
Je n'en ai pas les moyens.
Cela me donne beaucoup de plaisir.
Combien pouvez-vous donner?
Je ne peux pas aller au-delà.
Donnez selon vos moyens.

Again.
Begin again.
Go there again.
He will come again.
I told it to him again and again.
Give me as much again.

De nouveau; encore. [veau.
Recommencez, *or* commencez de nou-
Allez y encore une fois.
Il reviendra.
Je le lui ai répété vingt fois.
Donnez-m'en deux fois autant.

Agree, to.
We have agreed about the price.
They agree like cat and dog.
I will make them agree.
Do you agree to those terms?
Agreed upon.
That does not agree with me (my stomach).

Convenir.
Nous sommes convenus du prix.
Ils s'accordent comme chien et chat.
Je les mettrai d'accord.
Consentez-vous à ces conditions?
Convenu. D'accord.
Cela me fait mal, me dérange l'estomac

All.
It is all over.
After all.
You must take him all in all.
All the better; all the better for it.

Tout.
C'est fini.
Après tout, au bout du compte.
Il faut le prendre tel quel.
Tant mieux; il n'en sera que mieux.

It is all one to me. Cela m'est égal.
If that is all, be easy. S'il ne tient qu'à cela, soyez tranquille.
To be all things to all men. Se faire tout à tous.
All is well that ends well. La fin couronne l'œuvre.
All is not gold that glitters. Tout ce qui reluit n'est pas or.

Answer, to. **Répondre.**
What did he answer you? Que vous a-t-il répondu ?
He shall answer before God. Il en rendra compte à Dieu.
That answers my purpose. Cela fait mon affaire.
That answers several purposes. Cela sert à plusieurs fins.
That answered very well. Cela a parfaitement réussi.

Ask, to. **Demander.**
Some one asks for you. On vous demande.
Ask him to come in. Priez-le d'entrer.
Did you ask for Mrs. B. ? Vous êtes-vous informé de Mme. B. ?
How much do you ask for that coat? Combien faites-vous cet habit ?

Attend, to. **Faire attention.**
To attend to one's business. S'occuper de, vaquer à, ses affaires.
— a meeting. Assister à une séance, une assemblée.
— lectures. Suivre un cours.
— a sick person. Soigner un malade.
The odium which attends dishonor. L'odieux qui s'attache au déshonneur.
I will attend to you in an instant. Je serai à vous à l'instant.

Average, to average. **Moyen, moyenne.**
The average circulation of that journal is 30,000 copies a day. La circulation moyenne de ce journal est de 30,000 exemplaires par jour.
Our receipts average fifty dollars a day. Nos recettes montent à cinquante dollars par jour l'un portant l'autre.

Be, to (12, 13). **Être.**
What is that? Qu'est-ce que c'est que cela ?
What is that to you? Qu'est-ce que cela vous fait ?
How are you? Comment vous portez-vous ?
He is not well. Il ne se porte pas bien.
He is better. Il va mieux.
How is that business? Comment va cette affaire ?
How is business? Comment vont les affaires ?
This coffee is better than the other. Ce café est meilleur que l'autre.
Tea is better for me than coffee. Le thé vaut mieux pour moi (or me con vient mieux) que le café.

He is as good as she is. Il la vaut bien.
He is worth a great deal. Il est très-riche.
It is (of time or distance). Il y a (217, 218, 219).

Bear, to. **Porter.**
To bear some one ill will. En vouloir à qqn.
— malice against some one. Garder rancune contre qqn.
— it in mind. Le retenir, ne pas l'oublier.
— a good character. Jouir d'une bonne réputation.
— witness. Rendre témoignage.

Beat, to.
To beat a person black and blue.
— *a path.*
— *up eggs, cream.*
— *down the price.*
— *about the bush.*
— *something into his head.*
I beat him two games.

Become, to.
What has become of him?
That hat is not becoming to you.
Her dress is very becoming.
That is very becoming.

Better.
I have thought better of it.
You will be the better for it.
You will not be the better for it.
He grows better and better.
You will get the better of those difficulties.
Better late than never.
The better the day the better the deed.

Bill.
To settle a bill.
To run up bills everywhere.
The walls are covered with bills.
There is a bill on the house.
The play-bill.
The bill of fare.

Break, to (to render useless).
To break into pieces (to smash).
— (*asunder*).
— *an engagement.*
— *an oath.*
— *one's word.*
— *any one's heart.*
— *open a door.*
— *the bank.*
— *in a horse.*
— *news to one.*

Bring, to.
Bring the gun.
— *the dogs, the carriage.*
— *in dinner.*
To bring luck.
— *an action against s. b.*
— *word to s. b. of s. th.*
Time brings about many things.
His conduct brought this misery upon him.

Battre.
Meurtrir qqn. de coups.
Frayer un sentier.
Fouetter des œufs, de la crème.
Rabattre le prix.
Tourner autour du pot.
Lui fourrer quelque chose dans l'esprit.
Je lui ai gagné deux parties.

Devenir.
Qu'est-il devenu ?
Ce chapeau ne vous convient pas.
Sa robe lui sied bien.
C'est bienséant, c'est très-convenable.

Meilleur, *adj.* ; **mieux,** *adv.*
Je me suis ravisé.
Vous vous en trouverez mieux.
Vous n'y gagnerez rien.
Il va de mieux en mieux.
Vous vaincrez ces obstacles.
Mieux vaut tard que jamais.
À bon jour bonne œuvre.

Billet, *m.*
Régler un compte.
Faire des dettes partout.
Les murs sont couverts d'affiches.
Il y a un écriteau sur la maison.
Le programme du spectacle.
Le menu du dîner ; la carte.

Casser.
Briser en morceaux.
Rompre.
Rompre un engagement.
Violer un serment.
Manquer de parole.
Fendre *or* briser le cœur à qqn.
Enfoncer *or* forcer une porte.
Faire sauter la banque.
Rompre un cheval.
Préparer qqn. à recevoir des nouvelles.

Apporter ; amener.
Apportez le fusil.
Amenez les chiens, la voiture.
Servez le dîner.
Porter bonheur.
Intenter une action contre qqn.
Informer, prévenir qqn. de qq. ch.
Le temps accomplit bien des choses.
Sa conduite lui a attiré ces malheurs.

Business.
Mind your business.
You had no business to go there.
This will just do my business.
I shall make it my business
To be in business.
To set up a business.
He is a man of business.

Call, to.
Can you call on me to-night?
I shall call on him to-day.
I shall call on you when I come back.
Will you call at the office?
He calls for his money.
I shall call for you when I pass.

Care, to take; to care.
Take good care of your health.
Take good care of yourself.
Take care not to fall.
I do not care for it.
Take it; I do not care for it.
What do I care about it?
He does not care for any body.

Carry, to.
To carry about one's person.
— one's point.
— a jest too far.
— it high.
— coals to Newcastle.
— on a profession.

Catch, to, a disease.
To catch a cold, to catch cold.
— a Tartar.
A drowning man catches at a straw.
The house caught fire.

Come, to.
How did that come about?
He will soon come about.
That appeal comes home to our feelings.
It comes to the same.
That came in his way.
First come, first helped.

Company.
He does not go into company.
We have company at dinner.
He sees good company.
Will you give us the pleasure of your company this evening?

Affaire, *f.*
Occupez-vous de vos affaires.
Vous n'aviez que faire d'y aller.
Ceci fera précisément mon affaire.
Je m'en ferai une obligation.
Être dans le commerce.
Établir une maison de commerce.
C'est un homme qui s'entend aux affaires

Appeler.
Pouvez-vous venir chez moi ce soir?
J'irai le voir aujourd'hui.
Je passerai chez vous en revenant.
Voulez-vous passer au bureau?
Il vient chercher son argent.
Je viendrai vous prendre en passant.

Avoir soin; se soucier.
Ayez bien soin de votre santé.
Soignez-vous bien.
Prenez garde de tomber.
Je ne m'en soucie pas.
Prenez-le; je n'y tiens pas.
Qu'est-ce que cela me fait?
Il n'aime personne.

Porter.
Porter sur soi.
Accomplir son dessein.
Pousser trop loin une plaisanterie.
Le prendre sur un haut ton.
Porter de l'eau à la rivière.
Suivre, *or* exercer une profession.

Attraper, une maladie.
Prendre un rhume, s'enrhumer.
Être pris dans ses filets.
Un homme qui se noie s'accroche à tout.
Le feu prit à la maison.

Venir.
Comment cela est-il arrivé?
Il se remettra bientôt.
Cet appel va au cœur.
Cela revient au même.
Cela lui est tombé dans la main. [ceaux.
Aux premiers venus, les premiers mor-

Monde, *m.*; **société,** *f.*
Il ne va pas dans le monde.
Nous avons du monde à dîner.
Il fréquente la bonne société.
Voulez-vous nous faire l'honneur de passer la soirée chez nous.

Course.
To follow a course of lectures on chemistry.
In the course of the day.
We do not know what course to pursue.
He follows his own course.
A long course of years.
The first course was brought in.
The effect will follow of course.
Of course.

Cours, *m.;* **courant,** *m.*
Suivre un cours de chimie.
Dans le courant de la journée.
Nous ne savons quel moyen adopter.
Il suit son penchant naturel.
Une longue suite d'années.
On servait le premier service.
L'effet suivra naturellement.
Sans doute ; c'est tout naturel.

Crack, to.
This dish is cracked.
He cracked his whip.
The cracking of the burning wood.
To crack jokes.
He is a little cracked.

Fendre ; fêler.
Ce plat est fêlé.
Il faisait claquer son fouet.
Le pétillement du bois qui brûle.
Faire des plaisanteries.
Il a le timbre tant soit peu fêlé.

Cut, to.
To cut the wood ; to cut up the fowl.
— *out a coat.*
— *the air.*
— *capers.*
— *sticks (to clear out).*
— *short.*
— *acquaintance with one.*

Couper.
Couper le bois ; découper le poulet.
Tailler un habit.
Fendre l'air.
Faire des cabrioles, des gambades.
Déguerpir.
Trancher court.
Rompre avec qqn.

Day *(daylight).*
Every day ; every other day.
All the day.
In the course of the day.
It is daylight ; in broad daylight.

Jour, *m.;* **journée,** *f.*
Tous les jours, tous les deux jours.
Toute la journée.
Dans la journée.
Il fait jour ; en plein jour.

REM.—JOUR represents the astronomical day, as a unit ; it is used in counting, TROIS JOURS, *three days;* HUIT JOURS, *a week;* QUINZE JOURS, *a fortnight.* It is also used in adverbial expressions : DE JOUR ET DE NUIT, *by day and by night.* JOURNÉE represents the day in its course, from morning till evening ; it is used when duration is implied, hence with reference to events which may characterize it : UNE JOURNÉE MALHEUREUSE, *an unfortunate day.* This remark applies likewise to MATIN, MATINÉE, *morning ;* SOIR, SOIRÉE, *evening ;* AN, ANNÉE, *year.*

Disappoint, to.
I am disappointed at not seeing her.
I do not wish to disappoint him.
That affair has disappointed me.

Désappointer.
Je suis contrarié de ne pas la voir.
Je ne veux pas lui manquer de parole.
Cette affaire n'a pas répondu à mon at- [tente.

Do, to.
To do justice.
— *a service.*
— *one's duties.*
— *nothing of the kind.*
He will do nothing of the kind.
I have nothing to do with that.
How do you do?
That will not do for me.

Faire.
Rendre justice.
— service.
Remplir ses devoirs.
N'en rien faire.
Il n'en fera rien.
Je n'ai que faire de cela.
Comment vous portez-vous ?
Cela ne me va pas, ne me convient pas

Draw, to.
To draw lots.
— the breath.
— (pencilling).
— a circle.
— a deed.
— a tooth.
— water (from a well).
— wine (from a cask).
— upon a person (a draft).
— (tea or herbs).

End.
He is near his end.
To sit at the upper end.
To make the two ends meet.

REM.—FIN, end, conclusion. There can be but one end (conclusion) to any thing. BOUT, end, extreme point; LE HAUT (BOUT) ET LE BAS BOUT DE LA TABLE, the upper and the lower end of the table; À LA FIN DE L'ANNÉE, or AU BOUT DE L'AN, at the end of the year. (See REM. under Day.)

Engage, to.
To engage, to pawn.
— lodgings.
This seat is engaged.
He is engaged, busy.
We are engaged.
They are engaged (to be married).
She is engaged.

Enter, to.
To enter one's room, college.
— into conversation.
— one's name.
— a profession.
— business.
— upon the subject.

Evening.
In the evening.
An evening party.

Excuse, to.
Will you excuse me to your father?

Excuse me from coming this evening.

The magistrate excused the fine.

Expect, to.
We expect his arrival this evening.
We did not expect that (were not prepared for it).

Tirer.
Tirer au sort.
Respirer l'air.
Dessiner.
Tracer un cercle.
Rédiger un acte.
Arracher une dent.
Puiser de l'eau.
Tirer du vin.
Tirer sur qqn. (une traite).
Infuser.

Fin, f.; bout, m.
Il touche à sa fin.
Être au haut bout de la table.
Joindre les deux bouts.

Engager.
Engager, mettre en gage.
Arrêter, louer, un appartement.
Cette place est retenue.
Il est occupé.
Nous avons pris des engagements.
Ils sont fiancés.
Elle est promise.

Entrer.
Entrer dans sa chambre, au collége.
— en conversation.
S'inscrire.
Embrasser une profession.
Commencer les affaires.
Entamer la matière.

Soir, m.; soirée, f. (See Day, REM.)
Le soir.
Une soirée.

Excuser.
Voulez-vous m'excuser auprès de M. votre père?
Excusez-moi, dispensez-moi, de venir ce soir.
Le magistrat lui a fait grâce de l'amende.

Attendre; espérer.
Nous attendons son arrivée ce soir.
Nous ne nous attendions pas à cela.

I expect to see him by and by.
I expect to pay him a visit.
I expect to be back in a fortnight.

Face.
They laughed in his face.
I tell it to you before your face.
Would you do it before his face?
I have the sun in my face.

Fault.
Whose fault is it?
He has but one fault.
To be at fault.
To find fault with.
He finds fault with every thing I do.
It is not my fault that he does not succeed.

Feel, to.
How do you feel?

I do not feel as usual.

How does your hand feel?
I shall feel happy in being useful to you.
I feel for you.

Let me feel your pulse.
Try to feel him on that subject.

Fire.
Have you a fire in your room?
There is a great fire.
Our house has caught fire.
He will not set the river on fire.

Fit, to.
That coat fits you very well.
My tailor fits well.
To fit up a house, a workshop.

Gain, to.
To gain one's living.
— a reputation.
— one's end.
— the ascendency.
— the day.

Get, to.
I must get a pair of gloves.
He got what he deserved.
His handsome conduct got him that place.
I cannot get the money.
To get a cold.
— wind of a thing.

J'espère le voir tantôt.
Je me propose d'aller le voir. [jours.
Je compte être de retour dans quinze

Visage, *m.;* **figure,** *f.*
Ils lui ont ri au nez.
Je vous le dis en face.
Le feriez-vous en sa présence ?
Le soleil me donne dans les yeux.

Faute, *f.;* **défaut,** *m.*
À qui en est la faute ?
Il n'a qu'un seul défaut.
Être en défaut.
Trouver à redire à.
Il trouve à redire à tout ce que je fais.
Il ne tient pas à moi qu'il ne réussisse.

Sentir. [vez-vous?
Comment vous sentez-vous ? vous trou-
{ Je ne me trouve pas comme d'ordinaire.
{ Je ne suis pas dans mon assiette.
Comment va la main ? [utile.
Je m'estimerai heureux de vous être
Je partage, je prends part à, votre chagrin.
Permettez-moi de vous tâter le pouls.
Tâtez-le un peu sur ce sujet.

Feu, *m.*
Avez-vous du feu dans votre chambre ?
Il y a un grand incendie.
Le feu a pris à notre maison.
Il n'a pas inventé la poudre.

Aller bien.
Cet habit vous va parfaitement.
Mon tailleur habille bien.
Meubler une maison, monter un atelier.

Gagner.
Gagner sa vie.
Acquérir *or* se faire de la réputation.
Parvenir à sa fin.
Prendre le dessus.
L'emporter.

Obtenir.
Il faut que j'achète une paire de gants.
Il a reçu ce qu'il a mérité.
Sa belle conduite lui a valu cette place.
Je ne puis obtenir, *or* me procurer, l'ar-
Attraper un rhume, s'enrhumer. [gent.
Avoir vent d'une chose.

To get rid of s. b.	Se débarrasser de qqn.
— — *s. th.*	Se défaire de qq. ch.
— *wet.*	Se mouiller.
— *confused.*	S'embarrasser, se troubler.
— *away.*	S'échapper.
— *into a scrape.*	S'attirer de mauvaises affaires.
— *out of the scrape.*	Se tirer d'affaire.

Give, to.

To give credit.	Faire crédit ; ajouter foi.
— — *for discretion.*	Reconnaître la discrétion de qqn.
— *a look.*	Jeter un regard.
— *heed.*	Faire attention.
— *comfort.*	Consoler.
— *notice.*	Prévenir, avertir.
Give my love to your sister.	Faites mes amitiés à votre sœur.
He gave us the slip.	Il s'est échappé, il nous a plantés là.
Silence gives consent.	Qui ne dit mot consent.

Go, to. To go away. — **Aller. S'en aller.**

To go halves.	Être de moitié.
— *to work.*	Se mettre à l'ouvrage.
— *about it, to set about it.*	S'y prendre.
— *for nothing.*	Compter pour rien.
— *by rule.*	Faire les choses selon les règles.
— *down (of heavenly bodies).*	Se coucher.
— *up.*	Monter.
— *without a thing.*	Se passer d'une chose.
— *and inquire.*	Aller aux informations.
How goes it with you?	Comment cela va-t-il ?
Go by that.	Réglez-vous sur cela.
To go on foot, on horseback, in a carriage.	Aller à pied, à cheval, en voiture.
— *twenty miles, on foot, on horseback.*	Faire vingt milles, à pied, à cheval.
— *for a walk.*	Aller à la promenade, aller se promener.
I am going.	Je m'en vais.

REM.—S'EN ALLER, *to go away*, to leave the place where we are.

Half. — **Moitié,** *f.* ; **demi,** *adj.*

Give me the half of it.	Donnez-m'en la moitié.
Cut it into halves.	Coupez-le en deux.
To do things by halves.	Faire les choses à demi.
Half wine and half water.	Moitié eau et moitié vin.
Half way ; half way up the hill.	À moitié chemin ; a mi-côte.

Hand. — **Main,** *f.*

The work is done by the hand.	L'ouvrage se fait à la main.
The work is in hand.	L'ouvrage est en main, entre les mains.
Your letter came to hand.	Votre lettre m'est parvenue.
I have every thing here at hand.	J'ai tout ici sous la main.
Give us a hand.	Donnez-nous un coup de main.
Let us put our hands to the task.	Mettons la main à l'œuvre.
He is a good hand at it.	Il s'y entend bien.

Will you take a hand at cards? — Voulez-vous faire une partie de cartes ?
On the one hand; on the other hand. — D'une part ; d'autre part.
They are hand and glove together. — Ce sont deux têtes dans un bonnet.

Hear, to (327). — **Entendre.**

Heart. — **Cœur.**
That will break her heart. — Cela lui brisera le cœur.
To take a thing to heart. — Prendre une chose à cœur.
His heart is set upon it. — Cela lui tient au cœur.
To take of a thing to one's heart's content. — S'en donner à cœur joie.
To have the heart full of it. — En avoir le cœur gros.
To have the heart in one's mouth. — Avoir le cœur sur les lèvres.
Out of the abundance of the heart the mouth speaketh. — Quand le cœur es plein, il déborde.

Home. — **À la maison, chez soi.**
Mrs. B. at home, Thursday. — Mme. B. recevra jeudi.
Make yourself at home. — Faites comme si vous étiez chez vous.
He is at home everywhere. — Il est sans gêne partout.
To be at home (with things). — Être au fait.
— *(with persons).* — Être en pays de connaissances.
To be without a home. — Etre sans asile.
Charity begins at home. — La charité bien ordonnée commence par soi-même.
Home, sweet home. — Oh mon doux foyer !

Improve, to. — **Améliorer.**
To improve one's condition. — Améliorer sa condition.
His health has improved. — Sa santé s'est améliorée.
To improve a machine. — Perfectionner une machine.
Arts have greatly improved. — Les arts se sont bien perfectionnés.
To improve (one's mind). — S'instruire, cultiver son esprit.
— *(to make progress).* — Faire des progrès.
— *(to grow better in quality).* — Bonifier.
— *(in appearance).* — Embellir.
— *an opportunity.* — Profiter d'une occasion.

Intend, to. — **Avoir l'intention.**
I intend to go out. — J'ai l'intention de sortir.
He intends to go on a journey. — Il se propose de faire un voyage.
His father intends him for the law. — Son père le destine au barreau.
This compliment is intended for you. — Ce compliment s'adresse à vous.

Introduce, to. — **Introduire.**
To introduce a person into a house. — Introduire qqn. dans une maison.
— *one person to another.* — Présenter qqn. à qqn.
Allow me to introduce Mr. B. — Permettez-moi de vous présenter à M. B

Intrude, to. — **Déranger.**
I fear I am intruding. — J'ai peur de vous avoir dérangé.
If I intrude, say so. — Si je suis de trop, dites-le-moi.

Keep, to. — **Garder ; tenir.**
To keep silence or silent. — Garder le silence, se taire.
— *a thing secret,* — le secret d'une chose.
— *a store.* — Tenir un magasin.

To keep a boarding-house.   Tenir pension.
— a carriage.   — équipage.
— one's word.   — parole, sa parole.
— from harm.   Préserver.
— one's health.   Conserver sa santé.
— the laws.   Observer les lois.
— the road.   Suivre le chemin.
— a festival.   Célébrer une fête.
— order, discipline.   Maintenir l'ordre, la discipline.
— an army on foot.   Entretenir une armée.
— one waiting.   Faire attendre qqu.
— back.   Retenir.

Leave, to.   **Laisser.**
I leave these papers with you.   Je laisse ces papiers entre vos mains.
He left them all well off.   Il les a tous laissés dans l'aisance.
I leave you to think.   Je vous laisse à penser.
To leave, to part from.   Quitter.
He left us.   Il nous a quittés.
To leave off business.   Quitter les affaires, se retirer des affaires.
To leave, to start.   Partir.
We leave for Boston.   Nous partons pour Boston.
This is all I have left of it.   Voilà tout ce qu'il m'en reste.
I leave it to you.   Je m'en rapporte à vous.
I have left off going there.   J'ai cessé d'y aller.
To leave off smoking.   Renoncer à fumer.
He does not leave things undone.   Il ne laisse pas les choses à moitié faites.
Leave off, stop.   Arrêtez, en voilà assez.

Let, to.   **Louer; laisser.**
He let his house by the year.   Il a loué sa maison à l'année.
Let me alone.   Laissez-moi tranquille.
Will you let him go with us?   Voulez-vous lui permettre de nous ac-
I will let you know.   Je vous le ferai savoir.   [compagner ?
To let out a secret.   Laisser échapper un secret.
To let go.   Lâcher, laisser aller.

Like, to.   **Aimer.**
I like fruit.   J'aime le fruit.
I like these pears very much.   Je trouve ces poires excellentes.
How do you like that book?   Comment trouvez-vous ce livre ?
I do not like it much.   Il ne me plaît pas beaucoup.
I do not like to be in the country.   Je ne me plais pas à la campagne.
Do as you like.   Faites comme vous voudrez.
I should like to see him.   Je voudrais bien le voir.

Look, to.   **Regarder.**
Look at that.   Regardez cela.
Look at your watch (to see the time).   Regardez à votre montre.
To look well.   Avoir bonne mine.
— pleased.   — l'air content.
— gentlemanly.   — — distingué.

To look like some body.
That does not look like it.
To look down.
— *up.*
— *for.*
— *into.*
— *out.*
My windows look out upon the river.
Look out! (mind).

Make, to.
To make fun of a thing.
How much did you make by it?
To make a mistake.
— *believe.*
She made believe that she did not see him.
To make happy.
— *one's self ridiculous.*
— — *miserable.*
— *sure of a thing.*
— *good a claim.*
— *void.*
— *light of a thing.*

Marry, to (to take in marriage).
He married my cousin.
To marry (to join in matrimony).
The bishop married them.
To get married.
When will you get married?

Mean, to.
What do you mean?
He means it well.
I did not mean that.
I mean that you shall do it.

Mind, to.
Mind your business.
Do not mind what he says.
Mind what you say.
Mind well what I say.
I do not mind that (do not care).
Never mind.
Mind the door.
To mind the shop.
Mind your health.

Miss, to. Miss, n.
To miss the train.
— *a line.*
— *the street.*
A miss is as good as a mile.

Ressembler à q'qn.
Cela n'y ressemble pas.
Baisser les yeux.
Lever les yeux.
Chercher.
Examiner.
Donner sur.
Mes fenêtres donnent sur la rivière.
Prenez garde !

Faire (324).
Tourner une chose en plaisanterie.
Combien y avez-vous gagné ?
Se tromper.
Faire semblant.
Elle faisait semblant de ne pas le voir.
Rendre heureux.
Se rendre ridicule.
Se rendre malheureux.
S'assurer d'une chose.
Justifier, prouver une réclamation.
Annuler.
Traiter une chose légèrement.

Épouser.
Il a épousé ma cousine.
Marier.
L'évêque les a mariés.
Se marier.
Quand vous marierez-vous ?

Vouloir dire.
Que voulez-vous dire ?
Ses intentions sont bonnes.
Ce n'était pas là mon intention.
J'entends que vous le fassiez.

S'occuper de.
Occupez-vous de vos affaires.
Ne faites pas attention à ce qu'il dit.
Prenez garde à ce que vous dites.
Remarquez bien ce que je dis.
Je ne me soucie pas de cela.
N'importe.
Ayez l'œil à la porte.
Garder la boutique.
Songez à votre santé.

Manquer.
Manquer le train.
Sauter une ligne.
Se tromper de rue.
Faute d'un point Martin perdit son âne.

Morning.
In the morning.
Early in the morning.
At six o'clock in the morning.

Matin, *m.;* **matinée,** *f.* (See *Day*, Rem.).
Le matin, dans la matinée.
Le matin de bonne heure.
À six heures du matin.

Name.
What is your name?

That man has a good name.
A good name is better than riches.
To call a person names.

Nom, *m.*
{ Comment vous appelez-vous ?
{ Comment vous nommez-vous ?
C'est un homme honorable.
Bonne renommée vaut mieux que cein-
Dire des injures à qqn. [ture dorée.

Part.
To bear one's part of the danger.
That is perfect in all its parts.
He has no part in it.
In good part; in bad part.
On the part of.
Foreign parts.
On my part; for my part.
A lad of parts.
To act or play a part.

Part, *f.;* **partie,** *f.*
Supporter sa part du danger.
Cela est parfait dans toutes ses parties.
Il n'y est pour rien.
En bonne part ; en mauvaise part.
De la part de.
Pays étrangers.
De mon côté ; quant à moi.
Un jeune homme de moyens, de talent.
Jouer un rôle.

Party.
The political parties.
The ruling party.
Party spirit.
The contracting parties.
A pleasure party.
To be of the party.
To go to a party.

Parti, *m.;* **partie,** *f.*
Les partis politiques.
Le parti dominant.
Esprit de parti.
Les parties contractantes.
Une partie de plaisir.
Être de la partie, en être.
Aller à une soirée, en soirée.

Pass, to.
To pass judgment.
— censure.
— a law.
— an examination.
How did it come to pass?
This is past my comprehension.
These bills do not pass here.

Passer.
Prononcer un arrêt, un jugement.
Exercer la censure.
Voter une loi.
Subir un examen.
Comment cela est-il arrivé ?
Cela surpasse mon intelligence.
Ces billets n'ont pas cours ici.

Pay, to.
To pay a visit.
— one's respects.
— attention.
— one off in his own coin.
I paid him in his own coin.
It does not pay.

Payer.
Faire *or* rendre visite.
Rendre *or* présenter ses respects.
Faire attention.
Lui rendre la pareille.
Je lui ai rendu la monnaie de sa pièce.
Le jeu ne vaut pas la chandelle.

People.
The French people.
All the people of the place were there.
The people murmur against the great.
The country people.

Peuple, *m.;* **nation,** *f.*
La nation française ; le peuple français.
Toute la population de l'endroit y était.
Le peuple murmure contre les grands.
Les gens, *or* les habitants de la campagne.

Old people are suspicious.　Les vieilles gens sont soupçonneux.
He sees a great many people.　Il voit beaucoup de monde.
There were three people at dinner.　Il y avait trois personnes à dîner.
There were very few people at church.　Il y avait fort peu de monde à l'église.
People are never satisfied.　On n'est jamais content.

Piece.　**Pièce,** *f.;* **morceau,** *m.*
I will take a sample of this piece.　Je prendrai un échantillon de cette pièce.
Cut me a small piece of it.　Coupez-m'en un petit morceau.
To pull a thing to pieces.　Mettre une chose en pièces.
They cost me three dollars a piece.　Ils me coûtent trois dollars la pièce.
They have ten thousand dollars a piece.　Ils ont chacun dix mille dollars.
This is a piece of good news.　Voilà une bonne nouvelle.
It is all of a piece with his conduct.　Cela est d'accord avec sa conduite.

Place.　**Place,** *f.;* **lieu,** *m.;* **endroit,** *m.*
Put every thing in its place.　Mettez chaque chose à sa place.
Those are places I do not go to.　Voilà des lieux que je ne fréquente pas.
This is the place where we parted.　Voici l'endroit où nous nous sommes
This is the sore place.　C'est la partie souffrante.　[séparés.
His heart is in the right place.　Il a le cœur bien placé.

Play, to.　**Jouer.**
To play high.　Jouer gros jeu.
— for love.　— pour l'honneur.
Whose turn is it to play?　À qui est-ce à jouer ?
We have played three games.　Nous avons fait trois parties.
To play cards.　Jouer aux cartes.
— on the piano.　— du piano, *or* toucher le piano.
— on the harp.　— de la harpe, *or* pincer la harpe.
They played all the evening.　Ils ont fait de la musique toute la soirée.
To play a trick.　Jouer un tour à qqn.
— the great man.　Faire l'homme d'importance.
— the fool, the child.　— le fou, l'enfant.
— truant.　— l'école buissonnière.
The engine plays well.　La pompe fonctionne bien.

Please, to.　**Plaire.**　　　　　　　　[mère.
That conduct will please his mother.　Cette conduite fera plaisir (plaira) à sa
That news will please her.　Cette nouvelle lui sera agréable.
Are you pleased with that?　Êtes-vous content de cela ?
You are hard to please.　Vous êtes difficile à contenter.
Do as you please.　Faites comme vous voudrez.
Please tell me where he lives.　Ayez la bonté de me dire où il demeure.
You are pleased to say so.　Cela vous plaît à dire.
If you please.　S'il vous plaît.

Put, to.　**Mettre.**
To put an end to a thing.　Mettre fin à une chose.
— a question.　Faire une question.
— a person in mind of a thing.　Rappeler une chose à qqn.
— the cart before the horse.　Mettre la charrue devant les bœufs.
— by (for safety); to put by or up.　Serrer ; mettre de côté.

Put by your papers.   Serrez vos papiers.
I will put this money by.   Je mettrai cet argent de côté.
To put down.   Déposer, mettre bas.
    —   *a rebellion.*   Réprimer une rebellion.
    —   *a person.*   Imposer silence à qqn.
    —   *pride.*   Rabaisser l'orgueil.
To put off.   Remettre.
    —   *— to sea.*   Mettre en mer.
    —   *out on interest.*   Placer à intérêt.
    —   *— a person.*   Embarrasser qqn.
    —   *— of a situation.*   Renvoyer qqn.

Question.   Question.
Why do you ask me that question?   Pourquoi me demandez-vous cela?
That is not the question.   Il ne s'agit pas de cela.
To bring into question.   Mettre en doute.
To raise a question.   Soulever un doute.
To ask a question.   Faire une question.

Raise, to.   Lever.
To raise the hand, the voice.   Lever la main, élever la voix.
    —   *suspicion.*   Faire naître des soupçons.
    —   *envy.*   Exciter l'envie.
    —   *the dust.*   Soulever la poussière.
    —   *one's spirits.*   Ranimer son courage.
    —   *from the dead.*   Ressusciter.
    —   *money.*   Trouver, se procurer de l'argent.
    —   *the price.*   Augmenter, hausser le prix.
    —   *vegetables.*   Cultiver des légumes.

Rise, to.   Se lever.
The sun rises at six o'clock.   Le soleil se lève à six heures.
Vapors rise from the earth.   Les vapeurs s'élèvent de la terre.
Men rise by industry.   Les hommes s'élèvent par leur travail.
A tempest rose on a sudden.   Tout à coup il s'éleva une tempête.
He fell and could not rise.   Il tomba et ne put se relever.
The Greeks rose against the Turks.   Les Grecs se soulevèrent contre les Turcs.
The river rose an inch during the night.   La rivière a monté d'un pouce dans la [nuit.
The corn rises.   Le blé renchérit.
The funds are rising.   Les fonds haussent.

Say, to.   Dire.
To say mass.   Dire la messe.
    —   *one's prayers.*   Faire ses prières.
    —   *the lesson.*   Répéter, *or* dire la leçon.
That is to say.   C'est-à-dire.
I say!   Dites donc!
I dare say. I dare say! (In irony).   Je le crois bien. Ah bien oui!
I heard him say so.   Je le lui ai entendu dire.
It is in vain for you to say.   Vous avez beau dire.

See, to.   Voir.
To see company.   Recevoir *or* voir du monde.
I shall see you home.   Je vous reconduirai chez vous.

Will you see her to the steamboat? — Voulez-vous l'accompagner jusqu'au ba-
I will see it done. — Je verrai à ce que cela se fasse. [teau ?
I will see about that business. — Je m'occuperai, je m'informerai de cette
We see through their plans. — Nous avons pénétré leurs projets. [affaire.
I must see into it. — Il faut que je l'approfondisse.

Send, to.
To send away goods. — Envoyer, expédier des marchandises.
— *away ; to dismiss.* — Renvoyer ; congédier.
— *one about his business.* — Envoyer promener qqn.
— *for.* — Envoyer chercher.
— *word.* — Envoyer dire, faire dire.

Set, to.
Set those things in order. — Mettre. [choses.
To set people at variance. — Mettez ces choses en ordre, arrangez ces
— *agog.* — Brouiller les gens, les mettre mal en-
— *a bone.* — Mettre en train. [semble.
— *a watch.* — Remettre un os.
— *a great value upon a thing.* — Régler une montre, la mettre à l'heure.
— *a task, an example.* — Attacher un grand prix à qq. ch.
— *to think.* — Donner une tâche, un exemple.
— *diamonds.* — Faire penser.
— *snares.* — Monter, enchâsser des diamants.
— *a day.* — Tendre des pièges.
Let me set you to right. — Fixer un jour.
I shall set about it presently. — Permettez-moi de vous tirer d'erreur.
You set about it in the wrong way. — Je m'y mettrai tout à l'heure.
How must I set about it? — Vous vous y prenez mal.
The sun sets early. — Comment faut-il s'y prendre ?
To set the world at defiance. — Le soleil se couche de bonne heure.
— Se moquer du monde.

Settle, to, an account.
To settle one's business. — Régler un compte.
— *a question, a dispute.* — Régler or arranger ses affaires.
— *the mind.* — Résoudre une question ; arranger un dif-
— *, to take a fixed abode.* — Composer l'esprit. [férend.
— *in business.* — Fixer, établir sa demeure, se domicilier.
— *(of liquids).* — S'établir dans le commerce.
— *(of the weather).* — Se rasseoir ; déposer.
— *(of anger).* — Se remettre au beau.
It is a settled thing. — S'apaiser, se calmer.
A settled idea. — C'est une affaire décidée.
— Une idée fixe.

Shoot, to, with a bow.
To shoot at a person. — Tirer de l'arc.
— *with a bullet.* — Tirer sur qqn.
— *at a target.* — — à balle.
— *a man with a gun (to kill).* — — à la cible.
— — *(to wound).* — Tuer un homme d'un coup de fusil.
— *(military execution).* — Blesser — —
— *(of plants).* — Fusiller.
— Pousser.

Sit, to.
To sit down to table.
Sit down by me.
Birds sit upon trees.
I will come and sit with you.
He sat an hour with us.
That coat sits well on you.
Those fine airs sit badly on him.
Sit still.
Sit close together.

Sleep, to.
Did you sleep well?
In which room did you sleep?
To sleep with God.

Speak, to.
To speak plainly.
— through the nose.
— extempore.
— openly.
— the truth.
Did you speak?
To speak out.
Who is to speak now?
Her eyes speak her thoughts.

Stand, to.
He kept standing in front of us.
The old castle is still standing.
The house stands between two hills.
Do not stand in the sun.
Let that stand.
They stood their ground.
That color will not stand.
How does the matter stand?
As matters stand.
The fact stands thus.
I cannot stand this any longer.
This is more than I can stand.
What does that stand for?
I stand first on the list.

Stop, to.
My watch has stopped.
I stop here.
We stopped a month with them.

Strike, to, with a dagger.
To strike a bargain.
— the balance.
The clock struck ten.
The carpenters have struck.

Se mettre, s'asseoir.
Se mettre à table.
Asseyez-vous auprès (à côté) de moi.
Les oiseaux se perchent sur les arbres.
Je viendrai vous tenir compagnie.
Il a passé une heure avec nous.
Cet habit vous va bien.
Ces grands airs ne lui conviennent pas
Restez tranquille.
Serrez-vous, serrez vos rangs.

Dormir; coucher.
Avez-vous bien dormi?
Dans quelle chambre avez-vous couché?
Reposer au sein de Dieu.

Parler.
Parler or prononcer distinctement.
Parler du nez.
Improviser.
Parler à cœur ouvert.
Dire la vérité.
Disiez-vous quelque chose?
Dire sa pensée.
Qui est-ce qui a la parole?
Ses yeux expriment sa pensée.

Se tenir debout.
Il se tenait debout devant nous
Le vieux château est encore debout.
La maison est située entre deux collines.
Ne vous exposez pas au soleil.
Laissez cela, ne touchez pas à cela.
Ils tinrent bon.
Cette couleur ne tiendra pas.
Où en est cette affaire?
Au point où en sont les affaires.
Voici le fait.
Je ne puis endurer cela plus longtemps
Ceci met ma patience à bout.
Qu'est-ce que cela représente?
Je suis le premier sur la liste.

Arrêter.
Ma montre est arrêtée.
Je m'arrête ici.
Nous avons passé un mois avec eux.

Frapper d'un poignard.
Conclure un marché.
Faire la balance.
L'horloge a sonné dix heures.
Les charpentiers ont fait grève.

Our ship struck against a rock.	Notre vaisseau a donné contre un rocher.
To strike at the root of good principles.	Saper les fondements des bons principes.
— a blow at some one.	Porter un coup à qqn.
— in with a person.	Tomber d'accord avec qqn.
— off an engraving, a copy.	Tirer une gravure, une impression.

Take, to, the air.   **Prendre** l'air.
To take advantage of.   Profiter de, tirer parti de.
— advice.   Consulter ; suivre un avis, un conseil.
— care.   Prendre or avoir soin.
— — (to be on one's guard).   Prendre garde.
— cold.   S'enrhumer.
— comfort.   Se consoler.
— delight in.   Se plaire à.
— effect.   Produire son effet.
— the field.   Se mettre en campagne.
— hold of s. th.   Saisir qq. ch., s'emparer de qq. ch.
— notice.   Observer, remarquer, faire attention à.
— an oath.   Prêter serment.
— a part in.   Prendre part à.
— revenge.   Tirer vengeance.
— shelter.   Se mettre à l'abri.
— sides with.   Se ranger du parti de.
— one's way.   Faire à sa guise.
— it kindly.   Savoir bon gré de qq. ch. à qqn.
— it well, ill.   Prendre en bonne (mauvaise) part.
— it easy.   Ne pas se gêner.
— after somebody.   Ressembler à qqn.
— away, off, out.   Emmener ; emporter ; enlever ; ôter.
— out a tooth.   Arracher une dent.
— to a thing.   Se plaire à une chose, y prendre plaisir.
— to bad habits.   Contracter de mauvaises habitudes.
— to one's heels.   Prendre la fuite.
— to heart.   Prendre à cœur.
— to pieces.   Démonter.
— up another person's interest.   Épouser les intérêts d'un autre.

Throw, to ; to throw away.   **Jeter.**
To throw dust into one's eyes.   Jeter de la poussière aux yeux de qqn.
— in one's teeth.   Jeter au nez.
— things about.   Éparpiller les choses.
— away time, money.   Gaspiller son temps, son argent.
— o. s. away.   Se sacrifier.
— out hints.   Donner à entendre.

Try, to, on a coat.   **Essayer** un habit.
To try a friend.   Éprouver un ami.
— a man for theft.   Juger un homme pour crime de vol.
— to convince.   Tâcher de convaincre.
— to please s. b.   Chercher à plaire à qqn.
— to lift.   Tenter à soulever.
— to succeed.   S'efforcer de réussir.

Turn, to.
The machine turns on a pivot.
To turn pale, red.
His hair turns gray.
He turned soldier.
To turn French into English.
— prose into verse.
— to good account.
— the stomach.
— an honest penny.
— the tables upon one.
— away.
— in.
The question turns on this point.
He does not know which way to turn.
To turn upside down.
— one's thoughts inward.

Walk, to, fast.
To walk to church.
He is walking this way.
To walk (for amusement).
They walked out together
How far did you walk?
I walked ten miles.
He walked up to her.

Way.
To lose one's way.
To miss the way.
To give way.
Over the way, across the way.
He is coming our way.
The best way to accomplish it.
To put a thing the wrong way.
In which way is it to be done?
Do it in my way.
Do not put yourself out of the way.
There is nothing out of the way in that.
To have one's way.
To be in the way (of persons).
To stand in the way.
To keep out of the way.
To make one's way in the world.
— — — through the crowd.
The house stands out of the way.
The ways of Providence.

Tourner.
La machine tourne sur un pivot.
Pâlir ; rougir.
Ses cheveux deviennent gris.
Il s'est fait soldat.
Traduire du français en Anglais.
Mettre de la prose en vers.
Mettre à profit.
Soulever le cœur.
Gagner honnêtement sa vie.
Rendre la pareille.
Se détourner, s'éloigner, s'écarter.
Se coucher, se mettre au lit.
La question roule sur ce point.
Il ne sait où donner de la tête.
Renverser, mettre sens dessus dessous.
Rentrer en soi-même.

Marcher vite.
Aller à l'église.
Il vient par ici.
Se promener.
Ils sont allés se promener ensemble.
Jusqu'où avez-vous été ? (260).
J'ai fait dix milles à pied.
Il s'avança vers elle.

Chemin.
Se perdre, s'égarer.
Se tromper de chemin.
Céder.
De l'autre côté.
Il vient de notre côté.
Le meilleur moyen d'y parvenir.
Mettre une chose à l'envers.
Comment faut-il le faire ?
Faites-le de ma manière.
Ne vous dérangez pas.
Il n'y a rien de singulier en cela.
En faire à sa tête.
Être de trop.
Faire obstacle.
Se tenir caché.
Faire son chemin dans le monde.
Percer la foule, se frayer un passage.
La maison est écartée.
Les voies de la Providence.

IDIOMS AND PROVERBS.

PART SECOND.—FRENCH INTO ENGLISH.

Affaire, *f.*
C'est mon affaire.
Cela fera précisément mon affaire.
Il en fait son affaire.
Il a fait son affaire (*one's own b.*).
    —   — (*another's*).
Son affaire est faite.
    —   — (*unfavorable sense*).
Il a son affaire.
    —   — (*unfavorable sense*).
J'en viens à mon affaire.
Il est bien (mal) dans ses affaires.
Les affaires ont changé de face.
Les affaires vont mal.
C'est un homme qui s'entend aux affaires.
Voulez-vous que je me fasse une affaire avec lui ?
Il s'est tiré d'affaire à temps.
Je me croyais hors d'affaire.
J'ai bien affaire de lui.
Il n'a pas affaire à un sot.
Avoir affaire à la veuve et aux héritiers.
À demain les affaires !

Aller.
Comment va la santé ?
Comment va la malade ?
Elle va mieux.
Comment va cette affaire ?
Ce ressort ne va pas.
Ça va, ça ira. Cela ne peut aller.
Cet habit vous va bien.
Ce chapeau lui va mal.
Ces couleurs vont bien ensemble.
Cela ne me va pas.
Je vais le voir aujourd'hui.
Il en va (*imp.*).
Il en allait comme on s'y attendait.
Il n'en va pas de même ici.
Y aller. Il y va (*imp.*),

Business.
That is my business, that concerns me.
That will just do for (suit) me.
He takes charge of it ; he makes it pay.
He has succeeded ; he has done well.
He has done for him.
His fortune is made.
He has been done for.
He is suited, he has what he wants.
He has got his due.
I am coming to the point.
He is in good (in bad) circumstances.
The tables are turned.
Things are in a bad condition.
He is a man who understands business.
Do you want me to get into trouble with him ?
He got out of the scrape in time.
I thought I was out of the scrape.
What do I care about him ?
He has not to do with a fool.
To have to do with a very strong party.
Away with business for to-day !

To go.
How is your health ?
How is the sick lady ?
She is better.
How does that matter stand ?
This spring does not work.
That will do. That won't do.
That coat fits you.
That bonnet is not becoming to her.
Those colors harmonize.
That does not suit me.
I shall call on him to-day.
It comes off.
It came off as was expected.
It does not work the same way here.
To go about. It concerns.

Allez-y doucement.	*Go about it quietly.*
On y va, madame.	*They are about it, madam.*
Il y va de votre fortune.	*It concerns your fortune.*
Il y allait de sa vie.	*His life was at stake.*
S'en aller.	*To go away.*
Je m'en vais.	*I am going, I am off.*
Je m'en vais réparer mon erreur.	*I am going to repair my fault.*
L'hérésie s'en va croissant.	*The heresy is increasing.*
Allons ! mes amis, au travail !	*Come! my friends, to work!*
Il n'en sera pas fâché, allez !	*He won't be sorry for it, be sure!*
C'est un las d'aller.	*He is a lazy fellow.*
Cela va sans dire.	*That is a matter of course.*
Aller son chemin.	*To go about one's business.*
— grand train.	*To go fast ; to live fast.*
— à tout vent.	*To trim one's sails to fit the wind.*
Il ne faut pas aller par quatre chemins.	*One should not seek crooked ways.* [mend.
À force de mal aller tout ira bien.	*When things are at the worst, they will*
On va bien loin depuis qu'on est las.	*Never despair ; one should not give way*
[se brise.	*to discouragement.* • ⇒ [broken.
Tant va la cruche à l'eau qu'à la fin elle	*The pitcher goes to the well until it is*
Battre.	**To beat.**
Battre l'eau, *or* battre l'air.	*To go to useless exertions.*
— les oreilles.	*To deafen by talking.*
— froid à qqn.	*To give one the cold shoulder.*
— la campagne.	*To beat about the bush.* [shoulders.
— qqn. sur le dos d'un autre.	*To beat a person over another man's*
— le fer pendant qu'il est chaud.	*To strike while the iron is hot.*
Il a battu les buissons et un autre a pris les oiseaux.	*He beat the bush and another caught the game.*
Beau, bel, belle.	**Beautiful, fine, handsome.**
Le beau monde, les gens du bel air.	*People of fashion.*
De belles paroles ! de belles promesses !	*Fine words! fine promises!*
Il fera beau quand il me reverra.	*He won't catch me again very soon.*
Me voilà dans un bel état !	*Now I am in a fine condition!*
En faire de belles ; en dire de belles.	*To do foolish things ; to say foolish things.*
En conter de belles sur le compte de qqn.	*To tell idle stories about a person.*
Déchirer qqn. de belles dents.	*To speak ill of s. b.*
La donner belle à qqn.	*To furnish one a fine opportunity.*
La manquer belle.	*To lose or miss a fine opportunity.*
L'avoir beau, *or* l'avoir belle.	*To have a good chance.*
La bailler belle à qqn.	*To tell a person stories.*
L'échapper belle.	*To have a narrow escape.*
Coucher à la belle étoile.	*To lie in the open air.*
Avoir beau. [pas.	*To be in vain.*
Vous avez beau faire, vous n'y arriverez	*You strive to no purpose.* [believe him.
Il aura beau dire, on ne le croira pas.	*He may say what he likes, people will not*
À beau jeu beau retour.	*One good turn deserves another.*
Voilà un beau venez-y-voir !	*That is a fine thing to boast of.*
La belle plume fait le bel oiseau.	*Fine feathers make fine birds.*

FRENCH INTO ENGLISH. 335

Boire.
Boire dans un verre, à une bouteille.
— son soûl, sec.
— comme un templier, une éponge.
— le vin du marché.
— le coup de l'étrier.
Il y a à boire et à manger.
Qui bon l'achète bon le boit.
Le vin est tiré, il faut le boire.
Qui fait la faute la boit.
C'est la mer à boire.
Il n'y pas de l'eau à boire.

Bois, *m.*
Faire flèche de tout bois.
Ne savoir de quel bois faire flèche.
Être du bois dont on fait les flûtes.
On verra de quel bois je me chauffe.
Il a l'œil au bois.
À gens de ..., trompette de bois.
Trouver ... de bois.
La faim chasse le loup du bois.

Bon.
Un bon enfant ; un bon vivant.
Avoir bon pied, bon œil.
Faire le bon apôtre.
Se donner du bon temps.
Avoir le bon bout d'une affaire.
Trouvez bon que je vous en parle.
À quoi bon en parler ?
C'est bon ; il me le payera.
La garder bonne.
À la bonne heure !
À bon jour bonne œuvre.
À bon vin point d'enseigne.
Les bons comptes font les bons amis.
À bon entendeur salut !
Voilà ce qui est le bon de l'affaire.
Ce n'est pas pour bon ; c'est pour rire.

Bonnet, *m.*
Prendre une chose sous son bonnet.
Ce sont deux têtes dans un bonnet.
Il a l'air triste comme un bonnet de nuit.
Mettre son bonnet de travers.
Avoir la tête près du bonnet.
Jeter son bonnet par dessus les moulins.

Bouche, *f.*
Faire venir l'eau à la bouche.
Garder une chose pour la bonne bouche.

To drink.
To drink out of a glass, out of a bottle.
— one's fill, much.
— excessively, like a sponge.
— to the bargain.
— to the stirrup.
There is good and bad in that business.
The best goods are the cheapest.
You are in it and you must go through.
Errors, like chickens, come home to roost.
You may as well empty the ocean with a
That is a very poor business.   [bucket.

Wood.
To strain every nerve to succeed.
Not to know which way to turn.   [body.
To be very yielding, to agree with every
They will find out with whom they have
He looks out sharply.   [to deal.
Don't talk about colors to the blind.   [seer.
To knock at a door and to receive no an-
Hunger drives the wolf out of the woods.

Good.
A good fellow ; a good liver.
To be active and vigilant.
To play the good fellow.
To have a good time of it.
To have the right side of a question.
Allow me to speak to you about it.
What good can it do to speak about it?
All right ; he will pay for it.
To keep rancor.
Well and good ! All right !
The better the day, the better the deed.
Good wine needs no bush.
Short settlements make long friends.
A word to the wise.
That is the funny part of the business.
It is not in earnest ; it is for fun.

Cap.
To take something into one's head.
They are hand and glove together.
He looks like patience on a monument.
To put the wrong foot foremost.
To be excitable, irritable.
To throw off all restraint.

Mouth.
To make the mouth water.
To keep a thing for the last.

IDIOMS AND PROVERBS.

Faire la petite bouche.
Dire tout ce qui vient à la bouche.
Garder bouche close.
Il arrive beaucoup de choses entre la [bouche et le verre.

Bout, *m.*
Tirer sur qqn à bout portant.
Avoir un mot sur le bout de la langue.
Dire qq. ch. du bout des lèvres.
On ne sait par quel bout le prendre.
Être au bout de son rôle.
Venir à bout d'une chose.
Pousser les choses jusqu'au bout.
Mettre, pousser, qqn. à bout.
Sa patience est à bout.
Au bout du compte.
Au bout du fossé la culbute.
Au bout de l'aune faut le drap.
Au bout le bout.

Brebis, *f.*
Brebis comptées le loup les mange.
À brebis tondue, Dieu mesure le vent.
Brebis qui bêle perd sa goulée.
Qui se fait brebis, le loup le mange.

Carte, *f.*
Avoir carte blanche.
Prendre les cartes.
Brouiller les cartes.
Jouer les cartes sur table.
Le dessous des cartes.
On ne sait jamais avec lui de quelle carte
Perdre la carte. [il retourne.
Tirer les cartes.

Cas, *m.*
C'est là mon cas.
Faire cas de.
On fait grand cas d'elle.

Chandelle, *f.*
Économie de bout de chandelles.
Brûler la chandelle par les deux bouts.
À chaque saint sa chandelle.

Chanson, *f.*
C'est toujours la même chanson.
Voilà bien une autre chanson.
Chansons que tout cela !
Je ne me paye pas de chansons.
Si vous en avez l'air, vous n'en avez pas la chanson.

To make difficulties. [mind.
To say any thing that comes across one's
To keep the secret, to have a close mouth.
There is many a slip betwixt the cup and [the lip.

End.
To fire at one close at hand.
To have a word at the end of the tongue.
To say a thing condescendingly.
One does not know how to take him.
To be at the end of his rope.
To carry a thing through, to succeed.
To drive things to extremes.
To nonplus a person ; to drive one to ex-
His patience is at an end. [tremes.
After all.
When it comes to the end, then the crash.
There is an end to every thing.
It will last as long as it can.

Sheep.
Don't count your chickens ... they are
God tempers the wind to the shorn lamb.
A bleating sheep goes home ...
If you are too yielding people will impose [upon you.

Card.
To have full power.
To take the lead in a business.
To embroil matters.
To act or speak frankly. [ness.
The hidden game ; the secret of the busi-
One never knows what he is after.
To become confused.
To tell fortunes ; to lay cards.

Case.
That is my case ; that suits me.
To value, to esteem highly.
They make a great ado about her.

Candle.
Penny wise and pound foolish.
To burn the candle at both ends.
Do homage to all whose influence you may [need.

Song.
It is always the same old song.
That is quite a different story.
That is all nonsense.
I will not be put off with fine speeches.
That will do for appearances, but it is not the thing.

FRENCH INTO ENGLISH. 337

Chat, *m.*
Emporter le chat
Acheter chat en poche.
Appeler un chat un chat.
Se servir de la patte du chat pour tirer les marrons du feu.
S'accorder comme chien et chat.
À bon chat bon rat.
La nuit tous les chats sont gris.
Quand les chats n'y sont pas les souris dansent.
Jeter les chats aux jambes à qqn.
Il n'y a pas là de quoi fouetter un chat.
On ne peut prendre de tels chats sans Éveiller le chat qui dort. [mitaines.
Dès que les chats seront chaussés.
Chat échaudé craint l'eau froide.

Cat.
To take French leave.
To buy a pig in a poke.
To call a spade a spade.
To make a cat's-paw of a person.

To agree like cat and dog.
Tit for tat.
In the dark all cats are gray.
When the cat is away, the mice will play.
To make trouble for one.
That is a very trifling fault. [gloves.
Such a matter has to be handled with
To touch upon an unpleasant business.
Very early in the morning.
A burnt child is afraid of the fire.

Chien, *m.*
Jeter sa ❚❚❚❚ x chiens.
Donner ❚❚❚❚ x chiens.
Fréquer ❚❚❚❚ en et le chat.
Il ne fa ❚❚❚❚ se moquer des chiens qu'on ne soit hors du village.
Bon chien de chasse, chasse de race.
Chien qui aboie ne mord pas.
Entre chien et loup.

Dog.
To give it up.
To give up one's claim in contempt.
To see all kinds of people.
Don't halloo till you are out of the wood.

Like father, like son.
Barking dogs don't bite.
In twilight.

Cœur, *m.*
Se ronger le cœur.
Je veux en avoir le cœur net.
En avoir le cœur gros.
Le cœur me le disait bien.
Avoir qq. ch sur le cœur.
Avoir le cœur mort.
Savoir un homme par cœur.
Dîner par cœur.
De bon cœur ; de tout mon cœur.
Tout à vous de cœur.
À cœur ouvert, le cœur sur les lèvres.
C'est une affaire que j'ai fort à cœur.
Avoir mal au cœur, le mal de cœur.
N'être pas malade de cœur.
Prenez-le, si le cœur vous en dit.
Loin des yeux loin du cœur.

Heart.
To waste away with secret grief.
I will sift the matter to the bottom.
To have the heart full of it.
I had a presentiment of it.
To bear or have a feeling of resentment.
To be heart-sick.
To know a man by heart.
To go without a dinner.
Willingly ; with all my heart.
Wholly yours.
Frankly, openly. [heart.
That is a matter which I take much to
To feel sick at the stomach.
Not to have lost one's appetite.
Take it, if you have an appetite for it.
Out of sight out of mind.

Compte, *m.*
Le compte est juste ; le compte y est.
Cela n'est pas de compte.
J'ai reçu cent dollars à-compte.
Au compte de ces gens.

Account.
The account is right ; it is right.
That does not count.
I received one hundred dollars on account.
On the statement of those people.

Oui, je suis donc un sot, à votre compte. | Oh, yes; I am a fool, according to you.
Au bout du compte. | After all.
J'en suis quitte à bon compte. | I have got off easily. [due.
Je lui ai fait son compte. | I have settled with him, given him his
Son compte sera bientôt réglé. | His account will soon be settled. [him.
C'est pour son compte ; tant pis pour lui. | That concerns him ; so much the worse for
Je suis inquiet sur son compte. | I am uneasy on his account.
Je n'y trouve pas mon compte. | I do not find it to my interest.
Il était bien loin de compte. | He was very far out of his reckoning. [us.
Tenir compte à qqn. d'une chose. | To keep account of a service one has done

Connaissance, *f.* — Acquaintance ; knowledge.
À ma connaissance. | To my knowledge.
Parler avec connaissance de cause. | To speak as a judge.
Il a de grandes connaissances. | He possesses great learning.
Faire connaissance avec qqn. } To make one's acquaintance.
Faire la connaissance de qqn.
Ce sont des gens de notre connaissance. | They are people of our acquaintance.
C'est une de mes connaissances. | She is an acquaintance of mine.
Être en pays de connaissances. | To be among acquaintances.

Corde, *f.* — **Rope.**
C'est lui qui est la grosse corde. | He is the principal man.
Toucher la grosse corde. | To come to the principal point.
— la corde sensible. | To come to the point.
Il ne faut pas toucher cette corde-là. | You must not touch upon that subject.
Tirer sur la même corde. | To pull by the same string.
Tenir la corde. | To hold the end of the rope.
Danser sur la corde. | To be engaged in a dangerous business.
Avoir deux cordes à son arc. | To have two strings to one's bow.
Être usé jusqu'à la corde. | To be worn threadbare.
Cet homme montre la corde. | That man lays bare his business.

Corps, *m.* — **Body.**
Passer sur le corps de qqn. | To pass ahead over s. b.
Saisir qqn. à bras le corps. | To seize a person round his body.
Combat corps à corps. | A hand-to-hand fight.
Être penché à mi-corps par la fenêtre. | To hang half way out of the window.
Prendre le lièvre au corps. | To take the bull by the horns.
Faire bon marché de son corps. | To expose one's self to bodily danger.
Avoir une mauvaise affaire sur le corps. | To have a bad matter on one's hand.
Un drôle de corps. | An odd, eccentric fellow.
Se jeter à corps perdu dans une affaire. | To go headlong into a business.

Côté, *m.* — **Side.**
Il est sur le côté. | He is over ; he is sick, or he is in disgrace.
Mettre une bouteille sur le côté. | To empty a bottle. [a th.
Le côté faible (de qqn., de qq. ch.). | The weak side of a p. ; the weak point of
De mon côté. | On my side ; on my part.
Allez-vous de mon côté ? | Do you go my way ?
De quel côté vient le vent ? | Which way does the wind blow ? [fear.
De ce côté il n'y a rien à craindre. | From that direction there is nothing to

De tous côtés.
Du côté de la fortune.
Ne savoir de quel côté tourner.
Mettre les rieurs de son côté.
Regarder qqn. de côté.
Laisser de côté.
Donner à côté.
Passer à côté d'une difficulté.
Être à côté de la question.

Coucher.
Coucher qqn. sur le carreau.
La pluie a couché les blés.
Coucher le poil de qq. ch. —à qqn.
   — qqn. en joue.
   — par écrit.
   — à la belle étoile.
Se coucher.

Coup, *m.*
Faire d'une pierre deux coups.
C'est un coup dans l'eau.
Donner un coup de main.
Manquer son coup.
Ce discours porte son coup.
Tout cela ne se fait pas d'un coup.
Du premier coup ; d'un seul coup.
Pour le coup ; à ce coup.
À coups perdus ; à coups redoublés.
À coup perdu.
À coup sûr.
Un coup de main ; coup d'État.
Un coup de soleil ; un coup de feu.
Tirer un coup de fusil, de canon.
Le coup vaut la balle, l'argent.

Devoir (325).
Je lui en dois, *or* il m'en doit.
Fais ce que tu dois, advienne que pourra.
Il croit toujours qu'on lui en doit.
Qui doit a tort.

Diable, *m.*
Tirer le diable par la queue.
C'est là le diable.
Un bon diable ; un pauvre diable.
Ne faites pas le diable plus noir qu'il est.
Il n'est pas si diable qu'il est noir.

Dieu, *m.*
S'il plaît à Dieu.
Plaise à Dieu ! À Dieu ne plaise ! [aide !
Dieu vous bénisse ! Dieu vous soit en

On all sides.
As to fortune ; with regard to fortune.
Not to know which way to turn.
To have the best of the discussion.
To look down upon a person.
To leave aside.
To miss the mark.
To avoid a difficulty, not to touch upon it.
To miss the question.

To lay ; to sleep.
To strike one down, either dead or hurt.
The rain has laid the corn.
To smooth s. th. ; to flatter s. b.
To take aim at s. b.
To put down in writing.
To sleep in the open air.
To lie down.

Blow.
To kill two birds with one stone.
It is a useless attempt.
To lend a helping hand.
To miss one's blow.
That speech had its effect.
All that can not be done at once.
With the first blow ; at one blow.
For once ; this time.
At random ; with redoubled strokes.
In vain.
Most certainly ; to be sure.
A surprise ; a stroke of policy.
A sunstroke ; a shot.
To fire off a gun, a cannon.
It is worth while.

To owe.
I have got an account to settle with him.
Do your duty, no matter what may happen.
He is never satisfied with what one does for
Who owes is wrong.   [him.

Devil.
To be pecuniarily embarrassed.
That is the ugly part of it.
A good fellow ; a poor fellow.
Give the devil his due.
The devil is not so black as he is painted.

God.
If it pleases God.
May it please God ! God forbid !
May God bless you ! May God help you !

Ce que femme veut, Dieu veut. — A woman's will is God's will.
La voix du peuple est la voix de Dieu. — The will of the people is the will of God.
Qui donne aux pauvres prête à Dieu. — Who gives to the poor lends to God.
L'homme propose, Dieu dispose. — Man proposes and God disposes.
Chacun pour soi Dieu pour tous. — Every one for himself, and God for us all.

Dire. — **To say; to tell.**
On dit. Des on-dit. — People say; it is said. Reports.
Que veut dire tout cela? — What does all that mean?
Cela ne dit rien. — That does not signify any thing.
Y avoir à dire. — To be wrong; to be wanting.
Il y a bien à dire là-dessus. — That is far from being right.
Il y a bien à dire que je n'aie mon compte. — That is far from being my account.
Il n'y a pas à dire. — Nothing to be said about it, all right.
Trouver à dire (trouver à redire). — To find fault with.
Il ne trouve rien à dire à cela. — He finds no fault with that.
En dire. — To say so; to feel like it; to scold.
Si le cœur vous en dit, faites-le. — If your heart says so, do it.
Il lui en a dit. — He gave it to him (scolded him).
Se le faire dire. — To be slow in doing a thing.
Il ne se le fit pas dire deux fois. — He was very prompt to do it.
Dire la vérité. — To speak the truth.
À vrai dire. — If the truth must be spoken.
Pour ainsi dire. — So to say.
Pour mieux dire, or disons mieux. — Let us rather say.
C'est tout dire. — That is every thing.
Cela va sans dire. — That is a matter of course.
Voilà qui est dit. — That is settled, agreed upon.
Soit dit en passant. — It may be said by the way.
Qui ne dit mot consent. — Silence gives consent.

Doigt, m. — **Finger.**
Montrer qqn. du doigt or au doigt. — To deride a person.
C'est une bague au doigt. — That is a good thing; that is an honor.
Mon petit doigt me l'a dit. — My little finger told me of it.
Donner sur les doigts à qqn. — To give it to one.
S'en mordre les doigts. — To regret a thing; to be sorry for it.
Toucher du doigt or au doigt. — To see or understand a thing plainly.
Se mettre le doigt dans l'œil. — To do an injury to one's self.
Vous avez mis le doigt dessus. — You have hit the nail on the head.
Avoir de l'esprit au bout des doigts. — To be very skilful. [purpose.
Toucher une chose du bout des doigts. — To have very nearly accomplished one's
Savoir une chose sur le bout des doigts. — To know a thing perfectly.

Donner. — **To give.**
Se donner de la peine. — To take trouble.
— des airs, de grands airs. — To put on airs.
Donner à penser, à entendre. — To set one to thinking; to throw out hints.
— un œuf pour avoir un bœuf. — To throw a sprat to catch a whale.
Tel donne à pleines mains qui n'oblige personne. — Ill-bestowed kindness gets no thanks.

Je vous le donne en dix, en cent.
En donner à qqn., en donner à garder.
Tu m'en as donné.
S'en donner.
S'en donner à cœur joie.
Ne savoir où donner de la tête.
Donner tête baissée dans qq. ch.
— dans un piége.
— dans le luxe.
Je ne donne pas là-dedans.
Donner dans l'œil.
— dans, sur.
Mes croisées donnent sur le jardin.
Qui donne tôt donne deux fois.

Dormir.
Dormir en lièvre, les yeux ouverts.
Cet homme ne dort pas.
Dormir sur une affaire.
Réveiller le chien qui dort.
Il n'y a pire eau que celle qui dort.

Écorcher.
Écorcher une matière.
— une langue.
— qqn.
Il crie avant qu'on l'écorche.
Beau parler n'écorche point la langue.
Il faut tondre les brebis et non pas les écorcher.
Écorcher l'anguille par la queue.
Il n'y a rien de plus difficile à écorcher que la queue.

Entendre.
Faites comme vous l'entendez.
Cela s'entend.
J'entends que cela se fasse.
Faire entendre.
Il n'y entend rien.
Il s'y entend.

Être.
Il est tout à ce qu'il fait.
En être.
Il en est.
Où en êtes-vous ?
Voilà où j'en suis.
En êtes-vous là ?
J'en suis pour ma peine.
Il en sera ce qu'il vous plaira.
Y être.

You may guess ten times, a hundred times.
To deceive one, to tell him falsehoods.
You have imposed upon me.
To indulge one's self.
To indulge o's self to one's heart's content.
Not to know which way to turn.
To go headlong into a thing.
To be caught in a snare.
To indulge in luxury.
I do not indulge in that.
To dazzle ; to take one's eye.
To open into ; to look into.
My windows overlook the garden.
Who gives promptly gives twice.

To sleep.
To sleep with one eye open.
That man is very watchful.
To go about a business slowly.
To come back to an unpleasant business.
Still waters run deep.

To skin.
To treat a subject superficially.
To speak a language badly.
To skin a person alive, to cheat.
He cries before he is hurt.
Politeness does not hurt one.
We should shear the sheep but not skin them.
To begin at the wrong end.
The winding up of a business is the most difficult part of it.

To hear ; to understand.
Do as you think proper, or fit.
That is a matter of course.
I mean that that shall be done.
To give to understand.
He understands nothing about it.
He understands it.

To be.
He is wholly absorbed in his work.
To be of the party ; to be with it.
He is one of them.
How far have you got with it ?
This is as far as I have got.
Are you so far ? Do you believe that ?
I had my trouble for my pains.
That business shall be settled as you wish.
To be in ; to be at home.

IDIOMS AND PROVERBS.

Je n'y suis pour personne. — I am not at home to any body.
J'y suis pour une petite somme. — I am in it for a small amount.
Vous n'y êtes pas. — You have not got it.
J'y suis, m'y voici. — I have got it.
On ne peut pas être et avoir été. — You cannot eat your cake and keep it.

Façon, *f.* — **Make; fashion; shape.**
Combien faites-vous la façon ? — How much do you charge for the making?
C'est une façon de parler avec lui. — That is a form of expression with him.
Telle est ma façon de penser. — Such is my way of thinking.
C'est un meuble en façon de biblio- [thèque. — It is a piece of furniture in the shape of a [bookcase.
J'y parviendrai de façon ou d'autre. — I shall accomplish it some way or other.
Vivre à la façon des Anglais. — To live in the English style.
Ne faites pas tant de façon, je vous en [prie. — Do not use so much ceremony, pray.
Point de façon ; sans façon. — No ceremony ; without ceremony.
De la bonne façon ; de la belle façon. — Properly ; in fine style, at a fine rate.
Ce trait-là est de votre façon. — That is a trick after your own fashion.
On l'a traité de façon qu'il ne revien- [dra pas. — He was received in such a manner that [he won't return.

Faire (214, 215, 324). — **To do; to make.**
Faire le bien, le mal. — To do good, evil.
— un voyage, une opération. — To perform a journey, an operation.
— son chemin, du progrès. — To go ahead, to get along ; to progress.
— trois milles, à pied, etc. — To travel three miles, on foot, etc.
— les draps. — To deal in cloths.
— faillite, banqueroute. — To fail, to go into bankruptcy.
— la médecine. — To practice medicine.
— une maladie. — To go through a sickness;
— la reine, l'enfant, etc. — To act like a queen, like a child.
— diète. — To diet.
— un bon dîner. — To eat a good dinner.
— bonne mine, bon visage à qqn. — To be friendly to one.
— les yeux doux à qqn. — To look sweet upon one.
L'argent fait tout en ce monde. — Money is every thing in this world.
Combien faites-vous cet habit ? — How much do you ask for that coat?
Combien font deux fois deux ? — How many are twice two?
Faire de qqn., de qq. ch. — To dispose of s. b., of s. th.
Je ne sais que faire de lui. — I do not know what to put him to.
Que voulez-vous faire de ce cheval ? — What will you do with that horse?
En faire à sa tête. — To do as one pleases.
Ne faire rien de la sorte, n'en rien faire. — To do nothing of the kind.
Il n'en fera rien. — He will do nothing of the kind.
N'avoir que faire de. — To have no occasion for.
Je n'ai que faire de lui. — { I have nothing to do with him. / I have no business with him.
Qu'est-ce que cela me fait ? — What is that to me?
Que voulez-vous que j'y fasse ? — How can I help it?
Qu'y faire ? — What is to be done?
Cela fait beaucoup. — That makes a great difference.
Cela n'y fait rien du tout. — That is nothing to the matter.
Jean fait tout et bon à rien. — Jack of all trades and master of none.

FRENCH INTO ENGLISH. 343

Ne faire que ; ne faire que de.	To do nothing but ; to have but just.
Elle ne fait que rire.	She does nothing but laugh.
Il ne fait que d'entrer.	He has but just come in.
Se faire soldat.	To become a soldier.
Ce jeune homme se fait.	That young man is coming out.
Se faire à la fatigue.	To get accustomed to toil.
On se fait à tout.	One gets accustomed to every thing.
Cela ne se fait pas.	That cannot be done.
Comment cela s'est-il fait ?	How did that happen?
Il se fait tard.	It is getting late
Faire d'une mouche un éléphant.	To exaggerate very much. [c'est
— la mouche du coche.	To attribute to o. s. all the credit of a suc-
Ce qui est fait n'est pas à faire.	Done is done.
L'occasion fait le larron.	Opportunity makes the thief.
Qui bien fera bien trouvera.	As you sow so you reap.
On ne peut faire qu'en faisant.	It takes time to do things properly.
Paris n'est pas fait en un jour	Rome was not built in a day.
Faire et dire sont deux.	Saying and doing are different things.
Qui a fait l'une a fait l'autre.	They are cast in the same mould.

Rem.—The verb FAIRE may take the place of any preceding verb to avoid its repetition (113).

Je voulais partir, mais je n'ai pu le faire.	I wished to leave, but could not do it.

Fait, m.   **Fact; deed.**

Un fait accompli.	An accomplished fact.
Venir au fait, passer au fait.	To come to the point.
Prendre qqn. sur le fait.	To catch a person in the act.
Par voie de fait.	Through or by violence.
Pour la beauté du fait.	For the beauty of the thing. [posted.
Être au fait d'une chose.	To be acquainted with a thing, to be
Question de fait ; point de fait.	Question of fact ; point of fact.
C'est justement votre fait.	That is just what suits you.
Dire, donner son fait à qqn.	To give it to one.
De fait, dans le fait.	In reality ; really ; in fact.
Si fait.	Oh! yes.
La bonne volonté est réputée pour le fait.	To take the will for the deed.

Feu, m.   **Fire.**

Prendre feu.	To become excited.
Faire feu qui dure.	To live within one's means.
Jeter son feu.	To sow one's wild oats.
Il n'est feu que de bois vert.	Youth is the time for action.

Fil, m.   **Thread.**

Du fil en aiguille.	From one thing to another.
Avoir, donner du fil à retordre.	To have or to stir up difficulties.
Le fil de l'épée	The edge of the sword.
Passer au fil de l'épée.	To put to the sword.

Fin.   **End.**

Fin courant.	The end of the month.
La fin couronne l'œuvre.	All is well that ends well.
Qui veut la fin, veut les moyens.	The end justifies the means.

Fond, *m.* — **Bottom.**
Le fond de l'affaire. — *The bottom facts of the business.*
À fond. — *To the bottom; thoroughly.*
Couler une affaire à fond. — *To run a thing to the ground.*
Savoir une chose à fond. — *To know a thing thoroughly.*
À deux fonds; à fond de paille. — *Double-bottomed; straw-bottomed*
Faire fond sur qqn., sur qq. ch. — *To rely upon s. b., upon s. th.*
Venir au fond des choses. — *To sift matters to the bottom.*
De fond en comble. — *From top to bottom, to the ground.*
C'est une mer sans fond et sans rive. — *It is a matter beyond the reach of human* [reason.

Fort, *m.* — **Strong; the strong point.**
C'est un peu fort, ce que vous dites-là — *That is rather hard what you say.*
Il est fort en mathématiques. — *He is good in mathematics.*
Au fort de l'hiver. — *In the heart of winter.*
C'est là son fort. — *That is his forte.*
Il s'en fait fort. — *He boasts of it.*
Le plus fort de l'affaire est passé. — *The hardest part of the business is over.*
C'est plus fort que moi. — *I cannot help it.*
Voilà qui est fort — *That is too bad.*

Fortune, *f.* — **Fortune.**
Attacher un clou à la roue de la fortune. — *To fix the wheel of fortune.*
Venez dîner avec nous à la fortune du — *Come and take pot-luck with us.*
Être en fortune. [pot. — *To be fortunate, to be in luck.*
Contre mauvaise fortune bon cœur. — *We must bear up against bad fortune.*

Garde, *f.* — **Guard; care; heed.**
En garde. — *In custody.*
À la garde de, *or* sous la garde de. — *To or in the custody of.*
1. Prendre garde (*indic.*). — *To notice; to pay attention; to mind.*
Prenez garde à ce cheval. [tête. — *Mind that horse.*
— qu'ils se font signe de la — *Notice that they motion to another.*
— qu'on ne vous dit pas la — *Notice that they do not tell you the truth.*
2. Prendre garde (*subj.*). [vérité. — *To take care; to be careful.* [will say.
Prenez garde que vous entendiez ce qu'il — *Take care that you understand what he*
— qu'il ne sorte. [dira. — *— that he does not go out.*
— à vous tenir comme il faut. — *Be careful that you keep orderly.*
— à ne pas confondre les — *— not to confound matters.* [choses.
3. Prendre garde de (*with the infinitive*). — *To beware of; to take care not.*
Prenez garde de tomber. — *Take care that you do not fall.*
Être, se mettre, se tenir, en garde, *or* sur — *To be on one's guard; to guard (against).*
ses gardes (contre).
N'avoir garde de faire. — *To beware of doing.*
Il n'a garde d'y aller. [faute. — *He takes good care not to go there.*
Je n'avais garde de commettre cette — *I was not fool enough to commit that*
La garde. À la garde! — *The watch. Watch!* [mistake.
Monter la garde. — *To mount guard.*
Être de garde, de service. — *To be on duty.*
Être de garde, de bonne garde. — *To keep well (of fruit, etc.).*
Ce fruit est de bonne garde. — *That fruit keeps well.*

Garder.
Garder le lit, la chambre.
— un malade.
La garder bonne à qqn.
En donner à garder à qqn.
Garder le secret d'une chose.
— une poire pour la soif.
Se garder ; se garder de.
Ces fruits se gardent.
Gardez-vous d'en parler.

Gêner ; se gêner.
Cet homme nous gêne.
Il ne se gêne pas.
Ne vous gênez pas.
Si cela ne vous gêne pas.

Gré, *m.*
Trouver qq. ch. à son gré.
Au gré de ses désirs, de ses vœux.
Bon gré, mal gré, de gré ou de force.
Savoir gré *or* bon gré à qqn. de qq. ch.
— mauvais gré à qqn. de qq. ch.

Heure, *f.*
Il est une heure, deux heures vingt.
À l'heure.
Avoir l'heure.
Être sujet à l'heure.
L'heure des classes.
À toute heure.
À l'heure qu'il est.
L'heure du berger.
Un mauvais quart d'heure.
Le quart d'heure de Rabelais.
De bonne heure ; de meilleure heure.
Arriver à la bonne heure.
À la bonne heure !
Être à l'heure *(of clocks).*
Mettre une montre à l'heure.
Fixer une heure.
Retarder l'heure.
Rentrer à une heure indue.

Jeu, *m.*
Jeu de mots ; jeu d'esprit.
Accuser son jeu.
Avoir beau jeu.
Donner *or* faire beau jeu à qqn.
Cacher *or* couvrir son jeu.
Faire bonne mine à mauvais jeu.
Se faire un jeu de qq. ch.

To keep.
To keep one's bed, one's room.
To take care of a sick person.
To have a rod in pickle for one.
To impose upon one.
To keep a thing secret.
To lay up something for a rainy day.
To keep ; to beware of ; to refrain from.
That fruit keeps.
Take care not to speak of it.

To incommode ; to be under restraint.
That man is in our way.
He stands on no ceremonies.
Make yourself at home.
If it does not incommode you.

Will ; liking.
To find a thing to one's liking.
At one's heart's content.
Willing or unwilling.
To be pleased with s. o. for s. th.
Not to thank a person for a thing.

Hour.
It is one o'clock, two o'clock and twenty m.
By the hour ; on time.
To have the right time.
To be tied to time.
Time for recitation.
At any time.
At the present moment.
The propitious hour.
A disagreeable time.
Settling time ; trying time.
Early, in good time ; earlier.
To come in the right time.
Well and good!
To be right.
To set a watch.
To appoint an hour.
To appoint a later hour, to make it later
To keep bad hours.

Play ; game.
A play upon words ; witticism.
To tell one's game. [*opportunity.*
To have a good game ; to have a good
To play into s. b's hands.
To conceal one's game.
To put a good face on the matter. [*in it.*
To make light of a thing ; to take pleasure

Jouer bien son jeu.	To play one's cards well.
Mettre en jeu.	To bring out, to call into play.
Prendre une chose en jeu.	To take a thing in jest.
À beau jeu beau retour.	One good turn deserves another.
Le jeu ne vaut pas la chandelle.	It is not worth powder and shot.

Main, f. — Hand.

Coup de main.	Sudden attack; surprise; bold stroke.
Tour de main.	Sleight of hand.
À la main droite, or à droite.	To or at the right hand.
— gauche, or à gauche.	— left hand.
Un cheval à deux mains.	A horse fitted to drive and ride.
Avoir une belle main.	To write a good hand.
— la main faite, or rompue.	To have one's hand in (trained).
— — crochue.	To be light-fingered (thievish).
— — légère.	To be skilful.
— les mains nettes.	To have one's hands clean (uncorrupted).
Donner la main à qqn.	To give one's hand, to assist s. b.
— un coup de main.	To lend a helping hand. [other's hands.
Se donner la main.	To be hand in hand with; to play into each
Faire main basse sur.	To lay violent hands on.
Forcer la main à qqn.	To compel one to do a thing.
Graisser la main à qqn.	To bribe one; to give him a sop.
En lever la main.	To take one's oath of it.
Mettre la main au feu pour qq. ch.	To stake one's life upon a thing. [wheel.
— — à l'œuvre, à la pâte.	To set to work; to put one's shoulder to the
Prêter la main à qqn.	To assist s. b.; to countenance s. b.
Serrer la main à qqn.	To give one a friendly squeeze of the hand.
Toucher dans la main à qqn.	To give one's hand in token of acquiescence.
Tenir de bonne main.	To have from good authority.
Tomber sous les mains.	To fall in one's way.
En venir aux mains.	To come to blows.
Les mains m'en tombent!	I am very much surprised at it.

Mal, m. — Evil; harm; sore.

Les maux de la vie.	The ills of life. [head.
Le mal de tête; mal à la tête.	The headache; headache; pain in the
— dents; — aux dents.	The toothache; toothache.
Mal aux yeux.	Sore eyes.
— au bras, à la main.	Pain in the arm; sore hand.
— au cœur, or de cœur.	Sickness of the stomach.
Faire mal, or du mal à qqn.	To hurt s. b.; to injure.

Mettre. — To put; to set.

Mettre fin, ordre, bon ordre à qq. ch.	To put an end to, to put order in, a thing.
— qqn. à l'aise.	To set one at ease.
— le couvert.	To lay the cloth.
— de côté.	To put aside.
— qqn. au fait, au courant.	To make one acquainted with.
— — à même de faire qq. ch.	To enable s. b. to do a thing.
— — à la raison.	To bring one to reason.

Mettre au jour.	To publish ; to put forth.
— dedans, dehors.	To trick, to take in ; to dismiss.
— le tout pour le tout.	To risk every thing.
— sous les yeux.	To bring to notice, to make known.
— sa gloire à faire une chose.	To make it one's glory to do a thing.
— de l'eau dans son vin.	To lower one's pretensions.
— du foin dans ses bottes.	To feather one's nest.
Se mettre	To put one's self ; to sit down ; to dress
Se mettre à table, à son aise.	To sit down to table ; to take one's ease.
— bien.	To dress well.
— en colère.	To get angry.
— en état, à même de.	To put one's self in a condition to.
— au fait, au courant.	To make one's self acquainted with.
— bien avec qqn.	⎰ To get on good terms with one. ⎱ To conciliate one's good-will.
— mal —	To get on bad terms with one.
S'y mettre.	To set about it ; to turn to.

Monter.   **To ascend ; to go** *or* **get up.**

Monter à cheval, en croupe.	To get, to ride on horseback ; to get behind
— en voiture.	To step into the carriage.
— sur le trône, au trône.	To ascend the throne.
— en grade.	To advance.
Le vin monte à la tête.	Wine goes to the head.
La rougeur lui monta au visage.	Her face turned red.
Le blé monte. [dollars.	Corn is rising.
Les frais montent (*or* se montent) à mille	The cost comes to a thousand dollars.
Monter le blé au grenier.	To carry the corn up to the granary.
— un cheval.	To ride a horse.
— un atelier.	To fit up a workshop.
— une machine.	To set up a machine.
— une horloge.	To wind up a clock.
— une affaire.	To get up an affair.
— un diamant.	To set a diamond.
— un chapeau.	To trim a bonnet.
— un instrument de musique.	To put a musical instrument together.
— sa dépense, son train.	To increase one's expense.
— la tête à qqn.	To get another into excitement about s. th.
Qui monte la mule la ferre.	Who rides the mule pays the hostler.

Moyen, *m.*   **Means.**

Par le moyen de. Au moyen de.	By means of. In consequence of.
Il n'y a pas moyen de le faire.	There is no means of doing it.
Je n'ai pas les moyens de le faire.	I cannot afford doing it.
Avoir des moyens.	To have talents, to be clever.

Nez, *m.*   **Nose.**

Au nez de qqn.	In a person's face.
Avoir bon nez.	To be sagacious.
Donner sur le nez à qqn.	To mortify s. b.
Se trouver nez à nez avec qqn.	To find o. s. face to face with s. b.

Oreille, *f.*
Avoir l'oreille au guet.
Tirer l'oreille à qqn.
Se faire tirer l'oreille.

Part, *f.*
En bonne part.
Avoir part à ; prendre part à.
Faire part à.
— la part de.
Mettre à part.
Prendre en mauvaise part.
Avoir de bonne part.

Parti, *m.*
Homme de parti.   Esprit de parti.
Épouser un bon parti.
Prendre un parti.
C'est un parti pris.
Prendre parti pour.
Tirer parti de.

Partie, *f.*
Être de la partie.
Avoir affaire à trop forte partie.
Faire la seconde partie auprès de qqn.
— le coup de partie.
Prendre qqn. à partie.
Quitter la partie.

Passer.
Passer chez qqn.
En passer par là.
Il lui faut passer par là ou par la fenêtre.
Se faire passer pour.
Passer le temps à s'amuser.
Je lui ai passé cela.
Cela me passe.
Se passer.
Ces choses se passent tous les jours.
Se passer de.
Il faut se passer de bien des choses.

Porter.
Porter témoignage.
— sur soi.
— du fruit.
— de beaux habits.
— les cheveux longs.
— les armes.
— un coup.
— envie.
Le bienfait porte intérêt.

Ear.
To be on tip-toe.
To pull s. o's ears ; to dunn s. b.
To get o. o. dunned ; to be very reluctant.

Share ; part.
In good part ; in a good sense.
To have a share in ; to participate in.
To give a part to ; to impart to.
To make allowance for.
To set aside.
To take amiss.
To have from good authority.

Party.
Party man.   Party spirit.
To make a good match.
To make up one's mind.
His mind is made up.
To take part with.
To derive advantage from.

Party.
To be one of them.
To be overmatched.
To play second fiddle to s. b.
To strike the decisive blow.
To sue s. b. ; to lay the blame on s. b.
To throw up the game ; to relinquish one's [pursuit.

To pass.
To call on one.
To submit to it.
He must submit to that or worse.
To pass one's self for.
To trifle away one's time.
I forgave him that ; I let that go.
That is beyond my comprehension.
To happen ; to take place.
Those things happen every day.
To do without ; to dispense with.   [out
There are many things one has to do with

To bear ; to carry ; to wear.
To bear witness.
To have about one's person.
To bear fruit.
To wear fine clothes.
To wear long hair.
To carry arms ; to be in the army.
To strike a blow.
To envy.
A good deed bears interest.

Elle porte les culottes. | She wears the breeches. [hearing.
Dire qq. ch. à bout portant. | To make unpleasant remarks in a. o's
Le coup a porté juste. | The blow went home.
Se porter à des extrémités, à l'excès. | To go to extremes, to excess.
— bien, mal. | To be well, ill.

Prendre. | **To take.**
Prendre des airs. | To put on airs.
— le dessus. | To gain the ascendency.
— l'occasion aux cheveux. | To seize the opportunity. [tion.
— le tison par où il brûle. | To take up the difficult side of the ques-
— la mouche, or la chèvre. | To fly into a passion for a trifle.
— la clef des champs. | To escape, to take to one's heels.
— le mords aux dents. | To fly into a passion. [sleep.
— sur sa nourriture, son sommeil. | To retrench ; to take from one's food, one's
Le prendre sur un haut ton. | To carry it high.
— bien, mal. | To take it well, amiss.
— pour bon, pour dit. [laisser. | — for granted. [in what he says.
Dans ce qu'il dit, il faut en prendre et en | There is not much confidence to be placed
Ne savoir par où prendre qqn. | Not to know how to treat one.
Je vous y prends. | I have you there.
Le feu a pris à la maison. | The house has caught fire.
La fièvre l'a pris. | He caught the fever.
S'y prendre. | To set about it.
Il s'y prend mal. | He sets about it in the wrong way.
S'en prendre à. | To throw the blame on.
Il s'en prend à vous. | He throws the blame on you.
À tout prendre. | Upon the whole.

Propos, m. | **Talk.**
Ce sont des propos en l'air. | That is idle talk.
Tenir de sots propos. | To talk nonsense.
À propos. | Timely ; seasonably ; by the way.
À tout propos. À propos de rien. | At every turn. For nothing at all.
Il est à propos que vous le voyiez. | It is expedient that you should see him.

Remettre. | **To put back ; to replace.**
Remettre qqn. dans ses droits. | To reinstate a person in his rights.
— le bras à qqn. | To set s. b's arm.
— bien ensemble. | To reconcile, to make friends again
— au lendemain. | To put off, to defer till next day.
— à l'an quarante. | — till doomsday.
— qq. ch. à qqn. | To deliver, to hand s. th. to s. b.
— qqn. | To recognize s. b.
Se remettre. | To set to again ; to recover ; to come to.
S'en remettre à. | To rely on.
Je m'en remets à sa décision. | I rely on his decision.

Rendre. | **To render ; to give back.**
Rendre réponse. | To return an answer.
— justice, la justice | To do right ; to administer justice.
— service, visite. | To render service ; to pay a visit.
— malade. | To make sick.

Rendre la pareille. — To pay back in one's own coin.
— compte, raison de. — To account for.
— une pensée, une idée. — To express a thought, an idea.
Cette fleur rend une odeur agréable. — That flower exhales a fragrant odor.
Ce chemin rend à la ville. — That road leads to the town.
Se rendre. — To yield; to surrender.
— à son poste, auprès de qqn. — To go to one's duty, to s. b.
— à la raison. — To submit to reason.
Rendez à César ce qui est à César. — Give unto Cæsar the things that are [Cæsar's.

Tenir. — To keep; to hold.
Tenir boutique, pension. — To keep a shop, a boarding-house.
— équipage. — — a carriage.
En tenir. — To have caught it; to be smitten with.
Il en tient. — He has caught it; he is in for it, etc.
Tenir qqn. le bec dans l'eau. — To keep . h in expectation.
— — à distance. — — at a distance.
— — dans sa manche. — To have a person at one's disposal.
— — à quatre. — — one bound hand and foot.
Un principe qui tient dans tous les cas. — A principle that holds good in every case.
À quoi tient-il que cela ne soit ? — What is the reason that that is not so ?
Qu'à cela ne tienne. — Do not let that make any difference.
S'il ne tient qu'à cela. — If that is all.
C'est à n'y pas tenir. — I cannot endure it any longer.
Il tient à ses opinions. — He is tenacious of his opinions.
Tiens, tiens, comme vous y allez. — Bless me, how you go about it.
Tenez, j'aime encore mieux cela. — See here, I like this still better.
Un tiens vaut mieux que deux tu l'auras. — A bird in the hand is worth two the
Se tenir prêt. — To hold one's self in readiness
— à une décision. — To abide by a decision
Je m'y tiens. — I adhere to it.
S'en tenir. — To rely on; to abide by.
Je m'en tiens à ce qui a été convenu. — I abide by what was agreed to.
S'en tenir là. — To stop there.
S'en tenir au gros de l'arbre. — To side with the strongest.

Vouloir. — To be willing; to wish.
Je veux bien que cela soit ainsi. — I consent to it; I am willing.
Je voudrais bien la voir. — I should like to see her. [cela
Veuillez me dire ce que vous pensez de — Please tell me what you think of that.
Je ne veux pas de ces gens-là. — I don't want those people.
Je ne veux pas de cela. — I don't wish that.
Vouloir du bien (du mal) à qqn. — To wish a person well (ill).
En vouloir à qqn. — To bear s. b. ill-will. [of that.
Je lui en veux d'avoir parlé de cela. — I am angry with him for having spoken
À qui en veut-il ? — Whom does he complain of?
Dieu le veuille ! — God grant!
Faites ce que vous voudrez. — Do what you like; do your best.
Quand vous voudrez. — When you like. All right.
Que voulez-vous ? Que voulez-vous ! — What do you wish? Who can help it.
Vouloir dire. — To mean.

www.ingramcontent.com/pod-product-compliance
Lightning Source LLC
Chambersburg PA
CBHW030306240426
43673CB00040B/1083